The Copy Workshop Workbook

3rd Edition

©2002 Bruce Bendinger

ISBN# 1-887229-12-4

The Copy Workshop
2144 N. Hudson • Chicago, IL 60614
(773) 871-1179 FX: (773) 281-4643
www.adbuzz.com or **thecopyworkshop@aol.com**

The Next Edition.

WELL, HERE WE ARE. Another edition.

First, let's talk about how things changed since this book was first written.

"WELCOME TO THE REVOLUTION."

That's how the previous edition began.

Now that revolution's over. Did you notice?

Since this book's first edition in '88, the advertising business has gone through revolutionary changes.

Today, it's a business that's dramatically different.

It means much of what we'll be teaching is history.

But it's history you can use today.

FROM ADVERTISING TO MARKETING.

The good news is what was once a small business called advertising is now a big business – marketing.

And what was once a specialized craft – advertising copywriting – is now part of a big business function – marketing communications – or MarCom.

So the things you learn in this book will probably be very useful to you – even if you never write an ad.

WHAT HAPPENED TO ADVERTISING?

Creating successful advertising was always hard.

Now it's more challenging than ever.

Here's what happened since that first edition:

• **More Media Choices.** We all have more media choices. Have you noticed? Of course you have. Well, more media means more messages. And no one can pay attention to all those messages.

The result? The Age of Noise – full of "media fragmentation" and "message proliferation."

You know what that is. You grew up with it.

The good news: more need for more people to create those messages.

The bad news: more distraction. There's more competition for attention. It's harder to be heard.

HISTORICAL NOTE #1.

When I started in the business (1966), a lot of ad agencies had training programs. (Thanks, JWT.) Those days are gone.

This book was first written to fill that specific need – the original target for this book was a young writer already in an agency – sort of a Copy Chief in a book.

But that world changed.

Now, agencies count on schools like yours to do the training.

So, instead of a book for a few young copywriters at an agency, this turned into a textbook for thousands of college students – including you.

Which just goes to show you, that even when things go right, they don't always go according to plan.

First Call for Feedback...

By the way, it's hard to read the label when you're inside the bottle.

So we're hoping you'll do that for us – teach us as we try to teach you.

Got a comment? Got a question? Got something you're worried about? Don't wait. Send us an e-mail. thecopyworkshop@aol.com Thanks.

"The transition to a knowledge-based economy sharply increases the demand for communication and swamps the old image-delivery systems."

Alvin Toffler, *PowerShift*

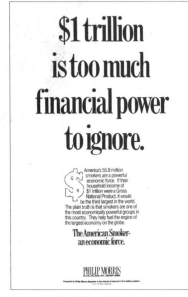
Alcohol and Tobacco.

Examples of ads for these products appear throughout the book.

Traditionally, they demonstrate state-of-the-art techniques. We've included examples to demonstrate the techniques – not endorse the products.

FIRST,
HE KILLED THE BOTTLE...

IF YOU DRINK,
DON'T DRIVE.

Cause-Related Advertising.

Many examples of exceptional ads for worthy causes are not featured.

Our focus is doing advertising that helps businesses stay in business.

Then, of course, you'll earn enough to support worthy causes.

• **Tougher competition.** Many advertising success stories come from people who were the first to do something. They usually had good products. And they probably had an expensive factory.

Today, it's easier for a competitor to copy your product, and if those competitors are still in business, they're pretty smart and pretty tough.

Advertising is about communicating competitive advantages. If there's more competition and less advantage, ads are often less effective.

Today, there are no easy businesses.

That's bad news and good news. It's tougher to do well, and it's needed more than ever. Got it?

• **Savvier consumers.** Now let's talk about you – you've seen it all and heard it all. Haven't you?

Chances are, you've been burned more than once by products that didn't live up to the ads.

Your first disappointment may have been an advertised toy or a cereal-box premium. That was the beginning of your ad education.

Remember. The people you'll be talking to are, in many ways, just like you – a bit cynical – and not all that easy to persuade.

• **Faster change.** When this book was written, people still used typewriters.

By the second edition, computers were common, but Web sites and e-mail addresses were new and novel. That's how fast the world can change.

For all these reasons – more media choices, tougher competition, savvier consumers, and faster change – a lot of advertising has become a lot less effective.

Yet each of these is also a reason for needing more and better communication.

And while individual ads may be less effective, advertising overall is a bigger part of our world.

IT'S AN AD AD AD AD WORLD.

Advertising has become more pervasive in the world we live in. It no longer sits obediently on the pages of your magazine or newspaper – or in a few thirty-second commercials on your TV or sixty-second commercials on your radio.

Advertising is growing dramatically – expanding into a wide range of fields that aren't even called advertising – direct marketing, public relations, and sales promotion – the thing many people call "IMC," Integrated Marketing Communications.

We call it The MarCom Matrix.

At the same time, some parts of advertising are contracting dramatically – many large ad agencies and retailers now offer fewer job opportunities.

HARDERFASTERBETTERMORE.

Alvin Toffler's *Third Wave* – the Post-Industrial Revolution – is crashing around us.

Everywhere you look, things are changing.

Time has compressed.

Now it's fast as a fax. Or faster.

e-mail anyone? Or is it quicker to hit the Web site?

Options have expanded.

When your parents were your age, they dealt with one phone company and their TVs tuned to just a few channels. And it wasn't that long ago.

Computers were for big-budget corporations or low-budget sci-fi movies.

Today, the list of possible media channels and marketing tactics is truly mind-boggling.

It's a marketplace that offers far more choices and far more ways to communicate.

For you, we hope that's good news.

And we hope this book helps you deal with that world – where effective communication is more important than ever.

Ethics.

Sad to say, this ain't no ethics book. (Or a grammar book, neither.)

One essential force of advertising and marketing is the search for advantage.

The "break the rules" spirit of the creative mind and the "bend the rules" history of many successful ad campaigns will continue to produce many examples of questionable ethics.

We've found that ethical questions are seldom those that confront you with bold moral choices – they just sort of sneak up on you.

Then you do the best you can.

Our best advice is to be of good heart and good intent in all you do.

In return, we offer our wishes for your good fortune and great success.

And this book.

An ad from P&G deals with the complex problem of diapers and recycling.

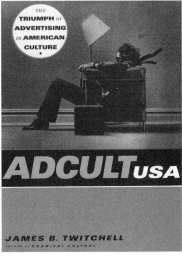

We like this book – AdCultUSA by James Twitchell. It won't help you write better ads, but it might help you understand the world in which you'll be writing those ads – and consuming them.

5

Introduction.

WE'VE NEEDED A BOOK LIKE THIS. It presents the essential creative and business principles needed for one of the toughest jobs in American business – writing effective advertising.

It was written by one of our industry's genuine creative talents – Bruce Bendinger.

I first met Bruce in 1970, when I was President of Leo Burnett. He came to us from one of Chicago's creative boutiques, where he'd won numerous awards.

We started him on one of our toughest accounts – P&G's All Temperature Cheer. Over the next two years, Bruce's team built Cheer into the #2 brand with ads that were engaging, yet effective.

In 1972, we named him a V-P and Creative Director. He was 27. At the time, the youngest ever.

Since then, Bruce has established himself as a top creative consultant, doing work for clients and agencies across the country.

We worked together again in Washington, DC, on Campaign '76, where he took a turn as Creative Director for the President of the United States.

And, over the years, we kept in touch.

Bruce also spent time as Sr. VP, Group Creative Director at FCB/Chicago, where he literally saved the Pizza Hut account for his agency – with work that helped turn that client's business around. No easy task.

When he sent me an early version of the book, I opened it with curiosity… and then delight.

It's great reading – this book demonstrates copywriting at the same time it teaches it.

And even though this book was written for advertising copywriters, I think there's something in it for everyone in our business.

Leonard S. Matthews, President 4A's
(American Association of Advertising Agencies) 1979-88

SECOND THOUGHTS…

Bruce asked me to add some observations on how things have changed in our industry since *The Copy Workshop Workbook* was first published.

First, the Weather's Better.

After retiring from the 4A's in New York, we moved to California, and I bought into a small agency in San Diego where my daughter worked.

My son joined us, and it once again proves to me that no matter what size agency you're in, this is a great business when you like the people you work with.

**Second, We Need This Book
More Than Ever.**

Fewer agencies of any size have the time or resources to train young professionals. It's even more true for a smaller agency like ours.

The smaller the agency, the bigger the problem – since you're also missing that group interaction where senior people help the cub copywriter learn on the job.

We have a number of copies of Bruce's book at our agency – and they get well-used by our junior people.

It's still the best "how-to" book I've ever seen.

(continued on next page)

Bruce set out to do a tough job.
I think he's done it wonderfully.
You're going to enjoy this book.

Leonard S. Matthews

Leonard S. Matthews
Former President, Leo Burnett
American Association of Advertising Agencies (4A's)
Chairman, Matthews, Mark San Diego, CA

How to Read This Book.

READ IT HOWEVER YOU WANT.

If you think you want to be a copywriter, use it like a good friend. Or a good boss.

If you're already in the advertising business, use it like a set of stretching exercises.

You can do the exercises if you feel like it. Or, better yet, apply some of the principles to your latest assignment – the one that's due tomorrow.

If you're a student, use it the way that your teacher tells you.

And, if you just picked it up because you're curious about advertising… enjoy yourself.

Because having a good time is one of the ways you make great advertising.

Bruce Bendinger

MATTHEWS *(Cont.)*

I've also found it a real help in getting account executives to understand the creative process.

In this New Edition, Bruce has added more emphasis on "Integrated Marketing." I think that's good.

But I think it's also worth mentioning that this is what the best agencies have done all along.

At Leo Burnett, if it was something that would help a client's business – we did it.

And so should you.

I hope this book helps you find new ways to help your clients.

Because media advertising isn't the only way to build our client's brands.

Finally, I'm a genuine fan of Bruce's writing in this book – it demonstrates the quality and attention that all our work deserves.

Because when we do work we can be proud of; when we do work that builds our clients' businesses; when we work as a team with people we like – there's not a better business in the world.

Len Matthews
Rancho Santa Fe

***Bruce Bendinger* on CBS Morning News.** *(Between the Ambassador to Iran and the precision jump-roping team – bet you missed it.)*

ReIntroduction.

*The world has changed since our first two editions. We asked a more recent head of the 4A's, **Ralph Rydholm,** to add his perspective.*

I MET Bruce Bendinger in a different time zone. I met him in the '60s. You remember the '60s, right? The break-all-the-rules, do-anything-you-want, the-whole-world-is-changing '60s!

A TIME WHEN WE STILL HAD SOME TIME.

The '60s were also a time when we still had some time. Time to learn the business. Time to learn how to make whatever talent we had actually work.

Time to try things on each other before we showed them to 250 million (or more) people.

Well, that time is gone. And so is the time. Today it seems there's hardly any time to learn the business.

Which is why this book – and Bruce Bendinger – are so important.

PRODUCTIVITY FROM DAY ONE.

Agencies don't have the time to train.

Now they leave that to the colleges and the special training schools.

In today's agency, you have to be productive from Day One.

Thanks to Bruce, you can get a clear picture of what you need to know (and how to learn it) faster.

*Ralph Rydholm,
former Chairman, TLK/EuroRSCG; former President, American Association of Advertising Agencies.*

Times have changed. Time has changed.

That's why it's the perfect time for this business of changing minds. And the perfect time for this book.

BE PREPARED. FOR CHANGE.

You can't go into this business today as unprepared as we were (no matter how good we thought we were at the time). Because it's a faster time.

Faster ups. Faster downs. Faster turnovers.

Which in our business has led to faster and faster deadlines, new clients every week, new mergers (and new conflicts), new pressures for new campaigns for new people at new (or old) clients in new media and there is no time left. No time at all.

THE SAME THING ONLY DIFFERENT.

But we still have to do the same thing we always did – find the way to cut through a clutter, change a mind, move someone to action, build a brand.

No matter what media you're working in.

Or how little time you have.

You have to do those same things – and this book will teach you the lessons we had to learn. Only faster.

And the great thing is, we *can* do it faster.

THE BEST BUSINESS IN THE WORLD.

Which is why, even in these times of no time, it's still the best business in the world.

Because you can still use all the talent you have, all the things you know, to move a mind. Or a heart.

So, in fact, it may be the best time yet.

You can create it faster, get it on air (or print, or the Web, or direct response, etc.) faster, move a consumer faster, build a brand faster, and, good news for you, build a career faster.

Well, I'm out of time.

Enjoy the book – there's a lot there for you.

Good luck.

And have a good time.

LOOK FAMILIAR?

Some of you may have had this book in an Introduction to Advertising class.

If you did, parts of this book will be familiar. You'll probably recognize some of the ads we talk about and some of the points we make.

We publish both books – and that book was very much influenced by this book.

A Small Revolution.

After helping change books on copywriting, we worked with other ad instructors to improve the way advertising was taught.

We hope *Advertising & The Business of Brands* gave you a solid introduction.

And we hope it helps you do well in this class. Hey, at least you'll recognize some of the pictures.

Can we help you? Call 773-871-1179 and real human beings at The Copy Workshop will do their absolute best to meet your needs. The computers have changed since this photo was taken, but the personal service is still the same.

9

THE OLD NEW EDITION.
The Copy Workshop Workbook was originally published in 1988. It was an early example of "desktop publishing."

Along the way, it became the #1 book on advertising copywriting. Go figure.

And it turned our little advertising consulting practice into a real publishing company.

The update was done in 1993, and we were startled to discover that something like a book on how to create advertising goes out-of-date almost as you write it.

Fortunately, a lot of good advertising stays good advertising and successful ad campaigns always have a lesson to teach us – no matter when they were done.

O nce upon a time...
copywriting was taught.

It was a skilled craft, acquired through years of apprenticeship and hard work.

But TV, the Baby Boom, and The Creative Revolution changed all that.

The shift from print to television created copywriters with outdated skills.

Then came the '60s.

The War Babies, our first TV generation, hit the ad business about the same time Bill Bernbach's writers and art directors were revolutionizing it.

Creative careers accelerated.

A memorable theme and a decent TV idea turned a writer into a Creative Supervisor.

Escalating salaries and rising expectations made apprenticeship unaffordable and impractical.

The economy changed.

The easy growth of the '60s slowed in the '70s, staggered into the '80s, roared into the '90s, and suddenly it's a new century.

Advertisers and agencies felt their worlds rocked by mergers. And slowly, the tempo grew faster.

Now it's a new century. Faster than ever. Tougher than ever. More choices. More chances.

For small advertisers, increased media noise makes it harder than ever to be heard.

For large advertisers, increased pressures make it harder to decide.

For agencies, the battle between the search for the lessons of what works best and the messy fact that what works best is often something you've never seen before just keeps making it harder.

And so it goes.

Haphazardly ever after...

Meanwhile…

YOU HAVE A JOB TO DO – as a copywriter.

That's what this book is about.

Our Mission is to help young men and women prepare for an industry that is undergoing revolutionary change.

Our Objective is to teach the skills necessary to create effective marketing communication .

Our Strategy is to present effective examples and the principles that make them work in an organized and easy-to-follow format.

Our Tactic is this book.

MISSION, OBJECTIVE, STRATEGY, TACTICS.

You may find this a new way of thinking and a new way of developing your writing – when we're done, it should make all the sense in the world.

A Message for Readers Who Aren't Writers.

THOUGH THIS BOOK IS FOR COPYWRITERS, there's something in it for almost everyone.

It's an easy-to-understand introduction to modern communication techniques.

It offers insights on how to get ahead in business.

It can help you learn to solve problems creatively.

It can help you work with others more effectively.

It can make communicating easier and more fun.

If you're in business, it might help you become a more effective marketing person.

If you're not, it can make you a smarter consumer.

This is the beginning of one of the most interesting journeys in American business.

Along the way, you'll learn new concepts and develop new skills. Hey, you might even enjoy it.

HISTORICAL NOTE #2.

Though a business practice since earliest recorded history, advertising grew and prospered in the USA.

In many ways, the spirit of advertising is uniquely American.

"The First American," Ben Franklin, was an ad man.

A writer, Thomas Paine, was a major force in "selling" the American Revolution with his persuasive little pamphlet, *Common Sense.*

In general, advertising took hold in American society due to a number of unique forces:

The English Language.

An adaptable, democratic, and easy-to-use language, English is now the world language of business.

Useful concepts and phrases are quickly adapted and adopted.

It's a language made for today's changing marketplace.

Economic Opportunity.

With an abundance of resources and opportunity, America had a population motivated to make the most of it and a government that encouraged and subsidized enterprise.

Democracy.

Think about it – the marketplace is about choice and change.

Consumers vote every day.

America was the best place to have a new idea and make it happen.

From America to the World.

A key player in this process has been the person who shapes these communications of commerce – the copywriter – an American original.

As we move to a world economy, the need for creative and motivating communication is now a worldwide opportunity. It started here.

THE FIRST SECTION.

The first step is to become a student of the craft of copywriting.

We'll look at early breakthroughs in advertising thinking.

Next, we'll look at forces shaping today's marketplace.

Then, we'll examine the creative or "ideation" process and show you some ways to develop even more flexibility in your thinking.

Finally, we'll talk about how verbal and visual communication have to work together.

DO YOU KNOW WHO THIS IS?
You'll know by the time we're done. **Claude Hopkins** is one of the people who helped invent copywriting.

You don't have to thank him. He made $185,000 a year back when cars cost $1,000 and there were no income taxes!

Every once in a while, art directors and copywriters bug each other. Chapter Six talks about the importance of visual communication.

Table of Contents:

INTRODUCTION.
Some brief words of welcome and purpose.

FOREWORDS.
Assignment #0. Assignment #1.

MORE WORDS.

THE TOUGH SECTION.

This section of the book deals with developing advertising strategy and introduces you to basic copywriting techniques.

You may find them a bit different from your regular writing habits.

Starting with Strategy.

The strategy section will teach you how the traditional P&G-style Advertising Strategy statement.

Then, it will introduce you to other formats – such as the original Y&R Creative Work Plan.

You'll see how they're different and all very similar.

Selling with Smarts.

There's a short but important section on what makes for a good Selling Idea. (And how to sell them once you have them.)

You won't find all the answers (if we had them, we'd be writing this book from our very large yacht), but you'll get started on the right foot.

Writing with Style.

Finally, there's an introduction to contemporary copywriting style – which varies from regular writing in a number of ways. Like sentence fragments.

"Where is that big black bag going with that little man?

**It's Leo Burnett with
a bag full of Selling Ideas.**

THE FUN SECTION!

We're going to write some ads – all kinds of ads – print, radio, and even TV commercials.

This section features approaches for print, radio, and television writing for the various media with Assignments and Exercises designed to put the principles you've learned into actual practice.

Outdoor in action.

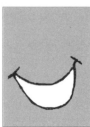

The Pitch. *One of the key formats you need to learn to create radio spots.*

Sales Promotion. *Find out more about a growing part of The MarCom Matrix.*

YOUR WORDS.

Why are these dogs laughing?

THE LAST SECTION.
We'll talk about working in the advertising business and building good working relationships.

We'll talk about how things can go wrong and how to make things go right. Hopefully.

We'll talk about opportunities outside of advertising. The good news – there are a lot of them!

We'll discuss building your "book," and getting a job.

Finally, we'll talk about how it all works together– and what it takes to make a great Campaign!

And we'll say more than once…
"Advertising is a team sport!"

THIS IS A COOL GUY.
Alex Osborn – the "O" in BBDO (Batten Barton Durstine and Osborn) is the person who invented what we call "Brainstorming."

It's one of the fairly cool things we'll cover in this section.

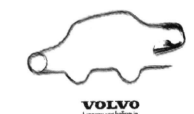

VOLVO
A car you can believe in.

This brand has stayed vital and relevant with an evolving brand image – from durability to safety.

Assignment #0:

THESE ARE SO EASY,
we won't even give them a number.

Do them anyway.

They're all designed to help you start
thinking about advertising.

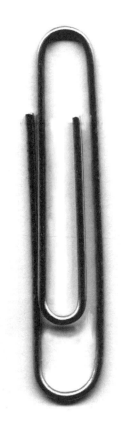

Speaking of Paper Clips…
Here's a classic copywriting assignment
from Sears.

Do it now – and then see how you'd do
it after reading this book.

Since this is a workbook, you might
want to clip your ads to this page.

#0/A. MAGAZINE EXERCISE.

- Pick two ads you LIKE.
  Tell us why you like them.

- Pick two ads you HATE.
  Tell us why you hate them.

#0/B. VCR EXERCISE.

Tonight, when you watch TV, save the commercials
and zap the programs.

Now, look at them again.

- Pick the two commercials you like best.
  Why did you like them?

- Pick the two commercials you like least.
  Why didn't you like them?

#0/C. SCRAP FILE(S).

- Start a file of ads you like.
- Start another file. Start saving ads or articles
  on subjects or businesses that interest you.

Think of it this way – if you had your own
agency, what accounts would you like to have.

Or, to think of it another way, what companies
would you like to be working for?

Start to save and clip.

#0/D. THE SEARS PAPER CLIP ASSIGNMENT.

- Create a print ad for a paper clip.
- Make a rough sketch of the ad.
  Write the headline(s) and body copy.

We want you to exercise your imagination.

But, remember, the purpose of the ad is to sell the
item. Limit ad size to 8" x10".

Assignment #1:

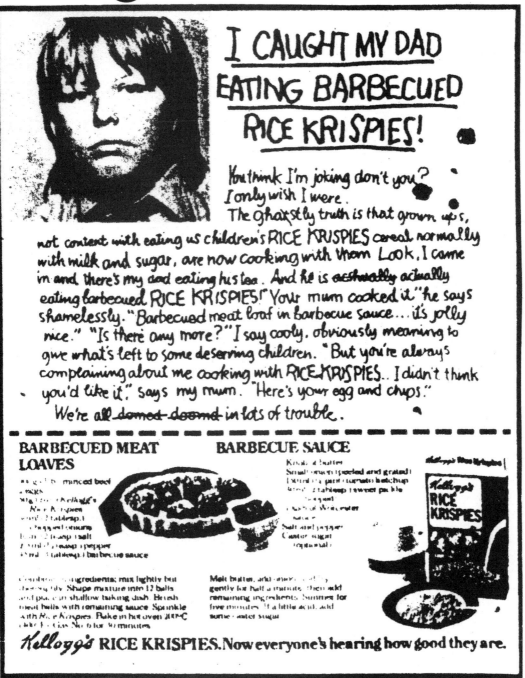

This ad for "Barbecued Rice Krispies" won awards in Great Britain.
It sold a few Rice Krispies, too. Now it's your turn. Create an ad like this one.

MAKE
THE LAYOUTS
ROUGH
AND
THE IDEAS
FANCY.

STAVROS COSMOPULOS

WHAT ABOUT LAYOUTS?

This book's about writing good ads, not how to make them look good.

We'll show you examples of good-looking and effective design, but we won't try to show you how to do it.

However, we do have some advice.

LEARN TO PRINT.

First, get your handwriting together. Next, find the writing instrument (pen, marker, etc.) you like and develop a good strong hand.

I use a hard-to-find type of Pentel and make everyone crazy when I run out. Find what works for you.

Then, practice your printing.

When you're in a meeting, you want to be able to present what you write in a clear, confident hand.

Start Paying Attention to Good Art Direction.

Nothing makes a copywriter look better than a terrific art director.

Get a relationship going. We'll have more to say about this in Chapter Six.

Find Out How Much Visual Talent You Have.

Find someone who knows what they're doing and see how you do.

You can probably learn how to do a brochure and newsletter.

Will you be able to do more?

Hey, you never know.

ASSIGNMENT #1 (Cont.)

First, pick your **product.**

Throughout the book, you'll be asked to "pick a product."

Sometimes the categories are very specific and some-times they aren't. In this case, your product is either:

A. **A product you like** –
Cereal, peanut butter, whatever.

B. **A service you might offer** –
Baby sitting, dog-walking, whatever.

C. **An event** – party, picnic, lunch, whatever.

D. **You** – think of it as a fun way to do a résumé.

HERE'S HOW TO DO IT:

1. **Find an appropriate picture of yourself** – snapshot, school picture, etc. That's your **visual.**

2. **Decide on your product.** Got it? Good.
If you can find a picture of your product, maybe that should be in the ad, too.

3. **Write a headline.** A quote, a story title, "true confessions" type of headline… whatever.

4. **Write some copy.** Tell us things we should know about your product. Why is it a good product? What's the "benefit" of your product? Write it like a story or a short theme.

5. **Add an extra something at the bottom:**
a coupon, your recipe for a great peanut butter sandwich, directions to the lunchroom… an offer… a contest … whatever.

6. **Put 'em all together in a layout.**
It should look sort of like the Rice Krispies ad. As you can see, neatness is optional.

There's only one absolute requirement.
Have fun.

YOU CAN USE THIS FOR YOUR LAYOUT.

Advertising's Ages.

FOUR A's OF ADVERTISING.

When advertising began, the primary concerns were:

Attention. Get noticed. *"You can't save souls in an empty church."*

Awareness. Be remembered. Early advertising experience showed that if consumers were already aware of your brand name, they were more willing to buy and try your product.

Attitude. Your advertising should make the consumer's attitude toward your product more positive. (Being liked does seem to make a difference.)

Action. Ads should work toward motivating action. Before you begin, you should have the desired consumer action clearly in mind. Know where you want to go. It helps.

AIDA.

Some call this sequence "AIDA."

That stands for: Attention, Interest, Desire, Action – it's the same thing as our "Four A's."

Claude Hopkins. Copywriter. In 1908, Lord & Thomas paid him $185,000 a year! He was worth it. His copy made millions for his clients.

IN THE BEGINNING, ad agencies were "agents." They sold advertising "space," primarily in newspapers and magazines, and collected a commission.

Advertising was *"keeping your name before the public."*

After all, customers who know your name are more likely to buy your product or brand.

Today, we call that "awareness," and it's still a priority of almost all advertising.

Then, in the early 1900s, a young man named **Albert Lasker** at the Lord & Thomas agency (now Foote, Cone & Belding) had a revelation.

The advertising business was *not* about selling space – it was about creating and selling what was *inside* that space – the advertising itself.

Advertising was *"salesmanship in print."*

Claude Hopkins, a Lord & Thomas copywriter, was advertising's first great salesman.

In his book *Scientific Advertising,* Hopkins described the attitude a successful copywriter must develop:

"Don't think of people in the mass.
That gives you a blurred view.
Think of a typical individual, man or woman,
who is likely to want what you sell."

Hopkins continues…

"The advertising man studies the consumer.
He tries to place himself in the position of the buyer.
His success largely depends on doing that to
the exclusion of everything else."

Times have changed.

The truth remains.

Talk *to* people.

One at a time.

PRE-EMPTION.

Hopkins is also credited with inventing an advertising technique known as "pre-emption." You take a product feature or a quality generic to the category, and, by pre-empting that feature, you make it yours.

Two early examples were "It's Toasted" for Lucky Strike and the claim that Schlitz beer bottles were sterilized with "Live Steam."

In fact, all tobacco was toasted and all beer bottles were sterilized with steam – "live steam" sounds more exciting. Hopkins knew how to add drama.

This advertising technique is still used today.

Can you think of some examples?

COPY BY HOPKINS.

Here's one of Hopkins' most famous ads – for Sunkist Oranges.

In 1916, this was a new idea for the average American – Orange Juice!

The headline was simple and, for the time, intriguing *"Drink an Orange."*

Benefits, Features, Support.

Now look at the first copy section.

First, Hopkins focuses on **consumer benefits** – good taste and good health.

Next, he focuses on **features** or **attributes** of the product, expressed as **product benefits** – such as "Nature's germ-proof package."

These function as **support** for the benefits of taste and healthfulness.

Note the use of informative captions throughout.

Closing Arguments.

Finally, he "Asks for the order" and closes with – an **offer.**

After Hopkins offered you good reasons to add orange juice to your diet, he offered you a "Juice Extractor" for *only 10¢.*

Hopkins and Albert Lasker actually had the juice extractor designed and manufactured.

They knew it would help increase the use of oranges. And it worked!

America's breakfast habits were changed forever.

IMAGE ADVERTISING.

As Hopkins was proving the power of words and "reason why," other advertisers were having great success by *showing it* rather than *saying it* with advertising driven by visual impact.

The visual – the image – does the majority of the work.

Fashion ads are a good example.

Selling with Visuals.

Important selling points can also be communicated visually.

Below, the Uneeda Biscuit boy tells consumers (mostly mothers) Nabisco's packaging keeps their crackers dry.

It's a visual product benefit with an easy-to-understand reason why.

Palmolive

The successor to ordinary toilet soaps in Particular Homes. Made of Pure Imported Olive and Palm Oils skillfully blended and combined with Cocoa Butter. **Palmolive** is not merely a cleanser, it combines all the virtues of the wonderful ingredients from which it is made. It allays irritation and inflammation and supplies the necessary oils for harsh skins and dry scalps.

Palmolive exercises the skin in that it stimulates the action of the many tiny pores and glands. The removal of all obstacles allows free circulation of the blood, and the delicate nourishment embodied in **Palmolive** supplies just the necessary impetus to restore the skin to its proper condition after cleansing it. Continued use will produce a beautiful, healthy, rosy complexion. There is no complexion that **Palmolive** cannot improve. If your dealer cannot supply you, send us his name and 15 cents and we will forward, prepaid, a full size cake.

Send four cents in stamps, to cover cost of mailing, and the *names of your grocer and druggist*, and we will send one of our beautiful oriental photogravures without advertising upon it, suitable for framing, size 10 x 16 inches. Address,

B. J. JOHNSON SOAP CO., 318 Fowler St., Milwaukee, Wis.

Hopkins also did "image" advertising.

Here, he took an unknown soap made of palm and olive oils, and created what was, for a time, America's leading beauty soap – Palmolive!

Despite the "reason why" copy, the real impact of this ad is visual. This is often the case in image advertising.

Once again, Hopkins uses an offer.

This time, the art from the ad!

A $100,000 Dish

New-Type Baked Beans Which College-Trained Scientific Cooks Have Spent Years in Perfecting

It has cost us at least $100,000 to perfect Van Camp's Pork and Beans.

Modern culinary experts—men with college training—have devoted some years to this dish. Able scientists and famous chefs have co-operated with them.

This Was Wrong

Old-style baked beans were very hard to digest. They were always under-baked. Yet the baking crisped them and broke them—made some hard and some mushy.

In the Van Camp kitchens each lot of beans is analyzed before we start to cook. They are boiled in water freed from minerals, because hard water makes them tough.

They are baked in steam ovens by live steam under pressure at 245 degrees. They are thus baked for hours—baked as beans should be—without bursting or crisping a bean.

856 Sauces

The zestful sauce which we bake with Van Camp's would itself give the dish distinction.

But these scientific cooks made 856 sauces before they attained this perfection. This ideal tang and savor came only through months of development.

A far greater accomplishment was to fit baked beans for easy digestion, while leaving them mealy and whole.

This Is Perfect

The result is a new-type dish which will change your whole idea of baked beans. It will multiply their popularity. Above all, it will not tax digestion. And it costs you less—all ready-baked—than do home-baked beans. Please order a trial meal.

VAN CAMP'S
Pork and Beans
Baked With the Van Camp Sauce – Also Baked Without the Sauce

Your first shave

will prove, beyond all doubt, the claims men make for this unique shaving cream

Let us send you a 10-shave tube to try

WE'VE built Palmolive Shaving Cream to a national business success by making few claims for it. We let it prove its case by sending a 10-day test tube free to all who ask. In that way, we've gained leadership in a highly competitive field in only a few years.

130 formulas tried

Before offering Palmolive Shaving Cream, we asked 1000 men their supreme desires in a shaving cream. Then met them exactly.

We tried and discarded 130 formulas before finding the right one. We put our 60 years of soap experience behind this creation. The result is a shaving cream unlike any you have ever tried.

Five advantages

1. Multiplies itself in lather 250 times.
2. Softens the beard in one minute.
3. Maintains its creamy fullness for 10 minutes on the face.
4. Strong bubbles hold the hairs erect for cutting.
5. Fine after-effects due to palm and olive oil content.

Just send coupon

Your present method may suit you well. But still there may be a better one. This test may mean much to you in comfort. Send the coupon before you forget.

THE PALMOLIVE COMPANY (Del. Corp.), CHICAGO, ILL.

MORE COPY BY HOPKINS.
Note the similarities in these two ads.
Claims and Positioning.
Each has dramatic fact-based claims.
"130 formulas/856 Sauces."

And, of course, "The $100,000 Dish."

Hopkins positions against competition. "Dish" positions against home-cooked beans. "First Shave" positions Palmolive against other shaving soaps.

"Asking for the Order."

For Van Camp's he says, *"Please order a trial meal."*

For Palmolive, a free sample. Each ad makes a small product important.

Famous Copywriters.

Helen Lansdowne Resor.

"She had a dozen ideas to the minute… and kept them coming so fast you couldn't possibly keep up and had to sit down afterwards with a pencil and paper and try to sort them out."

"She had a brilliant feminine mind that darted and dipped and swooped with terrifying speed and accuracy."

She wasn't the only "brilliant feminine mind" to succeed.

Other Prominent Women.

A time when women did not even have the vote, there were a number prominent in the early days of advertising.

In 1903, the magazine *Profitable Advertising* profiled 40 women copywriters, advertising artists, agents, and advisers. Among the women from those early days were:

• copywriter-turned-author **Helen Woodward** ("Through Many Windows") • **Louise Taylor Davis** (Y&R) • **Jean Wade Rindlaub** (BBDO) • the retail legend, **Bernice Fitz-Gibbon,** who wrote copy like – "It's smart to be thrifty" for Macy's and "Nobody, but nobody, undersells Gimbel's."

LET'S MEET A FEW OF THE COPYWRITERS who had a big impact on the early advertising industry.

Some developed effective approaches, some helped develop successful agencies. Some did both.

HOW'S THIS FOR A STORY?

Smart, talented young copywriter meets up-and-coming young account exec. They work together and marry.

Together, they build the world's largest ad agency.

Sound a bit far-fetched? It's true.

In the early 1900s, after graduating as her high-school valedictorian, **Helen Lansdowne** began writing retail ads in Cincinnati. First, she wrote for a newspaper and then for a local streetcar advertising company.

Then, she went to work with a bright young account exec who was making a name for himself developing ad strategies that appealed to the growing middle class. His name was **Stanley Resor.**

When J. Walter Thompson (JWT) hired Stanley to open a Cincinnati office, Helen went along.

At the time, many JWT clients had products that were purchased by women. Helen was the right person at the right place at the right time – with the right thinking.

"I supplied the feminine point of view," she said.

"I watched the advertising to see that the idea, the wording, and the illustrating were effective for women."

Even then, understanding and insight into the consumer made a tremendous difference in advertising effectiveness.

Her ads for Woodbury's Soap increased sales 1000% with "A skin you love to touch."

She was the first woman to appear before the board of Procter & Gamble.

She explained advertising to a room full of men who marketed and advertised to women.

Together, Stanley and Helen ran JWT. He ran client service. She supervised the creation of the advertising.

She never really had a title. But she didn't need one.

Helen supervised the legendary JWT office decor as well as the advertising. She nurtured and supervised a creative staff where women were paid and treated well.

And they wrote advertising that worked.

Brands and Celebrity. If you want your brand to be famous, one way to do it is connect that brand with famous people. And vice versa. Appearing in advertising was not only a way to capitalize on fame, it was also a way to become more famous.

SOFT SOAP & HARD SELL.

Here are two famous JWT campaigns.

Emotion and Poetry.

For Woodbury's, Helen Resor sold softness, romance, and sex appeal.

The line was simple and memorable, "A skin you love to touch," with an almost poetic rhythm.

Against that emotion, copy featured a skin-care regimen and an offer of product samples and the art from the advertisement.

The Art of the Testimonial.

For Lux, they sold glamor, luxury, fame… and sex appeal.

Helen Resor upgraded the testimonial format by getting famous people to endorse JWT products.

For Lux, the use of movie stars made a bar of soap glamourous.

Stanley Resor called it "the spirit of emulation." Helen called her friends.

Helen's Connections.

The first famous personage was Mrs. O.H.P. Belmont, a leader in New York society at the time – as well as a prominent feminist. She endorsed Pond's in exchange for a donation to one of her favorite charities.

Ads featured Mrs. Reginald Vanderbilt, the Duchess de Richelieu, and the Queen of Rumania.

Helen also invited a high-school chum to come work at JWT – James Webb Young. (You'll read a bit about him in Chapter Four, "How to Have an Idea.")

Caples, Getchell & More...

John Caples. BBDO's direct response and copy testing expert.

READ ALL ABOUT IT.

You can understand Caples' style just by reading the table of contents of his well-written well-organized book, *How to Make Your Advertising Make Money.*

TABLE OF CONTENTS:

HERE ARE SOME OTHER COPY PIONEERS – who invented and then improved the craft:

John Caples. He established some of the basic principles of successful direct advertising and shared them through books and an approach that applies to virtually all advertising.

Bruce Barton. He used his talent to grow one of the major advertising agencies... and more.

Ned Jordan. Here was a unique individual who combined copywriting and automobile manufacturing.

Stirling Getchell. His flame burned briefly and brightly. He pioneered techniques of positioning and photographic storytelling, which predated TV.

UNDERSTANDING WHAT WORKS.

Developing advertising is a learning process.

We learn about products, we learn about the competition, and we learn about people.

John Caples spent his career learning what works. Learn more about his legacy at www.caples.org.

For example, here are his thoughts on headlines:

"Headlines make ads work. The best headlines appeal to people's self interest, or give news. Long headlines that say something outpull short headlines that say nothing.

"Remember that every headline has one job – it must stop your prospects with a believable promise.

"All messages have headlines. In TV, it's the start of the commercial; in radio, the first few words; in a letter, the first paragraph.

To men who want to
Quit Work some day

"Come up with a good headline and you're almost certain to have a good ad."

"Can he really play?" a girl whispered. "Heavens, no!" Arthur exclaimed. "He never played a note in his life."

They Laughed When I Sat Down At the Piano
But When I Started to Play!~

ARTHUR had just played "The Rosary." The room rang with applause. I decided that this would be a dramatic moment for me to make my debut. To the amazement of all my friends I strode confidently over to the piano and sat down.

"Jack is up to his old tricks," somebody chuckled. The crowd laughed. They were all certain that I couldn't play a single note.

"Can he really play?" I heard a girl whisper to Arthur. "Heavens, no!" Arthur exclaimed. "He never played a note in all his life...But just you watch him. This is going to be good."

I decided to make the most of the situation. With mock dignity I drew out a silk handkerchief and lightly dusted off the keys. Then I rose and gave the revolving piano stool a quarter of a turn, just as I had seen an imitator of Paderewski do in a vaudeville sketch.

"What do you think of his execution?" called a voice from the rear.

"We're in favor of it!" came back the answer, and the crowd rocked with laughter.

Then I Started to Play

Instantly a tense silence fell on the guests. The laughter died on their lips as if by magic. I played through the first bars of Liszt's immortal Liebesträume. I heard gasps of amazement. My friends sat breathless—spellbound.

I played on and as I played I forgot the people around me. I forgot the hour, the place, the breathless listeners. The little world I lived in seemed to fade—seemed to grow dim—unreal. Only the music was real. Only the music and the visions it brought me. Visions as beautiful and as changing as the wind-blown clouds and drifting moonlight, that long ago inspired the master composer. It seemed as if the master musician himself were speaking to me—speaking through the medium of music—not in words but in chords. Not in sentences but in exquisite melodies.

A Complete Triumph!

As the last notes of the Liebesträume died away, the room resounded with a sudden roar of applause. I found myself surrounded by excited faces. How my friends carried on! Men shook my hand—wildly congratulated me—pounded me on the back in their enthusiasm! Everybody was exclaiming with delight—plying me with rapid questions.... "Jack! Why didn't you tell us you could play like that?" ..."Where *did* you learn?"—"How long have you studied?"—"Who *was* your teacher?"

"I have never even *seen* my teacher," I replied. "And just a short while ago I couldn't play a note."

"Quit your kidding," laughed Arthur, himself an accomplished pianist. "You've been studying for years. I can tell."

"I have been studying only a short while," I insisted. "I decided to keep it a secret so that I could surprise all you folks."

Then I told them the whole story.

"Have you ever heard of the U. S. School of Music?" I asked. A few of my friends nodded. "That's a correspondence school, isn't it?" they exclaimed.

"Exactly," I replied. "They have a new simplified method that can teach you to play any instrument *by note* in just a few months."

How I Learned to Play Without a Teacher

And then I explained how for years I had longed to play the piano.

"It seems just a short while ago," I continued, "that I saw an interesting ad of the U. S. School of Music mentioning a new method of learning to play which only cost a few cents a day! The ad told how a woman had mastered the piano in her spare time at home—and *without a teacher!* Best of all, the wonderful new method she used required no laborious scales—no heartless exercises—no tiresome practising. It sounded so convincing that I filled out the coupon requesting the Free Demonstration Lesson.

"The free book arrived promptly and I started in that very night to study the Demonstration Lesson. I was amazed to see how easy it was to play this new way. Then I sent for the course.

"When the course arrived I found it was just as the ad said—as easy as A. B. C.! And as the lessons continued they got easier and easier. Before I knew it I was playing all the pieces I liked best. Nothing stopped me. I could play ballads or classical numbers or jazz, all with equal ease. And I never did have any special talent for music."

* * * *

Play Any Instrument

You, too, can now *teach yourself* to be an accomplished musician—right at home—in half the usual time. You can't go wrong with this simple new method which has already shown almost half a million people how to play their favorite instruments *by note*. Forget that old-fashioned idea that you need special "talent." Just read the list of instruments in the panel, decide which one you want to play and the U. S. School will do the rest. And bear in mind no matter which instrument you choose, the cost in each case will be the same—just a few cents a day. No matter whether you are a mere beginner or already a good performer, you will be interested in learning about this new and wonderful method.

Send for Our Free Booklet and Demonstration Lesson

Thousands of successful students never dreamed they possessed musical ability until it was revealed to them by a remarkable "Musical Ability Test" which we send entirely without cost with our interesting free booklet.

If you are in earnest about wanting to play your favorite instrument—if you really want to gain happiness and increase your popularity—send at once for the free booklet and Demonstration Lesson. No cost—no obligation. Sign and send the convenient coupon now. Instruments supplied when needed, cash or credit. **U. S. School of Music, 812 Brunswick Bldg., New York City.**

U. S. School of Music,
812 Brunswick Bldg., New York City.

Please send me your free book, "Music Lessons in Your Own Home," with introduction by Dr. Frank Crane, Demonstration Lesson and particulars of your offer. I am interested in the following course:

....

Have you above instrument?.....................

Name...
(Please write plainly)

Address...

City.................State...................

Pick Your Instrument

Piano	Harmony and Composition
Organ	Sight Singing
Violin	Ukulele
Drums and Traps	Guitar
Mandolin	Hawaiian Steel Guitar
Clarinet	Harp
Flute	Cornet
Saxophone	Piccolo
'Cello	Trombone
Voice and Speech Culture	
Automatic Finger Control	
Piano Accordion	
Banjo (5-String, Plectrum or Tenor)	

**FROM COPYWRITER
TO CONGRESSMAN.**

The AdMan Nobody Knows.

He was a best-selling author, confidante of presidents, and a U.S. Congressman.

He was Chairman of the United Negro College Fund and the American Heart Association.

He was a copywriter – a preacher's son named Bruce Barton.

His name's still on the door at BBDO – Batten, Barton, Durstine & Osborn.

In addition to his work at BBDO, he wrote continually – articles (he began as a magazine writer) and books.

He combined his background in religion and advertising to write *The Man Nobody Knows*, a book that combined classic parables of Christianity with those of modern salesmanship.

It was a bestseller.

In *The Seven Lost Secrets of Success*, author Joe Vitale lists some of Barton's classic principles. They include:

• **Discover your real business.** Lipstick or romance? Tires or safety?

• **"Story selling."** Use parables and stories to deliver your message.

• **The value of sincerity and honesty in effective selling.**

A preacher's son, he, and many others, wrote sermons for America's growing business community.

The PENALTY OF LEADERSHIP

IN every field of human endeavor, he that is first must perpetually live in the white light of publicity. ¶Whether the leadership be vested in a man or in a manufactured product, emulation and envy are ever at work. ¶In art, in literature, in music, in industry, the reward and the punishment are always the same. ¶The reward is widespread recognition; the punishment, fierce denial and detraction. ¶When a man's work becomes a standard for the whole world, it also becomes a target for the shafts of the envious few. ¶If his work be merely mediocre, he will be left severely alone—if he achieve a masterpiece, it will set a million tongues a-wagging. ¶Jealousy does not protrude its forked tongue at the artist who produces a commonplace painting. ¶Whatsoever you write, or paint, or play, or sing, or build, no one will strive to surpass, or to slander you, unless your work be stamped with the seal of genius. ¶Long, long after a great work or a good work has been done, those who are disappointed or envious continue to cry out that it can not be done. ¶Spiteful little voices in the domain of art were raised against our own Whistler as a mountebank, long after the big world had acclaimed him its greatest artistic genius. ¶Multitudes flocked to Bayreuth to worship at the musical shrine of Wagner, while the little group of those whom he had dethroned and displaced argued angrily that he was no musician at all. ¶The little world continued to protest that Fulton could never build a steamboat, while the big world flocked to the river banks to see his boat steam by. ¶The leader is assailed because he is a leader, and the effort to equal him is merely added proof of that leadership. ¶Failing to equal or to excel, the follower seeks to depreciate and to destroy—but only confirms once more the superiority of that which he strives to supplant. ¶There is nothing new in this. ¶It is as old as the world and as old as the human passions—envy, fear, greed, ambition, and the desire to surpass. ¶And it all avails nothing. ¶If the leader truly leads, he remains—the leader. ¶Master-poet, master-painter, master-workman, each in his turn is assailed, and each holds his laurels through the ages. ¶That which is good or great makes itself known, no matter how loud the clamor of denial. ¶That which deserves to live—lives.

Cadillac Motor Car Co. Detroit, Mich.

EMPHASIZING THE POSITIVE.

Bruce Barton referred to advertising as *"the handmaiden of business."* He said, *"The advertisements which persuade people to act are written by men who have an abiding respect for the intelligence of their readers, and a deep sincerity regarding the merits of the goods they have to sell."*

The ad above, "The Penalty of Leadership," was one of the favorite ads of the period.

It was not written by Barton but by another well-regarded copywriter of the day, Theodore MacManus.

The tone is typical – positive and high-minded.

(By the way, MacManus had a young copywriter working for him named Leo Burnett.)

Often a bridesmaid but never a bride

EDNA'S case was really a pathetic one. Like every woman, her primary ambition was to marry. Most of the girls of her set were married—or about to be. Yet not one possessed more grace or charm or loveliness than she.

And as her birthdays crept gradually toward that tragic thirty-mark, marriage seemed farther from her life than ever. She was often a bridesmaid but never a bride.

That's the insidious thing about halitosis (unpleasant breath). You, yourself, rarely know when you have it. And even your closest friends won't tell you.

EMPHASIZING THE NEGATIVE.

Ads like the one above helped build Listerine into a major brand.

They "dramatized the problem" and pre-empted it by owning "halitosis," a semi-scientific word for "bad breath."

If your product solves a problem and you can, in some way, own that problem, your brand has a good chance of owning the solution.

Even today, agencies like Y&R are concerned with *The Problem the Advertising Must Solve.*

PROBLEMS, PROBLEMS.

New levels of disposable income and a new concern with hygiene were driving forces in the success of many new personal products:

A Cough is a Social Blunder

Drop that Cough
SMITH BROTHERS *of Poughkeepsie*
FAMOUS SINCE 1847

Cough Problems? *Smith Brothers Cough Drops dial up the social importance of not having a cough.*

Held back by Coffee . .
this boy never had a fair chance

Coffee Problems? *Postum, a non-caffeine hot beverage, positioned itself aggressively against coffee.*

"Here's an Extra $50, Grace
—I'm making <u>real</u> money now!"

Money Problems! *Correspondence schools used the promise of a better job.*

THE POWER OF LANGUAGE.

Is it prose, or is it poetry? The style and vocabulary are dated, but you can feel the appeal of this ad.

It tapped into classic imagery – The West– fast horses, fast cars, and, perhaps, fast women. "Word magic!"

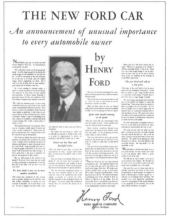

THE POWER OF PRODUCT.

Here's a very restrained ad by Ford introducing their Model A.

This ad set a very different tone.

By not showing the car, or telling the price, interest was heightened.

An estimated 10 million people visited the showrooms and 800,000 ordered the car in the first weeks.

THE POWER OF MARKETING.

By doing a better job of paying attention to consumer needs – and providing services like financing – GM became the new leader in a growing America's growing automobile industry.

Somewhere West of Laramie

SOMEWHERE WEST OF CLEVELAND...

The ad above was written by Ned Jordan – a copywriter who became an automobile manufacturer!

With ads like these, he literally created demand for a car which he had manufactured in Cleveland.

He sold thousands, and then he was smart enough to liquidate before the Depression.

This style of writing, sometimes called "word magic," helped start a whole new school of advertising, which lives on in ads for perfume and fashion.

"Look at All Three!
BUT DON'T BUY ANY LOW-PRICED CAR UNTIL YOU'VE DRIVEN THE NEW PLYMOUTH WITH FLOATING POWER"

**A STATEMENT BY
WALTER P. CHRYSLER**

THOUSANDS of people have been waiting expectantly until today before buying a new car. I hope that you are one of them.

Now that the new low-priced cars are here (including the new Plymouth which will be shown on Saturday) I urge you to carefully *compare* values.

This is the time for you to "shop" and buy wisely. Don't make a deposit on any automobile until you've actually had a demonstration.

It is my opinion that the automobile industry as a whole has never offered such values to the public.

In the new Plymouth we have achieved more than I had ever dared to hope for. If you had told me two years ago that such a big, powerful, beautiful automobile could be sold at the astonishing prices we will announce on Saturday... I'd have said it was absolutely impossible.

I have spent my life building fine cars. But no achievement in my career has given me the deep-down satisfaction

that I derive from the value you get in this 1932 Plymouth. To me, its outstanding feature is Floating Power. We already know how the public feels about this. Last summer it was news, but today it is an established engineering achievement.

It is my opinion, and I think that of leading engineering authorities, that any new car without Floating Power, and none its utter lack of vibration . . . then drive a car with old-fashioned engine mountings and you will understand what I mean. *There's absolutely no comparison.*

We have made the Plymouth a much larger automobile. It is a BIG car. We have increased its power, lengthened the wheelbase and greatly improved its beauty.

In my opinion you will find the new Plymouth the easiest riding car you have ever driven. Yet with all these improvements we have been able to lower prices.

Again let me urge you, go and see the new Plymouth with Floating Power on Saturday. Be sure to *look at all THREE low-priced cars and don't buy any until you do.* That is the way to get the most for your money.

FIRST SHOWING NEXT SATURDAY, APRIL 2nd, AT DESOTO, DODGE AND CHRYSLER DEALERS

The Campaign Concept. Once you have a winning idea, try to keep it going strong. Above, the first ad. Below, a follow-up for the next year's model.

Again "Look at All Three" and may the Best car Win!

WALTER P. CHRYSLER
makes a Frank Statement to Buyers of Low-priced Cars

IT'S A SIX AT $60 LESS THAN LAST YEAR

PLYMOUTH SIX IS SOLD BY   DESOTO, DODGE AND CHRYSLER DEALERS EVERYWHERE

GOT GETCHELL?

J. Stirling Getchell wrote one of the very first "Positioning" ads for Walter Chrysler – years before Avis.

Just one ad, "Look at All Three," established Plymouth as a major brand.

Somewhere East of Detroit.

The ad was part of a last-minute "pitch" by Getchell's new agency.

He did the work at his own expense and was able to photograph Walter Chrysler – before the ads he was writing were even finished…

"Look" was one of three ads – no one remembers the others.

The simple strategic appeal in the ad hit the public right.

Overnight, it made Plymouth a contender in the low-priced field.

Read the whole story in Julius Watkins' book *The 100 Greatest Advertisements.*

The Power of Change.

Important ads do more than sell products – they change the entire advertising environment.

The initial impact of each new style and each new approach changes the marketplace.

The Power of Continuity.

Notice how the first ad "positions" Chrysler as one of the three cars you should consider.

The second ad – which ran the next year – reinforces that position with Plymouth's new-found success.

Nothing succeeds quite like it.

Y&R: The First Modern Agency.

RAY RUBICAM.
He proved you could do good advertising and be a good human being – good news for us all.

His agency set new standards for creativity and quality – more good news.

STEINWAY

The Instrument of the Immortals

There has been but one supreme piano in the history of music. In the days of Liszt and Wagner, of Rubinstein and Berlioz, the pre-eminence of the Steinway was as unquestioned as it is today. It stood then, as it stands now, the chosen instrument of the masters— the inevitable preference wherever great music is understood and esteemed.

STEINWAY & SONS, Steinway Hall, 107-109 E. 14th Street, New York
Subway Express Station at the Door

STEINWAY.
This classic ad is an early example of image advertising. And, at the same time, it was a very hard-working ad.

It was written by Rubicam before he started his own agency, and it solved a tough business problem for Steinway – pianos had new competition – the phonograph!

Rubicam's advertising made the piano a status symbol as well as a home entertainment item.

Note the sense of proportion.

The ad is influenced by design considerations as well as copy.

CREATING ADVERTISING was mostly about writing copy. Then **Ray Rubicam** broadened the creative process at his agency – Young & Rubicam.

He involved research, hiring Northwestern professor George Gallup to study ad readership. Before writing the ads, they talked to consumers – at the time, a revolutionary change in agency behavior.

Most important, he involved art directors in the process, assembling the best team of copywriters and art directors in the industry.

Y&R set other standards, too, believing, *"Advertising has a responsibility to behave properly."*

Rubicam didn't like Hopkins' approach. *"You can sell products without bamboozling the public."*

To him, a good ad was, *"An admirable piece of work."*

His philosophy? *"Resist the usual."*

NEW WAYS OF WORKING TOGETHER.

Y&R was the first to institutionalize two processes that are critical to the modern advertising agency.

First, the visual/verbal interaction of writer/art director.

Second, **The Y&R Creative Work Plan.** It's the model for agency strategy systems used today.

It was an orderly way of gathering all the information available and distilling it down to a Key Fact and *"The Problem the Advertising Must Solve."*

LARGER CONCERNS.

Rubicam showed a concern for more than advertising. Y&R was the only large agency to actively support consumer groups.

His was one of the first major agencies to initiate stock and profit participation plans for employees.

All in all, he had an advertising career that was most certainly *"an admirable piece of work."*

"Oh, Doctor, I bet you tell that to all the Girls!"

IMPACT

AN AD AGENCY ADVERTISES.
Few "house" ads are this memorable.
Rubicam wrote it himself in 1939.
Art and Copy Work Together.
The visual/verbal approach was key
to the '60s "Creative Revolution."
Y&R did it first.

please do not lick this page!

*Advertising then was different. Slower.
But, gradually, the pace quickened.
20th Century technology was creating
new consumer miracles: appliances,
automobiles, filter-tips, and...*

ADVERTISING BUILDS BUSINESSES.

This period demonstrated the power of well-crafted advertising appeals to establish brand name products.

Many brands we know today were established during this period. Advertising was a key part of it.

Above, you can see the friendly approach Y&R used to establish Borden's dairy products – personifying the brand with "Elsie the Cow" (this predates the "inherent drama" approach of the Leo Burnett agency by decades) and "If it's Borden's it's got to be good." A simple memorable theme.

Ads had more copy – people read magazines cover to cover. How would you do this ad today?

TV!

33

Unique Selling Proposition.

Rosser Reeves. Chairman, Ted Bates & Co. Author, Reality in Advertising. *Inventor, USP.*

THE "USP" WAS advertising's child of the '50s.

Rosser Reeves was the father, and his book, *Reality in Advertising,* was the New Improved Testament.

The premise was simple. Find the unique benefit in your product. Hammer it home. Repeatedly.

"M&Ms melt in your mouth, not in your hands."

"Colgate cleans your breath, as it cleans your teeth."

In his Anacin TV commercial, heads full of hammers hammered home the Anacin USP. Repeatedly.

And Rosser Reeves' agency, Ted Bates & Co., sold carloads of Anacin, Colgate, and M&Ms.

Tools of the trade were: slogans, demonstrations, mnemonics, and repetition with an insistent rhythm.

And those tools built businesses. Repeatedly.

They demonstrated the power of television as an advertising medium. Repeatedly.

DEFINITION OF USP:

1. Each advertisement must make a proposition to the consumer. Not just words, not just product puffery, not just show-window advertising.

Each advertisement must say to each reader, "Buy this product and you will get this specific benefit."

2. The proposition must be one that the competition either cannot, or does not, offer.

It must be unique – either a uniqueness of the brand or a claim not otherwise made in that particular field of advertising.

3. The proposition must be so strong that it can move the mass millions, i.e., pull over new customers to your product.

"The Most Hated Commercial." This frame is from the classic Anacin commercial featuring "Fast! Fast! Fast Relief." "For headache, neuritis and neuralgia." (Whatever that is.) It cost $8,200 to produce. It made more money than Gone with the Wind. People hated it – but it worked.

Some commercials were fun to watch and fun to hear. "Use Ajax (Boom Boom) the Foaming Cleanser (Boom-ba-boom-ba-boom-boom-boom). Floats the dirt, right down the drain (Boom-boo-boom-boo-boo-boo-boom). You'll stop paying the elbow tax, when you start cleaning with Ajax (Boom Boom)..."

THE POWER OF CADENCE AND INCANTATION.

Reeves' USPs are almost magic formulas – ritual chants that are repeated over and over.

Note the rhythmic construction – words written to be said – over and over.

Your child needs *every one of the 12 Building Blocks of Life in Wonder Bread* to help him grow straight and strong. Eight slices of tender, delectable Wonder Bread served daily in a balanced diet provide your child with twelve food elements essential to his normal growth and development. And children love delicious Wonder Bread . . . eat all they need without coaxing!

Think of it! Just eight slices of Wonder Bread daily will give your growing child as much protein as a serving of beef . . . to build sturdy muscles; as much niacin as six sardines . . . for mental health; as much iron as three lamb chops . . . for rich red blood; plus nine more Building Blocks of Life; *vitamins and minerals* found in eggs, vegetables, liver and cheese. Wonder

Bread is not a substitute for these foods. It *belongs* with them in your child's diet.

WONDER ENRICHED BREAD is the perfect combination of nutrition and flavor.

Get your family started on Wonder Bread . . . and give them the 12 Building Blocks of Life found in the freshest, most fragrant, finest textured loaf you ever tasted.

WONDER BREAD
Helps Build Strong Bodies 12 Ways

The Limits of Logic. *The powerful TV commercials with their almost magical repetition and cadence didn't always make strong print. The incantation of "Wonder Bread Builds Strong Bodies 12 Ways" turns into psuedo-science. Still, the overall power of a proposition that turned a loaf of bread into a giant vitamin pill had its effect.*

THE POWER OF THE PROPOSITION.

Reeves influence was deeper with clients than creative departments – most creative people *hated* his ads.

But the discipline of the USP still remains with most package goods marketers. Though now you need to do a bit more than just say the same thing over and over

In fact, even Ted Bates & Co. added a new dimension to their USP. Now it's Unique Selling Proposition *plus* Unique Selling *Personality* – image. Time for the '60s.

Welcome to The Creative Revolution.

REEVES BELIEVES...

"Let's say you have one million dollars tied up in your little company and suddenly your advertising isn't working and sales are going down. And everything depends on it.

"Your future depends on it, your family's future depends on it, other people's families depend on it...

"Now, what do you want from me? Fine writing? Or do you want to see the God-damned sales curve stop moving down and start moving up?"

In his spare time, Reeves wrote short stories and poetry. But when it came to writing advertising, he was all business.

His only gauge was "will it work?"

His first lesson – *"You must make* the product *interesting, not just make the ad different."*

Copy: "Which hand has the M&M chocolate

candy in it? Not this hand– that's messy,

*but this hand... because **M&M Candies Melt in Your Mouth, Not in Your Hand."***

This was a side-by-side demonstration with a "reason why." It worked.

The Creative Revolution.

Leo Burnett and **Bill Bernbach**

David Ogilvy. Copywriter. *Even after he retired to a French chateau, his agency kept growing with intelligent ads and intelligent management that built worldclass brands.*

The man in the Hathaway shirt

THE HATHAWAY "STORY."

What does the eye patch do?

First, it adds "story appeal," increasing interest and readership.

Second, it creates distinctiveness and memorability. (After all, a shirt is a shirt.) It gives the shirt "an image."

Third, it gives the campaign continuity.

Last, eye contact. People look back at people. And one is better than none.

THE '60S WAS THE DECADE of "The Creative Revolution." Three people were instrumental in shaping this dramatic change in advertising.

All three of them were copywriters: **David Ogilvy, Leo Burnett,** and **Bill Bernbach.**

David Ogilvy…

hired a model with an eyepatch for Hathaway shirts and created an ad for Rolls-Royce with a headline that the world of advertising will never forget:

"At 60 miles an hour the loudest noise in this new Rolls-Royce comes from the electric clock."

The title of his book was memorable, too – *Confessions of an Advertising Man.* It was a modest bestseller and a superb new business tool. He and his agency followed with more books, such as *Ogilvy on Advertising* and *How to Advertise.*

Ogilvy was a student of the craft of copywriting. His work combined the lessons of Hopkins, Caples, and Reeves with his own unique wit and style.

Here is Ogilvy's paraphrase of Hopkins: *"I don't write to the crowd. I try to write from one human being to another human being in the second person singular."*

AN INVESTMENT IN IMAGE.

Yet, Ogilvy's contribution moved beyond the rational. It was emotional. Ogilvy had class. Image.

The style of the man in the Hathaway shirt.

The delightfully stuffy Commander Whitehead and "Schweppervescence," a tongue-in-cheek USP.

Rolls-Royce dignity with Brit wit as counterpoint.

Ogilvy did advertising that made you like and respect the advertiser. He believed *"Every advertisement is a long-term investment in the image of a brand."*

The Rolls-Royce Silver Cloud—$13,995

"At 60 miles an hour the loudest noise in this new Rolls-Royce comes from the electric clock"

What makes Rolls-Royce the best car in the world? "There is really no magic about it— it is merely patient attention to detail," says an eminent Rolls-Royce engineer.

1. "At 60 miles an hour the loudest noise comes from the electric clock," reports the Technical Editor of THE MOTOR. Three mufflers tune out sound frequencies—acoustically.

2. Every Rolls-Royce engine is run for seven hours at full throttle before installation, and each car is test-driven for hundreds of miles over varying road surfaces.

3. The Rolls-Royce is designed as an *owner-driven* car. It is eighteen inches shorter than the largest domestic cars.

4. The car has power steering, power brakes and automatic gear-shift. It is very easy to drive and to park. No chauffeur required.

5. The finished car spends a week in the final test-shop, being fine-tuned. Here it is subjected to 98 separate ordeals. For example, the engineers use a *stethoscope* to listen for axle-whine.

6. The Rolls-Royce is guaranteed for

three years. With a new network of dealers and parts-depots from Coast to Coast, service is no problem.

7. The Rolls-Royce radiator has never changed, except that when Sir Henry Royce died in 1933 the monogram RR was changed from red to black.

8. The coachwork is given five coats of primer paint, and hand rubbed between each coat, before *nine* coats of finishing paint go on.

9. By moving a switch on the steering column, you can adjust the shock-absorbers to suit road conditions.

10. A picnic table, veneered in French walnut, slides out from under the dash. Two more swing out behind the front seats.

11. You can get such optional extras as an Espresso coffee-making machine, a dictating machine, a bed, hot and cold water for washing, an electric razor or a telephone.

12. There are three separate systems of power brakes, two hydraulic and one mechanical. Damage to one will not affect the others. The Rolls-Royce is a very *safe* car—and also a very *lively* car. It cruises serenely at eighty-five. Top speed is in excess of 100 m.p.h.

13. The Bentley is made by Rolls-Royce. Except for the radiators, they are identical motor cars, manufactured by the same engineers in the same works. People who feel diffident about driving a Rolls-Royce can buy a Bentley.

PRICE. The Rolls-Royce illustrated in this advertisement – f.o.b. principal ports of entry – costs **$13,995.**

If you would like the rewarding experience of driving a Rolls-Royce or Bentley, write or telephone to one of the dealers listed on opposite page. Rolls-Royce Inc., 10 Rockefeller Plaza, New York 20, N. Y. CIrcle 5-1144.

STUDY THE AD ABOVE.

First, it's smooth as a ride in a Rolls. Though long, it's still tightly written. And rewritten.

Second, it's filled with interesting facts. (By the way, the headline came from a review in a British car magazine.)

Third, note the witty counterpoint – technical facts with a human touch. *"The engineers use a stethoscope," "No chauffeur required," "People who feel diffident about driving a Rolls-Royce can buy a Bentley."*

Finally, he ends with an offer. Just like Hopkins.

The Man from Schweppes Arrives!

SCHWEPPES PERSONIFIED.

"Personification" is an interesting advertising technique – a person represents the product or brand.

Here, Ogilvy used Commander Whitehead, an executive with the company that introduced Schweppes to the US.

In many ways, Whitehead *became* the product. Sophisticated. Attractive. Sociable – someone who mixes well at parties. Just like Schweppes.

Note the similar layout styles of the Schweppes and Hathaway ads – even the headlines are similar.

Ogilvy studied readership results and determined what he believed to be the best layout approaches.

Ogilvy did not believe in...
Periods.

He believed that they stopped readers.

By eliminating periods from headlines, he felt it was easier for readers to continue into the copy.

AN OGILVY USP.

"Dove is 1/4 cleansing cream."

By the way, did you know that Rosser Reeves was Ogilvy's brother-in-law? It's true – they were married to sisters.

THE OGILVY INFLUENCE.
The account went to another agency – it had become too small for O&M, but the heritage stayed – here's an example using media mogul Ted Turner.

IBM is one of the worldwide brands handled by O & M. On the left, a print ad working to own the idea of "e-business." On the right, French nuns talk about the Internet in a TV spot with the theme "Solutions for a small planet."

THE OGILVY HERITAGE.

Most important, David Ogilvy created an agency.

Today, Ogilvy & Mather is one of the world's largest. Much of their success is a result of Ogilvy's philosophy.

Today, his agency abounds with rules and guidelines, which will surprise no one who reads his books.

But Ogilvy himself says, *"I hate rules."*

In the beginning, Ogilvy's image-making was rule-breaking and helped create a whole new style of advertising.

Now O&M is part of a large agency conglomerate – WPP – a result of what Ogilvy says is his one regret – going public.

But his spirit and individuality are still a part of their heritage. They're still going like sixty.

And the loudest noise is the electronics.

A Brand-Building Partner. That's what Ogilvy's agency became. Above, two examples of the range of work they do to build the American Express brand. A niche ad, saluting a well-known tennis player as part of a sports marketing program, and a local newspaper ad, saluting restaurants that honor the card.

SOMEWHERE WEST OF OGILVY. Above and below, two examples of some Western Ogilvy work – Hal Riney ran their San Francisco office, which then became Hal Riney & Partners.

That's just one example of agencies started under the Ogilvy influence.

Above is Bartles & Jaymes, wine cooler *personifications.*

Below, some Riney long copy – note the rhythm and rhyme.

Why the beer from here is better than the beer from there.

If Oregon were like other places, you'd expect the beer here to be like other beers.

But in attitude as well as geography, our state is different from places like Wisconsin and Missouri. And that's why Portland-brewed Blitz-Weinhard is so different from the beers brewed in Milwaukee or St. Louis.

Natural beer, naturally brewed and naturally aged.

Over the last 30 years or so, science has revolutionized the art of brewing.

There are chemicals on the market which can shorten the time it takes to brew beer. And other chemicals which can preserve it once it's bottled. There are machines available to make beer ferment faster, and techniques to make it "age" quicker.

These are cost-saving innovations. But they're not a natural part of the brewing process, so they're not part of making Blitz-Weinhard beer.

At Blitz-Weinhard, we use no additives, no preservatives, no chemicals, and no shortcuts. Our product is naturally brewed, naturally fermented, and naturally aged.

This means it costs us more to make Blitz-Weinhard. But we believe natural country deserves nothing less than natural beer.

A small brewery.

Once, America's demand for beer was supplied by hundreds of small, local breweries. Today, brewing is heavily concentrated in the hands of a few large, national manufacturers with sizeable brewing plants located in different parts of the country.

But Blitz-Weinhard is made only at the original brewery in Portland. As a result, the total amount of beer we can produce is quite small by industry standards. This means we are able to brew with the extra time, care and attention required to produce the finest product possible.

The hops and barley are better here.

There's a type of barley which grows only in the Northwest, and it is held in high regard by brewers everywhere. It's safe to say that breweries in the East and Midwest would use more of this barley, but for the high cost of shipping it across the country.

Because we're close to the source, we are able to brew Blitz-Weinhard with more of this premium barley than any other beer we know of.

We also brew our beer with premium Cascade hops. This variety was developed by Oregon State University, and has been acclaimed throughout the industry as the equal of Bavaria's famed Hallertau hop. But the Willamette and Yakima valleys are the only areas suited to growing Cascade hops, and the relatively small crop assures a premium price—a price we are willing to pay in order to brew Blitz-Weinhard with the finest ingredients available.

Fresher beer is better beer.

Newly brewed beer must spend time in ageing vats to bring its flavor to maturity. Ageing is necessary to mellow the beer, and to bring out its sparkling clarity.

But once in the bottle, time is the enemy of good beer. In a matter of weeks, it can begin to lose its freshness. Eventually it will become stale and unappetizing.

Because our goal is to supply quality beer only to the people of Oregon, bottles of Blitz-Weinhard don't have to spend weeks or months being shipped long distances, or standing in warehouses. Brewery-fresh Blitz-Weinhard beer can reach the farthest point of our distribution within hours of leaving Portland.

Taste and tradition, guaranteed.

Blitz-Weinhard has been brewing premium beer for Oregonians since Territorial days. We are the oldest continuously-operating brewery west of the Mississippi, and throughout our 122-year history, we have tried to follow the basic guiding principle laid down by our founder, pioneer brewer Henry Weinhard:

"Spare no time, effort, nor cost to give our customers a perfect glass of beer."

In the spirit of these words, every bottle and can of Blitz-Weinhard beer carries a written guarantee of satisfaction. If you are ever displeased with our product, for any reason, your money will be refunded.

We're aware that other brewers don't offer a guarantee like ours. But when you think about it, there's no reason why they should.

After all, they're not the beer here.

The beer here.

Leo Burnett.

MEANWHILE, Leo Burnett was building an agency in Chicago, Illinois.

Leo, a loveable man in a freshly rumpled suit, had bowls of apples in the lobby, peas picked in the moonlight, and a slogan that was pure Leo:

*"When you reach for the stars,
you might not quite get one,
but you won't come up with
a handful of mud either."*

Leo's Logo.

Everyone loved Leo.

And they loved his advertising.

Leo put red meat on a red background.

He took a little canned vegetable company in LeSueur, Minnesota, and grew the Jolly Green Giant.

His Chicago agency took a New York cigarette with a British name and moved it to Marlboro Country.

Charlie the Tuna, Morris the Cat, the Pillsbury Doughboy, the Keebler Elves, Tony the Tiger, and all the other cute cartoon critters of Kellogg's were born at Leo's.

INHERENT DRAMA.

Leo believed in "inherent drama." He believed it existed in almost every product or service.

Leo believed in Middle America.

His "Chicago-style" advertising showed love and respect for people.

It felt homegrown and authentic.

It was. Leo called it *"The glacier-like power of friendly familiarity."*

That friendly strength, and the hardworking Middle Americans who thought the way Leo did, grew his agency into one of the largest in the world.

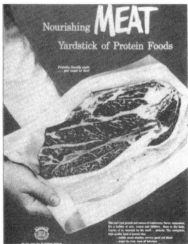

The Pillsbury Doughboy.

Now there's a big, brawny building in Chicago with his name on it, where thousands work every day.

And the apples are still in the lobby.

Leo. *Leo Burnett was influenced by the philosophy and writing style of an early boss. He worked for Theodore MacManus ("The Penalty of Leadership") in Detroit during the first wave of image selling.*

He knocked around the Midwest, ending up in Chicago in 1935 – the middle of the Depression. When he started his agency, people told him he'd be selling apples on the street. From then on, there was a bowl of apples in the lobby.

They represented "the agency's commitment to simple, honest communication and an optimistic vision of the future" (Morrison in The Ad Men and Women). *Slowly, this vision grew.*

Nourishing **MEAT**
Yardstick of Protein Foods

RED MEAT. RED BACKGROUND.
This was one of Leo's earliest ads and his first million-dollar account.

The power is Image. This small black and white rendition doesn't do it justice.

The selling idea is *Red!*

The "inherent drama" in meat.

THE BURNETT STYLE.

The agency was built on strong, simple instinctive imagery. Each with its own "inherent drama."

Let's look at some of the long-term advertising ideas that were born at the Leo Burnett Company.

Kinda Corny. Burnett's brand images provided built-in story value.

Even Little Ideas can grow into Big Ideas. The Keebler story is simple – they're made by elves. Suddenly the brand has a unifying idea that provides continuity at the same time it gives Keebler the flexibility to advertise a wide variety of cookies. Magic in action.

New Kid on the Block. Altoids. Another long-term campaign – just starting up.

Strong Simple TV Ideas. Burnett's heritage of visual impact also translates into television. Here are two frames from a long-term campaign for All-Temperature Cheer. A stain is removed with musical accompaniment.

THE MARLBORO STORY.

When the agency first received the assignment from Phillip Morris, everyone gathered around working to have the right idea – a "Big Idea."

Leo walked in with a copy of *Life* magazine. There was an article about the King Ranch in Texas – and it featured cowboys.

That's it, he muttered, and he insisted that a cowboy be one of the original ads – they featured men with tattoos.

Like this one.

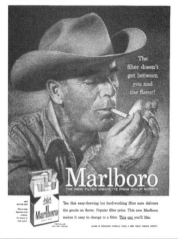

The Original Marlboro Man.

Early ads featured a range of models and TV commercials. The sexy voice of Julie London crooned, *"You get a lot to like from a Marlboro. Filter, flavor, Flip-Top Box."*

But the cowboy concept took hold and the "glacier-like power" kept building.

Today, it's the largest cigarette brand in the world – whatever your feelings about smoking, Marlboro is a huge advertising success.

It maintains the imagery – and flanker brands, like  Marlboro Light and Marlboro Medium, that extend that imagery.

And it all began with Leo's instincts about "inherent drama" when he saw that article in *Life*.

Blessings on thee, little man,
barefoot boy with cheeks
full of *Kellogg's* CORN FLAKES

Classic Work for Kellogg's.

NOT SO LONG AGO...
Leo Burnett leveraged early feminist issues for this Philip Morris brand with "You've Come a Long Way, Baby."

Yes, we have come a long way.

The Burnett Secret.

Here are what I believe were the four main reasons for the Leo Burnett agency's long-term success:

1. AGENCY TEAMWORK.

The people at Burnett worked together.

Creative and account people worked as equals.

They listened to each other and respected each other.

The creatives were smart. So were the suits.

2. CLIENT PARTNERSHIP.

The agency operated as a dedicated business partner.

They had the client's best interests at heart. Always.

This was not an act, it was a rock-solid belief.

This builds client respect and trust and unifies the agency around a single-minded goal – build the client's business.

3. LONG-TERM CAMPAIGNS.

Burnett knew how to stick with an idea. Eventually, this becomes a tremendous competitive advantage.

But the cumulative power takes time to build.

Of all advertising agencies, Leo Burnett has more long-running campaigns than any other. By far.

They could take a simple idea, like "fly the friendly skies" for United Airlines, and make it last for 20 years. Make that 30.

In fact, even after United left Burnett for another agency, some of that long-term equity is still being used.

They may or may not have had better ideas first year.

But, over time, Burnett really knew how to keep a campaign fresh.

They didn't change campaigns just because there was a new creative team or a new brand manager.

They knew that building the equity and image of a brand is a long-term job. And they did it.

Year after year after year.

4. HARD WORK.

Nobody outworked Burnett.

It was only possible to work as hard as the people at Burnett. It was impossible to work harder.

Some successful new agencies, such as Chiat/Day, have this same work ethic.

Once upon a time, when I worked at Leo Burnett, I received a compliment from The Creative Director of the World. *"You know why you're good?"* he asked.

"Why, no," I said, puffing up for some flattery about my unique talent or, perhaps, my keen intelligence.

"You've got stamina," said The Creative Director of the World. Nobody outworked the Leo Burnett Company.

CRITTER POWER.

Leo Burnett built long-term advertising proper-ties which captured the inherent drama of the brands.

Charlie the Tuna, the Keebler Elves, the Pillsbury Doughboy, and the Maytag Repairman each repre-sent a key Selling Idea and a long-term narrative framework. With these properties, you can keep telling the same story for your brand. Brilliant.

Burnett knows how to keep P&G smiling. A long-term relationship.

Dewar's Profiles ran for decades. Another long-term relationship.

YOU CAN'T WIN 'EM ALL.

The Oldsmobile brand is one that could not be saved with the Burnett magic. Despite years of effort, the brand kept losing share, and GM decided to termi-nate the brand.

Some blamed the cars, some blamed the advertising. It certainly wasn't lack of effort.

William Bernbach – Creative Director.

I found out
about Joan

Ohrbach's

DDB'S FIRST CLIENT.
Ohrbach's was outspent by ten other retailers, but their advertising gave them greater awareness than the competition, as DDB won awards for Best Retail fifteen years in a row!

This ad is a surprise, but you understand it instantly. Art direction was by Bob Gage, a disciple of Paul Rand.

Bill Bernbach.

Meanwhile, a copywriter from Grey Advertising opened up a New York agency that set new standards for the entire industry. Bill Bernbach (Pronounced Bern-*back*).

His agency, Doyle Dane Bernbach, set the tone for advertising in the '60s.

Some people called it "soft sell," but it wasn't.

It sold hard. It just wasn't rude.

Bernbach's work was smart. Intelligent.

It didn't talk down to people.

It was honest. Admitting faults and winning sales ("We're Only #2." "Ugly Is Beautiful.").

It was funny. It was classy.

And the graphics knocked you on your you-know-what.

Though started years ago at Y&R, it was DDB that made the writer/art director team the industry standard. The latest graphics, typography, and film techniques were used to create advertising that raised the craft to the level of art.

As Bernbach said, *"I warn you against believing that advertising is a science. It is intuition and artistry, not science, that develops effective advertising."*

Yet it was not art for its own sake.

"You must have inventiveness, but it must be disciplined. Everything you write, everything on a page, every word, every graphic symbol, every shadow should further the message you're trying to convey."

He wasn't just a leader, he was a teacher who seemed to know how to bring out the best in others.

His people created advertising and agencies in DDB's image: Julian Koenig, George Lois, Mary Wells, Helmut Krone, Ron Rosenfeld, and many others were part of the DDB Creative Revolution.

Today, his influence is still felt in every award show and almost every agency creative department.

What was it exactly?

He never wrote a book about it, and many of the best DDB ads were written by others.

Bill Bernbach broke the rules but never felt obliged to write new ones.

His philosophy was quite simple, really.

"Find the simple story in the product and present it in an articulate, intelligent, and persuasive way."

It was all based on an even simpler belief:

"The power of the idea."

THE DDB PHILOSOPHY.

• Nobody's waiting to hear from us.

• Advertising that nags its way into people's consciousness does only half as much as advertising should.

• Genuinely entertaining, involving, or dramatic advertising not only gets people's attention, it gets their affection.

• This kind of advertising multiplies every dollar an advertiser spends.

DDB CREATIVE APPROACH.

• Creativity is as important in developing a strategy as it is in communicating it.

• Creativity that doesn't reinforce the proposition in an ad or commercial isn't creative, it's disruptive.

• Execution isn't a vehicle for delivering a selling message, it *is* a selling message.

SOME DDB QUESTIONS.

• Does it communicate a message that is motivating?

• Is it fresh, appealing, intrusive?

• Is the style and tonality appropriate to the product and the point?

• Do you like the company that manufactures/sells this product?

• Will it help build a long-term personality for the product?

Lemon.

This Volkswagen missed the boat.

The chrome strip on the glove compartment is blemished and must be replaced. Chances are you wouldn't have noticed it; Inspector Kurt Kroner did.

There are 3,389 men at our Wolfsburg factory with only one job: to inspect Volkswagens at each stage of production. (3000 Volkswagens are produced daily; there are more inspectors than cars.)

Every shock absorber is tested (spot checking won't do), every windshield is scanned. VWs have been rejected for surface scratches barely visible to the eye.

Final inspection is really something! VW inspectors run each car off the line onto the Funktionsprüfstand (car test stand), tote up 189 check points, gun ahead to the automatic brake stand, and say "no" to one VW out of fifty.

This preoccupation with detail means the VW lasts longer and requires less maintenance, by and large, than other cars. (It also means a used VW depreciates less than any other car.)

We pluck the lemons; you get the plums.

The original headline was "This Volkswagen missed the boat." It became the first line of body copy. Julian Koenig started it (then he went to the track) and Rita Seldon finished it. Helmut Krone made it all work (you can read more about his contributions at the end of Chapter Six). Many DDB print ads featured a "klitchik," a clever last line of copy that tied to the headline. Check out the last line of this ad.

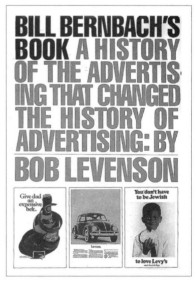

READ ALL ABOUT IT.

An excellent summary of the DDB legacy with terrific reproductions of the classic campaigns and the stories behind them.

You don't have to be Jewish

to love Levy's
real Jewish Rye

Save water.

Presented by Volkswagen, the car with the air-cooled engine that doesn't use any.

Or buy a Volkswagen.

THE POWER OF SURPRISE.

Surprise! DDB made bread exciting – Levy's Jewish Rye, to be exact.

Instead of backing away from the ethnic nature of the product, they met it head on.

As a result, they managed to say "The rye bread for everybody" in a tremendously arresting and distinctive way. There is also a powerful but subtle logic at work.

Since Jewish people eat (and bake) a lot of rye bread, naturally they'd be the rye bread experts.

Another facet of DDB style. Taste.

This approach could have been offensive, but it wasn't.

You don't have to be Jewish

to love Levy's
real Jewish Rye

News as Product News. Bernbach believed in using the timeliness of today's newspaper to make a point for his clients – he believed that advertising should be a bit sociological. Look how they did it. When New York had a water shortage, VW was there with an ad that humorously leveraged the fact that a Volkswagen had an air-cooled (rather than a water-cooled) engine. When the US had a gas shortage, Volkswagen capitalized on the event with this ad. They ran the art director's rough as the illustration. When the economy took a bit of a bump, they used it as an opportunity to advertise an economy car.

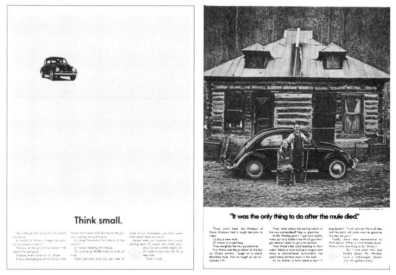

Think small.

"It was the only thing to do after the mule died."

IBM's "Think" and "Think Big" were common slogans of the times. DDB bucked the trend... just like Volkswagen. The "Think Small" ad was originally a "one-timer" for *Fortune*. It was so well received that consumer versions were written.

Not as fact-filled as Rolls-Royce, but, there was less to say. And less to pay.

A dramatically different layout approach by Helmut Krone (who also wrote the last lines of copy). It said, "Read Me." People did.

The "mule" ad shows how delightfully extendable the whole campaign was, with an understated humor that brought warmth, charm, and humanity to almost every situation where there was a Volkswagen.

Avis is only No.2 in rent a cars. So why go with us?

We try harder.
(When you're not the biggest, you have to.)

We just can't afford dirty ashtrays. Or half-empty gas tanks. Or worn wipers. Or unwashed cars. Or low tires. Or anything less than seat-adjusters that adjust. Heaters that heat. Defrosters that defrost.

Obviously, the thing we try hardest for is just to be nice. To start you out right with a new car, like a lively, super-torque Ford, and a pleasant smile. To know, say, where you get a good pastrami sandwich in Duluth. Why?

Because we can't afford to take you for granted.

Go with us next time.

The line at our counter is shorter.

The writer of this ad rented an Avis car recently. Here's what I found:

I write Avis ads for a living. But that doesn't make me a paid liar.

When I promise that the least you'll get from Avis is a clean Plymouth with everything in perfect order, I expect Avis to back me up.

I don't expect full ashtrays; it's not like them.

I know for a fact that everybody in that company, from the president down, tries harder.

"We try harder" was their idea; not mine.

And now they're stuck with it; not me.

So if I'm going to continue writing these ads, Avis had better live up to them. Or they can get themselves a new boy.

They'll probably never run this ad.

EL AL.

Here's another DDB trademark – *visual surprise!* DDB's art directors gave us a new way of looking at the same old page – like this. Surprise! A new way to say faster.

"We Try Harder!" What a wonderful theme. It communicated the benefit of being better without over-promise. And, it motivated personnel – an important and often overlooked function of advertising. This was one of the first modern "positioning" campaigns. A marvelous piece of logic. It made you believe you got a better deal and better service. It's an excellent example of '60s style copywriting by Paula Green, with help from Helmut Krone. Tight and delightful.

Are you working like a dog to get to the top? Shake hands with Avis.

When you're not top dog, you try harder. You work more hours. You worry more. You eat much too fast.

You go through the same thing Avis is going through. We're only No. 2 in rent a cars. We have to knock ourselves out to please people.

By not giving them anything less than fine cars like lively super-torque Fords. By worrying that one of our people might forget to empty an ashtray. Or clean a windshield. Or fill a gas tank. We try harder. But you'll never know how hard we try until you try us.

Walk up to our counter.

And give us some growing pains to keep our stomach pains company.

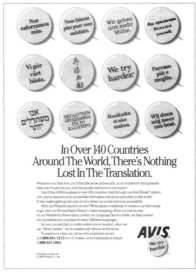

In Over 140 Countries Around The World, There's Nothing Lost In The Translation.

Wherever you find Avis, you'll find the same philosophy: a commitment to trying harder than ever to provide you with the quality and service you expect.

You'll find 4,900 locations in over 140 countries. And through our Avis Wizard® system, you can be assured of an immediate reservation just about anywhere in the world. It also makes getting into and out of a rental car as fast and easy as possible.

With our Preferred service at over 700 locations worldwide, it means a car that's ready to go. And our Roving Rapid Return® makes dropping off the car just as easy.

At our Worldwide Reservation Center, our Language Service Desk can help answer any questions you may have in many different languages.

So you can see that no matter where you're headed, when we say "We try harder," the translation will always be the same.

To reserve an Avis car, call an Avis employee-owner at **1-800-331-1212** for U.S. rentals, or for international rentals, **1-800-331-1084.**

AVIS
We try harder.®

Avis features GM cars.
© 1994 Wizard Co., Inc.

KNOW WHO THIS IS?

He's Paul Rand – one of the major influences on 20th century design – showing new ways of combining words and visuals.

Know who his favorite copywriter was? It was Bill Bernbach.

They worked together early in Bernbach's career on accounts like Ohrbach's – which became DDB's first account. Paul Rand was primarily a graphic designer.

Rand disciples like Bob Gage went to DDB and applied Rand's graphic design approach to advertising.

Find The W

The Nauga is ugly,

YOW!

For Naugahyde, George Lois created inherent drama in The Nauga!! An idea that *"bristles with visual imagery."*

but his vinyl hide is beautiful.

Naugahyde
vinyl fabric

What makes a great ad?

Ogilvy had guidelines.

Burnett had a feeling.

Bernbach had an idea.

We'll talk about ways to develop ideas and strategies later, but here's a quick review of some of the techniques that the '60s pioneers used.

REDEFINE THE PROBLEM.

Beginning with Y&R and refined at DDB, they were constantly turning the problems over in their minds.

This was a lot of the "creative" work done. While a lot of headlines were written along the way, the real job was articulating the underlying marketing issue the advertising had to address.

DRAMATIZE VISUALLY.

George Lois looks for *"words that bristle with visual imagery."* He's an art director who looks for *"the blending of verbal and visual imagery… that inexplicable alchemy which causes one plus one to equal three."*

Even much of David Ogilvy's work had strong visual elements: "Dove is 1/4 cleansing cream," Commander Whitehead, and the Hathaway eyepatch.

Writers thinking visually. Art directors looking for the right words – two things into one bigger thing.

LOOK INTO TODAY'S WORLD.

Though many of the ads now seem dated, they were contemporary when they ran.

They all featured contemporary language and a contemporary graphic style – whether cutting-edge or straight down the middle.

W!

UNDERSTAND THE CUSTOMER.

The creative work of the '60s had a genuine understanding of how people felt. About their lives. About products. About advertising.

Whether it was Ogilvy's intellect generating a tour de force on Rolls-Royce, or Leo's instinct putting red meat on a red background, *an understanding of the person who would respond to the ads* was a key part of their creation.

DDB's Avis campaign had this deep understanding of the customer. Think about it. The key customer for rent-a-cars is usually a salesman on the road – who probably has a bigger competitor. Like Avis!

That person knows in his own life exactly what it's like to "Try Harder." So while it was interesting that Avis admitted "We're only #2," the Wow connected with people in a very powerful way – because it was also about them!

The strength was not just the brains of clever copy or the beauty of brilliant art direction.

It had heart. It understood and respected the people it was talking to. So should you.

POW!

Campbell's visualizes a simple but meaty proposition for Chunky Soup – a soup aimed at men.

The product era.

These memorable visuals introduced Trout and Ries's classic *Advertising Age* article. The visuals made the point that advertising had evolved from repeating a USP-style message ad infinitum or adding

The image era.

memorable, but not always relevant, imagery. There were too many messages. In this new mental environment, the first step was understanding what was going on

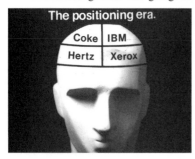

The positioning era.

Coke	IBM
Hertz	Xerox

inside the mind of consumers you were trying to reach. Their timing was perfect – their book became a business bestseller.

POSITIONING:
The Battle for Your Mind

THE 20TH
ANNIVERSARY EDITION
WITH COMMENTS
BY THE AUTHORS

AL RIES · JACK TROUT

Positioning.

"The Positioning Era Cometh," was the headline of Jack Trout and Al Ries's *Ad Age* article.

The premise was simple, and its promise of profit in the age of product proliferation was irresistable.

The key to success was *positioning* your product properly in the consumer's mind.

Positioning was a product of product proliferation. The '70s marketplace was a teeming pool of products and messages. Consumers were on overload.

P&G was an early practitioner, marketing detergents with distinct positions: Tide for clean, Bold for bright, and Cheer, renamed and repositioned as All-Temperature Cheer, for all-temperature washing.

ADVERTISING THINKING FOR MARKETERS.

Positioning was tailor-made for the brand management organizations that had become standard in the major advertisers' marketing departments. And, in fact, Trout and Ries began as brand managers at GE.

Did it work? Sure. But remember, much of the analysis came after the fact – it described campaigns that were already successful.

Positioning helped us understand why the DDB Avis campaign was effective, with a classic "Against" position featuring "We're only #2."

It also explained Burnett's instincts – capturing core category values with advertising that was full of inherent drama.

Finally, it was a helpful way of thinking for both clients and agencies. Whether they happened to believe in USP or image, it didn't matter.

It helped everyone involved find a common conceptual framework based on an eternal truth of advertising – understand the consumer.

HOW TO GET STARTED.

First, you must develop a "conceptual map" of your category inside the mind of the consumer. You need to find out what's important and what's already there.

While earlier advertising approaches worked to put new thoughts and concepts into consumers' minds, po-sitioning works to understand what's in there already.

The search moves from "within the product" (USP) to "within the ad" (image) to "within the prospect's mind."

That's where you create your position.

MARKETING THINKING FOR ADVERTISERS.

Since positioning is rooted in both marketing and creative advertising thinking, making it work demands cooperation between "creatives" and "suits."

It can help marketing and creative people find a common ground and a clear path of development.

By the end of the '70s, positioning was part of every major agency's vocabulary and part of how most agencies and marketers worked to solve their problems.

Trout and Ries continued to maintain their own leadership position in marketing thinking with more popular marketing books like *Marketing Warfare*

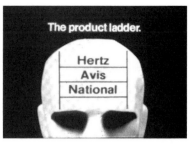

A CONCEPTUAL MAP.

Where is your product "within the mind of the consumer?"

That's the first question.

Often, the product category is already occupied by information, brands, and pre-existing attitudes.

For example, a car rental brand might have to deal with something like this. Is there room for another?

Yes and no. You have to find a way to establish a new position in the consumer's mind. That's what Budget did.

SUCCESSFUL POSITION.
WINNING PROPOSITION.

A distinct positioning and a new proposition for Lite Beer from Miller succeeded in a market where many (including DDB) had failed.

They solved the problem of trying to market "diet beer" to beer drinkers.

Their proposition, "Great Taste. Less Filling" provided a reason why – since it was less filling, you could drink more.

That, plus the fun use of ex-jocks in their TV spots, helped Lite to become the #2 beer brand – at least for a while…

What position do we want?

FIRST THOUGHTS...

At the very beginning of a project, a copywriter needs to think about what position is right for the product.

IT'S BEEN STUCK IN FIRST OR FOUR YEARS

ACURA

THE BEST POSITION.

Be first in the consumer's mind in a meaningful way. Dominant share of mind usually results in a dominant share of business. And vice versa.

MCDONALD'S.

Some of the best work of the '70s was Needham's work for McDonald's.

In many ways, a version of the Burnett/Kellogg's school of advertising, with "You Deserve a Break Today" and "We Do It All for You."

Great music, warm, human TV production, and, most important, a company totally committed to QSCV: Quality, Service, Cleanliness, and Value.

FOUR BASIC TYPES OF POSITIONING:

1. The Best or Leadership Position
2. The Against Position
3. The Niche Position
4. The New Category

Naturally, there are some combinations and variations. First, the basic positions:

The Best Position.

Become first in the mind of the customer.

Once you're there, it's hard to beat.

Just ask IBM's competitors.

Many beat IBM to the punch with better products. But, in the customer's mind, IBM held onto #1 for quite some time. They still maintain that position in the minds of many.

Hertz and McDonald's are two other excellent examples of this position. But wait, it gets better.

THE POWER OF LEADERSHIP.

From that leverage point, you can do things that no other brand in the category can really do.

Tide, Chevrolet, Budweiser, and McDonald's have a power in their messages that comes not only from what's being said, but from who's saying it.

OTHER WAYS TO BE #1.

As you can see by the Acura ad, you can say you're #1 without necessarily being the biggest seller.

That's why two other types of positions are important – Niche and New Category positions.

We'll cover them a few pages from now.

The "Against" Position.

It can be a tough road. But sometimes you don't have a choice. You suck it up and take 'em on.

Avis had the right idea. You do have to try harder.

SOME EXAMPLES:

Remember Plymouth's "Look at all Three?"

Sometimes, just by adding yourself to the competitive set, you accomplish an important task.

That's what "UnCola" did for 7Up.

Burger King and Pepsi are examples of really going at it. If you're going to sell more burgers or colas, you've got to go after somebody else's customers – and they've got more than anyone else.

The Pepsi Challenge was an Against position executed as an entire marketing effort – including taste tests at malls across the country.

Apple Computer, with a unique operating system, positioned itself against the entire world of PCs.

This position began with "The computer for the rest of us" and is continuing with their current "Think Different" campaign.

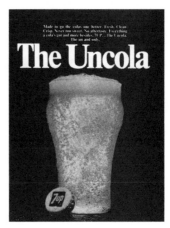

7UP VS. THE COLAS.

In the '60s and into the '70s, 7Up positioned itself against the brown cola drinks. Their research discovered that in the mind of the consumer, soft drinks meant colas.

The UnCola worked because it related to something already established in the consumer's mind.

#2 AS LEADERSHIP CLAIM?

Positioning is a way of thinking, not a set of hard and fast rules.

Here, Subway uses its large number of outlets to build its image in the mind of the consumer.

In the mind of the consumer, Subway is much farther down the product ladder.

So the #2 claim actually raises it a few notches in your perception, and it works to improve their position on the product ladder.

But, of course, just saying it isn't enough. So it shouldn't be surprising that this ad also came with a coupon.

AVIS. Classic Against. Among other things, it can leverage off natural sympathy for the underdog and resentment of the big bully. Can be difficult to defend.

THE MORE POTATO POTATO CHIP

HOW ARE YOU DIFFERENT FROM THE CATEGORY LEADER?

Here, a new product tries to establish a niche in the potato chip category with what they hope is a meaningful product advantage.

Sometimes it works.

Sometimes it doesn't.

Try Ireland's no.1 non-alcoholic brew.

DEFINE YOURSELF.

Here, Kaliber makes itself #1 by defining the category very narrowly.

SOME "NEW CATEGORIES."

In the relatively recent past, each of these has been a New Category:

- CDs • DVDs • PCs • VCRs
- Mini-Vans
- Granola Bars
- Overnight Delivery
- Lap Top Computers
- Portable Telephones
- "Gourmet" TV Dinners
- "Light" or "Lite" anything
- "Clear or Crystal" products

Can you name a new New Category?

Niche Positions.

If you can't have the whole pie, how about a slice?

That's the Niche position.

In general, this position establishes leadership in one aspect of a product category.

When it's the right match with a segment of the marketplace, you can be #1 with some of the people all of the time!

Many New Category products and "flanker" brands can also be viewed as Niche positions.

Success depends on identifying a target and doing a better job of matching your product to the needs and preferences of that target.

"Market segmentation" is one of the techniques used to help discover a profitable niche in the marketplace.

The New Category.

By establishing (or inventing) a new category, you give your brand a brand new opportunity to be #1 and take a leadership position.

It may be totally new, like FedEx, or, a new definition, like Michelob (super premium beer).

SOMETIMES NICHES TURN INTO CATEGORIES.

The marketplace is always changing.

SUVs were a niche, with just a few players.

Now it's a category, and everybody has one.

FedEx was a new category – soon, there were lots of competitors – including things you might not think of as competitors – like the fax machine.

FedEx's original business involved moving a lot of documents. But soon, everyone had one of those strange little machines spitting out rolls of fax paper.

And soon there was another new category – and a whole new category of retailer as well – office supply superstores!

RePositioning.

IF YOU DON'T LIKE YOUR POSITION, you may want to change your position – from one you have to one you want. That's "re-positioning."

During the '70s, marketers like Pontiac and 7Up, revitalized their products by repositioning.

ALL-TEMPERATURE CHEER.

The All-Temperature position took Cheer from #5 to #2 in the very competitive detergent category.

Cheer moved from a "whiteness" position ("New Blue Cheer") to a position that was associated with a new laundry practice – washing in all temperatures.

P&G repositioned (and reformulated) the product to match the change in laundry habits caused by new fabrics and brighter colors.

Contemporary "slice of life" commercials reflected new habits and new values, with kids and husbands helping with traditionally female household chores.

Earlier spots, with the same basic strategy, had marginally competent women confused by their laundry. They were then told to use Cheer by a male authority figure. The commercials didn't work, even though they did "Burke" (a type of "day after recall" research).

MORAL: The right positioning isn't everything. You need the right advertising!

Then, they kept the position fresh with a new approach. Using a demo from a P&G sales meeting, Leo Burnett developed a long-running series of commercials that used the same proposition over and over – Cheer got out spots in cold water.

Rolling Stone *works to reposition itself* from its initial *"hippie" reputation with this classic trade campaign.*

Arm & Hammer Repositioned Itself *into the refrigerator – turning baking soda into a refrigerator deodorant!*

It'll last longer than the payment book.

VOLVO'S FIRST POSITION.
Originally, Volvo positioned itself for durability, based on the fact that they were longer-lasting than, at the time, less-durable US brands.

Later, they evolved that position into a different niche – safety.

Combinations.

THE FOUR BASIC TYPES OF POSITIONS can have many combinations and variations. The following work was done by Roman Hiebing in *The Successful Marketing Plan,* one of the better marketing books available.

These are quite useful. Just remember some positions can be accurately described by more than one of them.

1. BY PRODUCT DIFFERENCE.

Generally, all positions work to establish some sort of brand differentiation within the category.

The difference between your product and the com-petition can be the basis for your position.

2. BY KEY ATTRIBUTE/BENEFIT.

There should be some sort of consumer benefit either stated or implied in your position.

For example,"The Quicker Picker Upper" positions Bounty as it communicates a clearly stated attribute/ product benefit.

Other more general attributes, such as quality, may have an implied benefit.

Many successful brands have been built by pre-empting the key attribute or benefit generic to the category. Leo Burnett does this often.

3. BY USERS OF YOUR PRODUCT.

Virginia Slims is an excellent example – particularly during its introductory period, when they were able to connect with emerging issues.

Many brands are built by heavy users – those who use a great deal of the product.

One aspect of product usage is a surprisingly accurate pattern known as **The 80/20 Rule.** That is, 80% of your business comes from 20% of your customers. For example, 20% of beer drinkers drink 80% of the beer.

Many brands are built with heavy usage and loyalty from a relatively small group of people.

**POSITIONING BY
PRODUCT DIFFERENCE.**

Every other cookie company had chocolate chip cookies. Archway had the #1 oatmeal cookie. That was the basis for this successful positioning.

**POSITIONED BY USER.
POSITIONED BY PROBLEM.**

The "Absolutely Positively" campaign from FedEx is an excellent example.

Though shipping had been around for years, FedEx was basically a New Category. All by itself, that was not meaningful enough in the consumer's mind.

By positioning themselves with *the right user* – business people who had to get it done – and by identifying exactly *the right problem* – a critical package that had to get there – they built a winning combination.

And a winning position.

4. BY TYPE OF USAGE.

Michelob was successful with "Weekends Are Made for Michelob." They weren't quite as successful with "The Night Belongs to Michelob." (Then again, some of this was due to the fact the beer market changed.)

Remember, these various types of positionings can be combined. Years earlier, Shaefer Beer combined Type of Usage with a Heavy-User position – *"Shaefer is the one beer to have when you're having more than one."*

5. POSITIONING AGAINST A CATEGORY.

Light beer can be positioned against regular beer; discount clothing stores are often positioned against department stores.

6. AGAINST A SPECIFIC COMPETITOR(S).

You can go against the overall leader, as Avis did, or against a specific competitor.

Truck marketers often play this game.

Ford goes against Chevy and vice versa.

Meanwhile, various small Japanese-made pickup trucks position against each other.

7. POSITIONING BY ASSOCIATION.

This is generally associated with image advertising. It can also be used to reinforce other attributes, such as a firm's heritage in the community being used to reinforce their caring and service – or even their old-fashioned recipes.

8. POSITION BY PROBLEM.

This is similar to positioning by benefit, only the problem is dramatized more than the solution.

Successful products fulfill needs – that need is often a problem that needs solving.

For example, calcium products that combat the effects of osteoporosis in women.

FedEx positioned itself against the problem with "absolutely positively…"

"BUCKET HEADS."
Church's Fried Chicken went after KFC users by calling them "bucket heads."
Funny? Yes.
Effective? What do you think?

Association with Celebrity. The right celebrity can reinforce your position.

"WHERE'S THE BEEF?"
Wendy's went after people standing in line at McDonald's by reminding them in a humorous way that there was a bigger beef patty on a Wendy's burger.
Funny? Yes.
Effective? Very.

Assignment #2:

THESE ASSIGNMENTS are designed to help you get in touch with some of the historical lessons we've covered. Some are pretty easy, and some are pretty tough.

1. DO A PARODY OF AN AD IN THIS CHAPTER.
   Use the product of your choice. This one's fun!

2. FIND ADS THAT REPRESENT THE DECADES.
   See if you can find ads that represent principles or techniques from the different periods. Start with some favorite magazines and the Sunday paper. Then, if you can find some old magazines, see what you find there.
   • Hopkins-style (person-to-person and pre-emption with some product-based news).
   • '50s-style USP.
   • '60s-style Image.
   • '70s-style Positioning.

3. HISTORY EXERCISE.
   Pick a product, any product. (I've done this exercise a few times, and I just pick something close at hand.)
   Do ads that demonstrate basic techniques from each period. It's a little tough, but it can be a lot of fun! And, you'll be amazed at how much more facile you become.
   Try it now and then try it again in a month or two.
   A. Do a Hopkins-style ad.
   B. Do a '50s-style ad. What is the USP?
   C. Do a '60s-style ad. What is the Image?
   D. Do a '70s-style ad. What is the Position?

4. "DO THE ZOO."
   Do ads for your local zoo.
   A. Do a simple poster.
   B. Do a USP for your zoo.
   C. Do one with copy about one of the animals.
   D. Develop a position for your zoo – in competiton with other entertainment options.

They laughed when I sat down at my Macintosh keyboard.

They snickered, "He can't run a Macintosh IIci. He knows nothing about Quark. Aldus Freehand will make a fool of him."

Then I booted up. And they shut up. Because they didn't know I had visited NovaWorks for some intensive training. I heard gasps of amazement as I produced letter-perfect layouts, meticulous mechanicals and powerful presentations. With NovaWorks, I turned into a Macintosh virtuoso virtually overnight. You can, too, by calling (212) 557-9199.

NovaWorks COMPUTER SYSTEMS, INC.

"They laughed when I sat down at the piano. So I sold it."

They laughed when I sat down at the piano. They stopped when I picked it up.

Let's not play around. Whether you're into Schwarzenegger or Shostakovich, no one gives you a better workout then Gold's Gym.

GOLD'S GYM AND FITNESS CENTER

They laughed when I sat down to write this assignment.
Here are some examples that people sent in.

Land-Rover 109 Station Wagon with Heat Shield Roof

"At 60 miles an hour the loudest noise in this new Land-Rover comes from the roar of the engine"

What makes Land-Rover the most conspicuous car in the world? "There is really no secret," says an eminent Land-Rover enthusiast.

1. "Except for rattles, I am against silence in a car," writes John Steinbeck, a Land-Rover enthusiast, "and I don't know a driver who doesn't want to hear his engine."

2. If this is so, then you may like the Land-Rover very much indeed.

3. Our 4 wheel drive (8 speeds forward, 2 in reverse) masterpiece is not money. Its throaty authority is assuring in times of stress, which nowadays is usually.

4. Nor is this claim true only at 60 miles an hour. A Land-Rover is more conspicuous even when it is standing still. With the ignition off.

5. The Land-Rover stands nearly seven feet tall. All its features tend to heroic proportion.

6. Therefore, when driving, you will simply loom over traffic which previously had scared the devil out of you.

7. This is not only safe and enjoyable, but you will exult to observe how other

drivers, awe-inspired by the Land-Rover's casual might, yield in deference.

8. (Small wonder that women are enormously fond of driving Land-Rovers. The easy command of such massive, maneuverable masculinity is heady stuff.)

9. You may have read of tests where "imported cars" fared badly in collisions? It's a pity we weren't in there to help out on the side. The Land-Rover is built to resist the charge of a bull rhinoceros; or a buff Lincoln for that matter.

10. The Land-Rover's sturdiness of construction (the under-frame resembles a reinforced section of railway track) makes it ideal for trackless wastes, car pools of small children, wretched ordeals, et cetera.

11. There are perhaps 14 Land-Rover hardy perennials ranging from safari cars and campers to police vans and getaway cars. Our most popular passenger models are the 7-seater Model 88 and the 10-seater Model 109 Station Wagons.

11-A. An attractive feature of the '66 Land-Rover is that it is precisely as attractive as the '65.

12. Both of these have capacious rear doors for unloading bulk or people. The unathletic may use the fold-down step.

13. The after compartment has facing seats. This arrangement, although somewhat reminiscent of riding in a paddy-wagon, is extremely sociable. Late at night, it is hilarious.

LAND-ROVER WITH & WITHOUT TIRE ON HOOD

14. The Land-Rover is available with a spare tire either mounted on the rear door or on top of the hood. The tires are identical in every respect save that it costs $7.40 more to have one on the hood.

15. People who feel diffident about driving a Land-Rover with the spare tire on the hood can buy the conventional Land-Rover and save $7.40.

PRICE: The Model 109 Station Wagon illustrated in this advertisement costs $3,906 on the Atlantic Coast, $4,092 on the Pacific Coast; at places in between, it costs in between. The Model 88 Station Wagon (shorter by 1 door) costs about $600 less.

If you would like to listen to the Land-Rover, or to the embarrassingly quiet Mark II Rover Sedan, or to the Rover 2000 Sports Sedan (which has "a little panty matter when idling that rises to a whispering roar in the lower gears," according to Mr. Steinbeck), please ask any dealer here listed. (L.R.) signifies a Land-Rover dealer; (R), a Rover dealer; (R & L.R), both.

Thank you.

©1965 Rover Motor Co. of North America, Ltd., Chrysler Bldg., New York 17.

A Rolls-Royce ad parody done by Howard Gossage (Ogilvy was amused).

READING LIST *(Cont.)*

The '60s.

Confessions of an Advertising Man & Ogilvy on Advertising
David Ogilvy

From Those Wonderful Folks Who Brought You Pearl Harbor
Jerry Della Femina
Simon & Schuster

When Advertising Tried Harder. The Sixties: The Golden Age of American Advertising
Larry Dobrow/Friendly Press

Bill Bernbach's Book: A History of the Advertising that Changed the History of Advertising
Bob Levenson/Villard Books

What's The Big Idea?
George Lois/Doubleday

The Book of Gossage
Howard Luck Gossage & others
The Copy Workshop

The '70s.
Positioning: The Battle for Your Mind
Al Trout/Jack Ries/McGraw Hill

The Image Makers: Power and Persuasion on Madison Avenue
William Myers/Times Books

Current Events.

SLAM-DUNK MARKETING!

A page on the back of *Rolling Stone* announces the premiere of the Charles Barkley vs. Godzilla commercial on the MTV Music Awards.

Is it an ad promoting another ad?

Is it a promotion? Is it an event?

Is it the shoes?

It's an excellent example of the thinking that turns the idea of Barkley vs. Godzilla into more than a TV spot.

Stations get PR footage on the shooting of the commercial – sports shows feature it along with the latest scores.

Charles Barkley is interviewed and asked about Godzilla. It's all in fun, but there's serious marketing going on.

Meanwhile, posters and promotional materials head toward the retail outlets (along with the shoes) to make it an event in the stores as well as in the media.

That's how Nike and their agency, Wieden + Kennedy, turn a single commercial into a multi-dimensional media event – including a monstrous amount of free media coverage.

THE PREVIOUS CHAPTER was about progress. This chapter is about change. Similar. Not the same.

Progress makes everything better for everyone.

With change, there are losers as well as winners.

In a variety of ways, this chapter is going to talk about changes in communication in a changing world.

In his book *PowerShift,* Alvin Toffler made an important point about today's economy – the value of information is approaching and surpassing the value of things. Think about it.

Mazda Miatas, Macintosh computers, and those new Nikes each contain a lot of information – computerized design and marketing investment – as well as the metal, plastic, rubber, and silicon you can touch.

Think about it. It's not just metal, it's *mental.*

It means the information content we add to manufactured goods is more important than ever.

It means people who produce useful information will be more important than ever.

Whether you produce ads, marketing plans, or Web sites, there's a need for you somewhere in this complex, fast-changing marketplace.

THINKING INTEGRATED.

Today's marketers have to develop a whole new way of thinking. So do copywriters.

There are more options. Messages can go through a wider range of channels. For example, think about all the different places you can see a Gatorade logo – or a Nike logo.

Today, you can also tailor your message to a wider range of groups – from consumers to fellow employees. You can do TV, snail mail, e-mail, or sponsor a concert.

With all those options, you have to pick the right ones, and then you have to make them work together. It's "IMC," **Integrated Marketing Communication.**

An excellent example of this integration in action was Apple's introduction of the Macintosh.

A LOT MORE THAN "1984."

There was a lot more to Apple's 1984 introduction than the spectacular "1984" commercial.

Though everyone seems to remember the commercial, it only ran *once* – during the Super Bowl.

Here's what else was going on:

For months, PR people had been briefing the technical and business press – stories were timed to break in newspapers and magazines.

They prepared informative print ads, multipage "FSIs" (Free Standing Inserts) and even sponsored entire magazines. Other TV commercials featured specific product features and benefits.

Three magazines were born – two monthlies, *Mac-World* and *MacUser,* and *MacWeek* – a trade weekly.

Other important groups, from retailers to software developers, were involved in special Apple programs. They were reached through: direct communications, events (such as demos and sales meetings), advertising in specialized media, and an outreach program Apple called "Evangelism."

In-store posters, brochures, banners, and T-shirts helped with the introduction. So did special interactive software programs that allowed customers to walk into a store and immediately interact with a Mac.

After the introductory period, a "test drive" sales promotion event let you walk out with one.

Apple's agency, Chiat/Day, and Apple's own in-house creative department worked together.

They even developed a common typeface…

"Apple Garamond" (Garamond condensed to 80%).

On January 24th, Apple Computer will introduce Macintosh. And you'll see why 1984 won't be like "1984."

[QuickTime version @ www.adbuzz.com]

Take Macintosh out for a test drive.

Ad for In-store Promotional Event.

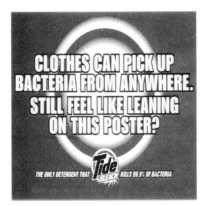

**LEADERSHIP BRANDS:
CAPITALIZING ON
BRAND EQUITY.**

In today's economy, leading brands are more valuable than ever.

Years of advertising and consumer familiarity build incredible equity in the marketplace.

For that reason, many of the mergers and buyouts you've read about involved very high values being paid for existing brand names.

After all, what would it cost today to establish a brand with the same aware-ness and familiarity of one that had been around for decades?

A Change in Philosophy.

Once, marketers like P&G would es-tablish a new brand – with its own unique benefit and position – every time it intro-duced a new product.

Now, it makes more sense for many brands to become families of related products.

Changing Channels.

Established brands also have a huge communication advantage.

Since they're already familiar, you don't have to say as much or work as hard to establish yourself "in the mind of the consumer."

So, a brand like Tide can have good results with short, relatively inexpen-sive messages on billboards using their familiar graphics and their familiar brand image.

"MARKETING IS EVERYTHING."

For company after company, marketing became the most important business function. As Apple consultant Regis McKenna noted, *"Marketing is everything."*

And, for more and more companies, it was.

Major Changes…

YOU CHANGE every ten years or so. So did advertising.

As we'll discuss later in this chapter, we must now communicate more quickly and more *visually*.

Advertising also changed because of:

• Changes in the marketplace.
• Changes in the media environment.
• Changes in our lives. Yours and mine.

As a result, traditional advertising became less effective. Here's what happened:

1. CHANGING MARKETS: "MATURITY."

Fast food and VWs aren't new anymore.

Today, you expect more than one kind of Tide.

PCs, VCRs, CDs, and e-mail are new technologies we now take for granted.

We've moved from growing categories, where almost every sales curve went up, to "mature" categories, where, whatever you're selling, most people have already got one.

That's a big difference – a huge difference.

In mature product categories, the growth that comes from people making new purchases and adopting new habits is essentially over.

Sales are "flat"– our purchase habits and brand preferences are more established. Sound familiar?

After you've decided on a brand, it takes more than a clever TV commercial to get you to change – particularly if you're satisfied with your current product choice.

It also means that people like you – younger and still in the process of making major brand decisions – are very desirable to marketers. (How many credit card come-ons were in your mailbox this week?)

It affects other things. In mature categories, established positions often make leaders harder to move.

In mature categories, advertising has a much more difficult task to accomplish – it's a tougher job.

When Volkswagen established itself in the '60s, with a unique car and unique advertising, it pretty much had the field to itself.

Then, VWs were better built and more reliable than most other foreign cars. Times change.

A unique car like the Mazda Miata quickly finds itself competing with other nifty convertibles.

You'll find the same thing happening with more cool small cars competing with the new VW and the PT Cruiser. These days, a new category can mature in a startlingly short period of time.

"A Zero-Sum Game."

In a mature category, it's a "zero-sum game."

For each winner, there's usually a loser.

It's *Marketing Warfare.*

As a friend said, *"Advertising today is selling corn flakes to people who are eating Cheerios."*

This more competitive marketplace is a major reason for the tremendous growth of sales promotion – the use of incentives to stimulate consumer purchase behavior and force distribution in a more crowded and mature marketplace.

That's the first big change – mature categories.

The second big change is in the world of media.

IT JUST FEELS RIGHT.
You bet it does.

Mazda saw an open niche in the marketplace and went for it – with a well-designed small convertible that was also designed to be profitable with a small production run.

The result – a unique new car that was like nothing else available.

And, guess what, the ads worked like gangbusters. Duh.

In about a year, other car makers responded with their own small convertibles – but by this time, Mazda Miata had established itself as the leader in this New Category.

In *Marketing Warfare,* Trout & Ries describe this as "flanking."

Look for undefended ground on the battlefield and take it.

SALES PROMOTION.
Adding an incentive – like special savings, an intriguing sweepstakes prize, or something extra – can increase sales on the short term.

This is particularly important when just an ad message may not be enough.

"Win/Free/Save."

These are the three major sales promotion techniques.

Perception.   Reality.

More media choices often mean smaller audiences – that's "fragmentation."

Millionaires aren't a dime a dozen. Actually, they run about 2¢ each.

GET MORE GEAR
Get the new catalog.

2. CHANGING MEDIA: "FRAGMENTATION."

There are more media choices. And, with one exception, each media choice costs more.

CPMs (Cost Per Thousand) in mass media have generally risen much faster than the rate of inflation.

It can cost two to three times more to reach the same number of people as it did ten years ago.

So, unless your new ad is two to three times more effective, it simply won't have the impact it did ten years ago. Ouch.

There's one exception – the Internet, but how often do you click on those Web ads?

Wallpaper isn't advertising. It's just wallpaper.

That's why advertisers and agencies are always looking for "breakthrough" concepts – ads that are many times more effective.

That's why strong programs, like the Charles Barkley vs. Godzilla example and the Mac intro, were built to communicate across media forms.

And that's why many marketers and agencies are looking at alternative media channels, alternative media delivery strategies, and alternative targets.

Finally, since it now costs more to reach (and persuade) new customers, why not increase effort against *current* customers? Why not indeed.

In many ways, the growth of direct-mail, "frequent-user" programs, niche media (like special interest magazines) and various forms of database marketing has been stimulated by the declining cost effectiveness of traditional mass media.

Why are we talking about this? Because as someone who creates media messages, you need to know about the environment you work in.

And that media environment is exploding.

The result is an abundance of opportunity and one huge problem – "fragmentation."

More media options mean less impact for any single message. Understanding this is easy.

Doing something about it can be tough.

But if you can use media more effectively, both you and the marketers you work for will benefit.

3. CHANGING CONSUMERS: "OVERCHOICE."

We've changed – as "receivers" and customers.

As the number of messages increases, we have to deal with "overchoice." Too many choices.

We become less responsive and more selective. It's simply impossible for us to respond to every message.

As a survival mechanism, we learn to ignore, or, more accurately, we learn to not pay attention.

We all do it. We have to. As Omnicom CEO Allen Rosenshine noted, *"Too much of advertising isn't simply bad, it's simply irrelevant."*

In addition, we're very good at selecting information when we need it. If your car has trouble starting on a winter morning, you quickly start to pay attention to the car battery ads you usually ignore.

We're all smarter consumers of advertising.

We use it when we need it. When we don't, we don't.

Our choice of car, cola, fast food, laundry detergent, and concert tickets is based on our own real-world experience and our own personal taste.

We use advertising for information, entertainment, and to pay for the media we enjoy. But we're not that easily influenced or persuaded.

Today, a good writer has to overcome:
- Mature product categories.
- Media fragmentation.
- Consumer overchoice.

It's not your imagination.

It's tougher than ever.

How About No Copy!
Jeff Gorman and Gary Johns "wrote" the billboard above and the print ad below for Nike.

They knew that, done right, no words could create a stronger communication!

HARDERFASTERBETTERMORE!
Another reason visuals work is that visual communication is faster.

FASTER THAN A SPEEDING CIVILIZATION.

And just in case you didn't think there was enough to worry about, it's all happening faster than ever, too.

Computer-based information and production technology have accelerated the pace of business.

For example, during the '80s, major amounts of business moved from Fed-Ex to fax machines in less than a year.

That's just one example.

There's no time for all of them.

TWO OTHER TRENDS.

Two other things happened to advertising in the '80s:

First, the effect of the stock market.

Second, an exciting change in what used to be called "secondary markets."

1. Stock Markets.

The first major change was due to something curious – price differentials between the New York and London Stock Exchanges.

At the time, the London Exchange valued agency stocks more highly. The P/E ratio (Price to Earnings) was twice that of the New York Exchange!

This meant Saatchi & Saatchi, based in London, could offer US stockholders almost twice as much.

They bought Ted Bates, Compton, Campbell-Mithun-Esty, Dancer Fitzgerald Sample, and others.

Can anyone do this trick? Yes.

Saatchi's accountant, Martin Sorrell, bought a shopping cart company – Wire Plastic Products (WPP).

It was small. It was cheap. It was listed on the London Stock Exchange.

In a startlingly short period, he bought Ogilvy & Mather and JWT, two of the world's largest agencies. Since then, he also picked up Y&R.

Other agencies merged as well.

And it changed the agency business.

2. Smaller Markets.

The business changed in another way.

Minneapolis and Portland are two dramatic examples of the tremendous improvement in advertising quality in smaller cities.

Production technology is no longer limited to large markets. Now every market has access to good typography, photography, and design.

And, while many big marketers have big bureaucracies devoted to "risk management," most small marketers know they need impact.

That's why there's often more opportunity for high-impact work with smaller clients, markets, and agencies.

You no longer have to go to New York to get a good job in advertising – or to do good advertising.

SOME ADS CHANGE HISTORY.

This advertising for Margaret Thatcher and the Conservative (Tory) Party in Great Britain was one key to their victory.

This change in government not only put Great Britain on a new political path, the response by the Labour Party to that success resulted in that party repositioning itself. The result? Tony Blair.

The tactics and techniques of advertising became a key part of the politics of a major industrial nation.

JESSE VENTURA, GOVERNOR.

The Governor of Minnesota is an ex-wrestler named Jesse Ventura.

A key part of his campaign was ironic, humorous, and very "po-mo" (post-modern) advertising that appealed to a turned-off electorate.

Ads featured Jesse Ventura action figures and Jesse "The Body" Ventura posed as "The Thinker."

A huge last-minute youth vote was one of the keys to his victory – as is the growing ability of celebrity to transfer from one area to another.

TWO FOR ONE.

The Pink Bunny interrupts a phony TV commercial for deodorant soap.

In one, the Bunny interrupted a real commercial – for Purina Cat Chow. (At the time, both brands had the same parent company – Ralston-Purina.)

THE PINK BUNNY ANNOUNCES A NEW AGE OF ADVERTISING.

Now advertising makes fun of advertising making fun of advertising.

With a very competitive point.

The charming "Pink Bunny" ads mask a very tough-minded business decision.

Eveready, and their agency, Chiat/Day, discovered that durability was not only the most important claim for batteries – it was the *only* meaningful claim.

The leading brand, DuraCell, was making exactly that point in their advertising – with a larger budget.

Client and agency made a tough decision – compete with category leader DuraCell on durability. The challenge wasn't do it different, but do it better.

When the ads first broke, research showed a high level of confusion. Eveready's Pink Bunny was being confused with DuraCell's battery-powered toys.

Client and agency stuck with it.

Over time, it worked, building Eveready's sales and the brand's reputation for durability. The Pink Bunny became one of America's favorite ad icons.

Tough marketing. Charming advertising.

That kept on going. And going…

TOUGH PROBLEMS.
TOUGH DECISIONS.

The Pink Bunny is a perfect example of the kind of tough-minded decisions you sometimes have to make.

Deciding to take on a larger competitor with a smaller budget and "me-too" advertising was a tough decision.

After that decision was made, client and agency had to endure about a year of research and trade magazine articles that reported consumers confusing Eveready advertising with the competitor's.

BUD LIGHT EVOLVED...

with "Party Animal" Spuds McKinzie.

The pleasantly goofy ads grew along with the brand – until Spuds T-shirts were being merchandised in two-year-old sizes. Hey, wait a minute!

Two-year-old sizes? This is for beer!

Suddenly, Spuds disappeared and beer advertising to younger target groups changed dramatically.

Cutty and denim.

The day was all business. The evening is all system. Instant with your favorite jeans, an understanding friend, and the smooth, mellow taste of Cutty Sark. A taste treasure.
Cutty Sark. You earned it.

THE PICTURE STORY.

With fewer words, you read in your own feelings and your own experiences.

The Viz Biz!

TELEVISION HAS TRANSFORMED SOCIETY. Some might argue it has transformed many of us neurologically, but we'll leave that to pediatricians and neurophysiologists. We merely observe the obvious.

We watch a ton of TV. And more and more, advertising has become visually driven.

Doug Warren, an agency president who'd left the business, made this observation on his return.

"We now live in a nonverbal society. Impressions are made on a visual basis. Language mainly serves to reinforce preconceived stereotypes.

Nothing new you say? I disagree.

The change over the past ten years is extreme and will grow stronger...

We respond in an ever-increasing degree on a strictly emotional level triggered by visual stimuli.

Talk all you will about your product's advantages, but the verbiage had better conjure up acceptable visual recall. People no longer have time (and there's growing inability) to isolate or critically examine facts."

He's right. Successful advertising is now more visual.

It's a move from verbally dominant to visually dominant communication… from logical left-brain "perception" to right-brain "reception."

Words became less important overall. Headlines became shorter – or even nonexistent.

Yet, it was right for the times. In magazines, more and more readers "viewed" print.

We are also a more visually sophisticated audience, with TV as our dominant input mode – experiencing ever more intense and condensed visual input.

'80s Scrapbook.

BETWEEN THE '80s AND '90s, computer-based visual assembly became possible – as a result, a wider range of visualizations became part of the art director's repertoire.

Later, a similar evolution happened in film and video, as computer power increased.

Product as Art. Advertising as Art. Art as Advertising. Here, early Absolut.

The Passionate Eye of Fashion. *The benefit is both the look of the clothes and the feeling of knowing that one is wearing something special. Building equity in the brand name is critical – and often best communicated without explanation.*

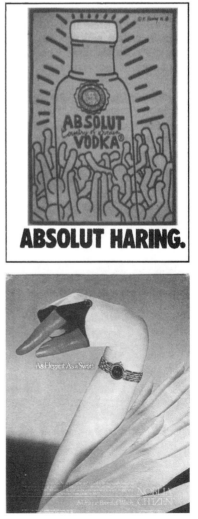

The Surreal Vision. *Schools of art re-emerge in advertising styles – with an assist from technology. Digitized photography expands the range of possibility.*

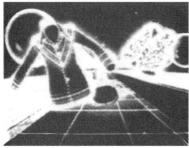

COMPUTER POWER.
Early TV spots like this one for Levi's used computerized motion control and film assembly to open new visual vistas.

THE POWER OF ROCK 'N' ROLL.
Popular music has a deep and positive connection with almost everybody.

This was demonstrated when the California Raisin Advisory Board had dancing raisins sing the Marvin Gaye hit, *I Heard It Through the Grapevine.*

Viz Biz Video.

WE'RE NOW A VISUAL CULTURE. From *Sesame Street* and the Rug Rat set to MTV for Generation Teen to high-tech commercials for upscale businessmen, television became a ravenous consumer of the newest video techniques. And so have we.

Today, the "channel-changer mentality" zips and zaps through the media environment.

Today we receive and perceive at an ever-increasing speed through an ever-wider range of media choices.

Here are some of the trends that kicked in:

THE ROCK VIDEO INFLUENCE.

Aggressive and surreal quick-cut imagery driven by a powerful music track. A shorthand symbolic language – heavy on the attitude.

This is both cause and result of an improved ability to receive and interpret visual information.

In addition, marketers now perceive rock 'n' roll as part of our contemporary cultural heritage and use it as a marketing tool.

Want to reach a target audience? Find the music they were listening to when they were about fourteen and you won't be too far off. That's one reason you'll hear old rock songs in ads for new luxury cars.

The same goes for old TV shows. Notice the little twinge you get when you recognize a bit of sit-com from your younger days.

THE GROWTH OF TECHNOLOGY.

Computers and video technology expanded the techniques available in video production.

What was once state-of-the-art is now available at most TV stations and video houses.

Complicated video effects are now easier and more affordable – and the trend will continue.

CELEBRITY.

Television now adds its own aura to those who stand center stage in our electronic window.

From manufactured celebrities, like The California Raisins, Spuds MacKenzie, and Bartels & Jaymes to well-established celebrities like Michael Jordan, Bill Cosby, and whoever's hot this week.

From nationally recognized supermodels to the celebrity status generated by local retailers and advertising spokesmen. It's electronic sizzle.

While the use of celebrities has been a common advertising technique, the game of fame in marketing has grown stronger.

The lines of celebrity blur, with public figures doing commercials while commercial stars become public figures.

It's all part of the growth of our visually driven media culture. Viz biz!

"Here's the Chief!" Wendy's cast founder Dave Thomas as their spokesperson, and he became a celebrity.

> **DONNA:** *Looking for a job, Mom?*
> **FERRARO:** *Very funny.*
> **LAURA:** *Well, I am.*
> **DONNA:** *So what's it this week Laura, marine biology?*
> **FERRARO:** *Are we still hoping to be a star of stage and screen?*
> **LAURA:** *Come on, Mom, it's a tough choice.*
> **FERRARO:** *Sure, it's tough when you can be anything you want to be.*
> **VO:** *When you make a choice, what's right is what feels right. Diet Pepsi.*
> **FERRARO:** *You know, there's one choice I'll never regret.*
> **DONNA:** *Politics?*
> **FERRARO:** *No, being a mother.*
> **VO:** *Diet Pepsi. The one-calorie choice of a new generation.*

FEATURE ATTRACTION.

This Nike spot became the movie *Space Jam,* featuring Bugs Bunny and Michael Jordan. And ads become pop culture.

WHO IS THAT LADY?

Today, you're used to politicians doing advertising pitches. But when this TV spot ran, featuring Geraldine Ferraro, who'd been a Democratic vice-presidential candidate, it made quite an impact.

This commercial is done in the "hyper-realism" mode first popularized by Pepsi during this period – it features tight framing, super close-ups, and intimate communication.

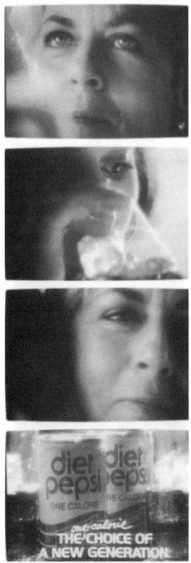

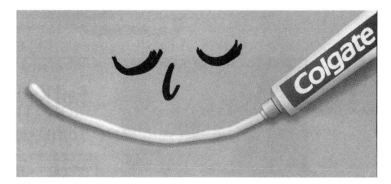

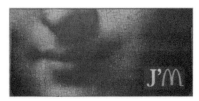

Simple visuals communicate powerfully in a language everyone understands.

A New Brand World.

THE BRAND AGE BEGAN IN THE '90s. A maturing marketplace, more expensive media, and more experienced consumers made a big change in advertising.

As alternative marketing communications options grew, and as the impact of individual ads lessened, marketers looked for ways to accumulate impact.

One of those ways was to refocus on the brand itself. As it cost more to establish a new brand, the value of existing brands grew.

THE GROWTH OF BRAND VALUE.

Here's another way to look at it. As we experience a shift in value from tangible things to information, we discover that the name and reputation of the product – the brand – is hugely valuable.

The advertised brand name has become of great importance to consumers, marketers, and investment bankers.

In many ways, the brand is the organizing concept of business. Though each business has ways of marketing products and making money, virtually every business is, in some way, building the equity of its brand.

Today, brands rule.

FROM ADVERTISING TO MARKETING COMMUNICATIONS.

Once, advertising was almost the only way a brand talked to consumers. Today, there are many options.

The same kind of thinking used to create great ads is now used to develop sales promotion, PR, direct marketing, events, and Web-based programs.

Now marketers are looking everywhere.

Nike, who first signed Michael Jordan, now signs up leading universities. Is it an ad? Not really.

Is it effective? What do you think?

For example, look at a key part of their strategy to create a major brand in a brand new market – golf. It's Tiger Woods.

CONTRADICTORY PRESSURES.

The pressure to solve problems with a breakthrough is constant and intense – so's the pressure to play it safe.

The challenge to reduce risks and conserve resources in a less effective environment competes with the challenge to break through the clutter and make an impact.

Often, that means risk – it's riskier than ever to change. It's riskier than ever *not* to change.

And that's why advertising – and all marketing communications – has become a much tougher business.

We need people who can think.

We need people who can communicate.

And we *really* need people who can do both.

MANY TARGETS, MANY CHANNELS.

Since the beginning, talking to your target as a single individual has been critical for effective communication. But now you may have multiple targets.

For example, software developers were critical for Macintosh's success – even though they're not exactly customers.

You have to reach large important target groups who may not have much in common with each other – including the way they'll use your product.

IMC. NOT NEW.

As Don Schultz of Northwestern University pointed out, one group of marketers practiced IMC (Integrated Marketing Communication) for years.

Small companies.

Smaller business-to-business marketers have been "thinking integrated" since marketing began.

The small business-to-business marketer knows how to integrate his communications all by himself:

- **Advertising in trade journals**
- **Direct mail to customers**
- **Conventions and trade shows**
- **Press releases to trade press**
- **Incentives for the sales force**

Whether or not all the right decisions are made, these marketers are fairly familiar with the marketing and selling options available to them.

Their ad agency often supplies a full range of IMC services:

- **Advertising • PR**
- **Brochures & Catalogs**
- **Sales Meetings • Trade Shows**
- **Newsletters • Corporate ID**
- **Package Design**

Other smaller businesses, such as single-store retailers, practice their own brand of IMC:

- **A sale (promotion)**
- **A newspaper ad**
- **A mailing to customers**
- **"Co-op" advertising**
- **Incentives to sales people**
- **Telemarketing**
- **Bus bench backs**
- **Flyers handed out in the mall**

All are IMC tactics appropriate for a small retailer.

Without even knowing it, they already "think integrated."

Bigger brands. Bigger problems.

For larger marketers, it's more complicated. Budgets are bigger, and so are organizational problems.

One person runs sales promotion, another runs PR, and someone else handles the advertising agency.

Simple things become complicated as larger marketing organizations try to "think integrated."

OUR CONCEPTUAL MODEL.

This is a useful way to think about The MarCom Matrix, with six major forms of MarCom: Advertising • Public Relations & Publicity • Sales Promotion • Direct Marketing • Event Marketing • New Media (which includes the Internet).

They all revolve around the "Idea."

What's the Idea?

It could be the idea of the brand, the idea around a current campaign, or a short-term event – like a product intro.

Put this in the back of your mind as you read the rest of the chapter.

Then, at the end of this chapter, we'll have an initial exercise where you try to develop an idea that works with every part of The MarCom Matrix.

SMOKING OUT
NEW OPPORTUNITIES.

Wrigley's Spearmint Gum saw a problem as an opportunity, taking advantage of increased smoking restrictions by positioning their product as an alternative for smokers.

With a strong simple visual device (substituting the No Smoking symbol for the "O"), they quickly communicate the thought "When You'd Like to Smoke But Can't."

The brand had been on an eight-year sales decline – until these ads.

The first year, sales *increased* 5%.

The MarCom Matrix.

ONCE UPON A TIME, when a manufacturer had a dollar for marketing, it was spent on advertising.

Today, there are a lot of things that can be done with a marketing dollar.

All these things add up to one big thing called "marketing communications" – MarCom for short.

Let's look at all the ways marketers communicate:

ADVERTISING.

The way you're most familiar with is advertising.

Communicating to consumers with an advertising message is still the biggest part of marketing communications. And it's usually the biggest part of the budget.

For the right product at the right time, advertising can still be a powerful force in the marketplace – even for a product that's been around for 100 years.

But advertising is no longer the only thing.

SALES PROMOTION.

For example, one way I can get your attention is to offer you something. A bribe. A free sample. A chance to win a prize. A rebate. A toy in your Happy Meal.

And that refrigerator magnet with the phone number of a local pizza place? That's a promotional product.

If you provided an incentive to a sales person, do you think that might affect their behavior?

You bet. That's a trade promotion.

These are all sales promotion tactics, and it's another big part of The MarCom Matrix.

In fact, for some products, they might spend more on sales promotion than on advertising.

MARKETING PUBLIC RELATIONS.

Did you see the new iMac on the cover of *Time?* Ever read a movie review? How about a review of software in a computer magazine? Or an article about a company in a business magazine?

That's "Marketing Public Relations," (MPR) and it's more important than ever.

Done well, MPR can result in press coverage that is worth millions in media exposure (what it would cost if you had to buy it) and the additional value of "third party endorsements" (when someone else says something nice about you, it has a bit more credibility than an ad).

DIRECT MARKETING.

Now let's take a peek in your mailboxes – the one where you live and the one on your computer.

There, marketers are directing messages at you for credit cards, computer accessories, and travel bargains for Spring Break. That's Direct Marketing.

EVENT MARKETING.

OK, now how about watching a sporting event.

Or maybe you'd like to go to a concert or a festival.

Or a NASCAR race.

AND THEY SAID WE COULDN'T GIVE IT AWAY.

Sales Promotion *uses an incentive to stimulate sales. With the right incentive, you can usually get people to try something once. After that, the product better deliver.*

The Direct Approach *can be very effective if you know who you're talking to. The most important thing is making the right connection with your target group.*

NASCAR *is just one of the new eventdriven marketing programs. It offers entertainment combined with huge sponsorship opportunities. It's a growing area of marketing communications with exciting opportunities for creative messaging.*

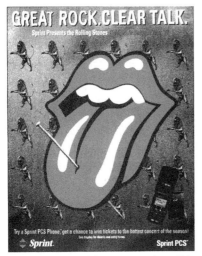

It's an event. It's a promotion. It's advertising. It's publicity. Strong ideas can play anywhere on The Matrix.

Bud World, anyone?

WHAT'S YOUR INTERNET STRATEGY?

Today, every company needs to have an Internet strategy in addition to an advertising and public relations strategy.

As this new media channel matures, you will see a growing range of effective applications that will add up to billions.

The Apple Store

Every marketer has to decide the role that New Media will play in their marketing. The Apple Store was part of Apple's commitment to do more business on the Internet. Retailers weren't happy.

Marketers are also involved with these events.

And the events are often marketers themselves – marketers working with other marketers.

In fact, the athletes and musicians that make these events special may also be involved in some aspect of marketing communications related to these events.

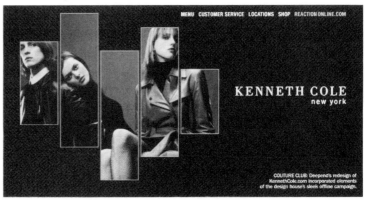

NEW MEDIA.

Finally, almost every marketer you can think of is trying to get the Internet to add effectiveness to their marketing. There may be other media ideas as well: a custom published magazine, a video, a CD – and whatever new combination is created tomorrow.

We'll call this all "New Media" and it covers all the new ways marketers are looking to communicate.

It's a new dimenstion to the media matrix we live in, as we shift from medium to medium – from the TV to your mailbox to your special interest magazine to that Web site a friend told you about.

Each represents an opportunity to communicate.

The techniques used to develop effective advertising can also be used to do these things effectively.

We've seen it demonstrated over and over – as media evolves into new forms, it opens up new ways for marketers to communicate.

New Media represents a whole new range of exciting opportunities – one that's expanding with possibility every day.

Matrix@Work.

NOW, MORE MARCOM OPTIONS THAN EVER!
Create a promotion. Stage an event. Publish a book.
Send in the coupon. Call the 800#. Watch the enclosed
video. Launch a new brand.

Never before have there been more choices and
more opportunities – from national ads to personalized letters in your mailbox – from catalogs to CDs.

There are also more media channels.

Today, it's more than crafting the right message –
it's crafting the right way to *deliver* that message.

SMART MARKETING BY SMARTFOOD.

When Frito-Lay purchased SmartFood, they bought
more than a brand. They bought a marketing plan.

To establish SmartFood as a unique, nontraditional snack-food brand, their smart agency, Mullen,
decided to do it with nontraditional media forms.

Instead of a TV spot, which would have appeared
with lots of other TV spots for snack foods, they
consciously chose alternative media channels.

Outdoor. Radio. Unusual direct mail. And sampling.

People dressed as six foot bags of SmartFood
distributed the product in high-traffic areas across
the country – from malls to ski slopes.

The result was a highly distinctive introduction
that created a highly distinctive brand personality.

In truth, SmartFood was just flavored popcorn –
tasty, but not tremendously new and different.

The choice of media channels differentiated this
product as much as the advertising itself. Smart.

BRIDGING THE GAP.

When this book was first written, The Gap was
just one of many jeans stores at the mall. But then…

With smart merchandising, fashions that were right
for the times, and ads that made their clothes look

CHANGING CHANNELS.
By putting their message in media you
wouldn't expect, and serving up their
message in ways you wouldn't expect,
SmartFood made extra impact in the
marketplace.

Ads for The Gap. *Their cool TV spots
aren't done by an ad agency, but by their
in-house advertising department.*

PRODUCT & PERSONALITY.
The Gap blends the two, featuring portraits of "cutting edge" individuals looking comfortable in The Gap's simple fashions combined with other clothes – just like in the real world.

The "Individuals of Style" campaign was developed by The Gap's own in-house ad department.

So were those neat TV spots.

Smart merchandising and smart advertising helped The Gap grow from a jeans store into America's second largest clothing brand.

They developed "flanker brands" – GapKids and Baby Gap – as well as two whole new brands – a restaged Banana Republic and Old Navy.

good, The Gap became a leading fashion brand.

They took the traditional tools of retail and turned an ordinary brand into a powerful fashion voice.

Even brands can have brands. They built up two more powerful brands – Banana Republic and Old Navy.

THE MILAN EPIPHANY.

Location. Location. Location. They say those are the three most important things in retail. But sometimes you need something else – vision.

Standing in a Milan coffee shop, Howard Schultz saw there was a place in America for coffee that was more than hot brown liquid poured from a pot.

With a design vision, merchandising, and imaginative tie-ins with things like jazz CDs, he created marketing communications with a bit of magic.

THREE KEYS TO SUCCESS.

In today's marketplace, you'll need three things:
1. Integrated Thinking. Your thinking should cover the full range of the marketing task – and the full range of opportunities. Integrated thinking helps you deal with the wide range of communication needs of a product like Macintosh – from high-impact TV to small newspaper ads for local dealers.
2. Smart Choices. You'll have to choose from a wide range of options – a range that keeps growing every day. The key is to make choices that connect.
3. Persuasive Communication. Marketing without communication seldom works. Persuasion is the key. And that means knowing how to talk to your target(s).

Howard Gossage.

HE WAS "MASTER OF THE MATRIX."

Gossage wrote ads – but his ads were more than advertising. His ads launched fads, contests, social movements, books, the Beethoven sweatshirt, and mountains of free publicity.

He introduced the world to the thinking of media guru Marshall McLuhan. His ads for the Sierra Club helped launch the modern environmental movement.

One Gossage ad almost formed a small Caribbean country – it was debated in the House of Commons.

Basically, Gossage understood how advertising could be made to play a part on a larger media stage – acting as a catalyst for a larger media presence.

When he conceived an ad, he also thought about how it could grow into something larger.

Today, that's part of what many call IMC and what we call The MarCom Matrix.

For example, he grew a small ad campaign for *Scientific American* into "The First International Paper Airplane Competition."

It created a huge PR buzz and was even made into a book! Gossage simply thought of it as a smart way to make the most of small ad budgets.

Gossage Today. This ad by the San Francisco agency Goodby Berlin Silverstein owes a debt to the work of copywriter Howard Gossage and art director Marget Larsen. It's a disarmingly unique and persuasive piece of communication, written literally from a "bird's eye view."

*"Nobody reads ads.
They read what interests them."*
Howard Luck Gossage

His agency was in an old San Francisco firehouse – no one knew how to start a bigger media fire with fewer ad dollars.

He was also concerned with larger issues – like mass media being taken over by mass marketers – hot dog vendors taking over a football game.

GOOD GOSSAGE!

Here are some other examples:

Beethoven Sweatshirts.

A small classical FM station asked Gossage to help them stay in business. The result – a Beethoven sweatshirt!

Gossage also used it as a tie-in with another client, Ranier Ale.

It was a classic Gossage event. "Coach Stahl wants you to walk to Seattle." After it began, newspapers treated it like a news story. Free PR!

Pink Air.

Pink Air spoofed advertising years before The Pink Bunny – it was a campaign for Fina Gas.

It had contests (Your Chance To Win 15 Yards Of Pink Asphalt), premiums (pink balloons and pink valve caps), and the world's longest slogan:

[Our Motto] "If you're driving down the road and you see a Fina station, and it's on your side so you don't have to make a U-Turn through traffic and there aren't six cars waiting and you need gas or something, please stop in."

Plus, there were coupons for pink valve caps, credit cards, and a "free sample" – a pink balloon with the Fina logo.

☞RESPONSE/INVOLVEMENT✍

Gossage's agency ran as many as seven coupons in one ad (for The Sierra Club).

He believed it was an important way to involve readers. It did!

BE THE FIRST ONE ON YOUR BLOCK TO WIN A KANGAROO!

That's how Howard Gossage got you to think about Australia's airline – Qantas.

Most of his ads included a response device. Gossage believed contests, offers, coupons and surveys were a great way to involve readers and dramatize some important aspect of the product.

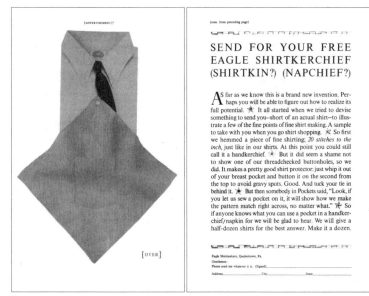

This "spread" was two sides of one page in the New Yorker. *You had to flip it back and forth to understand the offer, which was a strange, useless thing that demonstrated various aspects of Eagle's shirtmaking skills. The ad set new records for responses and even inspired a book (yes, a book), called* Dear Miss Afflerbach *or* The Postman Hardly Ever Rings 11,342 Times.

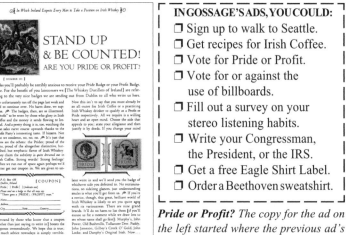

IN GOSSAGE'S ADS, YOU COULD:
- ❏ Sign up to walk to Seattle.
- ❏ Get recipes for Irish Coffee.
- ❏ Vote for Pride or Profit.
- ❏ Vote for or against the use of billboards.
- ❏ Fill out a survey on your stereo listening habits.
- ❏ Write your Congressman, the President, or the IRS.
- ❏ Get a free Eagle Shirt Label.
- ❏ Order a Beethoven sweatshirt.

Pride or Profit? The copy for the ad on the left started where the previous ad's copy left off. People looked forward to...

Assignment #3:

THE OBJECTIVE of this assignment is to get you thinking about the dynamics of today's marketplace – and the problems you'll have to solve.

1. DEALING WITH CHANGE.

A. Pick a Product. It doesn't matter what. Remember, the objective is to develop the right mindset.

B. Think about the Category. Is it growing or mature? Are your potential customers using something else? Do you already have a loyal customer base? Why do people buy? Describe the category and competitive situation in two sentences.

C. Think about the Best Way to Reach People. What are the best communication channels? Write down your top choices.

D. OK, What's the Best Way to Sell Them? Based on your initial instincts, what's the best way to get the job done? Later on, you will be provided with good information about products, competition, and consumer behavior. Right now, you want to develop the conceptual framework.) Write your general approach in a few sentences.

EXAMPLE: *Healthy Joints tablets (helps fight arthritis in older dogs). Growing category – dogs living longer, pet food superstores, growing pet health knowledge. Best ways to reach are point of purchase and visit to vet. Look for places w. high dog concentrations – particularly larger dogs. Best way to sell – Sampling w. coupons and information that says "Every dog 8 or older needs Healthy Joints every day." Adult dog food tie-in?*

2. VISUALS:

A. Bring in a Visual that you think works.

B. Start a File of visuals you think are strong.

C. Think Visuals first. See it before you write it.

ALVIN TOFFLER
Author of FUTURE SHOCK

POWERSHIFT

KNOWLEDGE, WEALTH, AND VIOLENCE
AT THE EDGE OF THE 21ST CENTURY

READING LIST.
Here are some books worth looking at. Each deals in its own way with the major changes in our economy and our society during this period:

Three by Toffler:
Future Shock (1971) • *The Third Wave* (1980) • *Powershift* (1990)

Toffler deals with the Post-Industrial Revolution, one of the three great revolutions in human history – which happens to be going on right now.

Each of these books makes an interesting contribution. The third, *Powershift,* builds on the first two – so, if you're pressed for time (and who isn't) – Toffler lets you catch up on the points he made in the first two, though you should read them all if you can find the time.

The Medium Is the Message (or Massage). Marshall McLuhan:
McLuhan is difficult (even he wasn't always sure what he meant), but thought-provoking. He was introduced to the media world by Howard Gossage.

Tony Schwartz is a copywriter turned media consultant who puts McLuhan into a practical context.

A brief discussion of his "Resonance Theory" appears at the end of Chapter Three. You might want to read…

The Responsive Chord
Tony Schwartz/Doubleday

Media: The Second God
Tony Schwartz/Random House

Finally, you can impress your friends by reading two *Harvard Business Review* articles, "Managing Our Way to Economic Decline" by Robert H. Hayes and William J. Abernathy, and "Marketing Is Everything" by Regis McKenna.

EXAMPLE: DOMINO'S PIZZA.
It's easy and it's fun. Let's say our idea is to combine Domino's Pizza and the game of dominoes. Here's what you'd write:

• **Advertising**. An ad with the headline "The Domino Theory." History of Domino's pizza, history of game. Ads would have coupon offer and some sort of game involvement.

• **Sales Promotion** (Win/Free/Save). Give domino pieces with every purchase. Find some way to build continuity – add "Lucky Domino" for extra value/prizes.

• **Public Relations.** Do giant toppling domino designs, have contests, film the event for a news release.

• **Direct Marking.** Send free domino and coupon to every customer in your database – or every student on campus.

• **Event Marketing.** Sponsor a big Domino Tournament, have demonstrations at student centers.

• **New Media.** Build a Web site with a downloadable domino game and an online tournament, offer software.

And don't forget a downloadable discount coupon.

Got it? Now you do one.

NEED HELP PICKING A BRAND?
Pick your favorite pizza, software you like, or an upcoming campus event.

Go to the store. Buy something off the shelf – barbecue sauce, a lesser-known beverage (not Coke or Pepsi), or even think about the store itself.

Remember, when you're out there working, you usually won't have much choice about what you work on – so don't worry about it.

Just pick something.

3. THE MARCOM MATRIX.

You may or may not think you have a good idea about all the MarCom options there are. But actually, you do. And you're going to prove it to yourself in this exercise.

First, pick a brand: _____.

Then, in the center circle, indicate a simple core selling idea for that brand.

In the other circles, which represent different types of MarCom, add a related idea, such as:

• An advertising headline   • An event idea
• A direct marketing tactic   • A publicity idea
• A sales promotion idea   • A new media idea
• An idea for publicity or PR   (for your computer)

Go ahead. You can do this.

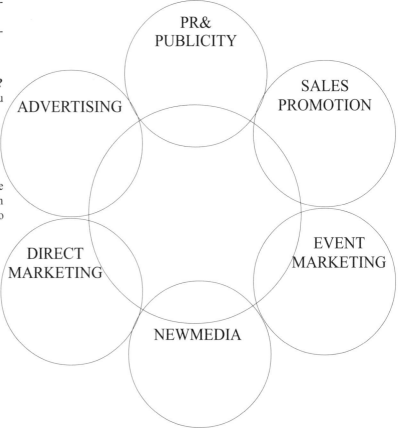

You might want to use this as a template.

Exercise: Personal Media.

Here's a "stretching" exercise to help you think about the range of IMC opportunities.

Discover your own "Personal Media Network."

1. Track yourself through a typical day – what "media" are part of your network?

Me

WAKE UP

SLEEP

2. When and where were the best opportunities to reach you? What's your Aperture?

3. How does your "Personal Media Network" differ on the weekend?

PERSONAL MEDIA NETWORK.

Keith Reinhard, head of DDB, wants you to think about your "Personal Media Network." That's the way you spend your media day.

What is the media experience from the point of view of the individual target customer?

Aperture™.

A related concept is Aperture™.

What is the best time to reach that person for your product?

It includes places and habit patterns – when and why they read, watch TV, or listen to radio.

For example, is the media for information, entertainment, or background?

It also includes things you might not think of as media, like the package itself.

Thinking like this can help pizza companies decide to advertise just before halftime on a football game.

Thinking like this can help you add in-store advertising to complement your TV schedule.

Helpful Hint.

A good way to get to know your target is to look at their media.

For example, if you have a business trade ad, look through the trade journals where your ad will appear.

Where can you be reached? And when?
To be effective, your message has to be at the right place and at the right time. Then, if it's the right message, you've got a shot.

THE PERSONAL TRUTH.

Dan Wieden, head of Wieden + Kennedy, wants his agency to discover the "personal truth" in the products they advertise.

How do they relate to the individual customer's feelings and experience?

Nike products cover a wide range of activities – each has a different reason for being in people's lives.

Nike advertising tries to match the personal values attached to those activities.

For example, their advertising to women is dramatically different from that aimed at competitive tennis players or older runners.

Thinking like this helps Nike advertising "ring true."

Even their celebrity advertising is crafted to allow you to empathize with the individual.

So the advertising's not just about Nike – it's about *you*.

"Just Do It" is a theme that gathers strength as each commercial adds its own "truth" to the Nike image.

Exercise: Personal Truth.

One of the ways we can develop insight into others is to develop insights into ourselves.

The excellent work for Nike is an example of advertising most people enjoy.

They work very hard to "Just Do It."

How do they persuade us?

Let's compare things we like and ads we like and see if we can't find the "truths" about both.

A. Make a list titled "Things I Like."

B. Make a list titled "Ads I Like."

C. Now, think a bit. What truths are there about advertising that persuade you? Not just things you want to own, but attitudes and images that touch you.

D. Write down a few truths that are true for you.

Learning what it takes to persuade ourselves is the first step in learning to persuade others.

Different Groups. Different Approaches. This "Design Your Own Shoelaces" promotion took a Foot Loose *(ever see the opening credits?) approach for a whole range of their casual footwear.*

Yo! It's Po-Mo!

THIS IS ABOUT POST-MODERNISM – or "Po-Mo."

There are po-mo movements in art, architecture, philosophy, literature, history, and sociology.

And, there's one in advertising. Sort of.

Post-Modernism began as *"a revolt against modernism* (duh)*, a rejection of progress, the power of reason, and the dominance of science and technology…"* (From "The Chaos of Meaning" by Ian Forth, BMP/DDB)

You'll find this sensibility in art galleries, rock lyrics, and even physics lectures that deal with "chaos theory."

MARKETING MODERNISM.

Meanwhile marketing, which pays for advertising, is essentially "modernistic" and "positivist."

Marketers view their own activities as "progress." They offer you products that solve problems, fashionable fashions, specials this week only, and generally work to keep business in business.

Marketing tries to be logical – there's a lot of money at stake. Marketing works to discover objective "truths" about the best way to do things – whether it's how to introduce a new running shoe with improved arch support, sustain consumption of a breakfast cereal that's been around for fifty years, or sell you a beer as soon as you're old enough to buy one.

On the Other Hand, It's Not a Simple World.

One person's progress may be another's environmentally unfriendly behavior.

One person's "better" may be sexist, racist, classist, exploitive, or worse yet, unfashionable when viewed from another perspective.

OK, it's time for a chart.

Addendum:

At the end of some chapters, we may add a few more things we think you need to think about.

Ad for a "po-mo" brand – Doc Martens.

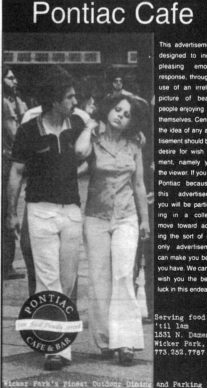

#31070

A SIDE-BY-SIDE COMPARISON.

On one side, we'll list some "modernist" and "progressive" values, and on the other, we'll list some post-modern perspectives.

Modernity	Post-Modernity
Order/Control	Disorder/Chaos
Certainty	Ambiguity
Content	Style
Tomorrow	Today
Similarities	Differences
Commodification	Customization
Universality	Individuality

See what's going on here?

Marketers are usually "modernistic."

They pretty much have to be. Because there's a lot at stake if you own a cereal factory.

But consumers nowadays, and young people in particular, may not be. After all, if you're just buying one box of cereal, what's the big deal.

Meanwhile, advertising is usually in the middle – working for the cereal manufacturer, trying to sell one box at a time to individuals.

Now let's talk about those individuals.

GENERATION PO-MO.

Today, most younger people understand and empathize with the chapter title from Doug Coupland's book *Generation X.*

That chapter was titled *"I Am Not a Target Market."*

Well, actually, you are a target market – we all are.

But that awareness, and that dissonance, changes things. And this awareness can be very different for different generations.

For example, even though I know I'm a target market, I don't have those feelings.

I can remember a time, as a child, when I was only occasionally a target market. For only a few hours a day, we could see TV for kids. Yay!

We'd plant our little blue-jeaned fannies in front of *The Howdy Doody Show.*

But, just like you, I discovered that you can eat just so many boxes of cereal – no matter what cool prize is inside. And we all discovered that the cool prize maybe isn't as cool as you thought it would be.

But you… Can you remember a moment when you didn't have a channel changer full of KidVid?

I'm guessing probably not.

You have a different attitude about the marketplace – very aware – but with very mixed feelings. Yes?

Well, that's po-mo.

TARGET MARKET AWARENESS.

So now let's look at the problem of advertising – the major way marketers speak to their target market.

The target is onto the game. They "get it." Don't you?

It isn't that you don't want to see an ad for something that might interest you – it's that you're aware of the fact that the marketer is doing what they're doing.

And, if advertisers don't send some sort of signal that "they know that you know," you may think they're pretty dim – or you may give them no thought at all.

You may buy the product, you may not, but the connection with the brand won't be as strong.

This awareness of being the target of marketing efforts is at the center of post-modern advertising.

CLAUDE HOPKINS RIDES AGAIN.

Remember Claude Hopkins? Remember his lesson?

It was to make that one-to-one connection.

It's still all about connecting with the consumer.

And the post-modern movement in advertising, which tends to be limited to certain specific types of products – those that appeal to younger consumers – is simply applying that lesson.

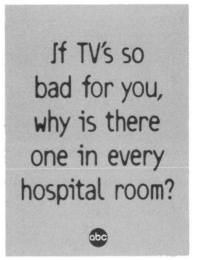

Po-Mo Promo. Here, ABC uses an ironic po-mo attitude to promote their "brand."

Po-Mo Attitude. Here, Simple.shoes takes a stand against modernity. Wonder if they have a Web site?

WHEN DO YOU PO-MO?

For certain products, in certain circumstances, good po-mo is critical for making a successful connection.

It's Claude Hopkins' one to one – with attitude.

Above, is a good example – a frame from a Sprite TV spot. They made up a phony soft drink, Jooky, and made fun of the claims and attitude.

It positioned Sprite as a more "honest" drink and more in touch with younger drinkers. Sprite sales grew.

Below, is a not-so-good example. The cutting-edge work for Subaru by Wieden + Kennedy didn't work.

Then again, the cars weren't much.

Better cars and more traditional advertising helped them get traction again.

And, at this point, it depends on the type of product.

You may have a po-mo mindset picking out Friday night's entertainment or the clothes you wear when you go out – but when you're figuring out the best way to finance a car – or pricing a trip for Spring Break – you're probably all business.

In the next chapter, "Two Brains are Better Than One," we'll spend a little more time on the concept that we can be very different people depending on what types of products we're thinking of purchasing.

"WHASSUP" WITH PO-MO?

The post-modern attitude tends to be ironic, knowing, and often self-referential.

It's the "we know that you know"syndrome. Done right, it's a shared joke.

"We know you get it. Wink. Wink. Nudge. Nudge." And you do – when it works.

This is the road that logically leads to "Whassup?"

"Whassup?" is about cameraderie and connection.

Good po-mo creates a loop of shared understanding.

Nike, because of its concern for the "personal truths" and values of its audience, contains aspects of po-mo.

It's also probably true that the crew at Wieden + Kennedy in Po-Mo, Oregon, is more in touch with these values than most.

PO-MO STYLE.

As Stephen Brown said in his very clever little book, *Post-Modern Marketing, "Post-modernism is characterized by style rather than by content."*

Getting the style or attitude right is critical.

What is that style? It's often a bit wry, or ironic, or cynical – but not always.

It's often "deconstructed" so that the audience can be involved in filling in the missing puzzle pieces.

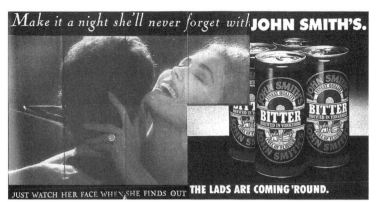

Make it a night she'll never forget with **JOHN SMITH'S.**

JUST WATCH HER FACE WHEN SHE FINDS OUT **THE LADS ARE COMING 'ROUND.**

The billboard on the left, for John Smith's Bitter, a British beverage, uses a number of po-mo devices.

It deconstructs a billboard, showing part of a John Smith's billboard over what looks like someone else's old billboard – with a very humorous result.

It's ironic and makes fun of ad cliches as it builds its own humor on top of it.

Get it?

This proves that you know that they know – or is it they know that you know?

And, since it's about style, not content, the critical ingredients in getting the recipe right are subjective –like art, attitude, and awareness.

So, how do you use po-mo? And when?

You use it like the beer they want you to buy when you're old enough – with moderation and when it's appropriate. Too much at the wrong time tends to have an unhappy result.

Because if you do it wrong, it shows that you don't know, you know?

Still, now you know po-mo.

But then again, we already knew that you knew.

Exercises & Discussion:

1. Describe the types of products where you think a po-mo appeal might be effective.

2. Describe people and products that are not po-mo.

3. OK, let's make a list:
   First, categories that are po-mo and not po-mo.
   Then, brands in categories that are and are not.

4. Look for some examples of advertising you think demonstrates good po-mo. How did they do it?

5. When are you a bit po-mo?
   When are you a modernist who believes in progress?

JESSE VENTURA
OUR NEXT GOVERNOR

PAID FOR BY VENTURA FOR GOVERNOR

GOVERNOR PO-MO.

Ironic, satirical commercials that made fun of establishment values and rhetoric were key ingredients in ads for Jesse Ventura, now governor of Minnesota.

Young voters, who responded to those appeals, were the key to his victory.

READ ALL ABOUT IT.

The book *Where the Suckers Moon* tracks the history of a Subaru new business pitch and the subsequent advertising by Wieden + Kennedy, who won the business.

Their innovative work had many po-mo aspects – such as deconstructed typography. One presenter mentioned punk music in the context of one of the Subaru models. It didn't work.

It can also be argued that the Subaru product that Wieden + Kennedy had to sell at the time wasn't all that terrific.

Then again, some have observed that the most popular car brand with younger consumers is "used," which is, after all, a po-mo brand.

YOUR "LEFT BRAIN"
Logical
Verbal
Math
Words
Facts
Memory
Asks "Why?"
Conservative

YOUR "RIGHT BRAIN"
Associative
Visual
Geometry
Music
Playful
Asks "What If?"
Imaginative

*

The two major modes of human brain hemisphere function were first described by psychobiologist Roger W. Sperry. His groundbreaking research was honored with a Nobel Prize.

**

The connection between the two sides of the human brain is called the *corpus callosum.* It literally lets the right hand know what the left hand is doing.

And… women usually have a much larger *corpus callosum* than men.

That's right, on average, women have many more connections between left and right brain hemispheres!

Two Brains Are Better Than One.*

YOUR BRAIN HAS TWO SIDES – left and right.

The left side of your brain is connected to the right side of your body. And vice versa.**

Basically, the left side is logical and verbal, rational and conservative. It does not take risks.

The right side is different.

It is intuitive, visual, liberal, and imaginative.

The left side reads.

The right side feels.

A well-organized Ogilvy-style reason why communicates to the left side of the brain.

Bill Bernbach's ads surprise the right side.

The right side listens to music. (But not always.)

The left side does math. (But not geometry.)

And, while both sides work together, it's important to consider how you will be communicating – emotionally or rationally.

Image or reason why.

Visually or verbally. Or both.

After all, just because you can't have it both ways doesn't mean it isn't.

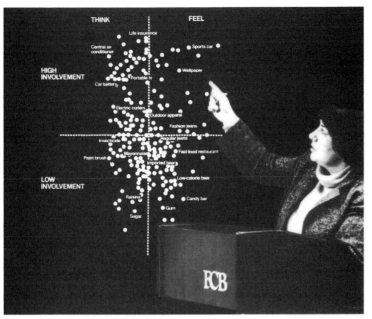

*Dona Vitale explains **The FCB Grid**. From the FCB annual report.*

	THINKING	FEELING
	THINK **HIGH** **INVOLVEMENT**	**FEEL** **HIGH** **INVOLVEMENT**
	THINK **LOW** **INVOLVEMENT**	**FEEL** **LOW** **INVOLVEMENT**

THE FCB PLANNING GRID.

The horizontal dimension goes from the rational to the emotional.
Thinking to **Feeling**.
And vice versa.

The vertical dimension is **interest** level – it goes from **low interest** to **high interest**.
Or vice versa.

The FCB Planning Grid.

THE RESEARCH DEPARTMENT at Foote Cone and Belding developed something called the **Vaughn Grid** (Richard Vaughn was Research Director in FCB's L.A. office – his original article can be found in the Addendum at the back of this chapter).

It's been called The FCB Grid for Advertising Planning, The FCB Planning Grid, or just, "The Grid."

The Grid takes this emotional vs. rational difference, plus a number of other advertising theories – economic, social, psychological, and responsive – and organizes the whole thing into a "playing field."

It's a pretty useful tool.

Some early examples, based on development work done by the FCB research department.

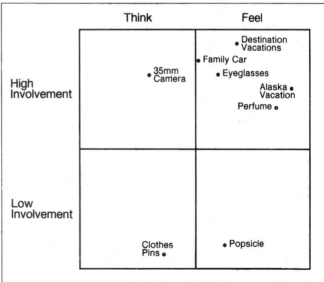

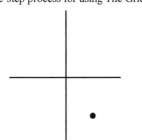

1. WHERE THE PRODUCT FITS.

First, place the product category in what you believe is the proper place on The Grid.

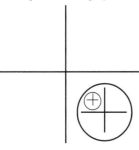

2. WHERE THE BRAND FITS.

Next, decide where your brand fits within the product category.

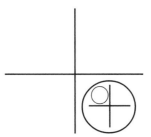

3. WHERE THE BRAND ATTRIBUTE FITS.

Finally, decide where the distinguishing product attribute of your brand fits.

So, for example, you could have a relatively emotional brand in a rational category. And vice versa.

HOW DO YOU USE THE GRID?

You use The Grid as a helpful technique and mental exercise for determining your advertising approach.

It helps you relate the type of product you're selling to the mind of your target consumer.

Because we're each a different type of consumer, depending on what we're buying. Consider ...

WHERE IS YOUR PRODUCT ON THE GRID?

Let's think about some different types of products and how they match up with the different quadrants:

Thinking/High Involvement: like a 35mm camera, a costly piece of office equipment, or perhaps the best terms for a student loan?

Thinking/Low Involvement: like clothes pins, a floor cleaner, or motor oil?

Feeling/High Involvement: like perfume, fashion, motorcycles, or cosmetics?

Feeling/Low Involvement: like a Popsicle, candy bar, or a soft drink?

Get the idea?

IT CAN BE BOTH.

As the Saab ad at the end of this chapter demonstrates, selling messages can contain elements of *both* thinking and feeling.

You may decide to sell your product in a rational way when others are selling theirs emotionally.

The key is to make a rational, strategic, or tactical decision – even if, ultimately, the logical conclusion is to be emotional.

There may be alternative hypotheses as to the proper placement of your product on The Grid.

This, in itself, can lead to interesting discussion and, hopefully, a better decision.

Thinking or feeling. High involvement or low.

All have their place. In the heart. And mind.

"Exploding the Dot."

Many advertising techniques involve developing mental flexibility. Learning one way of thinking about things. Then learning another.

Here's one that's *almost* the exact reverse of the FCB Planning Grid. It was developed while working with The Grid. After you determine where you want to place your dot/product on the Grid, "explode" it!

Turn your focus inside out and look at the forces pushing out in different directions. Sort of like this:

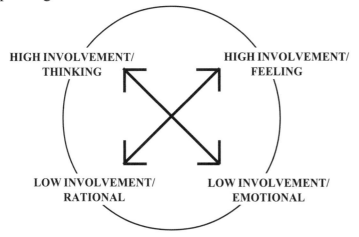

HIGH INVOLVEMENT/ THINKING

HIGH INVOLVEMENT/ FEELING

LOW INVOLVEMENT/ RATIONAL

LOW INVOLVEMENT/ EMOTIONAL

Often, these forces can be expressed as little "quotes" about the feeling or thinking involved.

Here's an example for Old El Paso, a leading brand of Mexican food.

In this case, The Grid can be a useful tool for opening up new ways of thinking about a product or product category.

READING LIST: TWO BOOKS ARE BETTER THAN ONE. MAKE THAT THREE.

Every day, there are more and more books examining aspects of left-brain and right-brain thinking.

There is a fascinating technique for teaching you to draw *upside down!* It generates right brain/visual connections in left brain/verbal people.

Writing the Natural Way by Gabrielle Lusser Rico helps you hook into associative areas of the right brain and unlock your writing creativity.

A Whack on the Side of the Head by Roger Von Oech, a Silicon Valley creativity consultant, is a lot of fun.

Whole Brain Thinking: Working from Both Sides of the Brain to Achieve Peak Job Performance, is a business book based on Roger Sperry's Nobel Prize winning research on split-brain theory, by Jacquelyn Wonder and Priscilla Donovan.

Read a few of them. You'll be a more effective and creative thinker.

And, you'll have more fun.

Maybe twice as much.

"EXPLODING THE DOT."
Example: Old El Paso Mexican Food.

HIGH INVOLVEMENT/ FEELING
Initial decision – High Risk – Fear of embarassment
Success – Creative Satisfaction
A creative way to enjoy a meal.

HIGH INVOLVEMENT/THINKING
Initial decision – High Risk– "What do I do?"
Meal Planning – New Recipes, Procedures.
A good way to serve good nutrition.

LOW INVOLVEMENT/RATIONAL
Success – Low Risk/No Risk
Good, Easy, Economical.
America's Favorite Brand of Mexican Food.
An economical way to serve good food.

LOW INVOLVEMENT/ EMOTIONAL
Fun & Flavor.
A fun, exciting meal.
"¡Ole!"

Assignment #4:

The E 320.
Where the rational mind
and the emotional mind collide.
Safely, of course.

THE
GOOD FOOD
COOKIE
archway.

**EXAMPLE: ARCHWAY
"THE GOOD FOOD COOKIE."**

We've used this example already in the Positioning section. And we'll use it again in the Strategy section.

Now we want to make the point that one idea can have different synergistic aspects within The Grid.

While the cookie category tends to be "lower right," Archway, a leading baker of oatmeal cookies, developed a "Good Food" position in the early '80s – a relatively "high think" position.

This matched up with other marketplace phenomena, such as increased concern about ingredients and good news about oat bran.

They also "exploded" their dot a bit.

Here are some examples of the range of programs they used:

High Think: mini-brochures containing nutritional information

Low Think: A promotional display program featuring a low price.

High Feel: "Be a Good Cookie" tie-in with Chilren's Miracle Network.

Low Feel: Slogans like "Did You Have Your Oatmeal Today?"

1. RIGHT TO LEFT.

Take a right brain (emotional) ad.
Make it a left brain (rational) ad.

2. LEFT TO RIGHT.

Pick a left brain (rational) ad.
Do the opposite.
Make it a right brain (emotional) ad.

3. GRID EXERCISE.

Draw The Grid.
Make a list of 10 different products.
Place them on The FCB Planning Grid.

4. BOTH SIDES.

The Saab ad on the right appeals to both.
Pick another product with *both* rational and emotional appeals.
Write an ad that appeals to both.
(It can be a spread.)

5. EXPLODE THE DOT.

Take the product from #4 and show the various forces at work in all four sections of The Grid.
Repeat the process with a second product.

A CAR FOR THE RIGHT SIDE OF YOUR BRAIN.

SAAB

The most intelligent car ever built.

A CAR FOR THE LEFT SIDE OF YOUR BRAIN.

The left side of your brain, recent investigations tell us, is the logical side.

It figures out that $1 + 1 = 2$. And, in a few cases, that $E = mc^2$.

On a more mundane level, it chooses the socks you wear, the cereal you eat, and the car you drive. All by means of rigorous Aristotelian logic.

However, and a big however it is, for real satisfaction, you must achieve harmony with the other side of your brain.

The right side, the poetic side, that says, "Yeah, Car X has a reputation for lasting a long time but it's so dull, who'd want to drive it that long anyway?"

The Saab Turbo looked at from all sides.

To the left side of your brain, Saab turbocharging is a technological feat that retains good gas mileage while also increasing performance.

To the right side of your brain, Saab turbocharging is what makes a Saab go like a bat out of hell.

The left side sees the safety in high performance. (Passing on a two-lane highway. Entering a freeway in the midst of high-speed traffic.)

The right side lives only for the thrills.

The left side considers that *Road & Track* magazine just named Saab "The Sports Sedan for the Eighties." By unanimous choice of its editors.

The right side eschews informed endorsements by editors who have spent a lifetime comparing cars. The right side doesn't know much about cars, but knows what it likes.

The left side scans this chart.

Wheelbase	99.1 inches
Length	187.6 inches
Width	66.5 inches
Height	55.9 inches
Fuel-tank capacity	16.6 gallons
EPA City	19 mpg*
EPA Highway	31 mpg*

The right side looks at the picture on the opposite page.

The left side compares a Saab's comfort with that of a Mercedes. Its performance with that of a BMW. Its braking with that of an Audi.

The right side looks at the picture.

The left side looks ahead to the winter when a Saab's front-wheel drive will keep a Saab in front of traffic.

The right side looks at the picture.

The left side also considers the other seasons of the year when a Saab's front-wheel drive gives it the cornering ability of a sports car.

The right side looks again at the picture.

Getting what you need vs. getting what you want.

Needs are boring; desires are what make life worth living.

The left side of your brain is your mother telling you that a Saab is good for you. "Eat your vegetables." (In today's world, you need a car engineered like a Saab.) "Put on your raincoat." (The Saab is economical. Look at the price-value relationship.) "Do your homework." (The passive safety of the construction. The active safety of the handling.)

1982 SAAB PRICE** LIST		
900 3-Door	5-Speed	$10,400
	Automatic	10,750
900 4-Door	5-Speed	$10,700
	Automatic	11,050
900S 3-Door	5-Speed	$12,100
	Automatic	12,450
900S 4-Door	5-Speed	$12,700
	Automatic	13,050
900 Turbo 3-Door	5-Speed	$15,600
	Automatic	15,950
900 Turbo 4-Door	5-Speed	$16,260
	Automatic	16,610

All turbo models include a Sony XR-70, 4-Speaker Stereo Sound System as standard equipment. The stereo can be, of course, perfectly balanced: left and right.

The right side of your brain guides your foot to the clutch, your hand to the gears, and listens for the "zzzooommm."

Together, they see the 1982 Saab Turbo as the responsible car the times demand you get. And the performance car you've always, deep down, wanted with half your mind.

*Saab 900 Turbo. Remember, test estimated mpg for comparison only. Mileage varies with speed, trip length, and weather. Actual highway mileage will probably be less. **Manufacturer's suggested retail price. Not including taxes, license, freight, dealer charges or options desired by either side of your brain.

This ad for Saab demonstrates how many products contain elements of the rational and emotional.

This is the original article by Richard Vaughn which formed the basis of The FCB Planning Grid. It also covers the "Learn/Feel/Do Circle," which we'll cover in the following Addendum.

Advertising Age Magazine

The Consumer Mind: How To Tailor Ad Strategies

Planning models are not all-purpose cures, but guides to organizing advertising goals.

BY RICHARD VAUGHN

Advertising is unlike the direct communications between two people which involves a give-and-take experience. It is a one-way exchange that is impersonal in format. To compensate, advertising must often make greater use of both rational and emotional devices to have an effect. People can selectively notice or avoid, accept or reject, remember or forget the experience, and thereby confound the best of advertising plans.

To understand how advertising works, it's necessary to explore the possibilities people have for thinking, feeling and behaving toward the various products and services in their lives. This isn't easy because we are all capable of being logical and illogical, objective and subjective, obvious and subtle simultaneously. Everything considered, it's not surprising that a unified theory of advertising effectiveness has eluded us for so long.

Four traditional theories of advertising effectiveness have long been prominent in marketing:

Economic: A rational consumer who consciously considers functional cost-utility information in a purchase decision. Economic theory says consumers act in their own financial self-interest. They look for maximum utility at the lowest cost. Rational, methodical calculation is presupposed, so price-demand equations are used to calculate aggregate consumer behavior. Consumers must have functional information to make a decision. This old, much-revered theory most often applies to commodity items. It is highly respected by economic forecasters and is the only theory widely publicized by U.S. government regulatory agencies.

Responsive: A habitual consumer conditioned to buy thoughtlessly through rote, stimulus-response learning. Responsive theory tells us consumers are lazy and want to buy with minimum effort. They develop habits through stimulus-response learning. The process is nonrational and automatic, as repetition builds and then reinforces buying activity for routine products. Information serves a reminder/exposure, rather than thoughtful purpose.

Psychological: An unpredictable consumer who buys compulsively under the influence of unconscious thoughts and indirect emotions. Psychological theory explains consumer behavior as ego involvement: The personality must be defended or promoted. This is essentially unpredictable, undeliberate and latent as psychic energy flows between the id, ego and super-ego. Implicit product attitudes are more important than functional benefits for products that touch people deeply.

Social: A compliant consumer who continually adjusts purchases to satisfy cultural and group needs for conformity. Social theory describes consumers as basically imitative. People watch what others buy and comply/adjust to get along or to be inconspicuous. It's an emotional, insecure behavior. Group role, prestige, status and vanity concerns are involved. Opinion leaders and word-of-mouth communication are important for the visi-

Richard Vaughn is research director, Foote, Cone & Belding/Honig, Los Angeles.

ble products affected.

While these theories have had proponents who defended them as sole explanations of consumer behavior, most marketers now consider them at best only partial explanations. These theories were most topical in the 1950s.

Which theory is right? They all have some truth. *Economic* motives dominate much consumer behavior, especially on expensive products and those with highly functional benefits. But *responsive* buying also prevails; many routine items require little or no thought, and purchase habits, once established, can serve indefinitely. *Psychological* issues complicate our understanding because many items can have "symbolic" overtones. The same is true of *social* motives since numerous products have public meaning. Thus, at various times and for different products, each theory might play a part in consideration, purchase and consumption behavior.

PURCHASE
CONVICTION
PREFERENCE
LIKING
KNOWLEDGE
AWARENESS

Consumer behavior models in the 1960s were patterned after the "Hierarchy of Effects" model (left). The Summary Adoption Process model appeared in 1971 (below).

ADOPTION
TRIAL
LEGITIMATION
ATTITUDE
COMPREHENSION
AWARENESS

While these theories have enough face validity to make them interesting, they lack the specificity to make them practical. Also, which theory to use in a situation and how to blend it with other theories are constant and frustrating problems.

Time and the efforts of consumer theorists have moved beyond these simpler explanations to more dynamic notions of how consumers respond to advertising.

Many consumer behavior models were developed in the early 1960s. They took a variety of forms, but most were patterned after Lavidge and Steiner's "Hierarchy of Effects" model in 1961.

This model proposed that consumer purchase of a product occurred via a sequential hierarchy of events from awareness through knowledge, liking, preference and conviction. It was a major step toward integrating the implications of the economic, responsive, psychological and social theories. In principle at least, rational concerns could coexist with habituation, ego involvement and conformity motives. Although research has been unable to verify the model, it has been conceptually useful and, because of its common sense qualities, remains today the intuitive, implicit model accepted by most marketing managers.

Andreason (1963), Nicosia (1966) and Engel-Kollat-

Blackwell (1967) proposed variant models, but the ultimate in thoroughness and complexity appeared in 1969 with publication of Howard & Sheth's "The Theory of Buyer Behavior." The model involved 35 to 40 variables grouped under input, perception, learning and output categories. Several research efforts validated the basic form of the model, but the predictive power was low because operational measures for many of the variables were weak.

Despite their detail, these second generation models remedied defects in the basic hierarchy model:

• Consumers might proceed through the sequence imperfectly (stop/start, make mistakes).

• Feedback would allow later events to influence earlier activities.

• Consumers could skip the process entirely and behave "illogically."

In a return to simplification, the following summary adoption process model appeared in 1917 (Robertson). It included the main features of earlier models.

This modified hierarchy model proposed that some consumers, under some conditions, for some products, might follow a sequential path. The dotted lines are feedbacks that can alter outcomes. Other decision patterns (on the right) track consumers as they violate the formal sequence of the hierarchy. Thus, consumers can learn from previous experience and swerve from the awareness-to-purchase pattern.

This scheme preserved the LEARN-FEEL-DO sequence of most hierarchy models but made it more flexible. It also helped explain purchase behavior without the presence of measurable product knowledge or attitude formation. Shortly after the arrival of this model, however, other hypotheses appeared.

The new theories are not models as much as explanations for conflicting results from consumer research. They are, respectively, "Consumer Involvement" and "Brain Specialization." They have been introduced to explain why consumers are interested in some purchase activities more than others and how consumers perceive different messages during purchase consideration.

Briefly, "Consumer Involvement" suggests a continuum of consumer interest in products and services. On the high side are those that are important in money cost, ego support, social value or newness; they involve more risk, require paying more attention to the decision and demand greater use of information. Low involvement decisions are at the other extreme; they arouse little consumer interest or information handling because the risk is small and effort can be reduced accordingly.

It's hard to define this concept because involvement can include consumption as well as purchase situations. Basically, the money, time, complexity and effort involved in buying and using products demand that the consumer make value judgments. Some decisions are important enough to get a lot of effort, others are not.

As the stakes rise, more attention must be given to the decision to avoid making a bad buy. The lower risk product has a lighter penalty for a mistake, and less anxiety about the outcome. The implication: Involvement level

(Continued on next page.)

Advertising Age, June 9, 19

The Consumer Mind

(Continued from Page 45)
affects receptivity to advertising.

"Brain Specializat on" proposes that anatomical separation of the cerebral hemispheres of the brain leads to specialized perception of messages. The left side is relatively more capable of handling linear logic, language and analysis—in short, the cognitive (thinking) function. The right side is more intuitive, visual and engages in synthesis—the affective (feeling) function. The implication: Advertising response will vary depending upon the thinking or feeling communication task involved.

This subject is quite topical, and enthusiasm for it is producing considerable marketing speculation. The physiological evidence is limited and there is no empirical support for it in a marketing context. However, it's not necessary to endorse right/left brain theory to use the principle that people are capable of both thinking and feeling reactions to stimuli.

Both of these theories have compounded the discussion about how advertising works. The balance of this article is an attempt to regain perspective.

In order to provide a structure that will integrate the traditional theories and LEARN-FEEL-DO hierarchy models with consumer involvement and brain specialization theories, a new approach to advertising strategy is called for. This requires building a matrix to classify products and services.

Here are the pieces for this new model:

- "Thinking" and "Feeling"
- "High" and "Low" involvement

This outline suggests that there are purchase decisions where thinking is most involved and others where feeling dominates; there are situations that are more important and those that are less so. The combination of these reference points produces a strategy matrix that encompasses most of the traditional theories as well as the various LEARN-FEEL-DO hierachy models just discussed.

Thinking and feeling are a continuum in the sense that some decisions involve one or the other, and many involve elements of both. The horizontal side of the matrix conveys this hypothesis and further proposes that over time, there is movement from thinking toward feeling. High and low importance is also a continuum, and the vertical side of the matrix displays this. It is suggested that over time, high importance can decay to relatively low-importance.

Four quadrants are developed in the matrix, with the dotted line in the following diagram indicating a soft partition between them. The solid line arrows visually depict the evolution of consumer tendencies as importance wanes and thinking diminishes with respect to particular products and services. The quadrants outline four potentially major goals for advertising strategy: To be informative, affective, habit forming or to promote self-satisfaction.

What does this matrix reveal? Each quadrant:

- Helps isolate specific categories for strategy planning;
- Approximates one of the traditional consumer theories (economic, psychological, responsive, social);
- Suggests a variant hierarchy model as a strategy guide;
- Implies considerations for creative, media and research.

The following detailed chart expands upon these points. Taking the quadrants separately, a number of strategy possibilities are suggested:

Quadrant 1: High involvement/thinking (informative). This implies a large need for information because of the importance of the product and thinking issues related to it. Major purchases (car, house, furnishings) probably qualify and, initially almost any new product which needs to convey what it is, its function, price and availability. The basic strategy model is the typical LEARN-FEEL-DO sequence where functional and salient information is designed to build consumer attitudinal acceptance and subsequent purchase.

The economic model may be appropriate here as well. A consumer here might be pictured as a "THINKER." Creatively, specific information and demonstration are possibilities. Long copy format and reflective, involving media may be necessary to literally "get through" with key points of consumer interest. If strategy research has defined the significant message to be communicated, recall testing and diagnostic measures will help evaluate the effectiveness of a proposed ad.

Quadrant 2: High involvement/feeling (affective). This product decision is involving, but specific information is less important than an attitude or holistic feeling. This is so because the involvement is related to the person's self-esteem (psychological model). Jewelry, cosmetics and fashion apparel might fall here. A functional example: Motorcyles. The strategy requires emotional involvement on the part of consumers; basically, that they become a "FEELER" about the product.

The model proposed is: FEEL-LEARN-DO. Creatively, executional impact is a possible goal, while media considerations suggest dramatic print exposure or "image" broadcast specials. Copy testing won't get much help from message recall since the effect is likely to be nonliteral; attitude shift testing or emotion arousal (autonomic, psychogalvanometer) tests may be more helpful in determining advertising effect.

Quadrant 3: Low involvement/thinking (habit formation). Product decisions in this area involve minimal thought and a tendency to form buying habits for convenience. Information, to the extent that it plays a role, will be any point of difference that can be meaningfully exploited. Most food and staple package goods items likely belong here. Brand loyalty will be a function of habit, but it's quite likely most consumers have several "acceptable" brands. Over time, many ordinary products will mature and descend into this commodity limbo.

The hierarchy model is a DO-LEARN-FEEL pattern which is compatible with the traditional responsive theory. It suggests that simply inducing trial (coupons, free samples) can often generate subsequent purchase more readily than pounding home undifferentiating copy points. This consumer can be viewed as a "DOER." Creatively what is required is to stimulate a reminder for the product. Media implications might include small-space ads, 10-second IDs, point of sale pieces and radio.

The ideal advertising test would be a sales measure or lab substitute; recall and/or attitude change tests may not correlate with sales and therefore be misleading. This is a troublesome quadrant because so many commonly used products and services are here and require very detailed and careful planning effort.

Quadrant 4: Low involvement/feeling (self-satisfaction). This low involvement area seems to be reserved for those products that satisfy personal tastes—cigarets, liquor, candy, movies. Imagery and quick satisfaction are involved. This is a DO-FEEL-LEARN model with some application of the social theory because so many products here fit into group situations (beer, soft drinks).

This consumer is a "REACTOR" whose logical interest will be hard to hold and short-lived. Creatively, it's basic to get attention with some consistency. Billboards, point of sale and newspapers might apply here. Copy testing will need to be sales oriented because recall and attitude change may not be relevant.

These comments are meant to be thought-starters rather than a formula for planning. The options clearly depend upon the category, brand, sales trends and marketing objectives. Also, it's not necessary to be restricted to just these four possibilities in using this matrix. For example, two other hierarchy models are available:

- Between quadrants one and three, a LEARN-DO-FEEL sequence might apply as consumers go directly from information to trial.
- Between quadrants two and four, a FEEL-DO-LEARN model suggests acting upon an initial feeling and purchasing.

Also, some products conceivably belong between quadrants 1 and 2 or 3 and 4, requiring elements of both learn and feel simultaneously. The options for placing products in the proper area are challenging indeed. But by thinking a product through the system, using available research and management judgment, the advertising strategy implications can become clearer and more manageable.

What this model says is that consumer entry into a product should be determined for information (learn), attitude (feel) and behavior (do) issues to develop advertising. We help do this using basic consumer research. The priority of learn over feel, feel over learn, or do over either learn-feel, has implications for advertising strategy, creative execution, media planning and copy testing.

To appreciate fully what this change means, recall that the LEARN-FEEL-DO sequence has been endorsed for years as the only "legitimate" model of advertising effectiveness. Its linearity has been forced into situations where it simply didn't apply. But it is only one of several models. Furthermore, it's no longer a straight line concept, but rather, circular.

Unfortunately, few advertising strategies are simple. Many products have learn, feel and do in varying degrees, best represented perhaps by overlap.

The fundamental hypothesis of this model can now be stated: An advertising strategy is determined by specifying (1) the consumer's point of entry on the LEARN-FEEL-DO continuum and (2) the priority of learn *vs.* feel *vs.* do for making a sale. Specifically, the strategy issue is whether to develop product features, brand image or some combination of both.

- To the extent a brand has hard news, with distinct features, and can link its name to them, the sale centers on "learning," with "feeling" and "doing" coming after.
- Lacking such information, where a product gives its users an identity via intangible/emotional features leading to an image, the sale centers on "feelings" and proceeds to "learning" and "doing."
- As brands endure and achieve fixed places in the consumer's mind, buying may become routine and consist primarily of "doing" with very little conscious "learning" or "feeling."

The more the strategy matches consumer purchase experience, the better the advertising will be "internalized" or "accepted." Advertising may now have to be the right communication "experience" for the consumer as well as the right "message."

Not all advertising works in the same way. Sometimes communication of key information and salient emotion will be needed to get a sale; at other times consumers will need one, but not both; and often buying may occur with little or no information and emotion. The purpose of strategy planning is to identify the information, emotion or action leverage for a particular product, build the appropriate advertising model and then execute it.

This planning model is not an all-purpose cure. It's a guide to help organize the advertising objectives for a product. The account team has to use product research to determine the brand's leverage and then build a strategy that incorporates creative, media and copy testing projects. If done properly, the parts should fit together. ■

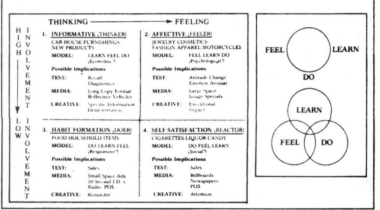

How Advertising Works: An FCB Planning Model

	THINKING →	→ FEELING
HIGH INVOLVEMENT	**1. INFORMATIVE (THINKER)** CAR-HOUSE-FURNISHINGS-NEW PRODUCTS MODEL: LEARN-FEEL-DO (Economic?) **Possible Implications** TEST: Recall, Diagnostics MEDIA: Long Copy Format, Reflective Vehicles CREATIVE: Specific Information, Demonstration	**2. AFFECTIVE (FEELER)** JEWELRY-COSMETICS-FASHION APPAREL-MOTORCYCLES MODEL: FEEL-LEARN-DO (Psychological?) **Possible Implications** TEST: Attitude Change, Emotion Arousal MEDIA: Large Space, Image Specials CREATIVE: Executional Impact
↓ LOW INVOLVEMENT	**3. HABIT FORMATION (DOER)** FOOD-HOUSEHOLD ITEMS MODEL: DO-LEARN-FEEL (Responsive?) **Possible Implications** TEST: Sales MEDIA: Small Space Ads, 10 Second I.D.'s, Radio; POS CREATIVE: Reminder	**4. SELF-SATISFACTION (REACTOR)** CIGARETTES-LIQUOR-CANDY MODEL: DO-FEEL-LEARN (Social?) **Possible Implications** TEST: Sales MEDIA: Billboards, Newspapers, POS CREATIVE: Attention

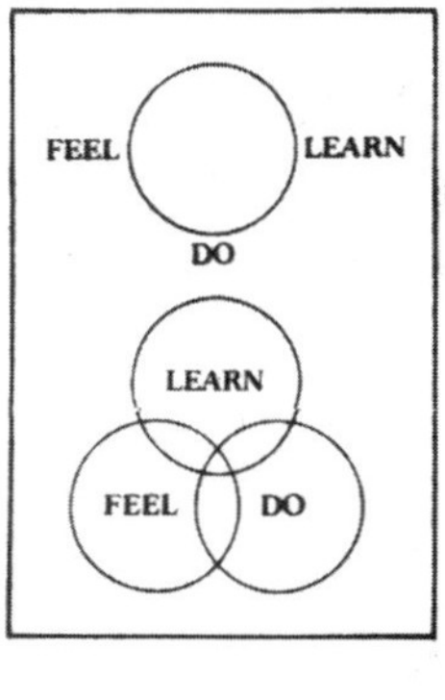

"Half my advertising is wasted – but I don't know which half." *

John J. Wanamaker

AT 50-80% OFF
THE ONLY THING
YOU CAN'T SAVE
IS OUR STORE.

The dresses are going. The skirts are going.
The fixtures are going. Shouldn't you be going too?

WE WROTE THE
BOOK ON FASHION.
UNFORTUNATELY,
IT ENDS WITH
CHAPTER 11.

At our going out of business sale you'll save
80% on European fashions. Au-revoir and Arrivederci.

*

Actually, the original quote was by Lord Leverhume, who founded Lever Brothers. Wanamaker was quoting him.

And, clever as they are, these "Going Out of Business" ads remind us that creating a business that works and advertising that works is a tough job.

**

"AIDA"

This is the more common acronym for the process: Attention, Interest, Desire, and Action

However, in our view, "interest" and "desire" overstate the case for many product categories.

"Awareness" and "Attitude" seem more accurate. And easier to remember.

Think Better Three Ways.

THIS ADDENDUM WILL COVER a few more ways to think about advertising!

First, some hierarchical views of how advertising works inside of people –

The Four A's and Four R's of Advertising.**

Then, a circular process called –

The Learn/Feel/Do Circle.

Finally, an "inside out" way of looking at how we relate to media messages – including advertising.

Resonance.

A IS FOR ADVERTISING.

When it works, advertising is more than the ads.

It's the beginning of a relationship.

It's something that happens *to* a person, whether reader, viewer, listener, or someone not paying much attention. It's not just the ad, it's *the response* to the ad.

It's not what happens in the ad, it's what happens *inside the person.*

That's how advertising works. Advertising that does not do that merely "talks to itself."

It may be handsome. The client may love it.

Hey, you might even win an award.

But it probably won't work very well.

As my psychology professor said (Yes, Professor Gilchrist, I was paying attention), you have to get "inside the other person's skin."

Once you start to see the world from that perspective, it becomes easier to think about how to create advertising that works.

1. The 4 A's & 4 R's of Advertising

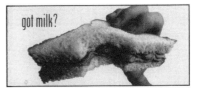

THIS SECTION NEEDS ITS OWN updated introduction, as my point of view has changed dramatically since this was first written a dozen years ago.

I began with a fairly traditional linear model of how advertising works – one that the industry has used for quite some time. Then, the changes we just talked about in Chapter Two caused me to modify my view.

You can follow that evolution as you see how I've moved from the "Four A's" to the "Four R's."

We'll start with the Four A's, the standard view of how advertising works. Then we'll move to the Four R's, which is how I think advertising works today.

THE FOUR A'S OF ADVERTISING.

The traditional view is that advertising works on four levels: Attention, Awareness, Attitude, Action.**

Let's take them one by one…

Attention.

First, advertising has to get *attention.*

Breaking through to get that attention is also one of the toughest jobs. And due to media fragmentation and the increase in the number of messages, getting that attention gets tougher every year.

You're not only competing with a lot of other mes-sages done by other skilled ad people, but people are very good at tuning out what doesn't interest them.

The thing to remember is that the ad doesn't necessarily have to jump out at you.

It's even better when people *jump in* to the ad.

When people notice your ad, to some extent, they remember it. And a certain percentage of these people will buy your product.

"It's important to be visually brave; to do something that goes beyond the ordinary and captures attention. That, as we know, is 50% of the battle; to turn the prospect's head, to pay attention to what's being said."

Susan Gillette, DDB Needham

"Nobody's waiting to hear from us."

Bill Bernbach

"Nobody reads advertising. People read what interests them. Sometimes it's an ad."

Howard Gossage

"Seventy-five percent of the benefit of advertising is that you advertise."

Jeremy Bullmore, JWT/London

One of the basic research techniques used to measure advertising's effectiveness is to measure awareness.

In its simplest form, you ask people what ads or products they remember.

As in, "Do you remember any beer commercials?" or "What brands of beer do you remember?"

The percentage of people who remember your brand or advertising is called awareness or "unaided awareness."

If your brand or commercial is not mentioned, the person is then asked, "Do you remember such and such a beer commercial, or such and such brand of beer?"

If the answer is "Oh, yeah," or something to that effect, this percentage is "aided awareness."

Generally, this will be a greater percentage than those who don't know your name or notice your ad.

Overcoming all the barriers to communication and getting attention is advertising's first job.

Awareness.

Second, advertising must build *awareness.*

You want the product that you're advertising to move from merely being noticed to being remembered.

You want your brand to occupy a space in the conscious or subconscious mind or memory.

This is usually a cumulative process, and building awareness is a constant goal of virtually all advertising.

It takes time, and as NW Ayer said over 100 years ago, "Keeping Everlastingly At It Brings Success." That often means sticking with it.

At this second level, your brand is beginning to have an ongoing existence *inside* people.

If they simply remember you, a greater percentage of these people will be disposed to buy your product.

If they remember the right thing about you, an even greater percentage of these people will be disposed to buy your product.

Attitude.

Third, advertising works to reinforce or change *attitude* – the feeling people have toward your product.

Attitude is more active than awareness.

When there's an attitude toward a brand, people can usually say how they feel – positive, negative, or neutral.

To state the obvious, you want to build a positive attitude toward your product.

However, some ads work to build up negative attitudes toward the competition, or the problem.

Political advertising is a good example.

But it's more than just advertising.

Ask for the Order. Look for ways to activate *the consumer and involve her (or him) in your ads. Invite them into your store – give them a reason to make the trip or to try your product for the first time.*

An attitude is usually an accumulation of experiences:

• An ad
• A product experience
• Imagery of the product name or package
• The product displayed at the point of purchase
• "Word of mouth" (A powerful force)
• All of the above (The MarCom Matrix)

In most cases, advertising has a major responsibility for building positive attitudes about the brand.

This process is often referred to as "building brand equity." And it often has a specific strategic focus – e.g., improve reputation for quality.

Action.

Finally, there is *action* – the relationship is externalized and the person actually acts!

He buys the product, sends for a brochure, or writes his Congressman. Sometimes you can move someone all the way to action in only one ad.

Direct Mail catalogs do this all the time.

People may purchase a product on the basis of one ad or a single piece of catalog copy.

Retail advertising has this focus. Retailers measure advertising effectiveness by store traffic and sales.

But with all advertisers, even those concerned with short-term sales, or even survival, the action of advertising is also a long-term cumulative process that builds with each ad.

For every advertiser, advertising is part of a long-term process… even when it's designed for short-term results. Once more, that process is…

gain *attention,*
build *awareness,*
shift *attitudes,* and …
motivate *action.*

The Four A's of Advertising.

"Every advertisement is a long-term investment in the image of the brand."

David Ogilvy

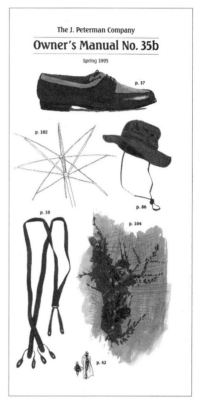

The Peterman Catalog *was very successful for a number of years with its inviting copy and unique items. Then, either due to the wrong product mix, too much expansion, or people just getting tired of it – after all, how many Australian bush jackets with a boomerang pocket does anyone need? But it was a great run, and if you can find an old Peterman catalog, you'll see some of the best catalog writing ever done. You should also check out the ones that are still in business, like Lands' End and L.L. Bean.*

Reaction. "This car has room for 324 people. (And trillions of germs.)" This message has a chance of getting a reaction for Keri Anti-Bacterial Hand Lotion in a crowded subway car.

Relevance. This visual, this topic, and this product are relevant to the target – the mother of a baby.

Relationship. Business is built on long-term relationships with customers. Effective advertising isn't the end of your job – it's the beginning.

FOUR R'S OF ADVERTISING.

My point of view has evolved.

Today, I practice what I call the "Four R's," which are: Reaction, Relevance, Response, Relationship.

Again, let's take them one by one.

Reaction.

People react – even if that reaction is no reaction. I have a new appreciation for the ability of today's consumer to scan the media environment and select what they choose to react to.

When you watch TV, page through a magazine, or go into a store, you notice pretty much everything – even if you don't think you do. Here's what happens next...

Relevance.

People (including you) select what is interesting to them. And we're all pretty good at it.

So the real challenge is figuring out what people find important to them. As Gossage said, *"People read what interests them. Sometimes it's an ad."*

Response.

If it makes the cut, people will respond to your message. And, in a world of "overchoice" it's a tough job.

Most people already have too many demands on their time and discretionary dollars. It takes more than ever to make it worth their while to respond.

That's one reason more marketers are using incentives to improve response rates.

It's more than "asking for the order." Ask yourself. What would it take to get you to respond?

Relationship.

Don't think of that response as the last step.

Traditionally, once that purchase was made, many advertisers thought their job was over. That's not true.

Some of the most avid readers of automobile advertising are those who just bought the car.

Retaining current customers is important for virtually every brand that wants to stay in business.

Think of that purchase as the first step.

After all, the most valuable person your brand has is that current customer – that's who's paying the bills.

And this is key to concepts from the direct marketing industry such as "relationship marketing" and LTV, which stands for "lifetime value." LTV is the total amount of what a customer is worth to a brand over the lifetime of that relationship.

Just think, what's your LTV with your favorite pizza place? Or the place you buy books and magazines.

Even with something fairly low cost, like the daily newspaper, your LTV is pretty substantial.

That fourth R needs to be a part of your thinking.

Advertising should be the first step in a growing relationship between the brand and those who use it.

Reaction. Relevance. Response. Relationship. Often, you can do them all at once. Here's a particularly interesting bit of communication – the media vehicle actually gives you a Free Ride. Nice.

2. The Learn/Feel/Do Circle.

The previous article by Richard Vaughn also mentioned something called "The Learn/Feel/Do Circle."

It's another dimension describing the ways people involve themselves with products.

The article showed three overlapping circles labeled *"Learn," "Feel,"* and *"Do"* (Fig. 1).

Learn. We read about a product in an ad, look at the label, or learn about it as we experience it.

Feel. We may have feelings about the product or product category. Some based on our experience, some on personal preference, and some on who knows what.

Do. We buy a product, use it, and experience it.

Generally, these three circles are shown as one circle, which we call The Learn/Feel/Do Circle (Fig. 2).

It's a sequence that can be very helpful in how we think about the role of advertising.

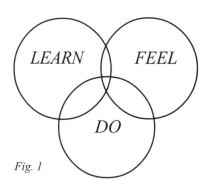

Fig. 1

THE LEARN/FEEL/DO CIRCLE

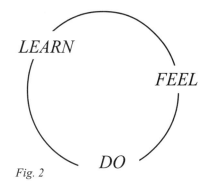

Fig. 2

103

DO/LEARN/FEEL.

For example, what is the process by which your customer gets involved with your product?

For a new snack food, you may try a free sample first (do), then, as you eat it, you find out how it tastes (learn).

Finally, there will be some sort of feel dimension – taste, sensate feelings (crunch/texture), satisfaction, and how this snack compares to others.

This process can continue.

The more you do, the more you learn, and the more you feel. Get it?

FEEL/DO/LEARN.

For a new perfume, the advertising might create feeling first.

Based on the imagery, you think it might be a nice perfume (feel).

So you try it at the perfume counter (do), and you find out whether you like it or not (learn).

More Than One Sequence.

And, of course, there are other ways around the circle – even if it's the same product and the same advertising.

You may notice a friend wearing a new perfume, then, since you're already aware of the perfume, you notice the ad, which reinforces the original memory, so next time you're at a store with a perfume counter…

TWO SIMPLE RULES.

Our little circle has two more simple rules.

1. You may enter at any point on the circle.

Your initial experience with a product may be learning, feeling, or doing (see sidebar).

2. You may go in either direction.

The sequence of experience can go in either direction – any way you wish. Think about it…

Think about the way people involve themselves with your product and with your advertising.

For example, a high involvement/thinking type of product may encourage you to try to "teach" people with a long copy ad – Learn/Feel/Do.

For an inexpensive snack food, perhaps you should encourage sampling – Do/Learn/Feel.

Different approaches may find you entering at different parts of the circle – even with the same strategy.

Think about how your target customer will relate to the product and the advertising.

Think of the point of entry and the sequence.

And realize that experience in the real world does not always duplicate the sequence you imagine.

You might find it helpful to think about all of this in the context of The MarCom Matrix.

The Learn/Feel/Do Circle is an excellent conceptual tool for thinking about the dynamic you wish to create for your brand:

What do you want them to learn?

What do you want them to feel?

What do you want them to do?

Now, how do they all work together inside of the consumer? That's *resonance*.

3. Resonance.

Advertising happens *inside* people.

As a writer and producer, Tony Schwartz has been responsible for some of the most powerful and effective ads ever made – the "Daisy" commercial helped create a landslide victory for Lyndon Johnson.

He has also made important contributions to the way we think about communicating.

THE "RESONANCE" THEORY.

When you achieve *resonance,* your external message connects with internal values and feelings. *"Resonance takes place when the stimuli put into our communication evoke* meaning *in a listener or viewer… the meaning of our communication is what a listener or viewer gets* out *of his experience with the communicator's stimuli."*

For example, how do you react when someone says, *"don't worry about the money"?* You immediately worry.

And that's the point. We need to understand how our messages work inside the other person's skin.

Resonance demands connecting with what is already inside the consumer's mind – not necessarily putting in something that is totally brand new or assuming that our words will be taken at face value. Schwartz says…

"It concentrates on evoking responses from people by attuning the message to their prior experience."

Hopkins would say,

"The advertising man studies the consumer. He tries to place himself in the position of the buyer."

And JWT says, *"It's not what you put in the advertising that counts – it's what people get out of it."*

End of Addendum.

THE DAISY COMMERCIAL.

A little girl is counting daisy petals. The track cross-fades into a missile countdown. We see a nuclear mushroom cloud. A calm voice tells us that in times like these we need Lyndon Johnson as president.

The power of the commercial wasn't in what was said, the power was in the internal processing of what was said.

What was said was that it was a dangerous world and you might want Lyndon Johnson to be president.

The response of viewers was, "Holy Smoke! Barry Goldwater (the other candidate, who'd advocated using nuclear weapons) might Drop The Big One!"

Johnson won in a landslide.

You never forget your first Girl.

ST. PAULI BREWERY, BREMEN

ST. PAULI GIRL
BEER

ADS TO REMEMBER.

The quick little emotional vibration off the double meaning in the St. Pauli Girl ad creates resonance.

At least, that's what happend to me. For you, it could be entirely different.

Pick out some ads that resonate with you – study how they work on you and how you respond.

How to Have an Idea.

ACTUALLY, THIS WHOLE BOOK IS ABOUT "CREATIVITY."

This chapter will introduce you to a few basic techniques and principles.

But, in truth, this entire book is about helping you develop your mental flexibility and capabilities.

So you can solve marketing problems effectively – and creatively.

It's Not Creative Unless It Sells.

NOT TRUE.

This was a popular ad agency slogan. Catchy, but incorrect.

An ad may be quite creative but not sell, and it may not be the ad's fault.

The product, or some other aspect of marketing, like pricing or distribution, or another product that's better, may be the reason. Not the advertising.

Could you sell an Oldsmobile?

An ad may delight both agency and client for its creativity and cleverness but miss the mark with the customer.

Creative, but not effective.

Finally, an ordinary and unimaginative ad may be quite effective if the message is strong and the product and value are above average.

So, even if the ad itself isn't very "creative," it may sell very well.

A CREATIVE QUESTION.

What might be substituted, combined, adapted, magnified, or put to other uses?

"WHAT IS CREATIVITY?" Every day, in speeches, seminars, meeting rooms, classrooms, and Creative Directors' offices, someone asks this question.

Answering it has become a minor industry in itself.

Since a completely satisfactory answer will never be given, this will continue to provide steady work for the chronically overqualified.

However, what we're interested in is how the mind associates and combines what we already know in fresh new ways.

It's called "having an idea," or "ideation," and a key part of your job will be to work with and develop ideas that help your client's business.

The business of advertising is about having ideas. So let's talk about it.

Here's what Arthur Koestler said in his book *The Act of Creation: "All great innovations consist of sudden shifts of attention and emphasis onto some previously neglected aspect of experience… They uncover what has always been there (yet) they are revolutionary."*

Leo Burnett said, *"Creativity is the art of establishing new and meaningful relationships between previously unrelated things… which somehow present the product in a fresh, new light."*

And James Webb Young, a well-known copywriter of his time, said it simply. *"An idea is nothing more or less than a new combination of old elements."*

The process appears to have six critical stages:

1. PREPARATION.

Collecting input. "Doing your homework."

During the preparation stage, information enters the left side (verbal/storage/memory) of the brain.

Simply put, the more information and background you have, the more potential connections you can make. More input = more possible connections.

As Pasteur noted, *"Fortune favors the prepared mind." "Luck is a matter of preparation meeting opportunity."*

2. FRUSTRATION.

However, unless the answer is obvious, the initial result can often be frustration – particularly if the answer is not achieved through simple logic.

So there you are. The left side doesn't quite know what to do with all this information. You're frustrated.

Emphasis shifts to the other side of the brain.

Some good news here. The longer you work at having ideas, the better you get. You've done more preparation. You have more to work with.

3. INCUBATION.

Now the right side of your brain goes to work with the information – consciously or subconsciously turning that information into new combinations.

You may actually want to sleep on it.

Mull it over. It's a natural process.

Another way of incubating is to stir things around as you discuss it with others. The kind of association and connecting your mind does by itself, is similar to what happens when a number of brains "kick it around."

In some ways, groups of people and creative teams duplicate this same incubation function.

4. ILLUMINATION.

AHA! The light bulb goes on!

Two previously unrelated elements connect.

Congratulations, you've just had an idea.

But don't always expect a blinding flash of light.

As Leo said, *"The secret of all effective original-ity in advertising is not the creation of new and tricky words and pictures, but putting familiar words and pictures into new relationships."*

James Webb Young. *JWT Copywriter. He developed a successful direct-mail business in his spare time. He wrote* A Technique for Producing Ideas. *It's only 61 pages long and a classic. Read it if you can find it.*

**LEARN TO BE #2
ON A GOOD IDEA.**

True story. The client and agency were in an idea session for a new TV spot.

Nike had just signed Bo Jackson, an outstanding athlete who was both a star NFL running back and a Major League Baseball player.

At one end of the table, they were having fun naming famous "Bo's."

Bo Derek, Beau Brummel, Little Bo Peep, etc. Someone said, "Bo Diddley."

The CD's ears perked up – Jim Riswold recognized an idea that could work.

By next morning, it was written.

The "Bo Knows" series was some of the best of the early Nike advertising.

This is how it often works. Though it wasn't the CD's idea, he knew what to do with it! Often, your biggest contribution can be helping to turn someone else's idea into a terrific piece of work.

107

Here are some tips I've found helpful. They're from *The Copywriter* by John Matthews. If you'd like the rest of the book, call The Copy Workshop, we have a few copies.

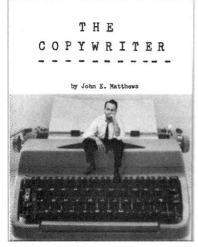

THE COPYWRITER
- - - - - - - - -

by John E. Matthews

**WHAT TO DO UNTIL
THE IDEA COMES.**

"The first trick is simply the mechanical process by which you write.

Do you use a typewriter, a ballpoint, a stubby black pencil, a tape recorder? [Note: This piece was written "BC," before computer – Ed.]

Whichever you use, try switching to something else whenever the blank moment comes up. Perhaps you'll discover that there's a strange and wonderful two-way communication between your brain and the writing mechanics.

Sometimes if you start talking instead of typing, the brain will get back in working order. (It's kind of like kicking a flat tire. It may not inflate the stupid thing, but it makes you feel you're 'taking action.')

Another category that works is called 'brain jiggling.' This covers anything that goes bumpety-bump-bump – from driving your car down a country road to taking a train ride.

All kinds of locomotion belong to this group – even jogging around the block. I admit that many pedestrians on Michigan Avenue (or Madison Avenue, for that matter) may think it odd to see an apparently civilized person jogging up the street. *(Continued on next page)*

5. EVALUATION.

Now, you have to decide if your idea is a good idea.

This is a major problem for many talented creative people – they have lots of ideas, but can't tell their good ones from their bad ones.

Here we bring back the critical/analytical left side for an opinion. Hopefully, a useful opinion.

Evaluating ideas is also one of the critical roles of the Creative Director.

The difference between having ideas and knowing which are the good ideas is equal parts evaluation and imagination, learning to be critical of your own work in a positive way.

It's also useful to learn to recognize the good ideas others might have – sometimes you can help make them better.

Evaluation might also involve additional ideation to shore up the weak spots of the initial idea or to take your idea one more step, by using it as part of a new combination.

6. ELABORATION.

Working it out.

Copy and layout.

This is the other hard part.

Having ideas, even good ones, is often pretty easy. Making them work is work.

And *that's* how to have an idea.

A "TEAM CREATIVITY" EXAMPLE.

Years ago, I ran into Gary Bayer, who'd been Creative Director on the very successful "Weekends Are Made for Michelob" campaign. I asked him about it.

"Well," he said. "We had a bunch of ideas up on the wall. One person had written 'Michelob is special,' and another had written 'Weekends are special.'"

That's how it happened. Good creative teams can create a left-brain/right-brain idea pressure cooker.

FIVE ADDITIONAL POINTS ABOUT
THE IDEATION PROCESS:

1. If Illumination doesn't come right away, you might not have done enough Preparation.

If your preparation is not complete, you may still be missing that critical element of insight.

Every successful copywriter talks a lot about becoming immersed in the product and in the prospect. This is *key* to the preparation stage.

Prepare thoroughly and then allow your intuitive process to sort it out. (Remember, incubation may take some time as well.)

A few thoughts while you tough it out.

Einstein said, *"The supreme task of the physicist is to arrive at those universal elementary laws from which the cosmos can be built by pure deduction. There is no logical path to these laws; only intuition resting on experience can reach them."*

Or as jazz pianist Thelonius Monk once said…

"Sometimes I play things I never heard myself."

You can do it. Be Prepared.

2. Selling an idea can be harder than having one.

A new idea can be threatening.

Koestler says this about the shock of new ideas:

"They compel us to re-value our values."

Others have *not* gone through your ideation process.

Sometimes the best approach is walk your audience through the process you went through – step by step – from preparation to frustration to illumination.

And then evaluation and elaboration.

Give them time to get comfortable with a new thought. (Like cheap underwear, the mind, once stretched, never reverts to its original shape.)

On the other hand, your idea might not be accepted because it's *too obvious!*

Just as a maze can be solved by going backward, the creative act is sometimes diminished in retrospect.

THE COPYWRITER *(Cont.)*

But we are not out to impress such pedestrian observers; the main thing is to get your brain working again.

[Note: Written Before Jogging – Ed.]

Another brain-jolter calls for walking down the street and entering the first shop you spot that you have no business in. Or have never been in for any reason whatever.

Now there's one school which contends that a couple of afternoon hours in a good movie will work wonders in regenerating creative cells.

I've always considered this 'cinema-system' most unimaginative; something which could be construed by laymen as merely the lazy Copywriter's excuse to goof-off an afternoon.

Much more ingenious and inspiring (and filling) is the system I have discovered of reactivating the brain via the stomach.

This system is extemely practical; it can be applied during your lunch hour.

It merely involves changing your luncheon habits drastically.

You frequent the Imperial House? Try Woolworth's lunch counter, a veritable creative wonderland!

Usually have a social lunch?

Make one anti-social.

I don't claim to know what makes this system work so well. But work it does. And it can save hours of waiting for a cold typewriter to thaw."

This is still pretty useful advice for breaking the idea logjam.

Ordering Information:

When we called John Matthews to ask for permission to use this piece, we asked him if he had any remaining copies of this old favorite of ours. (It was written in 1963, and I read it while taking one of my first ad courses.)

John called back a few weeks later to say he'd found the last few copies in his garage and he was sending them to us.

So… if you want to add this classic to your collection, you can now order *The Copywriter* from The Copy Workshop.

While Supplies Last.

WHY ADVERTISING NEEDS NEW IDEAS.

Marketers constantly search for the big advantage – a new selling idea can often create "enormous elasticity" in the effectiveness of media dollars.

Think about it. A breakthrough selling approach can be as much as *10 times* more effective than a predictable selling message – even when the strategy is the same!

Thus, the constant search for new selling approaches by advertisers and agencies alike.

Advertising is a risky business.

There is risk in shifting to a new approach and risk in sticking with an approach that may have worked in the past.

The marketplace changes with each message, competitive advantages are met with competitive responses.

Unique approaches breed hosts of imitators. The battle is constant.

The wars of the marketplace demand a constant supply of fresh ammunition – new Selling Ideas.

There is much to be gained by the short-term breakthrough.

And much to be gained building a consistent, long-term image.

Do you head into unknown territory or back to the basics?

The challenge of the marketplace is constantly changing – that's part of the adventure of advertising.

And as Leo Burnett reminds us, *"There's no such thing as a permanent advertising success."*

DO IDEAS WEAR OUT?

Sure they do. But, more often than not, clients and agencies tire of their advertising long before consumers.

Remember, you've seen your work hundreds of times more than the average reader or viewer.

And remember the success of agencies like Leo Burnett – keeping ideas fresh over the long haul.

The path that was once unclear is now there for all to see. "Aha" becomes "of course."

Leo Burnett had this to say about new ideas… *"Great copy and great ideas are deceptively simple."*

Trout and Ries agree. *"The best positioning ideas are so simple that most people overlook them."*

If that's the case, dramatize your concept's *simplicity.* (People don't have to know how clever you are.)

In every case, emphasize to the client or the people you work with how this idea relates to *their* needs and solves *their* problems.

Help *your* idea become *their* idea.

3. Your idea isn't always the right idea.

Try to be objective about your ideas. Many bright creative people are victimized by their inability to know their good ideas from their bad ones and to confuse *their* idea with the *right* idea.

This is compounded by a competitive reluctance to like other people's ideas.

Learning to tell good ideas from bad ideas is a tough skill to develop. And, since it's a bit like predicting the future, you'll never be perfect at it.

As a start, try to learn to like the best idea… no matter whose idea it is. And remember, it's more credible to speak up for someone else's idea.

Evaluation is another important part of this process. Get other opinions.

Try to become objective about your ideas. (It ain't easy.) Learn to keep going. Stay open to new insights and new ideas. What seemed like the destination may be only a stop along the way.

It may be a piece of a larger puzzle.

4. Just because you've got a good idea, that doesn't mean you know what to do with it.

Elaborate. Once you get that idea, even a great one, you have to work to make it work.

And you probably need help.

Learn to get others to help you make your idea work better and work harder. In fact, one other characteristic of successful ideas is a lot of people worked together to make it work. Bill Backer talks about "idea families."

Working together on ideas is one of the joys of this business. (As Norm Brown former chairman of FCB noted, "Work is fun.")

There are many ways to elaborate.

The root word is "labor." Once you get an idea, your job hasn't ended, it's just begun.

5. Oops! Maybe you already had the idea.

With many advertising and marketing projects, a lot of people and a lot of thinking have gone before.

The brand may already have some heritage, and some smart people may have already given this some thought.

There's good news and bad news. The bad news is that if it's already been thought of, some people will discount it. So even though the idea was never tried, it may already be viewed as a "failure."

The good news is one of best ways to do your preparation is take a look at all that's gone before.

True story. When I first joined FCB, producer Phil Hagenah said, "Let me play you something."

He took me to his office and played a demo of "The Ah Song," which had been put together for Pizza Hut by jingle writer Gary Klaff, based on a Bernie Washington idea – but it had never been used.

It was wonderful. (Thanks Phil, Gary, and Bernie.)

Well, I remembered that wonderful piece of music. About a year later, the agency was fired. Yow!

That piece of music was one of the critical elements in a campaign that both saved the account for

IDEA CHANNELS, IDEA FAMILIES, AND "THE POWER WHO CAN SAY YES."
These are some of the concepts that populate Bill Backer's *The Care and Feeding of Ideas.*

It's a fresh and practical approach to one of our most important jobs.

Published by Times Books

A NEW COMBINATION OF OLD ELEMENTS.
Garbage bag + Jack-o'-Lantern.

Turning lawn and leaf bags into pumpkins pumps up sales in the fall for plastic bag companies.

It was a simple idea.

Don't you wish you'd thought of it!

READING LIST:
Some books on how to have an idea:

The Act of Creation
Arthur Koestler/Pan Picador

The Care and Feeding of Ideas
Bill Backer/Times Books

A Technique for Producing Ideas
James Webb Young/Crain Books

DeBono's Thinking Course
Edward de Bono/Facts on File

The Office:
A Facility Based On Change
(Available through
Herman Miller Furniture)

Some of the books listed in the previous chapter also deal with the subject of ideation.

Idea Exercises:

1. PREPARATION.

List the types of source material you can assemble for preparation on a product assignment.

List other types of product-related experiences you can generate at the preparation stage.

2. FRUSTRATION.

Think about two times you've experienced frustration. How did you feel? How was it resolved.

3. INCUBATION.

Think about ways you can incubate alone.

Now think about who you'd want to work with in a group – to cook-up/incubate some ideas.

List some idea objectives and sit with that person.

4. ILLUMINATION.

Describe two times you've experienced illumination. Short paragraphs. What did it feel like?

5. EVALUATION.

How would you evaluate an idea?

How do you know if you're right or wrong?

6. ELABORATION.

What work do you have to do to put your idea in presentable form? Are you just going to "talk it," or can you prepare some sort of visualization of your idea?

The Idea Box:

Here's a low-tech approach from James Webb Young:
- Write each fact on an index card.
- One fact (or idea), one card.
- Keep adding cards and place them all in a box.
- Or, you can wrap them with a rubber band.
- Put them aside for a while.
- Then go back to the pile and review the cards
- Write down new ideas as they emerge.

Zen Copywriting.

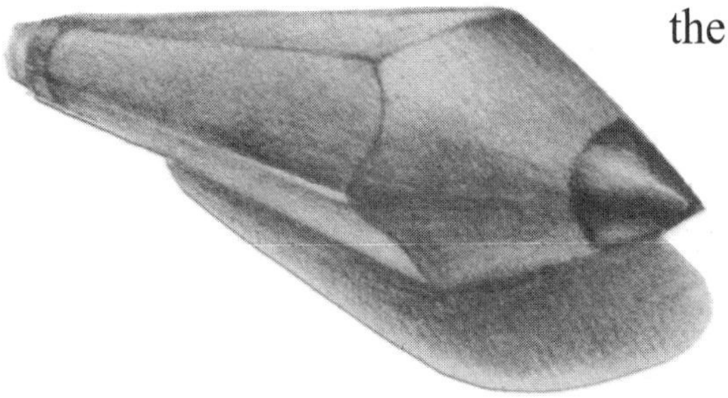

IN ZEN ARCHERY,
the archer and the act become one.
The copywriter's job
is much the same.

Imagine
the destination
before you begin
the journey.

Your job is to take
information
and images
and ideas
and make them
what they were
meant to be.

You must
organize them,
imagine them,
write them,
and
sell them.
As your journey progresses,
your destination will be seen more clearly.
As your skills develop, your arrows
will fly closer to the invisible
target's center.
That's your job.
Imagine
the future.
Make it
come
true

.

INSIDE & OUTSIDE.

When working on a problem, I try to go inside the problem.

Into the product.

Into the target consumer.

Into the relationship between people and product.

Yet, it's also true that the answer, or part of it, may be *outside* – at the cutting edge of art, fashion, or music.

Or a unique combination of concept and circumstance.

But, to get outside, I believe that sometimes you must go so far in that you come out the other side.

Just like in some parts of New Jersey.

Once you go inside a problem deeply enough, you can almost feel yourself standing outside.

A good copywriter should be able to go both ways… all at once.

That's why, as a copywriter, you must continually broaden your outside perspective at the same time you journey inside the products you advertise and try to get *inside* the minds of the people you talk to.

Q: How many Zen Masters does it take to change a light bulb?

A: Two.
One to change the light bulb.
One to not change the light bulb.

TWO KEY ASPECTS OF ZEN are:
- accomodating contradictory thoughts, and
- being in touch with the moment.

Both are important in advertising.

For example, we take small products that play a minor role in people's lives and make them seem important.

We must embrace that contradiction in many ways.

For example, this is a business where you must really take it seriously to be successful.

Yet, take it too seriously, and it makes you crazy.

You must embrace the moment.

Good advertising seems to have an intuitive sense of good timing. It seems to know the right moment – a knowing without knowing.

Some of this may be rooted in Bernbach's belief that good advertising was a bit "sociological."

And some of it is the fact that if your goal, your target, is people living their lives right now, well why shouldn't your message be in harmony with that simple reality?

It is often hard to explain.

But we tend to know it when we see it.

And feel it.

Ad Haiku.

Let's do some *haiku*.
It's Japanese poetry
of only three lines.

First five syllables
then in the middle seven
followed by five more.

It's five seven five
a rhythm made from phrasing
that doesn't need rhyme.

How do you haiku?
Feel the thought within the thing.
Put it on paper.

You can haiku, too
Just start at the beginning
let the writing flow.

Haiku. Assignment #5:

1. TRADITIONAL HAIKU.
   Based on an object or scene in nature.

2. DO A HAIKU.
   About a tool or kitchen appliance.

3. HOW TO HAIKU.
   Do a haiku about how to do something.

4. MOVIE REVIEW HAIKU.
   Do a haiku about a movie or TV show.

5. ADVERTISING HAIKU.
   Do a haiku about a brand name product.

ZEN READING LIST:
Want to know more about Zen?
   Don't get carried away, but I believe that a general understanding of Zen can help in doing your job.

The Way of Zen
Alan Watts
Vintage Books

Zen in the Art of Archery
E. Herrigel
Pantheon

**Zen and the Art of
Motorcycle Maintenance:
An Inquiry into Values**
Robert M. Pirsig

Shogun.
James Clavell
(The book is better than the movie.)

PAPER NAPKIN HAIKU.
This can be a lot of fun with the right group of people – at a restaurant, or wherever.
   Someone starts a haiku on a napkin (or a piece of note paper) and writes the first five syllables.
   The next person writes the next line – seven syllables.
   And a third person does the third line –   five syllables.
   Try it.

Q. How many art directors does it take to change a light bulb?
A. Does it have to be a light bulb?

Q. How many copywriters does it take to change a light bulb?
A. I'm not changing it.

Art Director Appreciation.

ADVERTISING IS A TEAM SPORT.

Copywriters and art directors depend on each other. No business relationship is closer.

Except perhaps in a trapeze act.

A major factor in how well you succeed in this business will be based on how well you work with an art director.

Earlier, we discussed the left and right sides of the brain. There is a parallel here in your contributions to the creation of an ad.

THE ART DIRECTOR IS VISUAL – Right Side.

THE COPYWRITER IS VERBAL – Left Side.

Your contributions reinforce each other.

This was part of Rubicam's revolution and the genius of the DDB approach.

The amount of time the two of you spend developing an ad can be different, too.

After you write something brilliant, like "New *and* Improved," the art director may have to spend hours making it look right.

A storyboard can take a day or two, particularly if the visuals have to be thought out and the rendering has to be of good quality.

After you sell the ad, the disparity continues.

For print ads, shooting, retouching, typesetting, and keylining are the art director's responsibility.

On the other hand, you have to spend more time with clients and account executives (you're the verbal one, remember?).

The point is, while the two of you are partners, even parents, your jobs are very different.

And the better you team up, despite these very real differences, the better the two of you will do. Together.

Here are a few hints for working with an art director:

1. DON'T FINISH TOO FAST.

Put thumbnails, roughs, and headline ideas up on the wall. Let it incubate.

2. TALK ABOUT TYPE.

Type is one important way to establish tone of voice. This is a key decision, and you're entitled to a vote! What attitude do you want your words to project? The typeface can even influence the headline itself. (And vice versa.)

Certain words look better in certain typefaces.

Talk about it. Learn about type.

Learn a page layout program on the computer.

Finally, talk about readability. If you wrote something worth reading, it should be readable.

Perhaps the body copy should be more readable.

Or… maybe you wrote too many words.

Learn to edit. Fewer words. Art directors like that.

3. STORYBOARD OR KEY FRAME?

Chances are, you don't need a storyboard right away.

Learn to present with "key frames."

An office filled with unsold storyboards is a monument to wasted time.

4. BE A FRIEND.

There may be much in your backgrounds that is different. Still, there will be much that you share.

And that will grow with time.

The two of you are literally the parents of your creations. You have responsibilities and obligations to each other and to the product of your combined talents.

Invest time and energy in that relationship, and it will pay off in the work you do. Together.

GRAPHIC DESIGNERS VS. ART DIRECTORS.

Fine artists and great graphic designers aren't necessarily good advertising art directors.

Fine design may arrange the page with pleasing proportion.

Fine art may express the artist's feelings and touch the heart (and the wallet) of the gallery-goer.

Good advertising art direction motivates action in ordinary people!

It grabs the casual reader and moves him in a desired direction.

It may invite him in, or pop off the page and poke him in the eye.

Whatever the effect, it can't just sit there looking nice.

It must be noticed.

The advertising art director uses art and design to accomplish these objectives. They are means to an end.

For the same reason, excellent journalists, novelists, poets, and playwrights aren't necessarily good copywriters.

And vice versa.

REMEMBER HIM?

Paul Rand was one of the great graphic designers – and, as we mentioned in Chapter One, his influence extended to advertising because of his influence with key players at DDB.

As design becomes a more important part of some brand strategies (think of how Apple uses design to gain competitive advantage), you may find it a more and more important part of your own MarCom Matrix.

5. THE MEETING IS THE MEDIA.

You probably think you do ads for print and TV. Wrong! *You do meetings!*

Your medium is not the magazine page or TV screen.

It's the meeting room wall and the walnut conference table. Sometimes it's your boss's office.

Here's the first thing you need to do…

Visualize the Meeting:

How big is the room? Where is the wall?

Where are the people you'll be presenting your ads to seated? Who are they?

You'll have to make an impact in that space.

Own the room with the power of your work.

Attack the Wall!

Give the meeting a headline. Get the theme up big.

Have a simple right-brain visual to go with all that left-brain verbiage. Remember, if you don't do the meeting right, the ads will never run.

Or worse. Another team wins.

Assignment #6:

1. THE ART CENTER EXERCISE.

Do an ad for Lava Soap that communicates with *only a visual!* No headline. No copy.

2. DO THE ZOO #2.

There's a whole world of terrific-looking animals. Write an ad for a local zoo, aquarium, or pet store using one of those wonderful visuals from nature.

3. VERBALIZE VISUALS. Pick three ads you like. *Verbalize* why you like them *visually.*

4. PLAN A MEETING.

Do a rough chart of the meeting room and display space. Outline visual materials you'll need.

These exercises are designed to help you learn to think more visually!

WORK BACKWARD!

Learn to become more of a visually driven writer.

Rough out visuals first.

Write words to pictures.

Try to think about products in a totally nonverbal way and see what essential communication imagery you discover.

Then, write the words.

See what happens.

KRONE ALONE

*In 1950, a 25-year-old designer saw The Art Directors Club annual exhibition dominated by a very new and very small advertising agency.
The designer's name: Helmut Krone. The agency: Doyle Dane Bernbach. The rest is history. Here, from a recent conversation,
are the singular views of DDB's executive vice president, a creative director, and a member of the Art Directors Hall of Fame,
with creative talent so extraordinary the late Bill Bernbach suggested he should be included in this series.*

On early ambitions:
I was interested in industrial design and architecture. At 21, I had two interviews scheduled. First, with a designer named Robert Greenwell who was doing freelance ads for a magazine. The second with Raymond Loewy. Greenwell offered me $40 per week. I said, "Gee, that's great." I never interviewed with Loewy. And never looked back. I tell my children, it's not so much what you do but how you do it. Kids today spend half their lives agonizing over their first move, first job. It doesn't matter, it's how you tackle your work. Stop worrying so much and just do *something*.

On advertising:
I was Bauhaus-based. My idol was Paul Rand. Advertising? If you had any respect for design—any self-respect—and you wanted to tell your mother what you were doing, you worked *around* advertising, but *not in it*. So I worked for Greenwell, in pharmaceuticals, in fashion, for publishers—but not for the hard-core advertising agencies. I had to wait for Bernbach to start his agency. I came here in 1954. I was 29, and one of four art directors.

On alternatives:
I have always said there were only two people for whom I could work: Bill Bernbach and myself. Bill did more than start an agency. He made advertising *respectable*, a profession, a high art. We argued a lot. With genuine disagreement but real affection. We could fight like cats and dogs because we *knew we were both after the same thing*.

On television and print:
I'm not crazy about *things that move*. I like things that stand still; that you can study, hold in your hand, look at, contemplate. That's what I hate about television commercials. They're happenings. They go by and you don't even remember the details. In a print ad, you can study them. There's a point to caring about details in print. If you can give a photo just an extra ounce of *caring*, just a touch of inspiration, it shows. While I do my share of TV, I'm known as the print maven around here. I really do like it. After all these years, the idea of the *page* continues to fascinate me.

On work:
Beauty and style are qualities I count as secondary. If they are in the work, they come along for the ride. The only quality I really appreciate is *newness*, to see something no one has ever seen before. New comes at 11 o'clock at night, after you've spent all day hunched over the board. I have worked with a couple of geniuses. I spend long hours making up for not being a genius.

On confidence and clients:
I am very insecure. Nothing I do ever turns out exactly right. It's never what I expected. I like to work with clients. I need their judgment. All I know is that what I'm doing is new. The client can tell me if it's right. I hate presentations: agency people filing in with a big portfolio, taking out their acetate-wrapped comprehensives and saying, "Here. Make a decision." I like to have clients work with me. I show them scraps of paper. I pull things out of the wastebasket, tissues off the wall. I say "What do *you* think? Should I keep going?" It's not a matter of giving clients what they want. It's a matter of making sure you're on the same wave length.

On working with writers:
I talk with the writer. We come up with a concept. The writer leaves. But I stay. I want to *top* the concept. I want to lay something on top of the concept that's totally unexpected. Most people go home. I don't. For my work begins *after* we've settled on a headline and picture. The next day, the writer will see the ad. It'll have the headline and the picture we discussed. But it won't look or feel the way they thought it would. And that's unnerving to some writers.

On staying ahead:
I try to have some idea of what I want to do even before I know what has to be done. So before I get an assignment, I know what my attack will be, even before I know the product. You can't explain this to a client. They don't understand the process. But I believe you can bend and twist the idea to fit the problem, and come up with something totally new. Does it sound crazy? Bernbach used to say, "First, you make the revolution. Then you figure out why." Thinking ahead isn't unfair to the client. It gives him a head start.

On ads as information:
I think people want *information*. They don't get it from advertising. Say you're buying a tape deck. Well, you're up against it—especially if you read the ads. You know the formula. A double-entendre headline. Nice photo. But *no real meat* in the ad. Because the people who did the ad don't think you *really* want to know. Advertising people argue that it's good to make it simple. But that's not the point. People want to know. Advertising ought to give them the information they need.

On the page as a package:
The page ought to be a *package* for the product. It should look like the product, smell like the product and the company. If it's a highly technical product—like the Porsche—that's how the page ought to look and feel. I tried to make the Porsche ads look a little like what you see when you raise the hood of the car. It's a *package* for Porsche. Every company, every product needs its own package.

On ideas and making them work:
Good ideas announce themselves. A bell rings. But that's just the start. To stage an idea at the level where I want to work, to do work that's *out at the edge*, you need to know about the tools. Type, photography, illustration, are tools. You need to know how they work, to know nearly as much about them as the people who specialize. For if you can't use the tools, you can't really make a good idea work.

On drawing pads:
Some people begin by drawing layouts. I can't work that way. I begin by *thinking*. I don't want to be influenced by that first scribble. Scribbles can box you in. Think first. I don't want to design *ads*. That's why I've spent my life fighting logos. Logos say "I'm an ad, so turn the page." I don't just leave out the logo. I give the client something better. And it doesn't look like an ad.

On The Wall Street Journal:
Form follows function. That was the Bauhaus revolution. The Journal is Bauhaus. Its form follows its function: information, organized for the reader, gathered for business reasons. I've said you ought to be able to identify your ads if you hang them upside down, forty feet away. The Journal *is* The Journal; there's no mistaking it. I've also said the graphic image ought to reflect reality. The Journal *looks* like business, and *is* business. Of course, I read The Journal. Of course, I like to see my ads in The Journal. I have had a lifelong fascination with *the page*, and no publication gives me a bigger page than The Journal. As an art director, I am in the business of *staging* ideas for our clients. The Journal does a magnificent job of *staging* advertising.

The Wall Street Journal.
It works.

Helmut Krone was one of the influential ADs at DDB.

This interview was for *The Wall Street Journal*. On the following pages, with Mr. Krone's permission, is another – a classic view of the art of art direction from one of the classics.

HELMUT KRONE TALKS
ABOUT THE MAKING OF AN AD

By Sandra Karl
Doyle Dane Bernbach, New York

Q. Is it true that you are a perfectionist?

A. I resent the charge. A perfectionist is someone who finishes the backside of a drawer, which I consider completely unnecessary. I spend a lot of time on the front, but I am definitely not interested in the backside of the drawer.

I feel that there's this imaginary line, and you have to get over that line. As soon as I feel I'm over that line, I quit. I don't go any further. I'll leave a thing without all the ends pulled in as soon as it's over that line.

Q. You mean you have a certain standard, and when you reach it, you stop?

A. Yes, just like everybody else. Now, maybe that line is in a different place for me. It all depends on where you place that line. For example, in engravings or television production, I feel that I'm not a stickler no matter what anyone says. If the page has the effect I was after, I'm not interested in petty little corrections.

Q. How did you come to work on Volkswagen when DDB first got the account?

A. I got on Volkswagen because I was the only one who'd ever heard of the car. I had one of the first Volkswagens in the U. S., probably one of the first 100, long before I ever worked here.

And just to show you how wrong a person can be—and how fallible I am—I was dead set against the Volkswagen campaign as we did it. I felt that the thing to do with this ugly little car was to make it as American as possible, as fast as possible. Like, let's get Dinah Shore also. What's that thing she used to sing? "See the U.S.A. in your Chevrolet." I wanted "See the U.S.A. in your Volkswagen." With models around the car and tv extravaganzas.

Q. But it was on Volkswagen that you changed the look of ads. You changed the way the copy looked.

A. Well, first let me say that on Volkswagen I felt so strongly that we were doing the wrong thing—even though I contributed my third to it, certainly—that I finished up three ads, went on vacation to St. Thomas, depressed, came back two weeks later and I was a star.

Q. You say you contributed your third. Not your half?

A. My third, Bill Bernbach's third and Julian Koenig's third.

In his 14 years at Doyle Dane Bernbach, Helmut Krone has, until now, refused interview requests. That hasn't kept him from winning nine New York Art Directors Club medals, dozens of other awards and the title of vp-director of special projects at the agency. After numerous tries by Sandra Karl of the DDB pr office, he agreed to an interview for the agency's house publication. Attired in his newest outfit—cowboy pants, suede shirt and neckerchief—he sat back and talked to Miss Karl about his work, how and why he does it. Here is the interview taken from the October "DDB News."

Q. What was Bill Bernbach's third?

A. Mostly in keeping me from doing the other. Also, the whole concept of speaking simply, clearly and with charm belongs to him. There was nothing new about the Volkswagen idea, the only thing was that we applied it to a car.

Probably eight years before that, Bernbach did an ad for Fairmont strawberries, where he showed a whole strawberry in the middle of a big page—just one life-size strawberry. And the headline was: "It seemed a pity to cut it up." What they were selling were the only whole frozen strawberries on the market, the point being that a strawberry has to be perfect in order to keep it whole.

Volkswagen is not any different from that ad that he did a long time before. The only thing different about it was its application to cars—and that's different enough. I took traditional layout A, which had always existed—two-thirds picture, one-third copy, three blocks with a headline in between. But I changed the picture. The picture was naked looking, not full and lush. The other small change was the copy, which was sans serif rather than serif.

Q. And nobody had ever done that before?

A. Not with that layout, no. It was an editorial look, but with sans serif type.

Q. The look of the copy was very different. The use of "widows" which we spoke of once before.

A. I actually cut those "widows" into the first Volkswagen comps with a razor blade and asked Julian Koenig to write that way. I deliberately kept the blocks from being solid, and when I felt that a sentence could be cut in half, I suggested it just to make another paragraph.

I wanted the copy to look Gertrude Steiny. The layout in that case actually influenced a new copy style, which Bernbach later referred to as "subject, verb, object."

Q. You mean the layout came before the copy style? The copy style came about because of the way it would look on a page?

A. Definitely.

Before then, it was usually the art

director's job to get writers to fill out "widows," so that they could have a neat, No. 2-looking gray wash on the page.

As far as layout is concerned—which I consider a lost art—I feel that almost no one is looking around for a brand new page, a new way of putting down the same old elements, a new way of breaking up that 7x10" area.

Q. You're saying that they should be?

A. Yes, but everybody wants to belong to the current club. There's safety in that, I suppose. And they want to show they're smart enough to recognize what's good, what's "in." They think being current, being fashionable is being new. And it's really the opposite of new.

If you get a medal in the Art Directors Club, the chances are that what you did was not an innovation. I'd say that about almost every medal that I've gotten. They were for innovations that were already a year or two old, and, therefore, easy to digest.

If people say to you, "That's up to your usual great standard," then you know you haven't done it.

■ "New" is when you've never seen before what you've just put on a piece of paper. You haven't seen it before and nobody else in the world has ever seen that thing that you've just put down on a piece of paper. And when a thing is new, all you know about it is that it is brand new. It's not related to anything that you've seen before in your life. And it's very hard to judge the value of it. You distrust it, and everybody distrusts it. And very often, it's somebody else who has to tell you that that thing has merit, because you have no frame of reference, and you can't relate it to anything that you or anybody else has ever done before.

Alexey Brodovitch at the New School was the one who put me on to "new." Students would bring in something to class that they thought was spectacular, but he'd toss it aside and say: "I've seen this once before somewhere." And he wouldn't even discuss it.

Q. What was his reaction when you did something he'd never seen before?

A. I never did anything he'd never seen before while I was in his class. I wasn't ready.

And now that I've done all that talking about "new," let me contradict myself and take a swing at the current trend toward "doing your own thing."

I asked one of our writers recently what was more important: Doing your own thing or making the ad as good as it can be. The answer was: "Doing my own thing." I disagree violently with that. I'd like to propose a new idea for our age: Until you've got a better answer, you copy. I copied Bob Gage for five years. I even copied the leading between his lines of type. And Bob originally copied Paul

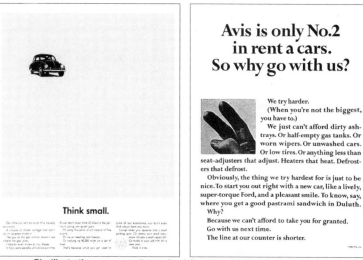

Think small.

Avis is only No.2 in rent a cars. So why go with us?

We try harder.
(When you're not the biggest, you have to.)
We just can't afford dirty ash-trays. Or half-empty gas tanks. Or worn wipers. Or unwashed cars. Or low tires. Or anything less than seat-adjusters that adjust. Heaters that heat. Defrosters that defrost.
Obviously, the thing we try hardest for is just to be nice. To start you out right with a new car, like a lively, super-torque Ford, and a pleasant smile. To know, say, where you get a good pastrami sandwich in Duluth. Why?
Because we can't afford to take you for granted.
Go with us next time.
The line at our counter is shorter.

Big illustration area, small type in Volkswagen ad was reversed for Avis.

Rand, and Rand first copied a German typographer named Tschichold. The thing to do when you get a requisition is to find an honest answer. Solve the problem. Then, if through the years a personal style begins to emerge, you must be the last to know. You have to be innocent of it.

Q. I'd wanted to ask you about the Avis layout. That was new too, wasn't it?

A. Yes. I remember going home on the train one night with Bob (Gage). Everybody at that time was doing Volkswagen layouts. In fact, the headlines were getting smaller and smaller, and the fashion at the time was to write three meaningful words, so strong in themselves that you could set them in very small type.

We had a discussion about this on the train, and he said: "How much smaller can headlines get before they become invisible?" And I thought about it. I was working on Avis currently and looking for a page style. Now that's very important to me, a page style. I feel that you should be able to tell who's running that ad at a distance of 20 feet.

Q. Just by the page style?

A. Just by the page style. You can tell a Volkswagen ad from a distance of 30 feet, and an Avis ad from a distance of 40 feet.

Anyway, to get back to this headline thing. I started thinking about what he'd said, how absurd it was getting with these headlines getting smaller and smaller. So what I did was I took the Volkswagen style and turned it inside out: The headline became big, and not in the middle, I put it on top. The picture became small, and the copy became large. It was very carefully, methodically done, very coolly arrived at. It was *not* inspired. It was a mathematical solution. I made everything

that was big, small, and everything that was small, big.

Q. Anything else?

A. Why don't you come clean and ask me why I'm so slow.

Q. Okay. Why are you so slow?

A. I have no defense, only a reason. Though a New Yorker, I had a German upbringing. And I'm the recipient of the best of such an upbringing as well as the victim of the worst part of it.

A German son is always wrong until he's proved himself to be right. He is a know-nothing and has everything to prove. It gives you a certain insecurity which is the opposite of "chutzpah." You tend to rework things and believe they're never good enough, because, after all, you're a "know-nothing."

David Ogilvy once said: "An agency ought to be on time, just like a good tailor." But in defense, I'd like to say that I've got the best tailor outside of Rome—and he's always late!

Q. Do you enjoy it, the work?

A. I don't know. I go back and forth. Advertising is stupid. Advertising is great. Advertising is unnecessary. Advertising is the most vital art form of our day. It depends on what week it is I think they're both true.

I didn't plan out my existence. "I'm going to do this for two years, this for three years, and then I'll be a vice-president, and so on." I never heard of stock options.

All I did was keep my nose on the board. I worked my ass off. I worked just like my father and mother worked. My father was an orthopedic shoemaker and my mother was a seamstress, and I believe that they were probably the best shoemaker and seamstress in America. I believe that with all my might. And I guess that's how it all happened. They used to work their heads off. And people said they were the best. #

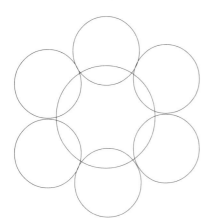

FILL IN THE BLANKS.

Above is our graphic for The MarCom Matrix. Can you fill in the blanks?

First, if you have the time, list them (don't peek) and then write one sentence about what they do for a brand.

Next, could you tell me if any of these areas interest you – and why?

We don't want a major essay here, just a quick idea of what places you might like to play in the MarCom Marketplace.

Finally, as you keep reading this book, tell us where you think you might want even more.

And we'll keep working to fill in those blanks. OK?

Thanks for your help.

Wait. More Feedback!

Those were some of our questions. What are your questions?

Do you have questions about techniques. About where it's going?

And, after you've finished this book, you may have even more questions.

So, stay in touch and let us know what you're thinking.

That's how we get smarter. Thanks.

Bruce Bendinger
copywork@aol.com
(that's my other e-mail address)

Feedback:

GOT A MINUTE? We'd like to get a little feedback from you. OK? Here are a few initial questions…

A. Assuming you can predict the future, how do you think creating messages will be a part of your life?

B. Right now, what kind of job would you like to have after you graduate? (Or have you graduated?)

C. What do you write with? Please list items and rough percentages (computer, 60%; ballpoint in notebook, 30%; miscellaneous doodles, 10%).

D. How's your handwriting? Do you like your handwriting? Do you write or print?

Now a few questions about the first part of the book.

1. HISTORY.
• What do you most remember?
• Do you feel you understand positioning?

2. CURRENT EVENTS.
• What did you think about the way things are changing? What stuck? What was confusing?
• What ads do you think should be in this chapter?
• Do you understand The MarCom Matrix?

3-4. TWO BRAINS/HOW TO HAVE AN IDEA.
• Do you understand The FCB Grid?
• Did you read the Addendum? Well?
• What ideation techniques work for you?

5. DID YOU HAIKU?
• Why is Zen important? Or is it?

6. ART DIRECTOR APPRECIATION.
• How do you feel about your visualizing skills?

AND FINALLY…
What would you like to know more about?

Send to thecopyworkshop@aol.com

More Words.

This section of the book will deal with:

1. Basics of strategic thinking and salesmanship.

2. Principles of effective copywriting style.

3. Copywriting for different media.

How to Copywrite.

"Advertising is salesmanship in print."
John Kennedy. Copywriter.

The quote is dated. The reality remains.
  Salesmanship.
  The ad you write has to *sell*.
  It must persuade.
  Persuasion is more than communication. It is active. It doesn't just inform.
  It influences. It motivates. It *moves*.

Understanding the customer helped
build a whole new market for cigarettes.
  Note the continued use of the preemptive "It's Toasted" theme line.

COPYWRITING…
  A skilled craft.
  Verbal carpentry.
  Words on paper.
  Scripts to time.
  And one more thing… *Salesmanship.*
  Our first lesson is:

SALESMANSHIP=STRATEGY+STRUCTURE+STYLE.
  While we'll cover a wide range of topics, it's really all about persuasion and salesmanship.
  Styles may change, but this will stay the same.
  Good salesmanship will always be a combination of artistry and common sense, hard work and easy answers, smart thinking and dumb luck. And, most of all, thinking about the person you need to persuade.
  Things may get complicated, but there are still simple fundamentals everyone can learn.
  And while there will be many exceptions to general rules, you gotta know 'em before you can break 'em.
  This is the general process –
  You'll develop a Strategy. Copywriting is strategic writing. It's designed to accomplish something.
  From that Strategy, you'll generate a Selling Idea. Copywriting is persuasive writing.
  Then, you'll give it Structure.
  Copywriting is writing that understands the reader.
  It needs to connect with the people you're writing to.
  Finally, you'll do it with Style. After all, it's hard to do all those other things if it isn't enjoyable to read.

STRATEGY + STRUCTURE + STYLE.
  That's SALESMANSHIP.
  And that's your job.

First, let's talk about Strategy. And the first thing we should say about that is this... *there are many types of Strategies.*

MARKETING STRATEGIES.

Many companies have a large, complex document called a Marketing Strategy.

This covers a wide range of things related to selling products, such as pricing, distribution, and other factors of the marketplace.

There are also Promotional Strategies, which focus on promotional tasks, and Public Relations Strategies, which focus on communication goals for publicity and unpaid media.

There are even Packaging Strategies.

In this book, we will focus primarily on developing and executing an *Advertising* Strategy.

ADVERTISING STRATEGIES.

Advertising works with a shorter document. It may be called an Advertising Strategy, a Communication Strategy, or Creative Platform – or something else.

It is part of the larger Marketing Strategy.

An Advertising Strategy generally indicates what the advertising should communicate and to whom it will be addressed.

From this point on, when we say "strategy," we mean advertising strategy. But remember, you may be in a meeting where that's not what they mean at all.

OBJECTIVE, STRATEGY, TACTICS.

Discovering the Objective is your real first step.

Before you can have a Strategy, you must have an Objective. Developing a Strategy begins with clearly defining what you want to accomplish.

The Objective is a statement of the task that must be done and, sometimes, the Problem to be solved (i.e., "The Problem the Advertising Must Solve").

M.O.S.T. = MISSION, OBJECTIVE, STRATEGY, TACTICS

Some definitions and examples:

Mission – Principles by which a company is run.

Example: Apple Computer's stated mission is *"Our goal is to put Macintosh computers in the hands of as many people as possible."*

A mission helps a company maintain focus in a complicated business environment.

Objective – A specific task to be accomplished.

An Objective Statement for a Marketing Strategy might be: *To double unit sales of low-end computers next quarter.*

An Objective Statement for an Advertising Strategy might be: *To convince decision-makers (parents and small business owners) that our entry-level computers offer the added-value of the Macintosh operating system.*

Defining Objectives is key to developing good Strategies.

Strategy – How you will meet an Objective. There may be alternate strategies to choose from – even when objectives are clear.

Example: *Our strategy will be to:*
a. *increase advertising*
b. *offer price-off incentives*
c. *provide easier financing*
d. *lower the retail price*
e. *some or all of the above*

The chosen (or "recommended") strategy is the best hypothesis as to how to meet the objective.

"On-Strategy" – When something is "on-strategy" it conforms to the strategy (hypothesis).

"Off-Strategy" – When it is "off-strategy" it fails to conform to the recommended strategy. It may or may not meet the objective and may represent an alternate hypothesis.

Tactics – Specific planned actions that execute the Strategy.

Ads, sales materials – the whole range of marketing communications tools are *tactics.* So is a sales call.

Example: *Advertising featuring Mac Classics starting at $999.*

While the final result is a straightforward sequence, the path to achieving it can be more like putting together a puzzle – or solving a mystery.

Clues – bits of information – help you along the way. Perhaps an insight into your consumer, an interesting product fact, a bit of brand heritage, or even something you pick up from the competition's advertising.

You often find yourself testing hypotheses – like a scientist or a detective.

Even when you miss, you learn.

So you aim better next time.

BACKING OUT A STRATEGY.

"Backing out a strategy" is the sequence of writing an ad first and then creating (or "backing out") the Strategy implied by the ad.

A lot of people say you're not supposed to do this, but an awful lot of professionals do it anyway, so let's talk about it.

It's simple. You write the ad.

Then, you write the Strategy.

Some persuasive and creative people are inherently strategic, so there's usually a Strategy contained within the work.

Hal Riney, one of the most successful contemporary copywriters, says, *"I don't know what the Strategy should be till I do the creative."*

So what's the problem?

You've got *a* strategy. But you don't know if you've got *the* strategy.

And even someone as good as Hal Riney doesn't get it right every time.

Discover the Objective.
Develop a Strategy.
Generate a Selling Idea.
Write it with Style.

The ad you write is an execution of your Strategy – it is a "tactic."

It's what you do after you go through the process: determine an Objective, develop a Strategy, think of a Selling Idea, and, finally, execute the tactic – the ad.

Through it all, remember, advertising is communication written with a consciousness of the *receiver.*

Writers may write for themselves.

Copywriters write with others in mind.

It's *receiver-driven* communication.

STRUCTURE:

The presentation of your idea must have a structure that is easy for the person receiving the message to follow and understand. It's simple.

Tell 'em what you're gonna tell 'em. Tell 'em.

Tell 'em what you told 'em. Beginning. Middle. End.

A BEGINNING.

Getting Attention.

Inviting Involvement.

Establishing Context.

A MIDDLE.

Developing Your Sale.

Adding Support or Credibility.

Reinforcing Memorability.

AN END.

Building Awareness.

Shifting Attitudes.

Motivating Action.

Achieving the Objective.

Your last step isn't a step at all.

It may be a hop, a karate kick, or a pirouette.

It's Style.

And, once more, this is our message:

Salesmanship = Strategy + Structure + Style.

OK, let's try to figure out what we have to do first.

Discovering The Objective.

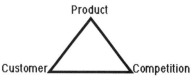

THE STRATEGIC TRIAD.
Your Objective is in there somewhere.
Product. Customer. Competition.
Your Strategy will address all three.
It will tell us why customers will choose your product in preference to that of the competition.

This often involves solving a Problem – but before you can solve a problem, you have to figure out what it is.

This copywriter understood the consumer problem. A dramatic but thoughtful ad, with empathy and insight into the difficulty of maintaining and losing weight and the fact that many "diet" products don't taste very good. A Product Benefit *that leads to a* Consumer Benefit.

WHERE are you going?　　Developing Strategy begins here – determining the job you have to do.

Sometimes that Objective is clear.

But often, your first job is to figure it out.

Here are some ways to help you get started.

1. THINK ABOUT THE CUSTOMER.

The better you know the person you're talking to, the better you'll understand what you must accomplish. Remember Hopkins: *"The advertising man studies the consumer. He tries to place himself in the position of the buyer."*

Try to envision the Target Consumer.

Try to become that person.

What is his or her state of mind?

Perhaps total ignorance. If that's the case, *awareness* may be your Objective.

Building awareness is an implicit part of almost every ad Objective.

But consumers aren't ignorant.

More likely, they already have some thoughts about your brand, about the product category, and, probably, about the competition.

You have to get at those thoughts.

• **Demographic information** can help, but you must use it as a tool to imagine the real live person.

• **Psychographic information** can help. VALS (Values and LifeStyles), can provide valuable insights and

ANNOUNCING THE TASTE YOU USED TO CHEAT FOR.

Bald, rubbery, hard-boiled eggs. Endless vistas of cottage cheese. The relentless boredom of carrots and celery.
Conventional diet food is enough to drive you off a diet.
Happily, Weight Watchers 19 New Frozen Meals are good enough to drive

you on.
Like this Chicken Oriental in a snappy soy-spiked ginger sauce with crunchy Chinese vegetables.
Lean, juicy beefsteak smothered in a thick, brown gravy.
Lasagna dripping with spicy tomato sauce.

Yes, even Sausage Pizza. Now you can have them. Even if you're on a diet.
So if you're really serious about dropping those extra pounds, our exciting new taste can help.
After all, how can you go off your diet, if the taste you want is on it?

WEIGHT WATCHERS
19 NEW FROZEN MEALS.
TRY IT.
YOU'LL DIET.

127

TARGET TALK.

As you might notice, we alternate between the words Customer, Consumer, Target, Target Consumer, Target Audience, and Prospect. They are basically the same concept. You may work at a company that prefers one or the other. We felt you should become familiar with all of the terms. Here are some other important definitions:

Consumer/Customer/Target (also referred to as Target Audience, Target Consumer, Target Customer, Prospect).

All of these refer to the person most likely to buy or influence purchase – the person at whom the marketing communication is usually aimed.

Sometimes, the consumer and the purchaser are different, like baby food or expensive office equipment.

In these cases, the Target is often called the "Decision-Maker."

Demographics. Specific quantitative information about the target: age, sex, income, etc.

Psychographics. Qualitative information about the target, sometimes based on quantitative survey information, more often based on smaller qualitative studies, sometimes based on judgement. Lifestyle, attitudes, etc.

Usage. Information based on use of product, product category, or competitive products.

Examples: *Heavy users of car wax, bifocal wearers, users of Lotus 1-2-3, etc.*

help you get to know your customers. VALS offers a way of looking at and getting to know people who may not be a lot like you.

• **Focus groups** can help. You can listen to real people talk about their real lives and how the products you want to sell them fit into their lives.

• **Usage information** can help. This is information that helps you understand how the product fits into people's lives.

Sometimes it can be as simple as talking to people who've purchased the product.

In general, good customers and "heavy users" can be a valuable source of good ideas.

However you do it, you need to get to know the people you'll be writing to and selling to.

2. THINK ABOUT THE PRODUCT.

Describe the product and what it does.

For example, let's say you're working on…

• Toothpaste plus mouthwash.

• A convenient diet product.

• A radial tire.

We've just listed Product Features (sometimes called Features or Attributes).

They are, quite simply, features of the product.

Now, how do these features become benefits for the person you'll be talking to? Like this…

• Cleaner breath.

• An easy way to lose weight.

• A safer ride.

Just think of the benefits that these features deliver. These are Product Benefits – benefits *of* the product to the consumer.

If the Product Benefit is meaningful, you'll probably want to communicate it to your Target.

Factors That Influence Purchase Behavior.

What's most important to customers?

It's dry!
But so shiny it looks wet.

Mr. Clean's lemon fresh formula never leaves dull streaks when it dries, even when you don't rinse. Mr. Clean cleans your whole house right down to the shine.

Mr. Clean. The man behind the shine.

FACTORS THAT MOTIVATE PURCHASE BEHAVIOR.
Sometimes it's a Product Benefit.
  Here's one from P&G for Mr. Clean.
  Note the *visualizing* of the benefit.
  This ad also performs a second function – building Mr. Clean's powerful but friendly *image*.

One big job will be determining "Factors That Influence Purchase Behavior."

Simply put, why do people buy this type of product?

You may find a generic benefit which encompasses the whole category – like durability for batteries.

Or you may find a category, like shampoo, where there are a number of factors ranging from hair manageability to price to dandruff control.

Advertise Your Advantage.

Historically, products that advertise their advantages do well… when the advantage is worth advertising.

Communicating the Product Benefit to the Target Audience may be your Objective.

Or perhaps that is only a step on the ladder leading to a benefit *within* the consumer –

• Fresher breath could translate to greater personal attractiveness and better relationships.

• A smaller dress size could mean greater personal attractiveness and better relationships.

• A safer ride makes you feel more confident that you are doing all you can to protect your family.

These are "Consumer Benefits."

They are benefits that the consumer receives when they use your product. Communicating the Consumer Benefit may be your Objective. It often is.

GIVE A TOY A CHILD FOR CHRISTMAS.

KAY BEE STOREWIDE CHRISTMAS SALE

CONSUMER BENEFIT.
Again, note the *visualizing* of the benefit.
  This ad uses a headline device I call "The Double."
  It turns a common phrase inside out and gives it new meaning.
  The visualization has great appeal for the target – parents.
  A very nice ad.

Half man. Half beast.

LADDERING.

ATTRIBUTES, FEATURES, BENEFITS & VALUES.

Much strategic discussion focuses on what factor to emphasize. Sequencing these factors is called "laddering."

Here are generally agreed upon definitions – listed "bottom to top:"

Attribute (Product Attribute). Characteristic of product, usually inherent or natural – *Applesauce comes in wide-mouth glass jars.*

Product Feature. This is usually based on some manufactured or designed aspect – *Applesauce spoons smoothly out of the wide-mouth jar.*

Product Benefit. A benefit to the consumer, usually based on a Product Feature or Attribute – *Applesauce is easy to serve.*

Consumer Benefit (Customer Benefit). A benefit usually based on how the Product Benefit delivers a positive result to the consumer – *I save time, and my children get extra nutrition (which tastes good – so they'll eat it).*

Values. The human dimension reinforced by the benefit – *I'm a good mother because I serve Applesauce.*

Laddering is the process of moving through this sequence. The general method is to ask people *why* the Feature (or Benefit) is important. The answer generally moves you up the "ladder."

Where On The Ladder?

A continuing issue is where to focus.

Generally, the "lower" on the ladder you are, the more product-specific your message and the more you are differentiating your product.

The higher up you are, the more you are dealing with what's important in the consumer's life – and the more generic your benefit. (All nutritious foods reinforce nurturing values!)

This is a major strategic decision. We offer only definitions. Not answers.

UP AND DOWN THE LADDER.

One of the best ways to identify the advantage to advertise is through a process called "laddering."

The "lower" levels tend to be about the product and the "higher" levels about consumers.

The highest level is something we call "Values."

Values are about internal needs and self-image.

Every product we use relates in some way to values that are important to us.

The part of us that nurtures.

The part of us that wants to succeed.

The part of us that wants to have a good time.

Values can be important – but remember, they're not exclusively about your product.

Most nutritious food products reinforce nurturing maternal values and most fashion and personal care products are about a positive self-image.

Think. How does the benefit *within* the product manifest itself *within* the consumer? And what aspect of the sequence is "ownable?"

Inherent drama. Leo Burnett (and others) solve this by using unique visualizations for generic benefits (e.g., the Maytag Repairman for washing machine durability or the Pink Bunny for battery durability), the benefit becomes, to some degree, ownable for your brand.

And, along the way, the brand develops Values.

More than one place on the Ladder?

Sure. Unique combinations can be powerful.

Examine the whole ladder – from Attributes to Features to Product Benefits to Consumer Benefits to Values – and look for unique strengths.

Find out what is most meaningful.

You may discover your Objective is communicating that unique dimension – or combination.

Or… maybe you keep looking.

3. THINK ABOUT THE COMPETITION.

The competition is also important.

Most marketing plans and strategies consider what they call "source of business."

If you win, who loses?

Sometimes new usage will be the source of overall business. For example, as soft drink consumption grew, people drank less water. Then, as bottled water consumption grew, people drank less tap water.

Even if you don't compete directly in your advertising, you should consider what other similar products are already *inside* the consumer's mind as well as what habit patterns are already out there.

Think about what's going on in the marketplace.

Category Insight. On the way to developing insight into your brand, you may want to develop insight into the category overall.

This is the first step in positioning.

POSITIONS…

To start this part of the process, think about what goes on *inside* the consumer's mind when he or she thinks about the product category.

Where is your product on the product ladder?

Where are you on the Positioning Grid? In a perfect world, where do you want your product to be?

Ask those questions. Do some positioning.

Establishing a distinct position for your brand versus the competition may be The Objective. If it is…

1. Don't underestimate the expense and effort it might take to achieve that position.

2. Realize establishing that position may not generate increased sales (e.g., "diet beer").

To be successful, Trout and Ries maintain,

"Your position must be:
1. A unique position
2. With broad appeal."

Everyone has competition…

…and it's survival of the fittest.

USPS VS. FEDEX.
Before they started cooperating, FedEx and the US Post Office ran very competitive ads for their services.

Now they both compete with UPS.

CONSUMER INSIGHT & ACCOUNT PLANNING

From advertising's earliest days, insight into the consumer has been key.

However, as marketing and advertising became more specialized, clients and agencies became more and more removed from their customers and "understanding the consumer" became more and more difficult.

During the '70s, British agencies addressed this problem with a new agency function called "Account Planning."

Simply put, the account planner "becomes" the customer.

Through interviews, "ethnology," and other forms of insight generation, the planner brings the Target Consumer into the agency.

The account planner helps you find the *"Sweet Spot"* and helps you hit it.

The best planners are able to represent the target group in a way that inspires fresh, new insights.

Jay Chiat, of Chiat/Day, imported the Account Planning system and gives it credit for much of his agency's success.

Today, some sort of account planning or "consumer insight" function is common at many US agencies.

The Consumer Insight Classic!

HITTING THE SWEET SPOT

How Consumer Insights Can Inspire Better Marketing and Advertising
By Lisa Fortini-Campbell, Ph.D.

Hitting The Sweet Spot, *by Lisa Fortini-Campbell, Ph.D. – the first US book on Account Planning. [From The Copy Workshop.]*

…AND PROPOSITIONS.

Rosser Reeves addresses the competition in his USP (Unique Selling Propostion).

"The proposition must be one that the competition either cannot or does not offer.

It must be unique – either a uniqueness of the brand or a claim not otherwise made in that particular field of advertising."

Person… product… and competition.

THE SWEET SPOT & THE STRATEGIC TRIAD.

"Consumer Insight" is one factor that can help you unify these elements.

One type of Consumer Insight concept is called *"The Sweet Spot."* You want to hit it.

But first you have to find it.

Finding it is the result of insights into the consumer, the consumer's feelings and attitudes about the product category, and feelings and attitudes toward your specific brand.

Consumer Insight + Brand Insight = Sweet Spot.

These same three factors – customer, product, and competition – are the general basis of many types of business strategy development.

Together, they are often referred to as the "Strategic Triangle" or "Strategic Triad."

Your Objective is most likely involved with some combination of these same three factors: customer, product, and competition.

But, in advertising strategy, there is a fourth dimension which you must consider.

Now you must think about… *the Problem!*

4. THINK ABOUT THE PROBLEM.

Ask yourself a very simple question…

"What's The Problem?" What's the *real* problem?

Is it the product (Yikes!), the image, lack of awareness, the sales force, the ad budget, or simply unrealistic expectations?

Sometimes it's the ads and, almost always, the ads are the easiest thing to change.

But there are often a few other factors squirming around in the stew. Peel the onion.

Put yourself in your client's shoes, your customer's mind, and the account exec's briefcase.

Turn the situation upside down and inside out.

And vice versa. Let it incubate.

You might even ask a few more questions.

Why? Because there is *danger* here!

Don't Solve The Wrong Problem!

It is not uncommon to have large numbers of bright, well-informed people focused on the wrong problem.

It's not uncommon to find situations where people passed the real problem and solution a long time ago.

Trout & Ries noted, *"The best positioning ideas are so simple that most people overlook them."*

And Leo Burnett observed, *"Great copy and great ideas are deceptively simple."*

Simple, but not easy.

THE PROBLEM THE ADVERTISING MUST SOLVE.

In their Creative Work Plan, Y&R focuses on *"The Problem the Advertising Must Solve."*

In virtually every agency planning system, some part of the document addresses this issue in one way or another. Think about it. What's the Problem?

INTERESTING PROBLEMS CAN MAKE INTERESTING ADS.

Above, the message is dramatized with humor and a powerful visual.

Below, a dramatic contrast in words create impact.

Each ad qualifies its target charmingly and disarmingly. And each appeals to the instincts of a certain type of person.

PROBLEM/CONSUMER BENEFIT.
"Morning Breath" was an engaging way for Scope to tell a simple story that contained a combination of strategic elements: the consumer problem and the product solution.

Plus a Competitive Claim.

Some Scope commercials also position the brand against the leading competitor (Listerine) by mentioning "Medicine Breath."

VISUALIZE THE PROBLEM.
In this case, a bad haircut.

A good use of humor. While it sort of makes fun of models and fashion, it allows any of us who've had a bad haircut to smile without being embarrassed, and to consider getting a better haircut at Sassoon's.

And because they connected with us, we accept their implied claim that their haircuts are better.

Jay Chiat notes,

"The creative process is really a very structured thing that has to do with problem-solving."

George Lois says,

"You should be able to distill a marketing problem – which precedes the advertising solution – into one simple sentence."

What Problem can the *advertising* solve?

There are a lot of problems out there, but what problem should advertising address?

The right answer to this question can give your whole advertising program a clear focus.

While The Problem may be contained within the Strategic Triad, it often seems to have a life of its own.

And getting a handle on that slippery little devil is often key to getting your Objective right – so you don't just have *a* strategy, but *the* Strategy.

Sometimes, you'll find The Problem has already been identified. Only people don't realize it.

I suggest a little historical research: old memos, old ads, people who used to work on the business.

There are discarded ideas and valuable insights scattered about just about everywhere.

Some are good ideas orphaned by circumstance.

Some are *terrific!* (Remember the Pizza Hut story?)

If you can make one of them get up and walk, your reputation may be enhanced by the miraculous nature of your deed and the gratitude of those whose ideas you have saved.

Be sure to acknowledge the original authors of the idea!

This can be a tricky area. Some will be appreciative. Others will not.

By making a point of giving credit, you will at least protect yourself from being branded as a thief.

Meanwhile, remember that your obligation is to see to it that the product gets *the best ideas available.*

No matter whose.

Wherever you find it, whoever thought of it, whatever it is, you must know the answer to the question – **"What's The Problem?"**

You have to understand the problem before you can solve the problem.

Once you have an answer, you may proceed.

You now understand The Problem.

Solving The Problem is often the Objective of your advertising. It usually combines key aspects of product, customer and competition.

A cautionary note – your conclusions may not lend themselves to widespread publicity.

For this reason, it is not uncommon to have both stated and unstated Objectives.

For example, the *stated* Objective might be,

"To give the sales force a rallying cry."

The *unstated* Objective might be, *"Now that we've got the product fixed, let's get the sales force to try and get it back into the stores again."*

Or, worse yet, you may have to reconvince turned-off customers who have already been burned once, while dealing with a client who refuses to acknowledge the problem. Now *that's* a Problem.

If you're still not sure of your Objective… go back to where you started…

THINK ABOUT THE **CUSTOMER.**
THINK ABOUT THE **PRODUCT.**
THINK ABOUT THE **COMPETITION.**
THINK ABOUT THE **PROBLEM.**
now…

5. COMBINE THEM.

That's right, think of everything. All at once.

Sometimes the answer is simple and obvious, and sometimes not. Look for patterns of reinforcement.

Use your *"nonlinear thinking tool."*

THE BUD LIGHT PROBLEM.
Their problem was at the bar, when the customer said, "Gimme a light" – which could mean Miller Lite, the leading light beer (at the time), or any light beer.

How could they communicate in a fresh, memorable, and persuasive way that people should order a Bud Light?

That was the problem.

The answer was the "Bar Call" campaign, originally planned as a few ten-second commercials.

This simple (and humorous) solution became a successful campaign that built the brand (causing Lite problems).

For Bud Light, it was advertising that effectively solved The Problem.

Q. WHAT'S BAND-AIDS' STICKY PROBLEM?

Let's say you're at Y&R, working on Band-Aid brand bandages.

What's the problem your advertising should solve?

You already have dominant share and have product in the medicine cabinets of most of America.

Your major usage is by mothers of active young children (2-10, the "Owie Age"), who use them to deal with the common cuts and scrapes of childhood.

Awareness is high.

Image is positive.

People, for the most part, already have the product in the house.

What, then, is "The Problem the Advertising Must Solve?"

Look for the answer at the end of this chapter…

Pattern Recognition.

"Pattern recognition" is the ability to see something based on incomplete information.

It's the way some people recognize new and emerging trends *before* the hard data is in.

Sometimes it's called intuition. Basically, it's coming to a conclusion based on a few clues.

Advertising thinking is often like that.

Pattern recognition can be key to identifying new marketing and advertising opportunities.

It may be a trend in art or fashion, or a changing lifestyle. It may be rooted in old-fashioned values or it may be a new-fashioned product.

It may be one person in a focus group, one customer, or a salesperson out in the field.

The challenge is to recognize it.

Feel the forces at work. Think of it like a chess board, or as a playing field…

Positioning opportunities that have been left open by the competition. Problems unsolved.

Benefits undramatized. Needs unmet. Targets to hit.

Look for ways to turn negatives into positives.

Your Objective will be at a conjunction of forces.

THE LITE EXAMPLE.

It's worth mentioning again. The product became a success only after numerous expensive failures.

Finally, the Lite agency turned a consumer negative, "diet beer," into a benefit, "you can drink more."

After the fact, it seems simple.

The Objective...

when discovered, will be simple and *synergistic*.

While The Objective of a marketing plan may be a specific numerical sales goal, the objective for an advertising strategy should be a clear and simple communications goal.

It should be clear and simple, even if the process might not have been simple at all.

Your Objective should be a simple statement of something that can be done relatively soon that will create a *dynamic system* that will help your brand achieve its goal.

Meeting The Objective will create or reinforce forces that will move your business forward.

Because once you know where you're going, you can start to figure out how to get there.

For example:

• Solve the "Diet Beer" Problem.

• Solve the "Gimme a light" Problem.

• Get women to use more Band-Aids.

Whatever your Objective, it should be clear, it should be simple, and you must have one before you can take the next step.

STRATEGY.

How you get there.

The path you must travel...

A. HOW TO GET MOTHERS TO USE MORE BAND-AIDS.

Y&R discovered an important opportunity – after the Band-Aid was initially applied, a scab formed and the old Band-Aid (which was now a bit dirty) was taken off and the scab protected the cut.

However, re-applying a Band-Aid to protect the scab promoted better healing. The cut was not re-opened and the scab was not knocked off (or picked off by the child). On average, cuts healed faster when a Band-Aid was used for this purpose.

The Problem became: Mothers do not realize that they can promote better healing by re-applying a Band-Aid to protect the scab.

Advertising which focused on this point promoted increased usage, which resulted in increased sales.

A QUICK CHECKLIST:

Things to do to discover your Objective:

1. Think about the Customer.

A. Consumer Information. Customer profiles, demographics, product usage studies, sales data.

B. VALS. Values and lifeStyles.

C. Focus Groups.

D. Talk to consumers one-on-one.

2. Think about the Product.

A. Use the product.

B. List Product Features and Product Benefits.

C. List **Consumer Benefits** and **Values.**

D. Do some **Laddering.**

3. Think about the Competition.

A. Do a "Store Check." Look at the competition in the marketplace. Compare package, price, in-store promotions, and performance.

B. Clip Competitive Print Ads. Make a clip file. If possible, tape a few competitive TV commercials.

C. Look for Articles. Read "the trades."

D. Talk to Customers. Find out why they like your competition. Find out the competition's weaknesses.

4. Think about The Problem.

Here are some common problems:

A. Low Awareness. Consumers unaware of product. (If it's a good product, a good problem to have.)

B. Old Product Didn't Perform. Or outperformed by competitive product. (If current product doesn't perform, try removing self from Problem.)

C. Pricing Problem. (Hard to solve with ads alone.)

D. Distribution Problem. Consider trade as target.

E. "Political" Problem. Obvious answer not recognized, irrational bias, office politics, etc.

F. Budget Problem. Not enough money to do job, unrealistic expectations, too many things to do, etc.

G. Advertising Problem. Previous ads did not "work." (Find out why before you write new ads.)

Be strategic.

Think long term, even when you're thinking short term. Analyze. Scrutinize. Weigh. Know how one thing affects another, and how all the pieces fit together. Buying a fund? Buying a company? Ask Merrill Lynch. We'll help you see the big picture.

Be bullish.

visit us at ml.com

© 1999 Merrill Lynch & Co., Inc.

THE ART OF STRATEGY.

In strategic development, market facts of varying accuracy and relevance are linked with hypotheses of varying validity in a long complex sequence.

In the process, many business people forget that a strategy is a hypothesis.

It's a theory, a blueprint, a road map.

It's a "best guess."

It's an art, not a science.

Strategy.

HOW do you get there?

That's strategy. It's a subject taught at great length and expense in business schools across the nation.

Seminars abound. Sober businessmen endorse its healthful benefits.

STRATEGY AND THE WEATHER.

Sometimes, strategy is like the weather – where everyone talks about it, but less is done than most will admit.

And sometimes it's not like the weather at all – because everywhere you go, it seems to be pretty much the same. Brand names for less. Better than the rest.

Best value. Quality and service.

Today, many businesses seem to have pretty much the same strategy. Because the forces at work and the people who work there are also pretty much the same.

A BIT OF HISTORY.

Once upon a time, some companies had MBAs and marketing departments and some didn't.

Strategies offered important differentiation.

Once upon a time, manufacturers were able to make things very different from the competition – and maintain that difference with patents or production secrets.

There were fewer products, but they seemed more different. Remember Hopkins? When he was writing, baked beans in a can was a big deal. That was then.

Today, all companies have MBAs. Most marketers are marching to the same strategic drum. Sometimes it seems the only thing they can't copy is the brand name.

A successful copywriter has to know strategy.

Your Selling Idea has to emerge from that strategy.

You have to know strategy because every new ad idea, particularly the brightest and most startling, is first judged by one simple standard. *"Is it on strategy?"*

Here's how Kenichi Ohmae, author of *The Mind of the Strategist,* described the process:

*"In business as on the battlefield,
the object of strategy is to bring about the
conditions most favorable to one's own side.
In strategic thinking, one first seeks a clear
understanding of the particular character
of each element of a situation, and then makes the
fullest possible use of human brainpower
to restructure the elements
in the most advantageous way.
Phenomena and events in the real world
do not always fit a linear model.
Hence, the most reliable means of dissecting a
situation into its constituent parts and then reas-
sembling them in the desired pattern
is not a step-by-step methodology
such as systems analysis.
Rather, it is that **ultimate nonlinear
thinking tool,** the human brain.
No matter how difficult or unprecedented
the problem, a breakthrough to
the best possible solution
can come only from a combination of rational
analysis based on the real nature of things,
and imaginative reintegration
of all the different items into a new pattern,
using **nonlinear brain power.**"*

TACTICS, STRATEGIES & OBJECTIVES.

Strategists ask, "What should I do?"

Tacticians ask, "What *can* I do?"

The strategist is concerned with consistency and payout over the long haul.

The tactician is concerned with effectiveness and short-term results.

Sometimes the tactics available to you can determine what strategies and objectives are possible.

Marketing Warfare and *Bottom-Up Marketing* by Trout and Reis are good sources for examining this "bottom-up" way of thinking.

Sometimes, tactics can help you discover the best strategy. As mentioned, Hal Riney says, *"I don't know what the Strategy should be till I do the creative."*

Below is Kenichi Ohmae's graphic description of strategic thinking.

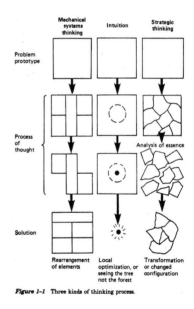

Figure 1-1 Three kinds of thinking process.

From The Mind of The Strategist *by Kenichi Ohmae. (A great book!)*

139

That's how Helmut Krone, the DDB Art
Director, described himself to us.
  He is.
  He's one heck of a strategist.
  And it's one of the main reasons his
ads worked so well.
  It's more than fine design.
  It's strategy.

A Strategy is
- Simple
- Clear in Intent
- Contains no executional
  elements.

THE PROCESS OF STRATEGIC DEVELOPMENT

can be complex. Yet, its essence is simple.

Simply put, an Advertising Strategy answers the question, *"How do you sell the thing?"*

A successful copywriter is a successful salesperson.

And, to survive in the complex world of an advertising agency, you *must* become involved in developing, understanding, and *selling* strategy.

Strategies are instinctive to good salesmen.

"That suit looks good on you."

"You're going to love this restaurant..."

"An offer you can't refuse."

P&G defines it this way...

*"Advertising Strategy is that portion of a
brand's marketing strategy which deals with
advertising copy.*

*It is a statement which identifies the basis
upon which we expect consumers to purchase
our product in preference to competition."*

A successful strategy must have the potential to persuade. Remember Bernbach:

*"Advertising is fundamentally **persuasion.**"*

Your strategy must be able to generate movement in the marketplace. It must *sell*.

THE P&G COPY STRATEGY MEMO.

On the following page is a copy of a memo which outlines the basic thinking on Copy Strategy that is taught to trainees at P&G and to people who work for their many ad agencies.

Those who leave P&G for other jobs take these lessons with them, as do agency people who work on their business.

This memo has become a standard industry view on the topic of Copy Strategy.

Copy Strategy.

A copy strategy is a document which identifies the basis upon which we expect consumers to purchase our brand in preference to competition. It is the part of the marketing strategy which deals with advertising copy.

The fundamental content of a copy strategy emerges directly from the product, and the basic consumer need which the product was designed to fulfill.

A copy strategy should state clearly the basic benefit which the brand promises and which constitutes the principal basis for purchase.

While not mandatory, the strategy may also include:

- A statement of the product characteristic which makes this basic benefit possible.

- A statement of the character we want to build for the brand over time.

PURPOSE OF A COPY STRATEGY.

Copy strategy provides guidance and direction for a brand's advertising. It should be a long-term document, not subject to judgment changes.

The copy strategy provides guidance and direction for the agency's creative people. It prescribes the limits within which an agency is to exercise its creative imagination, while being flexible enough to allow latitude for fresh and varied executions.

The copy strategy provides a common basis upon which to evaluate and discuss merits of an advertising submission in terms of intent and idea content.

A clear copy strategy can save a great deal of creative time and energy, because it identifies those basic decisions which we do not intend to review and rethink each time we look at a new piece of advertising.

CHARACTERISTICS OF A GOOD COPY STRATEGY.

Here are some things which characterize a good strategy statement:

- **It's clear.**

The basis upon which the consumer is being asked to buy our brand in preference to others should be quite clear to everyone involved.

- **It's simple.**

Key here is that the number of ideas in the strategy be kept to a minimum.

- **It's devoid of executional considerations.**

The copy strategy identifies *what* benefits we are to present to consumers, avoiding executional issues which deal with *how* these benefits are to be presented.

-**It's inherently competitive.**

The copy strategy should provide the answer to the question "Why should I buy this product rather than some other?"

How to Write a Strategy.

THE PURPOSE of this section is to show you a basic format for writing an Advertising Strategy.

We can't tell you how to write the *right* strategy, but we can tell you how to write one that:

1. makes sense
2. is written in a format that will be clear to everyone who reads it.

Writing strategies takes practice.

The more you do it, the better you'll get.

Just being aware of strategies that worked (and failed) in the past can be a big help.

It also helps to work with good people – developing a Strategy is usually *a team effort:* research, account management, clients, creatives, even consumers (in the form of focus groups or account planners) can be a part of that team.

As a mental process, it involves logical analysis, intuitive thinking, high-minded hypothesizing, and tough-minded negotiation.

And even though it's often complicated and frustrating, developing a strategy can be tremendously exciting and satisfying – as you work with others to shape the future of a business.

Let's get started.

SOME COMMENTS ON CONVENTIONAL WISDOM ABOUT STRATEGIES.

It is generally believed that…

1. Strong strategies = strong tactics.
This is probably true.

But what if your strategy is *not* getting you strong, motivating communications that are meaningful to the consumer?

- Perhaps the people creating the tactics aren't good enough.
- Or, perhaps, the strategy itself is not inherently persuasive.

If a strategy is strong, you *should* be looking at a wide variety of persuasive communications based on that strategy.

If you're not, it's not unreasonable to conclude that you should be taking another look at the strategy as well as the people who are executing it.

2. A mediocre execution of a correct strategy is better than an excellent execution of an incorrect strategy.

Sure, but, again, there are limits to what is generally accepted to be true.

For example, a commercial that makes fun of your Target Customer probably won't work very well – no matter how on-strategy it might be.

Concurrently, some alternate strategies may be just as persuasive (i.e., "as correct") as the recommended strategy.

In this case, all bets are off.

On-Strategy or Off-Target?
Remember this clever visual? It tells its target (people who eat Kentucky Fried Chicken) that they're "Bucket Heads." It's on-strategy, but how persuasive do you think it is?

THERE ARE NUMEROUS FORMATS for writing an Advertising Strategy.

We'll cover others at the end of this chapter, and your instructor may want you to use a different format. Don't worry.

As you will discover, they have common characteristics.

The one we'll start with is a simple format that was used for years by clients and agencies such as P&G and Leo Burnett. It has three parts:

1. AN OBJECTIVE STATEMENT.

The Objective is stated *within* this first section of the Strategy. It identifies the brand's Target Customer and states the Objective, which is usually (but not always communicating a meaningful Benefit.

2. A SUPPORT STATEMENT.

This indicates the support you will use to "prove" your benefit. It may be a "reason why" for that benefit, or it may be something else.

3. A STATEMENT OF TONE OR "BRAND CHARACTER."

This may describe the desired "selling attitude" of the advertising or the long-term values of the brand. It looks like this.

**Advertising will [verb]
[Target Customer] that [Product/Brand]
is/will/provides
[Statement of Benefit].**

Support will be [Support/Reason Why].

**Tone will be
["Selling Attitude" Adjectives].**

– or –

**[Brand] is
[Description of "Brand Character."]**

> Advertising Strategy is that portion of a brand's marketing strategy which deals with advertising copy. It is a statement which identifies the basis upon which we expect consumers to purchase our product in preference to competition.

P&G says a strategy "customarily contains the following information."

1. A statement of the basic benefit which the product promises and which constitutes the principal basis for purchase of the brand.

2. A statement of the product characteristic which makes it possible for the product to deliver this basic benefit.

3. A statement of the character we strive to build for the product.

STRATEGY FORMATS.

This section contains a number of commonly used advertising strategy formats in addition to this one.

You'll find them at the end of this chapter. They are:

- **The Y&R Creative Work Plan**
- **GE Focus System**
- **Leo Burnett Strategy Worksheet**
- **DDB ROI System**
- **Creative Action Plan**
- **Creative Briefs**
- **Blueprints and Backgrounders**

Finally, there's an IMC Strategy Discussion. We'll talk about how to develop strategies for The MarCom Matrix.

1. Objective Statement.

The Objective of Energizer's Pink Bunny advertising was to establish leadership in the generic category benefit of durability by out-executing the competitive brand – DuraCell.

OUR ADVERTISING OBJECTIVE STATEMENT starts simply: **"Advertising will…"**

Obviously, it will *do* something. We need a verb.

"Convince," "persuade," and "communicate" are the verbs most commonly used.

"Remind" has also been used. For example, "Put a Jell-O out tonight" was a Reminder Strategy.

We prefer "convince." It demonstrates confidence and reminds us that we are talking about *persuasion,* something that will occur inside the consumer's mind.

PART ONE. TARGET CUSTOMER.

Next, the Strategy defines who we're talking to…the Target Customer. Hopefully, this will be more than a simple statement of demographics.

"Women 18 to 45" may be correct, but "mothers" or "traditional homemakers" may be closer to a real description of your target.

"Usage" is another good way to describe your target.

It's often helpful to include some phrase describing the type of person you're targeting.

Remember, you're talking to a *person,* a real person. Describe that person.

Your description may be qualitative (taste-oriented, price-conscious, etc.) or quantitative (18-45, A&B Counties, etc.). Or both.

It may be broad, it may be narrow, but try to give your target a *dimension.* Look for important characteristics that your Target Customers have in common.

Even broadly based products have targets that can be described with insight.

Y&R places great emphasis on this – they call it "Prospect Definition." They believe it's critical to understand what's important to consumers.

STEP BY STEP: ARCHWAY "GOOD FOOD COOKIE" ADVERTISING STRATEGY.

Background: In the early '80s, Archway Cookies, a small national brand, was caught up in "The Cookie Wars."

Large marketers, such as Frito-Lay and P&G, entered the cookie category while Nabisco and Keebler defended their positions aggressively.

Archway moved to a strategy based on a niche position.

While other cookie companies competed with chocolate chip and other chocolate varieties, Archway developed a strategy based on the brand's strength in *oatmeal-based* cookies.

"FOR YEARS I HID MY INTELLIGENCE SO GUYS WOULD LIKE ME. THEN I NOTICED THE ONLY GUYS WHO LIKED ME WERE STUPID."

Insight into your target is critical for developing effective communication. Here, a magazine uses that insight to communicate to their target customers – advertising executives.

They believe prospects should be defined in terms of: product usage, demographics, and psychographics (lifestyles, attitudes, etc.)

Often, simple descriptions of the target are backed with additional in-depth information.

For example, your strategy may refer simply to *"men who drink premium beer."* This will be backed with additional information – such as attitudes toward sports, women, and their job.

Broadly defined targets may have important subgroups described in support material.

Here are some typical examples:

Women who wash confidently in all temperatures.
Working mothers.
Fashion-conscious women, 18-35.
Young adults concerned about nutrition.
Adults who wear eyeglasses.

Now, add the name of your product.

That should be easy.

So far, your strategy reads

"Advertising will [convince]
[Target Customer] that [Product]
is/will/provides…

Now it gets tough.

ARCHWAY COOKIES
OBJECTIVE STATEMENT.
Part One. Target Customer.
Advertising will convince
adults who eat cookies…

Though much cookie consumption is by children, Archway is basically an adult product.

This was supported by a wide range of market research as well as focus groups that addressed this specific issue.

A key question – were adults naturally "migrating" to the brand, or was Archway an "old" brand with an eroding customer base.

Research focused on this key issue. The answer – adults naturally "discovered" Archway Cookies as they looked for something "more homemade" and less sweet.

Additional barriers were discovered to increased consumption by children, such as cost per cookie.

Information about Archway purchasing habits, which skewed older and female, was used to assist in media selection.

A decision was made to advertise both to older consumers, who were the most loyal Archway customers, and to younger adults who were migrating into Archway's market.

**ARCHWAY COOKIES
OBJECTIVE STATEMENT**
Part Two. Benefit.
*...that Archway Oatmeal
Cookies are uniquely
nutritious and delicious.*
Strategy is about choice.

Archway's major strategic decision was to focus mainly on their popular oatmeal cookies.

Rather than advertise the whole line, the decision was made to focus on oatmeal-based varieties (over 30% of sales).

The benefit was actually based on an Attribute – oatmeal.

Oatmeal naturally has good nutritional characteristics and, even more important, a wholesome, positive image with our target consumers.

The decision was made not to overstate "healthy" aspects, but rather to depend on the inherent "good nutrition" of oatmeal – this was a unique claim in the category.

Taste was added to the benefit claim to remind everyone that we were talking about cookies, but was a secondary part of the benefit statement since it was generic – cookies taste good.

PART TWO. BENEFIT STATEMENT.

So, what is the Objective? The Advertising Objective.

What is the movement within the consumer's attitude or awareness which, if accomplished, will result in meeting your Marketing Objective (usually selling more product) and turning a Target *Consumer* into a Target *Customer.*

Sometimes, in the case of products with a clear dimension of difference, it's communicating product *superiority* in a persuasive fashion.

It might be a general (or generic) superiority or it may be superiority with a specific dimension of product performance.

Very often, your objective will be communicating some form of superiority, uniqueness, or differentiation in a convincing way. This dimension of superiority should be meaningful in terms of purchase behavior.

The movement may be psychological – such as "confidence" or "satisfaction."

It might be tangible – "feels soft" or "tastes terrific!"

Your product might be:
- Easier – Convenience Strategy
- Cheaper – Economy Strategy
- Better quality for the price – Value Strategy

Your product might be a service, or a combination of product and service, which adds other dimensions.

Sometimes it's rational, sometimes it's emotional – every time it's important.

A key consideration is that it be *meaningful* – again, a *"factor that influences purchase behavior."*

Many well-supported strategies have failed because, when you got right down to it, the difference was not meaningful to the consumer – or not worth it.

Either it wasn't important enough, or it wasn't worth the extra price (products that do more often cost more).

Ask this question – What is it we want the person to believe or feel about our product or service?

And, will that be enough to move them toward a purchase decision? Here's an example for Cascade:

**"Advertising will convince
automatic dishwasher owners
that Cascade provides
virtually spotless end results."**

This is a clear statement of what they want their advertising to communicate.

In this case, their Objective is communicating the benefit of "virtually spotless end results."

The movement in the consumer's mind is increasing conviction that Cascade delivers in this dimension of product performance.

The word "virtually" clearly communicates that neither the advertising nor Cascade can promise or deliver *completely* spotless results.

If you have a clear idea of the movement in the consumer's mind you wish to achieve, you understand the Objective.

In the case of products without dramatic differences or with multiple benefits, this might not be as clear. (A common strategic problem.)

Once you've developed your Objective or Benefit Statement, your strategy reads

**"Advertising will [convince]
[Target Customer] that [Product]
is/will /provides
[Objective/Benefit]."**

You've just finished the first section of the Strategy.

A simple statement that sets out the mission to be accomplished by your advertising.

But saying it isn't enough. You need help.

"Support will be…"

DISCOVER THE BENEFIT.

In general, you will want to discover the benefit a consumer derives from the product.

You may wish to ask yourself these questions:

1. Is it a Product Benefit?
   i.e., "spotless end results"

2. Or is it a Consumer Benefit?
   i.e., "I'm a good homemaker"

3. Or is it both?
   i.e., *"cleans down to the shine and isn't that a nice reflection on you?"*

A statement of the basic benefit which the product promises consumers and which constitutes the principal basis for purchase of that brand.

147

2. Support Statement.

THE SECOND SECTION OF THE STRATEGY begins **"Support will be…"**

Generally, Support is the *reason* you can provide the benefit mentioned in the Objective Statement.

For example...

"Virtually spotless end results will be attributed to the sheeting action produced by the Cascade formula."

The Objective is communicating the benefit, which is the reason for buying Cascade.

Support is the *reason* you provide the benefit.

Sometimes this is clear and simple – Cascade's "sheeting action" is a reason why.

And sometimes it isn't simple at all.

Many ambitious strategies have failed because of an unrealistic attitude toward this critical issue, promising more than they could deliver. Others failed to prove what they promised to skeptical consumers.

Still others priced themselves higher than people were willing to pay.

The Strategy may have sounded great in the meeting but could not be made into effective advertising.

LINKAGE.

Finally, Support and Objective are *linked.*

What can you deliver as Support for your benefit? The link may be logical – like Cascade's sheeting action.

Or the linkage may be an effort of imagination and determination – like Marlboro becoming linked to the imagery of Marlboro Country.

One important concern is establishing *linkage* throughout the strategy.

This means you must *link* an Objective that can be accomplished with Support that can be delivered.

ARCHWAY COOKIES SUPPORT STATEMENT

Support was based on the inherent nutritional characteristics of oatmeal cookies with additional emphasis on other emerging health concerns – such as palm oil.

A low-calorie claim was added later ("ounce-for-ounce lower in calories than most other cookies in your store.")

Archway's other varieties were used as further support for Archway uniqueness.

Support will be:
Archway Cookies are made with nutritious oatmeal,
Archway Oatmeal Cookies are naturally low in sodium and fat – they contain No Palm Oil.
Archway has many unique varieties.

Longer ads, like 60" radio spots, and package copy went deeper into the Support section.

Shorter ads, like in-store posters, concentrated on the first points.

Whether your Support is a product-based fact or pure imagination and attitude, these two parts of your Strategy must be well-connected.

Here are some of the common issues related to developing Support.

PRODUCT BENEFIT VS. CONSUMER BENEFIT.

One of the most common debates in advertising strategy development revolves around this issue.

When the strategy features a Consumer Benefit (you're a good mother), the support is often a Product Benefit ('cause you serve your children tasty and nutritious…)

The discussion goes something like this…

Is the Objective communicating a Consumer Benefit (or Value) with the Product Benefit as the Support ("You're a Good Mother because you serve Yum Nut Peanut Butter to your kids.")?

Or, should we communicate the Product Benefit with a reason why as the Support ("Yum Nut tastes better because it's made with more nuts.")?

Strategically, this is a good question. And a good case can often be made for both sides of the argument.

Remember P&G's theme for Jif Peanut Butter?

It's "Choosy Mothers Choose Jif." Then, they gave some sort of "more peanuts" reason why as support.

CAN YOU COMMUNICATE IT ALL?

Can you communicate consumer and product benefits and reason why?

Sure you can.

But you may need a longer format – like this magazine ad for Parker Pen.

Product Benefit as Support for Consumer Benefit.

Great manufacturing is the reason why. Great writing is the benefit.

LOOKING FOR SUPPORT?

Often, while discovering the Objective, material for Support has been generated in the process:

- Product Facts
- Product Benefits
- Consumer Needs
- Consumer Benefits
- Competitive Advantages
- Positioning Opportunities
- Whatever It Takes to Solve The Problem

149

It's Better. See!

The P&G Philosophy.
Better Products. Strong Strategies. And, if possible, *Visual Demonstration* of Benefit or Superiority.

"The key to successful marketing is superior product performance.

If the consumer does not perceive any real benefits in the brand, then no amount of ingenious advertising and selling can save the brand."

Ed Harness
Former P & G Chairman

Consumer Benefits are generally regarded as strategically superior – yet, in one survey done by Y&R, TV commercials that focused on product Attributes or benefits were judged more effective and distinctive.

The only thing certain is that this will continue to be the subject of strategic discussion.

FEATURES AND ATTRIBUTES.

Product Benefits may also be called Features.

We usually think of a Feature as a reason why for a benefit. (Are you following this? Let it settle in, feel how they're all connected on the ladder.)

Finally, an Attribute is just sort of a generic quality of the product – peanut butter is made from peanuts. Though this doesn't mean you can't leverage that fact into some meaningful communication.

Peanut butter is made from peanuts. Certain types of candy bars contain peanuts. People who buy these products like peanuts.

So you might find a way of dramatizing this attribute, and it could be a key part of your strategy.

TYPES OF SUPPORT.

Here are some different types of support statement:
Reason Why.

This type of support is often a product fact, such as Cascade's sheeting action. Classic package goods strategies try to provide a logical reason why.

As P&G would say, *"A statement of the product characteristic which makes it possible for the product to deliver this basic benefit."*

P&G brands are based on superior product performance supported by an extraordinary commitment to marketing superior products.

This is not always possible.

Many products compete in areas where there is no specific "reason why." Or, where the reason why is either not motivating or "ownable."

A statement of the product characteristic which makes it possible for the product to deliver this basic benefit.

A "Reason Why." Support Statement.

For example, in the floor wax and floor cleaner category, it's hard to really own clean shiny floors. If this is the case, you have to look for another type of linkage.

Combinations.

Sometimes a *combination* of facts can support a single and specific benefit.

> **"Support is that Special K is
> low in calories and sugar,
> high in protein."**

These two characteristics combined help support Special K's "healthy weight loss" benefit.

It's common to link two Product Benefits to create a Consumer Benefit or a larger Product Benefit. Here are three examples:

A. The Value equation links quality and price.

Price/Quality = Value

B. Liquid laundry detergents combine special cleaning properties (removal of stains or collar soil) with general cleaning effectiveness to build their position.

C. Convenience plus good taste is a common combination for many prepared foods. Yet, the benefit is relatively single-minded ("Easy to serve a great tasting meal.")

Permission to Believe and Nine-Wheel Logic.

This is a subtler type of support – the logic is trickier. 9-Lives tasting good enough for finicky Morris lets you believe the products perform as advertised.

You're caught up in the story, and there's something about Morris that reminds you of your cat, so you give the advertiser "permission" to make the claim.

You know it's not the shoes, but you like the TV spot and the style of the shoes and you extend that permission to yourself.

For example, sometimes color or some visual cue is added to products to visualize a colorless technical improvement. (See the "Nine Wheel Logic" sidebar.)

Combined Support *(low fat and high taste) lets Subway deliver the Consumer Benefit of weight reduction.*

NINE WHEEL LOGIC.

Here's how the story goes.

You're standing by the railroad tracks with your small son and a steam locomotive goes chugging by. (It's an old story.)

Your son asks, "Why does that big train go so fast?"

Well, you can't really explain how a locomotive works, and even if you could, a little boy wouldn't understand and doesn't really care. So you say, "Look at all the wheels."

And that's a good answer. One thing – the wheels – symbolizes something else – the power of the locomotive.

See what we're getting at?

You can't explain the new detergent formula in the time allowed, and even if you could, who would listen. So you put "green power crystals" in the otherwise colorless detergent formula and you can communicate quickly and clearly, and everyone "gets it."

And that's Nine-Wheel Logic.

Altoids. *Nine-Wheel Logic at work.*

Is that all I am to you, a "Reason Why?" Or am I "Permission to Believe?" It's hard to know sometimes. I like to think of myself as "Inherent Drama."

Imagery at Work. *Marlboro's ownership of the West is now so complete that even small pieces can communicate the entire range of imagery. Here, a graphic variation for a flanker brand.*

The Keebler Elves. *They're cute and entertaining, and we give them our "permission." And they keep going...*

Image.

Here, Support is almost ephemeral. At the same time, the linkage may be quite powerful.

Objective and Support are often linked by imagination, artistry, and ad budgets.

The linkage between Marlboro and the imagery of Marlboro Country is an act of will supported by heavy media expenditures. The heritage of the name is of English nobility – it's not Western at all.

The "lifestyle" imagery of many campaigns, seeks to place the product in a certain type of environment with certain types of people.

Fashion advertising does not try to persuade you by talking about the fabric or their unique stitching process, but by projecting a look (visual support) and an attitude. And maybe someone famous.

Some aspects of image may be based on a brand's long-term heritage. And that heritage may contain its own "permission to believe."

Years ago, I saw the very first Keebler Cookie commercials presented. I said, "Are they kidding?" Years later, you sort of nod your head and accept it.

We don't really believe Keebler Cookies are made by elves in hollow trees, but we give them permission, and as we do it, we buy into the image of the brand.

The result of those feelings and attitudes on the part of consumers can be substantial. It can be as strong and powerful as a logical "reason why."

GENERIC BENEFIT. UNIQUE SUPPORT.

In theory, the more unique and distinctive your Support, the more it will be Support for your Product. The benefit may be generic, but with unique Support (a unique proposition, visual support, or other inherent drama) it can be a unique construct.

Or, as The Pink Bunny demonstrates, perhaps it is the uniqueness of your advertising that does it.

As Rosser Reeves' USP clearly states, your Support should be "unique."

"The proposition must be one that the competition either cannot or does not offer.

*It must be **unique** – either a uniqueness of the brand or a claim not otherwise made in that particular field of advertising."*

That's the theory. In reality, many successful brands manage to reinforce their leadership and dominate by staking claim to a generic benefit supported by a generic attribute – one common to the category.

Many dominant brands have established strong positions with generic benefits.

This is the modern version of Claude Hopkins' pre-emption, Rosser Reeves' USP, and Leo Burnett's inherent drama.

One of the key issues in developing a winning strategy is determining what benefit position you can establish and how you can support it.

LINKING LOGIC AND EMOTION.

Remember The FCB Grid a few chapters ago?

In many cases, there is both emotional and logical support for your brand.

Have you heard the radio commercials for Motel 6? The advertising combines the emotional aspect of being a "smart shopper" and a "frugal American" with the facts of Motel 6's low prices.

Done right, they can even turn a lack of Features (no mint on your pillow) into a Benefit.

This link of logic and emotion can happen anywhere in a strategy and in the development process.

The emotional benefit of your family's safety, which the tires cannot guarantee, can have the logical support of the construction of the tires.

And the proof of the tire's quality? The high price!

A little radial tire logic, I guess.

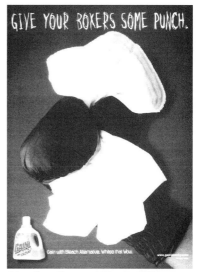

Bleach as Reason Why for Whiteness. *A strong brand like Tide can often have good results with a fairly generic claim. A smaller brand like Gain will not get the same punch – even if the ad is quite nice.*

Target Customer as Support. *This is a common Positioning Strategy. Do you see the linkage here?*

A strong benefit delivered with a sweet yet powerful visual. See how the various aspects of tire purchase are linked?

*The theme was "Everything You Always
Wanted in a Beer. And less."*

LOOK FOR MORE LINKAGE.

To strengthen your Strategy further, it is often helpful to establish *additional linkage* between the Benefit and the Target.

For example, "Less Filling" was a benefit that appealed to Lite Beer's Target – the heavy beer drinker. So did the visual support – ex-jocks who enjoyed it.

Like a good ad, a solid Strategy *resonates.*

All of the elements work together to build the sale.

DOES IT ADD UP TO A PROPOSITION?

Here are some further considerations:

Is Support Single-Minded?

A laundry list of attributes is not Support. Support in a Strategy should reinforce a single-minded path to the Objective.

Multiple Benefit Strategies (i.e., "Tastes better/ Costs less") must be clearly superior to those that focus on a single benefit.

However, by *linking* two pieces of Support, it is sometimes possible to achieve a single-minded benefit. (Remember the Subway ad a few pages ago?)

Is Your Support Clear?

When you read the Strategy, do you understand *why* a person should buy this product?

Does it make sense? Does it seem important?

And finally… **Does It Feel Like You Can Sell the Product with It?**

After all, sooner or later, you've got to write an ad. Will your Support support you?

This may seem like an obvious question, but the "presold" nature of the people writing strategies often makes them more eager to be persuaded than the consumers to whom they'll be advertising.

If your Support is supportable, write it down.

(If it isn't, keep working.)

Now your strategy will read:

Advertising will [convince] [Target Customer] that [Product] is/will/provides [Objective/Benefit].

Support will be [Support].

That's what you say.

Tone is how you say it.

Reason Why Support.
Product performance as Support for a Consumer Benefit. "No Cavities!"

Ultimate. "The Ultimate Driving Machine" was basically a Product Benefit supported by the design and "road feel" of BMWs.

ARCHWAY COOKIES OBJECTIVE & SUPPORT.

Most often, communicating a benefit will be your Objective.

In the Archway strategy, oatmeal implied a nutrition benefit that was unique to the cookie category. Note the ways in which the first two statements are *linked*.

Advertising will convince adults who eat cookies that Archway Oatmeal Cookies are uniquely delicious and nutritious.
Support will be:
Archway Cookies are made with nutritious oatmeal.
Archway Cookies are naturally low in sodium and fat – they contain no Palm Oil.
Archway has many unique varieties.

Even *unique* is used as linkage. Unique varieties can be Support for unique taste (uniquely delicious).

This is not an accident. When opportunities arose related to their popular Ginger Snaps, the strategy could accomodate it.

155

3. The Tone or Brand Character Statement.

YOUR STRATEGY MAY ALSO HAVE a third part – a Tone or Brand Character Statement.

Over the years, there has been a movement away from "Tone" or "Tone and Manner" Statements, which describe the character of the advertising, toward statements which describe the character of the brand – *"long-term brand values."*

This is particularly true with clients such as P&G, who view Advertising Strategies as long-term documents which, ideally, should last a number of years.

Over that period of time, P&G believes that while the *tone* of the advertising may vary, the *values* represented by the brand should remain constant.

WHEN TO USE A TONE STATEMENT.

There are many cases where a Tone Statement can be a very helpful addition to the Strategy.

Many clients are not P&G, and if the advertising isn't "working," your Advertising Strategy may be in a more or less constant state of revision.

In these cases, Tone Statements can be very helpful as you work to get the strategy right.

Tone Statements can be a place for additional insights into the Target or as a description of the best advertising style for the product category.

In situations where you are trying to reposition a brand, reach consumers in a new way, go after a new target, or deal with a "rejector base" (former customers who no longer purchase your brand), "long-term brand values" may actually be a hindrance and a Tone Statement more helpful.

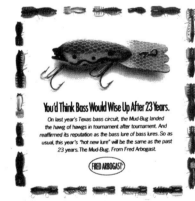

You'd Think Bass Would Wise Up After 23 Years.

On last year's Texas bass circuit, the Mud-Bug landed the hawg of hawgs in tournament after tournament. And reaffirmed its reputation as the bass lure of bass lures. So as usual, this year's "hot new lure" will be the same as the past 23 years. The Mud-Bug. From Fred Arbogast.

(FRED ARBOGAST)

The Right Tone.
The Right Brand Character.
This award-winning advertising has the right tone for its target – men who fish. It also strengthens the Brand Character.

Whether you use a Tone or Brand Character Statement, your ads should do both jobs well.

WHEN TO USE A BRAND CHARACTER STATEMENT.

Currently, Brand Character Statements are preferred by major marketers and agencies.

As virtually every company has placed increased emphasis on the long-term value of their brands, a statement which addresses the issue of "what is our brand's equity?" is increasingly important.

For flanker brands, there may be a Brand Character Statement based on some variation of values of the "mother" brand. Or, more likely, a single Brand Character Statement will be the standard for all.

When your brand advertises to diverse groups, a Brand Character Statement can help focus on values that endure across groups.

By the way, when writing a Brand Character Statement, be patient – developing one that everyone can agree on may take a little time.

Even though a number of people may *feel* the same way about a brand, they may express it differently.

Brand Character Statements can be tough to write, and Tone Statements are relatively easy.

In summary…

Tone Statements are short-term and about the Advertising.

Brand Character Statements are long-term and about the Brand.

You should learn to write both.
We'll start with the Tone Statement.

MORE ON TONE VS. BRAND CHARACTER…

I like Tone Statements for the same reason P&G *does not* like them – they are "about the advertising."

After all, this is an Advertising Strategy we're writing.

I've found that Tone Statements can offer an important opportunity for people to talk about how they think the advertising should "feel" just as you're getting ready to create it.

This can be important input during creative development and a helpful reference frame when the advertising is presented.

That's why, as a practical matter, Tone Statements can be very helpful.

157

DEVELOPING THE ARCHWAY TONE STATEMENT.

The Tone Statement was used to define the way Archway Cookies should be advertised. They were not vitamins or a nutritional supplement – they were cookies, a dessert and snack item eaten for enjoyment.

Within that context, Archway wanted to identify with good nutritional habits.

Here's how it worked out…

ARCHWAY COOKIES TONE STATEMENT.

*Tone will combine
the importance of good nutrition
with the fun of cookies.*

A major internal concern was that we didn't forget that cookies taste good and are fun – that's why people buy them.

In this regard, the Archway Tone Statement related to their Objective Statement.

It also clearly signalled that commercials should have entertainment value – not just nutritional value.

The Tone Statement.

The Tone Statement can begin simply,
"Tone will be…"

Tone is the *how* of the Strategy. It is the key to the type of advertising you will create. A key strategic question in developing the Tone Statement…

"How will you relate to your target?"

The Tone of your Strategy will be the first step in determining the style of your advertising.

More from Bernbach:

"Great execution becomes content.

It brings what you have to say to the eyes and ears of your audience believably and persuasively."

For a period of time, DDB strategies contained what they termed a "Tone and Manner" Statement.

The right Tone will help put you on the right track to great execution.

Stating the desired Tone will be based on your knowledge of your product, how to talk to your target, and the competitive environment.

Sound familiar? It's the Strategic Triad – only this time it's about feeling and attitude.

The Tone Statement functions as a right-brain/emotional description of your Strategy.

Here are two examples:

**Tone will convey the spicy fun
of Popeyes' New Orleans heritage.**

(Popeyes Famous Fried Chicken, '81-83)

**Tone will be compatible with today's competitive
fast-food environment.**

(Popeyes Famous Fried Chicken, '85-'87)

The change was a result of a change in the competitive environment (other spicy chicken products).

In retrospect, Popeyes may have overreacted – but it's hard to know that when it's happening and your biggest competitor is coming at you.

158

A good Tone Statement is a guide for how to talk to your target. The descriptions in your Tone Statement should be *meaningful* to your target and helpful to the people creating and judging the advertising.

In addition, it's not uncommon to revise that Tone section as you find out more about how to talk to your target. Often, the facts of an Advertising Strategy are right before the feelings are.

And sometimes the "feel" of the marketplace can change, while everything else – like your product your benefits, and your support – remain the same. (That's what happened to Popeyes.)

While not executional, the Tone Statement helps guide the execution in the proper direction, and it indicates the type of communication which, on judgment, the target will respond to.

Once you've completed your Tone Statement, your Strategy is written.

It reads…

> **"Advertising will [convince] [Target Customer] that [Product] is/will [Objective].**
>
> **Support will be [Support].**
>
> **Tone will be ["Selling Attitude" Adjectives]."**

And that's how a complete Advertising Strategy looks when you use a Tone Statement.

Now let's talk about the alternative…

SOME EXAMPLES OF TONE STATEMENTS:

Tone will reflect the fun of the pizza-eating experience.

Tone will be fashion-conscious and "state of the art."

Tone will be intrusive and bring excitement to a major improvement in a low-interest category.

This Brand is a Character. *What do you think the Tone Statement might have been for Slim Jim? Here, where the brand has been personified, Brand Character Statements become even more important.*

A statement of the character we strive to build for the product.

The Brand Character Statement.

Clients such as P&G and agencies like Y&R do not believe in Tone Statements.

Y&R says, *"As usually written they are meaningless. If the rest of the Strategy is clear, they are unnecessary."*

At Y&R, they address this issue with something they call the Prospect Definition, which treats the target in depth. (We'll cover the Y&R Creative Work Plan in an Addendum which follows.)

At P&G, they've evolved to what they call Brand Character Statements, which describe the enduring values of their brands – these values are viewed as an important part of a brand's equity in the marketplace.

Here are some Brand Character Statements for a few familiar brands:

Crest is the dedicated leader in improving dental health for the family.

Coast is a product that is exhilarating to use.

Pampers – pre-eminent reputation as the leader in baby care… a warm and affectionate attitude toward babies.

Camay – the soap of beautiful women.

These statements describe the "enduring values," "long-term values," or "core values" of the brands.

Little Characters for some Brand Character. *Kids eat a lot of Oscar Mayer products, and little kids are a big part of the Oscar Mayer brand character.*

ARCHWAY COOKIES BRAND CHARACTER.

"The Good Food Cookie."
This positioning line was also their Brand Character Statement.

In developing a Brand Character Statement, review all the relevant aspects of the brand history: packaging, graphics, target customer values – everything you can think of.

Then, distill it to its essence.

Try to describe the brand as you would a person – look for the adjectives and phrases that best personify the brand. What does your brand stand for?

Within all this information you should find the elements you need.

Brand Character Statements can begin, *"The Character of the Brand will be seen to be"* or in whatever way seems appropriate.

As you can see by the previous statements, they may simple start, **[Product] is…**

Remember, this is a long-term document.

Don't worry if it takes a while.

And don't worry if you have to revise it a few times till you finally get it right.

And (instead of a Tone Statement), this is the third element of your Advertising Strategy.

Now your strategy reads…

> **"Advertising will [convince]**
> **[Target Customer] that [Product]**
> **is/will [Objective].**
>
> **Support will be [Support].**
>
> **[Product] is**
> **["Brand Character" Statement]."**

And that's an Advertising Strategy with a Brand Character Statement.

Now let's try writing a few.

STRATEGY READING LIST:
Some of the better books in this field.

The Marketing Imagination
Theodore Levitt/MacMillan

**Positioning &
Marketing Warfare**
Trout & Reis/McGraw Hill

**The Mind of The Strategist:
Business Planning for
Competitive Advantage**
Kenichi Ohmae
Penguin Business Library
(My personal favorite)

**The Y&R
Traveling Creative Workshop**
Hanley Norins/Prentice-Hall
(now out-of-print)

**The Making of
Effective Advertising**
Patti & Moriarty
Prentice Hall

**Planning for R.O.I.:
Effective Advertising Strategy**
Wells, William D/DDB Needham
Prentice-Hall

Planning for R.O.I. Workbook
Prentice-Hall

Also recommended:

Passion for Excellence
Peters & Austin/Harper & Row

Small Is Beautiful
E.F. Schumacher/Harper & Row

Further Up The Organization
Robert Townsend/Alfred A. Knopf

NEW PRODUCTS.
"A new product is a strategy brought to life."

Thinking up new products is good exercise for thinking up new strategies.

New products are usually developed with a specific Target Customer in mind offering a unique benefit – usually with a product-based reason why.

Its reason for being is usually a need in the marketplace. Let's try a few.

Here are some helpful hints:

- Focus on a problem that needs solving. Invent a product that solves it.
- Think of current trends and growing needs.
- Your best ideas may come from a familiar area.
- Your new "product" could also be a new service. Or a combination of product and service – like lawn care.
- A **good name** is most often one that *communicates the benefit.* A good name can also help make a new product successful.

For the moment, you can ignore
- Technology limitations
- Price considerations
- Size of the market (many new product ideas are developed for small and/or emerging markets)

By the way, in the real world, *80% of new products fail!*

So good luck.

Assignment #7:

1. INVENT A NEW PRODUCT.
- What is it?
- Who is your Target Customer?
- What is The Benefit?
- Is it a Product Benefit or a Consumer Benefit?
- What is Support for your Benefit?
- What problem does your product solve?
- What should the Tone be?
- What about Brand Character?
- What is the *name?* (It should describe your product in an appealing way.
- Does this suggest any advertising themes?

2. WRITE YOUR STRATEGY.
   Product Description:＿＿＿＿＿＿＿＿＿＿
＿＿＿＿＿＿＿＿＿＿＿＿＿＿＿＿＿＿＿＿

Brand Name: ＿＿＿＿＿＿＿＿＿＿＿＿＿

Advertising will ＿＿＿＿＿＿＿＿＿＿＿
＿＿＿＿＿＿＿＿＿＿＿＿＿＿＿ **that**
＿＿＿＿＿＿＿＿＿＿＿＿**is/will/provides**
＿＿＿＿＿＿＿＿＿＿＿＿＿＿＿＿＿＿.

Support will be ＿＿＿＿＿＿＿＿＿＿＿
＿＿＿＿＿＿＿＿＿＿＿＿＿＿＿＿＿＿.

Tone will be ＿＿＿＿＿＿＿＿＿＿＿＿
＿＿＿＿＿＿＿＿＿＿＿＿＿＿＿＿＿＿.

Brand Character is ＿＿＿＿＿＿＿＿＿
＿＿＿＿＿＿＿＿＿＿＿＿＿＿＿＿＿＿.

For fun, write an "on-strategy" advertising theme

＿＿＿＿＿＿＿＿＿＿＿＿＿＿＿＿＿＿.

Here's a New Product Based on an Old Product! Tom Brancky at Starkist realized that tuna could be convenience food. The result – a Tuna Salad Lunch Kit. Instant understanding by consumers and instant sales accelerated by engaging coupon ads like this, which combined established brand heritage with a brand new idea – that was already familiar!

Strategy Worksheet:

PRODUCT: _____

PRODUCT DESCRIPTION: _____

_____

_____

TARGET CUSTOMER: _____

_____

_____

PRODUCT BENEFIT(S): _____

_____

_____

CONSUMER BENEFIT(S): _____

_____

_____

SUPPORT: _____

_____

_____

TONE OF ADVERTISING: _____

_____

BRAND CHARACTER: _____

_____

ADVERTISING THEME IDEAS: _____

_____

_____

_____

MISC: _____

_____

ALTERNATE STRATEGIES.

These are the three major determinants for alternate Strategies:

- **Competition (Source of Business)**
- **Target Customer**
- **Message Selection (Benefit)**

Here are some examples:

Competition.

Stove Top Stuffing could have competed with all side dishes, but Stove Top decided to focus on the most popular side dish, which was the major "source of business," potatoes.

"Stove Top Stuffing, instead of potatoes" clearly defined the competition as it communicated the benefit – a nice change of pace.

Target Customer.

Many years ago, P&G advertised Jif Peanut Butter to kids.

After all, most peanut butter was consumed by kids, and they influenced similar purchases – like cereal.

However, P&G found the purchase was made by *mothers.* The result?

"Choosy Mothers Choose Jif."

Message Selection.

Attributes, Features, Product Benefits, Consumer Benefits, Values – a single product offers many choices.

Apple began advertising Macintosh as *"The computer for the rest of us."*

While appealing to many early Mac adopters, this "Against" positioning alienated many business people – a key market for Apple's Objectives.

BBDO's line, *"The power to be your best"* communicated to both targets.

Apple's current theme, *"Think different"* focuses on their creatively oriented target and also reflects the views of current management.

Assignment #8:

PICK AN EXISTING PRODUCT.

1. MAKE A LIST.

- Target options
- Benefit options
- Support options
- Tone options
- Brand Character options

2. WRITE YOUR "BEST BET" STRATEGY.

Advertising will _____

_____ **that**

_____ **is/will/provides**

_____.

Support will be _____

_____.

Tone will be _____

Brand Character is _____.

Advertising Theme:

_____

_____

3. WRITE A "NEXT BEST BET" STRATEGY.

Advertising will _____

_____ **that**

_____ **is/will**

_____.

Support will be _____

_____.

Tone will be _____

Brand Character is _____

Advertising Theme:

_____

Assignment #9:
Business Building Ideas.

GOOD IDEAS BUILD BUSINESS. Whether it's putting a box of Arm & Hammer Baking Soda in your refrigerator or making some Rice Krispies Treats, ideas like these can lead to powerful advertising.

YOUR ASSIGNMENT:

Have an idea that will build a company's business. Then, write an ad about it.

It might be:

* A new use for the product
* A new target for the product
* Something else

There are two requirements:

* Your idea should be for an existing product or service.
* Your idea should be one that generates "plus" business.

It's a simple assignment, but it's one that will help teach you to think about advertising problems in an important way – because everyone is looking for ideas that build business.

Having trouble picking a product?

Grab something close at hand.

Or have someone pick it for you.

Remember, in the real world, you have little control over assignments.

But here's a hint.

Products with the strongest benefit and the greatest competitive advantage usually generate the strongest strategies.

DUAL TARGETS AND SECONDARY BENEFITS.

Programs can often have more than one target. For example, many products have to communicate to the trade as well as the consumer.

After all, if it's not in the store, it doesn't matter how good the ad is.

And, a single product may have different customers who buy it for dramatically different reasons – an example, Apple Computers.

If you have dramatically different target groups, you may have to integrate more than one Strategy into the advertising process.

Remember, secondary targets can be of primary importance.

Here, Lee Jeans talks to the trade.

And it's a good fit.

FROM SECONDARY USAGE TO NEW PRODUCT.

Kellogg's discovered consumer familiarity with the Rice Krispies Treats recipe created a ready market for both a ready-to-eat cereal and a popular snack.

Notice how the ad also addresses a potential problem – people might think of it as dessert, not breakfast.

That's why secondary copy works to reassure mothers with a chart indicating "Less sugar than most kids' cereals."

CONVENIENCE STRATEGIES.

Convenience is becoming ever more important for "time-poor" consumers.

Convenience strategies generally focus on some factor of product usage and performance and related benefit.

Faster, easier, less mess, etc.

Support may be simple and single-minded (new formula), or more complex (new formula, new package with competitive performance results).

Pick a convenient product and write a strategy for it. You may also need a bit of "quality reassurance." But the communication should be simple.

After all, it's all about being easy.

SUPERIORITY STRATEGIES.

These focus on a dimension in which your product is better than something else.

It may be a competitor, your own previous product, or no product at all!

Support is often a reason why.

Take a product that you think is better (it might be more expensive) and write a strategy that proves it.

IMAGE STRATEGIES.

They're tough to write because the focus and benefit are less tangible.

The focus may be *attributes* (independent magazine for independent women).

The linkage may be *associative* (like a pop star and soda pop).

You can try to be *assumptive,* or *pre-emptive.* (Think of a brand that's acting like a leader without having to prove it.)

Sometimes, as in the case of much fashion advertising, it's pure *attitude.*

Pick a product you like in an image category and write a strategy for it.

Assignment #10:

1. CONVENIENCE STRATEGY.

Product: _____

Advertising will _____

_____ **that**

_____ **is/will/provides**

_____ .

Support will be _____

_____ .

Tone will be _____ .

2. SUPERIORITY STRATEGY.

Product: _____

Advertising will _____

_____ **that**

_____ **is/will/provides**

_____ .

Support will be _____

_____ .

Tone will be _____ .

3. IMAGE STRATEGY.

Product: _____

Advertising will _____

_____ **that**

_____ **is/will/provides**

_____ .

Support will be _____

_____ .

Tone will be _____ .

4. SERVICE STRATEGY.

(Bank, law firm, baby-sitter, shop by phone, etc.)

Service: _____

Advertising will _____
_____ **that**
_____ **is/will/provides**
_____ .

Support will be _____
_____ .

Tone will be _____ .

5. BASED ON YOUR STRATEGY, WRITE AT LEAST ONE THEME LINE FOR EACH OF YOUR PRODUCTS.

Convenience Product: _____
_____
_____
_____

Superiority Product: _____
_____
_____
_____

Image Product: _____
_____
_____
_____

Service/Name: _____
_____
_____

Service "Products:" _____
_____
_____

SERVICE STRATEGIES.

Services are a combination of tangibles and intangibles.

For example, a restaurant has both the tangibles of food and price and the intangibles of service and ambiance.

An airline sells you a seat. But the intangibles of efficiency, comfort, and feelings of safety are more important.

The ticket price is a tangible, but what is the convenience of the schedule?

Financial services offer a difficult combination. Most benefits (like "make you rich") cannot be claimed with certainty.

Financial services are both high-interest (it's your money, so you're interested) and dull (a lot of talk and numbers that are hard to understand, complicated by legal restrictions). This can make simple communication difficult.

Features like "friendly service" are hard to guarantee. Service, as Theodore Levitt points out in *The Marketing Imagination*, is *"generally only recognized in its absence."* People notice bad service, but they take good service for granted.

Your service may emphasize tangibles or intangibles. Or both.

Making Services Tangible. Here, a bank offers a specific product with a specific benefit.

In this short section, we'll briefly cover "Briefs" and other strategy documents.

Backgrounders, Blueprints, Briefs, & Work Plans.

THERE'S NO SINGLE "RIGHT" WAY to write an Advertising Strategy – though you will find most Strategy systems have a lot in common.

Let's look at a number of popular formats:

Y&R Creative Work Plan.

This classic system begins with four elements:

1. **A Statement of the Key Fact...**
based on an analysis of all pertinent facts.

2. **A Definition of the Problem...**
which the advertising must solve in light of this Key Fact. This is *"The Problem the Advertising Must Solve."* This should be a *consumer* problem and stated from the consumer point of view.

3. **The Advertising Objective.**
This stems from the Problem.
All of this information helps you develop...

4. **The Creative Strategy.**
In the Y&R system, the Strategy is *"designed to achieve the objective, which will solve the problem that the key fact has defined."* The Key Fact and the Problem are related.
For example, research might show that people think your product has an inferior taste, even if they haven't tried it. *The Problem the Advertising Must Solve* then becomes…
"Our brand has a poor taste reputation."
This would then relate to the Objective –
"To overcome our poor taste reputation with consumers."

WRITING THE WORK PLAN.

At Y&R, writing the Work Plan is the job of the Creative Director.

This may be one of the reasons for their exceptional record of unique, on-target work.

The Work Plan must be written before creative work begins. Its prime purpose is *"to set creative people free... in the right direction."*

The Young & Rubicam Traveling Creative Workshop
by Hanley Norins (Prentice-Hall)
A comprehensive presentation of the first great agency strategy system.

168

Y&R Creative Strategy.

The Strategy must include:

A. Prospect Definition.

This defines prospects in terms of:
- Product usage
- Demographics
- Psychographics

Sometimes, facts are not available. If that is the case, use an "educated guess."

B. Principal Competition.

The Principal Competition Statement gives *"a clear idea of the arena in which your product will do battle."*

In the case of a new or unique product, use a "reason for being."

C. Promise/Consumer Benefit.*

The best argument your brand can offer.

The Promise Statement has four guidelines:

1. The Promise should be phrased in terms of *"what the product will do for the consumer."*

2. The Promise should be as *competitive* as possible.

3. The Promise should *motivate* prospects in the direction that will accomplish your Objective.

4. The Promise should *not* be written in actual advertising terms.

D. Reason Why.

A statement that *supports* the Promise. Each statement must be "sharp, clear, and specific."

* In some versions of the Work Plan, this is known as the "Promise," in others, it is termed the "Consumer Benefit."

WORK PLAN AT WORK

Here's an example – a Creative Work Plan for Sanka.

1. KEY FACT.

29% of coffee-drinking households say they are concerned about caffeine, but resist trying Sanka Brand.

2. CONSUMER PROBLEM THE ADVERTISING MUST SOLVE.

Prospects don't think Sanka Brand would taste as good as caffeinated coffee, and they also resist its somewhat medicinal image.

3. ADVERTISING OBJECTIVE.

Convince prospects that *Sanka does indeed taste as good as caffeinated coffee* and has the added benefit of being caffeine free.

4. CREATIVE STRATEGY.

A. Prospect Definition:

Our prime prospects are mildly concerned about caffeine but haven't switched to decaffeinated coffee. They are probably somewhat more hyper than the average coffee drinker, more health aware, and perhaps even self-conscious about giving in to a decaffeinated coffee.

B. Principal Competition:

The regular coffee prospects are currently drinking. Secondarily, any other decaffeinated coffee they may consider switching to.

C. Promise/Consumer Benefit:

You will be surprised how good Sanka tastes, and it has the advantage of being caffeine free.

D. Reason Why:

In blind taste tests, Sanka brand decaffeinated coffee is at parity and sometimes superior to competitive caffeinated coffees.

GE FOCUS SYSTEM
1. Focus on the Receiver.
2. Focus on the Proposition.
3. Dramatize the Proposition.

GE Focus System.

GENERAL ELECTRIC is a client that produces numerous communications in-house.

Their Advertising and Sales Promotion Operations division developed a simple three-step process that helps them do effective work.

One big advantage of this system is that it can be implemented quickly. At GE, you could be writing consumer information on light bulbs one day and technical ads for atomic power plants the next.

Here's how the system works.

1. FOCUS ON THE RECEIVER.

First, you must know the receiver.

Singular, not plural.

You must know this audience as a person, with needs and wants beyond your product.

2. FOCUS ON THE PROPOSITION.

"The Proposition relates what we know about the product to what we've learned about the receiver."

The Proposition is a strategic statement, not a headline. But, if you just set the proposition in type and ran it with a picture of the product, "you'd have something useful."

GE believes it relates to a Key Fact (Y&R) and a position (Trout & Ries) the way they are perceived by the receiver.

3. DRAMATIZE THE PROPOSITION.

With the proposition as the basis, the challenge becomes "break the boredom barrier."

Find a way to communicate the Proposition in a dramatic way.

THREE KINDS OF THINKING.
This classic system calls for three different kinds of thinking:

Thinking about the receiver involves *analytic* thinking (and empathy).

Thinking about the Proposition requires *strategic* thinking.

Finally, dramatization demands *creative* thinking.

Leo Burnett Strategy Worksheet.

**THIS FORMAT
BREAKS THE MOLD.**
Many successful Burnett campaigns do not fit traditional strategy formats.

This format was developed to accomodate unique components in their campaigns based on Leo's concept of inherent drama, which is stated here as "key drama."

This unique visual property allows Burnett's campaigns to capture generic benefits with unique executions.

This worksheet allows you to include these unique properties as well as more traditional approaches.

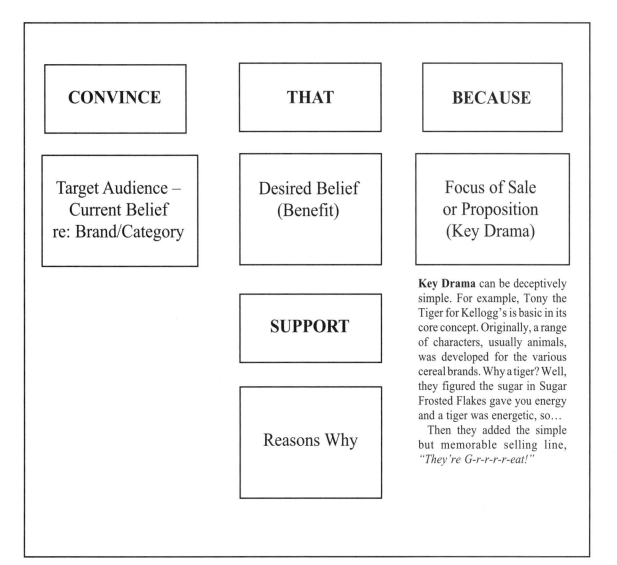

CONVINCE

Target Audience –
Current Belief
re: Brand/Category

THAT

Desired Belief
(Benefit)

SUPPORT

Reasons Why

BECAUSE

Focus of Sale
or Proposition
(Key Drama)

Key Drama can be deceptively simple. For example, Tony the Tiger for Kellogg's is basic in its core concept. Originally, a range of characters, usually animals, was developed for the various cereal brands. Why a tiger? Well, they figured the sugar in Sugar Frosted Flakes gave you energy and a tiger was energetic, so…

Then they added the simple but memorable selling line, *"They're G-r-r-r-r-eat!"*

The "R.O.I." System.

ROI stands for "Return on Investment."

At DDB/Needham, it also means that *"great advertising is distinguished by three fundamental qualities: Relevance, Originality, and Impact."*

Their ROI Strategy System is similar to the Y&R Work Plan, but there are important exceptions – particularly in the inclusion of certain tactical elements (demonstrations) and a media section.

The system is built on five questions:

1. What is the purpose of the advertising?

The ROI process focuses on the specific desired behavior and source of business.

2. To whom will the advertising be addressed?

The target section should have both demographic and psychographic information.

DDB/Needham looks for "aiming points," which allow you to think specifically and personally about your target. An example would be "Cereal eaters who are interested in sports" for Wheaties.

3. What competitive benefit will be promised, and how will that promise be supported?

This is a traditional benefit/reason why section.

4. What personality will distinguish the brand?

This may be treated simply or in great detail.

5. When, where, and under what circumstances will the target be most receptive to the message? What media will deliver that message to the target at the lowest possible cost?

ROI integrates media planning into the process.

A key part of this is the concept of *"aperture,"* the time that *"a customer is most likely to notice, be receptive to, and react favorably to, an advertising message..."*

The Creative Action Plan.

CREATIVE RECOMMENDATION.
This useful format is recommended by Dennis Altman.

He worked at DDB during The Creative Revolution, at Y&R, and a number of other top agencies, as well as his own.

He wrote the chapter on creative in *Advertising & The Business of Brands.*

And, he's the author of a bestselling humor book from the '60s, *The Executive Coloring Book.*

Now, as Professor Altman, he teaches advertising creative, direct, and IMC at the University of Kentucky.

Client:

Name of the product, service, or idea we're selling.

Target:

Description of target audience.

Demographics, geographics, psychographics, etc.

Competitive Snapshot:

Quick overview of the marketplace.

Key competitors and their positions.

Selling problems, if any.

Old thought/New thought:

What target thinks now/What we want them to think.

Main Claim:

The big thing to say. It could be a Customer Benefit, a Product Benefit, or a whole new way to use the product.

Customer Benefit is: What *customer* derives from product (clean breath, white teeth, prestige, relief, confidence).

Product Benefit is: *Actual* claims the product can make (*"Prevents dental plaque," "Gets up to highway speeds in 4 seconds," "Unbreakable, aged in oak, America's favorite"*).

Support:

Proof-points that justify claims *"Approved by ADA," "all-steel construction, sugar-free, all-natural."*

(Any real tests, charts, facts, documentation, research, to back up claims.)

Tone:

Mood of ad (informative, urgent, beautiful, entertaining, sexy, funny, warm, professional, classy, worldly, etc.).

Added Tools:

Road map, cutaway, coupon, comparison, prices, etc.

& Account Planning The Creative Brief.

Agencies like Chiat/Day added a third force to the creative development process.

In addition to account executives and creatives, they now have "account planners."

The planner is responsible for the advertising's *target audience relevance.* A key part of the process is developing "The Creative Brief." Here is a sample outline:

1. What is the Opportunity and/or Problem the advertising must address?

A brief summary of why you are advertising.

Take consumer point of view, not "sales are down," but "consumers are choosing cheaper alternatives."

2. What do we want people to do as a result of the advertising?

Try to make this as specific as possible.

3. Who are we talking to?

Try to develop a rich description of the target group.

Indicate beliefs and feelings about the category.

Avoid demographic information only.

Add personality and lifestyle dimensions.

4. What's the Key Response we want?

What *single* thing do we want people to feel or notice or believe as a result of the advertising?

5. What information/attributes might help produce this response?

It could be a key product attribute, or user need the brand fulfills, etc. Avoid a laundry list.

6. What aspect of Brand Personality should the advertising express?

7. Are there media or budget considerations?

8. This could be helpful...

Finally, provide any additional information that might affect the creative direction.

Backgrounders.

BEFORE you write a Strategy, a "Backgrounder" can help organize information in one place.

Here's an example of a Backgrounder for a local or regional business.

This one's for a local TV station or cable company. You can write one to suit your needs.

WHAT'S A BACKGROUNDER?

Before you can write a Strategy, you often need a lot of background – information about the brand.

A Backgrounder is usually some form of questionnaire designed to collect and organize that information so the Strategy can be developed.

---

1. Name and Location.
For a local advertiser, one of the most important communication tasks is your Name and Address (maybe your phone number, too).
Name:
Location(s):

Addresses and/or Location Identifiers (Intersections, etc.):

Phone Number:
Do you have any unique graphics, such as logo or signage?
(Attach copies. Indicate source of "master" graphics.
Do you have any existing slogans or advertising themes?
(Attach examples of print ads, flyers, brochures, and/or scripts.)

2. Products and Services.
Tell us about what you make and sell and/or what services you provide. Don't just make a list – let us know some of the things that make your company special – because those are some of the things you'll want to tell potential customers or clients.

Do you have any existing materials that describe your products or services? (Attach brochures, menus, catalogs, etc.)

3. Your Customers.
Tell us about your customers.
Chances are your new customers will be a lot like the customers you have now. They'll live in the same area and have many of the same characteristics.
Let us know what you think is special about you and your company.

Do you have any letters or customers' comments?
(Attach examples – not originals!)
By the way, don't forget that good advertising can also reinforce current customers' attitudes as well as bring in new customers.
That means, with a good commercial, you should see your current customers more often, as well as new customers.
If you'd like to know more about your customers, just ask them.

IF YOU'D LIKE TO KNOW MORE ABOUT YOUR CUSTOMERS...

Just ask. Here's a handy start at a good questionnaire.

Don't be reluctant to do a few one-on-one interviews.

A lot of people think they're better than focus groups. Not to mention quicker and cheaper.

So, get out your clipboard and go talk to a few customers.

CUSTOMER QUESTIONNAIRE
How long have you shopped at_____?

When did you first discover _____?

What was your first impression?

Why do you keep coming back?

What would you say to a friend who had never tried _____?

What similar places do you shop, and why do you like these places?

"People do not experience products or their performance directly through advertising."

It can come from sampling or past experience, but not advertising.

"From advertising, people experience images of the users – *people the advertiser associates with the product. Often these images are mixed together.*

The key thing we must remember is this: It's all images.

Advertising is all vicarious experience for the viewer."

WHY "PRODUCT" AND "YOU."

Here are some good reasons supporting the BBDO point of view:

"Product" image alone is limited because:

• Many product edges (advantages) are short lived, and quickly met by competition;

• Many product edges, as perceived by advertisers, are not important to consumers;

• Many product claims address category issues, but not underlying consumer problems;

• Performance claims often provide little added value;

• Finally, differentiating claims can sometimes have the opposite effect – and lead to perceived parity. This is particularly true when imagery and experience do not match.

The "You" image is critical, because:

• It takes positioning beyond logic into the realm of emotion;

• It adds value to performance claims;

• It can build product relevance and personality;

• It puts product truths and benefits into a meaningful framework for the consumer.

The "You" image takes the consumer beyond fact, and into feeling.

It can build brand loyalty and help provide competitive insulation.

BBDO.

THE BBDO SYSTEM is, in many ways, a more complex and complete version of GE's Focus System (GE is a BBDO client). It goes like this:

1. Know Your Prime Prospect

2. Know Your Prime Prospect's Problem

3. Know Your Product

4. Break the Boredom Barrier

See how the sequence works when a variety of research techniques are applied.

Note how BBDO uses the word "image." By this they mean images in the advertising. As the quote on the left indicates, they believe "it's all images."

1. KNOW YOUR PRIME PROSPECT.

BBDO research works to understand the market *from the consumer's point of view,* using a tool they call a "Market Structure Audit."

For example, in the gum market, they discovered that gums compete on flavor (i.e., cinnamon vs. cinnamon). So Big Red competes with Dentyne. Period.

Once the competition is defined, BBDO focuses on what they call *the prime prospect: Who* currently consumes competing products?

It's important to view prime prospects not just as demographic statistics, but as human beings – consider how they live and what they do with their time.

BBDO uses research tools such as Lifestyle Indicators and Photo Sort for insight into user dynamics and imagery.

They believe understanding "You" in terms of *attitudes* versus *lifestyles* is key to the differentiation of selling messages. Understanding attitudes can provide deeper insights into the consumer and lead to true differentiation.

2. KNOW YOUR PRIME PROSPECT'S PROBLEM.

BBDO believes the best way to get a purchase decision in your favor is to solve a problem for the prospect. They use a "Problem Detection System" to develop insight into these problems.

For example, when asked what they want in dog food, consumers most often responded with "nutrition" or "good taste." No surprise there.

But when asked what problems they have had with dog foods, consumers complained about their dog's bad breath and the food's odor or mess.

You can see from this example that this could lead strategically to some radically different approaches.

3. KNOW YOUR PRODUCT.

The "Product" position is developed by the client and agency with research input, such as the Market Structure Audit and Problem Detection Study.

Like all marketers, they isolate key performance characteristics, but rather than offering category benefits, they focus on solving consumer problems – approaching the product from a "Problem" standpoint, as opposed to a "benefit-attribute" standpoint.

It's not problem/solution. For example, Dodge's "product problem" for their prime prospects is "too many cars look alike and are boring."

4. BREAK THE BOREDOM BARRIER.

See how the Dodge campaigns of "Different" and "Grab Life By the Horns" combine a "Product" (Performance) image with a "You" (User) image while solving the "boring cars" problem.

If you can pinpoint a problem that is frequent and pre-emptable, you have some grist for the development of a not-so-obvious strategy.

For BBDO all execution is strategic. The result of their approach is "Imagery That Works."

BBDO POSITIONING.
BBDO combines these elements:
Brand Equity.
Brand Equity trade-off analysis helps determine which are the most important "Product" imagery problems vs. the competition and which are the most important "You" imagery problems.
"Product" + "You" Positioning.
With this information, they develop the "Product" image and the "You" image that will position the product.

SOME EXAMPLES:
Pepsi Cola. The "Product" stance is Leadership. The "You" attitude is Contemporary ("Hot," "In").

The resultant combination has been an evolving campaign, beginning with "The Pepsi Generation," continuing through "Pepsi. The Choice of a New Generation," "Generation Next," and, most recently "Joy of Cola."

Though they have evolved through variations on this basic product stance, the core position has stayed the same.

Gillette Dry Idea Antiperspirant. The "Product" stance is that it "goes on dry, stays dry." But this did not differentiate this superior performing product until the "You" attitude was added: Control, Aspiration.

The resulting theme was, "Never Let Them See You Sweat," with a campaign featuring young entertainers.

General Electric. The "Product" stance is "contemporary products of good quality."

The "You" attitude is Contemporary ("Hot," "In") and Quality ("The best I can afford").

The campaign uniting these elements is "We Bring Good Things to Life."

Information for this section was excerpted from *The Making of Effective Advertising* by Charles Patti & Sandra E. Moriarty ©1990 Prentice-Hall

Just as an ad reflects the personality of an advertiser, your Creative Strategy, Brief, or Blueprint can say something about you and your company.

Your approach to Strategy is a big part of how you do your job.

You'll "own" your Strategy even more when you have a Strategy format that you can call your own.

SECOND THOUGHTS.

Don't forget secondary audiences and secondary benefits.

In many businesses there is a second audience that's very important.

For the food marketers, it's the grocery trade.

For computers, it's dealers and "opinion leaders."

For office equipment, it's secretaries and "decision-makers."

Many complex products, like computers and office equipment, may have additional benefits or features that appeal to those making the final purchase decision.

For example, if both copiers are reliable, which has the best service?

Or the best price?

Or the best lease?

Or…?

Assignment #11:
Build Your Own Brief.

1. WRITE A FORMAT THAT WORKS FOR YOU.

You may feel free to borrow from any part of this section and use any combination of elements.

Your format may be a single form or a two-part process (e.g., Backgrounder & Brief).

2. GIVE YOUR FORMAT A NAME.

Have that name reflect the "Brand Personality" you wish to project.

Again, you may borrow from elements already presented in this section.

3. FILL OUT YOUR BRIEF.

Take a product you know something about and see if your format works.

4. DO A LITTLE "HYPOTHESIS TESTING."

Now, see how your format works for a few other products you're familiar with.

If you're really feeling ambitious, write some ads

The MarCom Matrix...

HERE'S HOW TO ADJUST your strategy statement.

Go from this...   ...to this.

Advertising will [convince]
[Target Customer] that
[Product]
is/will [Objective/Benefit].
Support will be [Support).
[Product] is
[Brand Character Statement]

[Target Customer]
[Product]
[Benefit].
[Support].

[Brand Character Statement]

TARGET CUSTOMER, PRODUCT, BENEFIT, SUPPORT, & BRAND CHARACTER.

These are still the building blocks for all of your MarCom strategies, though the emphasis may vary.

Once you've determined these core strategic elements, developing the individual substrategies can be relatively straightforward. Then you can move to the real challenge – determining the best tactics.

We'll cover sales promotion, MPR, and direct in later chapters.

STRATEGIC CONCERNS FOR OTHER ACTIVITIES IN THE MARCOM MATRIX:

Marketing Public Relations.
Publics. (PR word for target)
Channels. What are the right media opportunities for the brand and the strategic message?
Creating Media Interest. Remember, when you're not paying for the media space, you really have to be interesting.

Sales Promotion.
Incentive (Appeal, Cost, Payout). It's easy to "give it away," you need to offer an incentive that will pay out.
Secondary Targets (Trade, etc.). The objective may be to get retail display, so that consumers will be exposed to the brand at the point of sale.

Direct Marketing.
Target Database. You're "as good as your list." And the better you know and understand the target, the better you can direct your program.
Offer/Incentive. What's the deal?
The right offer can increase responses dramatically.
Message Emphasis. Saying the right thing also has an impact, though the list and the offer are more important.
Testing & Results Measurement.
This is key. Smart direct marketers always want to keep testing to make sure they are using the optimum combinations of target, offer, and message emphasis. So they keep testing.

Event Marketing.
Brand Character. Is the event appropriate for the brand?
Target Involvement. Will the event connect the brand with the right people?
Coordination with other activities. The event may feature additional advertising, PR, promotional, or even database capture activities.

New Media (Internet).
Business Objective. Is it a site for sales and transactions, consumer involvement, PR "buzz," investor information, or...
This is the *critical* initial decision.
Once that has been determined, an effective program can be developed.

IS A TIGER A "BIG IDEA?"
It was for a cereal and a gasoline.
How about a lion or a panther?
Who knows? Nobody.
Hey, "Nobody" may be a Big Idea, too.

FROM "GRRRR!" TO "R-R-R-R!"
"R-R-R-Ruffles have R-R-R-Ridges"
is still a memorable Selling Idea.

Selling Ideas.

FIRST A STRATEGY.

Next, a "Selling Idea" that's based on that strategy.

We discussed "How to Have an Idea." Now let's have an idea that emerges from our strategy.

First, your idea should be a *Selling* Idea.

SELLING IDEAS VS. BIG IDEAS.

Some say it should be a "Big Idea," but my own opinion is that this tends to confuse the issue.

Ideas become Big Ideas only in retrospect – *after* they've performed in the marketplace.

In the beginning, it's all conjecture.

But, to some degree, we're all competent to judge a Selling Idea. It's an idea that sells. Duh.

Is a tiger an idea? Tony the Tiger sells Sugar Frosted Flakes by saying, *"They're Grrrrreat!"*

"Put a Tiger in Your Tank" sold the power of Exxon. Both emerged from strategies about power and energy.

Some of it depends on the strength of the idea itself, some on how well you execute, and some of it depends on having a bit of luck in the marketplace.

So, how *do* ideas sell?

CHARACTERISTICS OF SELLING IDEAS.

P&G studied this a bit. They made some observations that you might find useful.

The Purpose of a Selling Idea:
 • *To register the brand's strategic objective –
 memorably – over the competition.*

What Is a Selling Idea?
 • *It's the primary executional ingredient
 and the main thread of executional continuity.*

Sounds simple. It's something that communicates your brand's advantage, and it's the idea that holds your campaign together. So far, so good.

Three Characteristics of Selling Ideas.

P&G found that successful Selling Ideas seemed to do well against "Three Principle Variables:"

1. Substance – This has to do with *meaningfulness* or desirability to the consumer.

2. Credibility – Capable of being believed. However, it's OK if it's a bit of a challenge. (Don't forget what we talked about related to "permission to believe.")

3. Provocativeness – The way the idea is expressed is *"a thought-provoking method of expression."*

How do you judge a Selling Idea?

Here are some questions you might ask:

- Is it faithful to Strategy?
- Does it have genuine substance?
- Is it credible yet challenging?
- Is it provocative?

Here are some of the conceptual areas where we seem to find effective Selling Ideas:

1. DRAMATIZE THE BENEFIT.

If you have no other type of idea than this one, you can do very well in advertising.

These ideas can be served up as: slogans… dramatic Demos… mnemonics… Tony the Tiger saying, *"They're Grrrreat!"* and even Mr. Whipple squeezing the Charmin. (Sorry, Luke.)

They *dramatize* the benefit.

George Lois looks for words that *"bristle with visual possibilities."* Dramatize and visualize.

It is worth saying again. If you have no other type of idea than this one, you can do very well in advertising.

2. A DISTINCTIVE SELLING PERSONALITY.

The Volkswagen campaign did this marvelously well.

Each ad projected a personality consumers could identify with. Unique. Smart. Frugal. And honest about being a little bit ugly.

This may not be a favorite ad campaign. But it's a memorable one. In a low-interest category (toilet paper), P&G was able to present their simple "softness" strategy over and over simply by having Mr. Whipple – who would certainly ask shoppers not to squeeze the fruit – ask "Please don't squeeze the Charmin." How successful was it? After "retiring," the actor was brought back. Many saw it as the return of an old friend.

Sprint dramatized the Product Benefit *of quality sound by literally letting us hear a pin drop over the phone.*

Our image.

WHAT COLOR IS YOUR BRAND?
With Levi's, it's easy to know.

Dockers made it easy, too, in TV spots that used "word jazz."

Think. What color are you?

That little bit of honesty gave their other claims more credibility and made the brand more likeable.

A lot of the brands you like project a personality that you connect with. Currently, Nike and Budweiser are very successful making that connection.

Positioning campaigns often do this.

The reassuring calm of a manufacturer concerned with your safety, or the outrageousness of a youth-oriented snack like Slim Jim – "definitely not part of a balanced breakfast."

Avis and Dr. Pepper ("I'm a Pepper") used a selling attitude to reinforce their position.

The position itself can be a personality.

Much fashion advertising does this with a visual personality. From good old Levi's to the latest designer jean. They sell style… with style.

Beers also seek to achieve a personality… only in the case of beer, many of them seem to be fighting to have the *same* personality.

There's a good reason for this. Many of them have the exact same target consumer.

3. A UNIQUE SELLING ENVIRONMENT.

Selling environment relates to selling personality, but it's subtler.

Marlboro moved from the "Marlboro Man" to "Marlboro Country" – an environment. It includes cowboys, but it's been enlarged to include all the feeling of the American West.

Sunkist Orange Soda became a major soft drink by utilizing imagery and an environment with almost universal appeal for its audience: California, the beach, The Beach Boys, girls in bikinis, surfing, and the Sunkist name.

Design can create a selling environment.

An ad can be a selling environment all in itself.

When you think about it, your typeface, the overall sense of design, even a photographic attitude (like Nike) can create this selling environment.

Design can send a strong selling message.

With increased visual emphasis, your graphic environment becomes more important.

Apple, a company that has strong design as part of its strategy, does this with product advertising that both complements and dramatizes their products.

Color values can reinforce your Selling Idea.

Like Levi's and The Blues. Or Dockers' "Colors."

Is color a Selling Idea? Yes it is.

Leo Burnett knew it instinctively.

Red meat on a red background.

Is it the picture or the frame?

Sometimes this environment is the idea itself and sometimes it's complementary to the main Selling Idea.

For example, McDonald's selling environment – the best-run, friendliest, cleanest food chain in the industry (QSC&V – Quality, Service, Cleanliness and Value) – played a consistent role in most of their advertising.

4. SOMETHING ELSE.

Sure, why not? For example, *Dramatize the Problem.*

"Halitosis," a dramatic way of saying "bad breath," built the Listerine business.

Then it was "morning breath" for Scope.

FedEx dramatized their benefit, delivering a package on time, by giving the Problem unique dimension. Happy people getting happy packages wasn't going to do the job.

Name awareness mnemonics may also be Selling Ideas. Like Ken-L-Ration Kibbles 'n Bits.

Or Rolaids. Or local retailers who sing their phone number over and over and over again.

We're taking time to make a simple point.

A Selling Idea Is an Idea that Sells.

A McSelling Idea. *The simple use of "Mc" is able to give McDonald's incredible branding flexibility. Simple but powerful bits of imagery, like "Mc" and their Golden Arches provide McDonald's with their own look and their own language,*

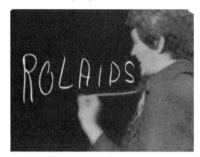

How do you spell "sell?"

Mnemonic Devices. *These are memory devices, usually with a rhythmic "hook." In this case, the last part of the name repeated over and over and over, gave the brand an engaging approach that helped them make the most of a small budget.*

Dramatize the Problem. *Here, Lubri-derm dramatizes the problem of dry skin with a high impact visual – an alligator!*

One Day It's Frogs…
For a while, the Budweiser Frogs were big. Their Bud-weis-er mnemonic was a lot of fun. But it didn't last. One reason was that was all they could say.

The Next Day It's Lizards.
Enter Louie the Lizard – able to add dialogue and bad jokes (probably a lounge lizard). Strong selling ideas can come from anywhere. Some might become Big. Some might last a year or two. And some are the ones you had just before you had the next one.

Seems simple, doesn't it?

Yet, in the complex advertising process, an abundance of opinion and uncertainty can cloud this simple issue. If you're not feeling confident about things, nothing seems good enough.

When things are going great, a lot of stuff seems to work… frogs, lizards, whatever.

Then again, if you're feeling a little too confident, you may accept something that isn't good enough to get the job done. And you've got a problem that needs no help to be dramatized.

(See why we had you read a little Zen?)

IN CONCLUSION.

Your advertising should have a Selling Idea.

That idea, which will emerge from the Strategy, should probably be simple and easy to understand – even though the process of getting there may have been long and hard.

Many ad people labor long and hard searching for a breakthrough so advanced that almost no one can understand it or describe it.

Work hard, but do not be confused.

Selling Ideas should be strong and simple.

"Great copy and great ideas are deceptively simple," said Leo Burnett, whose agency came up with many "Big Ideas." Or, perhaps more accurately, they grew many ideas into big ideas.

Build your Selling Ideas strong and simple and they may grow up to be big ideas.

But in the beginning, your Problems will be:

• First, having an idea that sells.

• Second, selling your Selling Idea.

From having the Selling Idea, we're going to move to *selling* that Selling Idea…

The next part of your journey…

Selling Idea Exercises:

This exercise is to help you realize how hard it is to connect with (and remember) a motivating idea.

1. **List the most memorable ad campaigns you can remember. How many can you list?**

   In your own words, write down the Selling Idea.

2. **Name an advertisement (or promotional) message that motivated you to act in the last 90 days.**

3. **Can you name two Selling Ideas (or slogans) that dramatize a Product Benefit?**

   Other products probably offer the same benefit. How did these make their benefit seem unique?

4. **Name two brands that project a selling personality or a selling attitude that you like.**

   How are they different from others in the category?

5. **Name two Selling Ideas used by a service.**

   Is there a symbol involved? What is it?

   What does it mean? Look up the word "semiotics."

6. **Name two Selling Ideas that dramatize a Problem.**

   Other products may solve the same problem.

Assignment #12:

Take the Strategies and Theme Lines that you wrote in Assignments #6, #7, and #8.

Pick your three favorites. If you have no favorites, write some new ones.

1. DEVELOP ONE SELLING IDEA FOR EACH PRODUCT AND STRATEGY.

   How do they develop visual drama?

   How do they reinforce name awareness?

   How do they communicate the benefit?

2. PRESENT YOUR SELLING IDEAS AS PRINT CONCEPTS, TV KEY FRAMES, OR BOTH.

"A surprising solution to a marketing problem, expressed in memorable verbal and/or graphic imagery – is the authentic source of communicative power."

George Lois

WHAT'S THE BIG IDEA?
How to Win with
Outrageous Ideas that Sell
by George Lois

Words from the master. George Lois knows how to create logos, advertising, advertising agencies, publicity, and controversey.

Each chapter in this readable book highlights one of George's slightly outrageous (and usually very successful) Selling Ideas – like Mick Jagger saying, *"I Want My MTV!"*

The book is out of print, but you should be able to find a copy.

"Where is that big black bag going with that little man?"

*"Plan the sale
as you write the ad."*
Leo Burnett

Sales Power!
How to Sell Your Ideas.

WE WISH THIS CHAPTER weren't necessary. We wish all you had to do is have a good idea and take a bow while the world agrees and admires you for your brilliance.

The world isn't like that. So this chapter is necessary.

How well you sell ideas is as important as how good those ideas are. Maybe more important (sorry).

So, how *do* you sell ideas?

First, it's pretty complicated.

Second, it's pretty simple. It starts with understanding *the other person's point of view.* And helping them feel confident (and excited) about the possibilities represented by your idea – which, like all ideas, is still unproven in the marketplace.

SELL BETTER FIVE WAYS.

To help make something complicated a little simpler, here are a few helpful hints on selling ideas we'll call "Sales Power." We built this little list with "S.P." initials to make it a little easier to remember:

- STRATEGIC PRECISION
- SAVVY PSYCHOLOGY
- SLICK PRESENTATION
- STRUCTURAL PERSUASION
- SOLVING THE PROBLEM

Let's go step by step.

1. STRATEGIC PRECISION.

First, your Selling Idea must be on-strategy.

Whether the Strategy was developed instinctively by an individual or at great length by a committee, your idea should be perceived as an expression of that Strategy. So...

STRONG STRATEGIES MAKE STRONG SELLING IDEAS.

If they're not coming, it may be you, or… it may be the Strategy.

If that's the case, look at the Strategy, look at the work, and try to figure out what's wrong.

Good luck.

186

Before You Talk about the Idea, You Have to Talk about the Strategy. Consider this as a rule.

It could be as simple as...

"Our Strategy is to build awareness among teen-agers for your new clothing store."

Or it could be a full-blown presentation – what we call a "Dog & Pony Show."

Strong Strategies Make for Strong Selling Ideas.

An idea that relates strongly to your Strategy has the potential to be a strong Selling Idea.

Emphasize that strength.

And once you get the idea, and believe in it, that's the first thing you say to sell the idea.

It's a good idea because it's on-strategy. (Of course, you'd better be prepared to tell people why the Strategy is right as well.) Show that you know the Strategy before you start to sell that idea.

Then, as you sell your idea, you'll be communicating that you understand the Strategy and believe it.

2. SAVVY PSYCHOLOGY.

As you present to people, think how *they* feel.

Not how you feel.

Presenting good ideas is like writing good advertising – it's receiver-driven.

In fact, your presentation begins long before your present. Learn to involve others in your Selling Idea.

That's the next step to selling ideas. It starts early.

Everyone wants to get with a winner – including your boss and your client. It might be as simple as communicating that you have a winning idea.

Invite early input from the AE and the research department. (Use it at your discretion.)

Look for information that bolsters your case.

It will help your audience (and your fellow workers) feel more confident.

As Leo said, *"Plan the sale as you write the ad."*

WHAT IF YOUR IDEA ISN'T ON-STRATEGY?

Then you must either have a different idea, or... a different Strategy!

Do not ignore this risky second option. Here's why:

Some strategies look nice on paper and sound nice in the meeting room, but when it comes time to execute them, they don't lead to strong executions.

For example, FedEx could have had a strategy that emphasized the benefit of on-time delivery.

Yet, happy normal people receiving their packages on time may not be powerful persuasion (Emery tried this, with no great success). So FedEx *dramatized the problem!*

Suddenly, the executional stage opens up – memorable comedic dramas and characters develop into a powerful and *resonant* campaign that every businessman can relate to.

Because every businessman has experienced the pressure of the deadline, when it *"absolutely positively has to be there overnight."*

ACCOUNT PLANNERS = CONSUMER PSYCHOLOGISTS.

Here's where account planning can really help.

A good account planner brings consumer insight into the equation when you need it most.

You can gain early insight into how the consumer feels about the category and how they'll react to the advertising.

Savvy Psychology in action!

"Selling is an art of passion. When you're passionate about an idea, it shows."
Tom McElligott

Look for ways to make your idea better. And look for others who will support your idea.

Someone else may have a valuable addition to your idea – and may also become a valuable ally.

And as you pay attention to the psychology of your audience help them focus on the psychology of the target customer. They pretty much always have the same question… *"What's in it for me?"*

In fact, that's *everybody's* question.

Understanding that question is solid psychology – show how your Selling Idea answers it.

Try to show how good your Selling Idea is from the target customer's point of view.

Through it all, remember, your idea has to meet *their* needs. Not yours.

Relate your idea to the needs of your audience.

3. SLICK PRESENTATION.

Next, you must become accomplished at presenting your Selling Idea to others.

A good presentation makes people *want* to do the ads. If you sell well, people see themselves.

Two team members are vital partners for success at this stage of the game – the account executive and the art director.

First, the account executive.

Remember, he or she wants to win, too.

Get together to rehearse or discuss your presentation, even on an informal basis.

It'll help you *both* get ready for the meeting.

Even if it's on a cocktail napkin on the flight to the client meeting, rehearse the meeting with the AE. Often, you can get the AE to make some of the key arguments on behalf of the Selling Idea.

And help get ready for any tough questions.

But, these days, talk is not enough to carry the day.

It's only part of it – the rational/verbal.

It's the emotional/visual part of your presentation that will really do it. *Show Time!*

A Great Presentation Needs Great Art Direction.

That's why your other important partner is the art director. He'd better like the idea – and it should show – with great graphics, loving layouts, juicy comps, terrific key frames or storyboards, and maybe a few extras.

How about a big title card with the campaign theme? Maybe a button for the sales force?

Your work should sell itself – *visually.*

How tight should layouts be?

Look at it this way. A good layout or storyboard, just like a good presentation, should make you *want* to do the ad.

It doesn't have to be tight – but it must be enticing.

Remember, the Meeting Is the Medium!

That means you've got to get good at presenting your own work. And that means you have to get good at putting presentations together.

Like copywriting, it's a skilled craft.

4. STRUCTURAL PERSUASION.

You persuade by meeting other people's needs.

They might not do it for you, but they'll certainly do it for themselves.

So let's talk about what you're going to talk about. Remember Bernbach...

"Persuasion is not a science, but an art."

Art has form. So does persuasion.

Your point of entry is critical.

This is the beginning. Context.

It's *"tell 'em what you're going to tell 'em."*

In everything you communicate, whether it's the first sentence in your ad or the opening thought in your presentation, you must be concerned with that vital first step.

IT'S TRUE!

One of the main reasons most people don't present well is that most people are afraid to present.

It's natural.

Avoidance is natural, too.

You have to work on presenting even though you probably don't want to.

It's natural.

To cheer us up before a meeting, an account exec friend would pat someone on the shoulder, smile warmly, and say, *"Remember... we're all in this alone."*

At least he was honest.

Hey, Good Luck.

There Are Two Times In Life When You're Totally Alone. Just Before You Die. And Just Before You Make A Speech.

VANDER ZANDEN, INC.
Executive Speechmaking And Storytelling.

HERE ARE SOME OF THE THINGS I GO THROUGH.

I take notes – lots of 'em.

When other people talk, I make notes. It's helpful, and it's clear to everyone that I'm listening.

Just like Leo, I'm planning the meeting as well as the ad.

I usually start with a rough outline of the presentation with titles and subheads for each part of the presentation sequence.

As it's coming together, I try to think about the toughest questions that will be asked and try to have answers ready.

I'm always looking for ways to strengthen the Selling Idea and the presentation using other's suggestions.

It makes the Selling Idea stronger and the selling team larger.

The more people who believe in the Selling Idea, the better the chance it will sell.

WHAT *DO* YOU SAY FIRST?

The first step is a lulu!

The first step you take affects every move you make.

Attention and involvement.

Resonance. Impact.

Whatever it takes.

Be careful. As they say, you only get one chance to make a first impression.

Remember…
Clients have clients.
Every client has a problem.
Your job is to help their business.

**PRACTICE
THIS SEQUENCE:**

Start where people *are.*
Problems and Opportunities.
Objectives and Strategies.
Then… the Selling Idea.
Conclude with how it
Solves The Problem.

Remember, in today's cluttered communications environment you're competing for people's attention – even in a meeting. First impressions are critical.

So, what *do* you say first?

Do you say, "Here's my great idea"? Wrong!

Think about it…

For example, when dealing with an opposing point of view, the first thing you might want to do is agree with that opposing point of view.

It can encourage those who might not agree with you to hear the other side of the story.

You might start with "Here's the problem."

Or, you might acknowledge other points of view before your own… whatever.

But whatever you do, have an idea of what you're doing and where you're going.

You have to think about what you're going to say first and how you will lead into the work.

Help them move from where they are to where you want them to be.

To do this, organization and sequence are essential.

That's why it's *vital* that you develop the habit of structured, organized thinking. So people can follow what you're saying.

Don't forget the importance of the emotional/ visual part of your presentation to make those points.

And remember, you only have one first chance.

5. SOLVE THE PROBLEM.

Clients have needs. And clients have clients.

Chances are, the Big-Shot you're presenting to works for an Even-Bigger-Shot who likes to ask tough questions about the advertising.

Make it easy for your client to answer those tough questions.

You must give him answers as to how this Selling Idea and these ads *Solve The Problem.*

Every client has a problem.

Hey, if he didn't, he wouldn't need you.

And that's the last helpful hint...

**Solve the Client's Problem,
and You'll Sell the Selling Idea.**

The more your Selling Idea can be seen to solve *their* problem, the better the chance *your* Selling Idea will become *their* Selling Idea.

And that's how to sell ideas.

Now, we'll talk about doing it with *Style*.

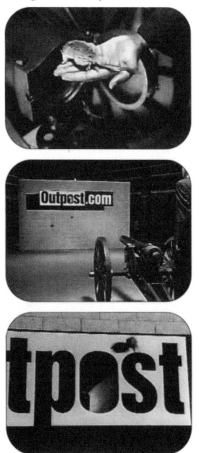

Clever, but what's the point?

"THE PROBLEM THE ADVERTISING MUST SOLVE."

It's easy to say that the problem is "we have declining share and a small budget." And, it's probably true.

And it's also probably true that "We need great advertising to overcome our problems." But that's not the point of figuring out what the problem is.

Or, what the problem is that the advertising can solve.

You need to frame it in terms of a consumer problem, not a brand problem or a business problem.

"A Maalox Moment" is a consumer problem. Whether we have those moments or not, we understand what the proposition is.

We can't make this point too many times. It's not about you, it's about the person on the other side of this page.

"People Aren't Aware."

Lack of awareness is certainly a problem, one almost every brand has to some degree. But, again, if there isn't a reason for the consumer to be aware, well, what's the point.

We can shoot a gerbil into our logo, as an Internet brand called Outpost did not too long ago, but if there's no consumer need and no consumer action to meet that need, well, again, what's the point?

And that's the point.

As you work to develop Selling Ideas and *sell* Selling Ideas, the best place to be is inside the mind of the consumer.

So you can turn him or her into a customer. Got it?

Here's what we'll do:
First, we'll cover the
Four R's of Copywriting.
Next, basics of modern
copywriting style.
Then, we'll have some
fun as we work in print,
radio, and TV.

"Most great advertising
is direct.
That's how people talk.
That's the style
they read."

Jerry Della Femina

How to Write with Style.

YOU MUST TALK PERSON TO PERSON. You must develop a short, straightforward writing style.

You must talk *to* people, not at them.

How do you do it?

Today's lesson is:

Readin'
Writin'
Rhythm 'n
Re-Writin'

How to Read with Style. Here's an ad from a campaign Jerry Della Femina did for the newspaper industry. The real message is simple and direct. Newspapers are cool. Cool people read them.

OUR FAMOUS FORMULA
Discover the Objective
Develop the Strategy
Create a Selling Idea
And… finally
Do it with Style!

The Science of Hopkins. Take this easy test. Compare modern copywriting style to that of Claude Hopkins. Then, send for a Free Offer!

What Is Style?

Impact. Image. Involvement. Awareness. All those other words we use in when we try to sell our ideas depend on advertising that's special.

Because advertising must be more than well-structured information.

It must have enthusiasm and artistry.

Here's a thought from Bill Bernbach:

"There are a lot of great technicians in advertising. And, unfortunately, they talk the best game.

They know all the rules.

They are the scientists of advertising.

But there's one little rub.

Advertising is fundamentally persuasion… and persuasion happens to be not a science, but an art."

It's difficult to think things through to the point where Objective and Strategy are understood and the structure of the sale is clear.

Yet, you must do more.

Bill Bernbach had more to say:

"We're all concerned about the facts we get and not enough concerned about how provocative we have made these facts to the consumer."

Hopkins agrees: *"Try to give each advertiser a becoming style. To create the right individuality is a supreme accomplishment."*

Objective and Strategy.
Structure and Style.
Put them all together.
That's Salesmanship.
And that's your job.

Tom McElligott's Style. A terrific copywriter and founder of Fallon McElligott, one trait of Tom's early award-winning print was using old pictures with contemporary copy. Did you know that his father worked for the Episcopal Church? Ads done for Dad!

AN EDITORIAL.
In school, most of your writing assignments were exercises in grammar, vocabulary, and reading comprehension – done for the approval of a teacher.

Often, it had to be a certain number of pages – so brevity was penalized.

So you were taught to overwrite!

Furthermore, you're probably carrying around the baggage of years of over-exposure to overwritten material.

In school, long words are preferred to short ones. Complex concepts win out over simple statements.

The lecturing language of education is preferred to the rhythm of conversation.

This verbal inflation has been encouraged by bureaucrats, lawyers, politicians, and the academic community.

Advertising works in the real world.

Instead of performing for marginally interested teachers who are, let's face it, paid to read what you write, you must talk to totally uninterested consumers.

You don't have to demonstrate your broad vocabulary, flaunt your superior intellect, or get a good grade.

Everything just got very simple.

Do writing worth reading.

End of editorial.

In the church started by a man who had six wives, forgiveness goes without saying.

The Episcopal Church

The New Writing.

New Fashions in Fashion. They help inspire new fashions in writing. Street fashion? Street language!

The Art of Bernbach. Visuals and words combine to create surprising impact. This ad cleverly says El Al is "making the Atlantic 20% smaller." Now this ad might seem a bit subtle, but think about the target – people reading the New Yorker *and considering a trip to Israel. For this target, the style was right.*

AS THE WORLD GOT WIRED, a brand new writing style emerged. Post-television copywriting.

Today, we read, hear, and feel our way through a flow of information. We inhale, skim, and absorb.

We take bites, bits, and chunks and change the channel. We turn the page, or tune out till we see or hear something of interest.

We've evolved from readers to "viewers."

Even when we read, we graze as we gaze.

Today, we're all more selective and demanding consumers of information – even if we insist on a diet of tabloid junk food.

More and more, we choose our news.

Channel changer in hand, we zip and zap as we interact with our information.

It's casual and natural.

Contemporary copywriting must connect with these new realities.

Literary traditions based on novels, short stories, essays, and other pre-electronic forms are replaced by those based on news, movies, music, and the cadence of conversation.

Yet, most writing is still taught as a logical, literary, left-brained skill – writers practicing their art for interested readers.

Copywriting is different.

In copywriting, the most important person is not the writer, but *the receiver.*

Got it? Good.

Readin'.

BEFORE YOU CAN WRITE CLEARLY about a subject, you have to understand it.

As a copywriter, you will find yourself continually becoming an expert on things you know little about – so you can then write about them with authority.

It means assembling information. Digging for facts – the preparation stage of the creative process.

Much of the difficulty of not knowing what to say is rooted in not having anything to say.

This can be a difficult problem for a copywriter, particularly with so-called "parity" products, older products and other advertisers without much news.

It seems like it's all been said before.

Nonetheless, your writing must have *substance.*

Interest is maintained with content as well as style.

Credibility must be earned. And that takes work.

Read all about it. Take notes. Make lists.

Read memos, fact sheets, magazine articles, and anything else you can lay your hands on.

READ PRODUCTS.

Involve yourself with the product. Dig.

As Julian Koenig said, *"Your job is to reveal how good your product is, not how good you are."*

A True Story.

One night, copywriter Dan Nichols dumped a box of cereal on his kitchen table and counted the raisins!

And that's how *"Two Scoops of Raisins in a box of Kellogg's Raisin Bran"* was born.

The best way to unearth a new and interesting advertising campaign is to dig into the interesting facts about the product itself. And the agency which digs deepest usually comes up with the most pay dirt.

YOUNG & RUBICAM, Inc. Advertising

LOOKING FOR THE CAPO D'ASTRO BAR.

(This ad classic is from a newsletter article by Bud Robbins, copywriter.)

Back in the '60s, I was hired by an ad agency to write copy on the Aeolian Piano Company account.

My first assignment was for an ad to be placed in the *New York Times* for one of their grand pianos.

The only background information I received was some previous ads and a few faded close-up shots… and, of course, the due date.

The account executive was slightly put out by my request for additional information, and his response to my suggestion that I sit down with the client was, *"Jesus Christ, are you one of those? Can't you just create something? We're up against a closing date!"*

I acknowledged his perception that I *was* one of those, which got us an immediate audience with the head of our agency.

I volunteered I couldn't even play a piano, let alone write about why anyone would spend $5000 for *this* piano when they could purchase a Baldwin or Steinway for the same amount.

Both allowed the fact they would gladly resign the Aeolian business for either of the others, however, while waiting for that call, suppose we make our deadline.

(continued on next page)

I persisted and, reluctantly, a tour of the Aeolian factory in upstate New York was arranged. I was assured that "we don't do this with all our clients" and my knowledge as to the value of company time was greatly reinforced.

The tour of the plant lasted two days, and although the care and construction appeared meticulous, $5000 still seemed to be a lot of money.

Just before leaving, I was escorted into the showroom by the national sales manager. In an elegant setting sat their piano alongside the comparably priced Steinway and Baldwin. *"They sure do look alike,"* I commented.

"They sure do. About the only real difference is the shipping weight – ours is heavier."

"Heavier?" I asked. *"What makes ours heavier?"*

"The Capo d'astro bar."

"What's a Capo d'astro bar?"

"Here, I'll show you. Get down on your knees."

Once under the piano, he pointed to a metallic bar fixed across the harp and bearing down on the highest octaves.

"It takes 50 years before the harp in a piano warps. That's when the Capo d'astro bar goes to work. It prevents that warping."

I left the national sales manager under his piano and dove under the Baldwin to find a Tinkertoy Capo d'astro bar at best. Same with the Steinway.

"You mean the Capo d'astro bar really doesn't go to work for 50 years?" I asked.

"Well, there's got to be some reason why the Met used it," he casually added.

I froze. *"Are you telling me that the Metropolitan Opera House in New York City used this piano?"*

"Sure. And their Capo d'astro bar should be working by now."

Upstate New York looks nothing like the front of the Metropolitan Opera House where I met the legendary Carmen Rise Steven. She was now in charge of moving the Metropolitan Opera House to the Lincoln Center.

(continued on next page)

You won't find the answer staring into space, getting stoned, feeling alienated, insecure, or above it all.

You must get *into* the product – just like the Capo d'astro bar, they all have a story to tell.

READ PEOPLE.

It's some of the most interesting reading you can do.

The product you're working on is surrounded by people – clients, customers, and competitors.

The have a story to tell, too.

And you never know where you'll find those stories.

One day, I was suddenly working for a retailer of women's clothes – the kind you wore to work.

I asked my sister, guessing she was in the target.

Not only was she in the target, she'd been to that retailer's wardrobe coordination seminar, and after half an hour in her closet, I understood a good part of the story I had to tell.

Some good news.

People like telling you stories about themselves.

They like it when someone is interested in them – even if it's a stranger "working on a project."

Learn to be interested in others, and they will reward you with stories worth telling.

READ PICTURES.

It's all becoming more visual, remember?

Learn to do some visual reading.

Add art shows, magazines, movies, television, and Web sites to your "reading list."

Can you create your target's visual environment?

Read their magazines. It can be as simple as paging through some of the trade magazines you'll be in.

Go to the dealership. Or the retailer.

Take a look at the world of the people who use your product and pay attention to what you see.

You may come back with that picture that's worth a thousand words.

ORGANIZATION, MAN.

I don't know if you want this next bit of advice.

If you take it, you'll end up with piles of "stuff."

But here goes… since the creation of ideas is based on new combinations of previously expressed ideas, the greater your resources, the greater your chances of achieving the best combination.

My own technique is to accumulate piles of notes, random scribblings, memos, magazine articles, competitve ads, and product literature. Folders help.

I let my subconscious incubate and organize during this period. And I start as soon as possible.

Because even when due dates seem far off, they sort of sneak up on you.

When the pile is a certain size, or the deadline is approaching rapidly, I'm ready to write.

First, I try to organize the material in an orderly, rational way, which gives me a chance to review it again and see if some initial ideas still hold up.

I'll generally use an outline, which I continually revise and update. I think the computer helps, but when you're writing by hand, you tend to write a little less and scribble and scratch out.

I usually write by hand for about two-and-a-half scribbles. During this time, as the details pile up, you continually refocus on what's important.

Then, having dealt with the material to some degree in a right-brained *and* left-brained way (making notes as you go), see where it takes you.

Alternate between looking for more details and then looking at what's most important.

Over time, you'll find yourself working with an ever-growing database, and you'll find that experience will help you get there faster with fewer clues.

You'll also end up with lots of files. Sorry.

It's life on the learning curve.

CAPO D'ASTRO (Cont.)

Ms. Stevens told me, *"About the only thing the Met is taking with them is their piano."* That quote was the headline of our first ad.

The result created a six-year wait between order and delivery.

My point is this.

No matter what the account, I promise you, the Capo d'astro bar is there.

"In art, the only thing you can teach is the mechanics.
When it comes to creativity,
that you do by trial and error,
by exposing yourself
to different things.
I think also you must have
the kind of sponge
that absorbs."

Paul Rand

"Good writers come in all sizes, shapes, and ages. What they all seem to have in common is the ability to hear, to listen, to understand – and to distill what they hear and learn into something that's human and persuasive."

Jay Chiat

GOOD ADVICE.

In A *Technique for Producing Ideas,* James Webb Young recommends two types of reading:

1. General Reading.
To expand the range of experience critical in idea producing.

2. Specific Reading.
Related to the products, people and problems at hand.

OLD ADVICE.

For complex projects, some people recommend the use of note cards.

I think that was before computers.

FIND YOUR VERB!
This verb helped position a new liquid detergent against powdered detergents.

A FRESH NEW VERB…
brings extra energy and a bit of extra excitement to a familiar and not all that exciting product.

ACTIVATE THE BENEFIT.
"Turn up the Volume" adds energy to Agree's conditioning benefit.

Writin'.

YOUR NEXT STEP is to build a working vocabulary for your product and your brand.

You may or may not have your Selling Idea yet.

Either way, you need to collect the vocabulary you'll be working with:

- Nouns, verbs, and adjectives
- Slang and jargon
- Interesting ideas
- Facts and figures
- And figures of speech

These are the building blocks for your copy blocks.

Much of this material will originate in your notes and the process of reading about your product and working on your Strategy.

In general, you should probably avoid using a thesaurus. You should try to avoid obscure words and look for exactly the right words.

As Mark Twain said, *"It's the difference between lightning and lightning bug.*

Here's what you should look for:

1. FIND YOUR VERB!

Your job is to *move* people.

The first things you should look for are verbs associated with your subject.

Verbs *activate* your writing – they are key to successful persuasion.

Many successful campaigns have been based on active verbal constructions:

"We Try Harder"
"Fly the Friendly Skies"
"Let Your Fingers Do the Walking"
"Got Milk?"

Can you think of a few running right now?

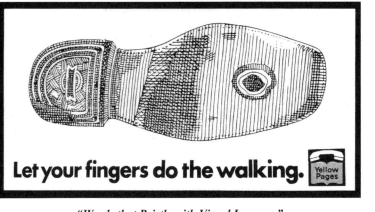

Let your fingers do the walking. *Yellow Pages*

"Words that Bristle with Visual Imagery."
This campaign ran for decades.
It communicated the Yellow Pages benefit very memorably.

The joint is jumpin'.
The San Diego Zoo

VERBS *ACTIVATE* ADS!
Write in the active voice.
Jump. Fly. Act now! Do it.

GO JUMP ON A LAKE.
YAMAHA

T-Birds priced to fly.

$35⁹⁰ a day weekday $22⁹⁰ a day weekend

The 1 way to rent a car.

Proof man was meant to fly.

New Intercooled
Mitsubishi Starion ESI Turbo

YES, IT WILL FLY.

THE 740 TURBO
By Volvo

Off-the-road

The proliferation of flying cars in *Newsweek* concerns me. Air traffic controllers don't deserve the added stress.

First the April 1 issue, with ads from Mitsubishi, Hertz and Volkswagen.

Then the VW ad runs again in the April 8 issue, along with one from Volvo.

Dr. Jung may have been right about a collective unconscious.

Jay W. Hillis
President, Uplifting Ideas
Seattle

Reprinted from *Advertising Age.*

GTI flies away with the Motor Trend Car of the Year Award.

The New GTI. $8,990. It's not a car. It's a Volkswagen.

199

2. ADD ADJECTIVES.

Be selective. Advertising adjectives need to be like Baby Bear's porridge. . . "Just right."

They should clarify, inform, and intensify.

They should resonate with the target.

They should relate to the Strategy.

After adding up all the adjectives that meet your objectives, ask one question.

Is there one adjective strong enough to sustain your campaign? It may be the only one you need.

AN ABSOLUTELY TRUE STORY.
The original line for FedEx was "When it has to be there overnight."

As TV Director Joe Sedelmeier was casting the commercial, one actor did an absolutely marvelous job saying "Absolutely. Positively."

Joe had the actor keep saying the words over and over. It had "Velcro."

It caught the ear and dramatized both the problem and the benefit.

The agency realized this added extra drama and intensity to the need for FedEx, and extra memorabilty to their theme.

ABSOLUT SUCCESS.

Many brand names are based on adjectives – it's a good name awareness device.

Absolut Vodka is an award-winning example.

But be sure you don't jeopardize your brand name.

It makes lawyers absolutely crazy.

ADJECTIVE AS HEADLINE.

These handsome ads for Centurion bikes communicate three lines of bikes quickly and charmingly.

The powerful cumulative effect if this tactic is affordable for the brand in a medium like a bike specialty magazine.

Rhythm. Rhythm. Rhythm. See how repetition can build a positive feeling about a brand?

Simple counterpoint between the adjective in the brand name and a product serving suggestion.

Adjective du jour.
Sometimes, certain words,
just like certain people,
become cool.
Go figure.
Sometimes, it can work.
Here's a good example.
Or, an extreme example.

SHOULD I MAKE UP WORDS?
Well, it's worked and it's failed.

As this book goes to press, Volvo is trying it with their ReVolvolution campaign. Clearly, they're trying to grow the brand image from the conservative boxy styled "safety" position into one that is more performance-oriented.

It's not clear how much "Velcro" there is in "ReVolvolution."

Then again, how much controversey is in "Couintreauversial."

What do you think?

STOREHOUSE SMALL SPACE.
These ads for Storehouse rephrase familiar phrases and make easy puns to add extra style.

Note that each phrase ties into a selling feature of the featured product.

THE NATURAL WAY TO WRITE.

Here's an interesting way to start thinking about a topic. Explored in *Writing the Natural Way* by Gabriele Lusser Rico (1983, Houghton Mifflin).

She shows you how to tap into the associative connections in both sides of your brain with a technique called "clustering," a nonlinear brainstorming process that you can do on a sheet of paper. It looks like this...

Instead of an outline, you start with "Clusters" of words and concepts that form chains and patterns of meaning.

She helps you focus on "cadence," the natural rhythm of words, to "attune the inner ear of your design mind."

A fascinating book.

Highly recommended.

3. PICK UP THE PIECES!

Find unique combinations of words and ideas that relate to your brand, your product category, and Strategy.

Pick 'em up and jot 'em down. Assemble:
- **familiar phrases**
- **cliches and puns**
- **endorsements**
- and **reasons why.**

Build your arsenal.

It's a jungle out there.

The Double. *By reversing one aspect of a common cliché, a negative can become a positive in an intense and startling way. Here, Volkswagen does it.*

4. ORGANIZE YOUR THINKING.

Now you're ready to write. Finally.

You have many of the pieces of the puzzle.

Now you have to put them together.

Take a short break. Think.

Utilize the incubation stage of the creative process.

Think about the path you must travel...

Take your time.

Focus past initial concerns… like what headline to write… or when your assignment is due.

Think of the target with your arrow in the center.

Now, describe your destination.

Think of themes.

And variations.

Start writing.

Go ahead.

We'll wait.

A Slightly New Way of Thinking About Soup. For a while, "Soup Is Good Food" revitalized Campbell's business.

Once your thinking's organized, doing more ads is a lot easier.

Rephrase Familiar Phrases. The gentle pun, replacing "Care" with "Fare," was a natural extension of Campbell's "Soup Is Good Food" campaign.

Another Double Meaning Ad – With a Single-Minded Strategy. This ad accomplishes its objective as tastefully as possible. The double meaning helps. To some people, this is important information. Their problem might not be your problem. Think target. Try to see the world through their eyes – not yours.

**DOUBLE FEATURE.
FROM HONDA.**

"Are you using the right car for your gasoline?" features a "verbal double" which takes a familiar phrase and turns it around to add double meaning.

The "Folds flat for easy storage" ad features a "visual double" where the double-meaning works off the visual.

AFTERWARDS, IT'S OBVIOUS.

Often, we see breakthrough work and we say, "Well, of course."

But before the awards and the sales results, it's not obvious at all.

5. DIS-ORGANIZE YOUR THINKING.

As you write, you can almost double your output if you challenge yourself.

Is what you wrote right? What if it's the opposite?

Continually challenging your own writing can open up new opportunities and perspectives.

See what happens when you turn things inside out or upside down.

An example: "Got Milk?"

For years, nice ads talked about how good milk was for you. Year after year, the same basic message went out – and people got tired of it.

When the folks at Goodby took a look at the problem they found that the usual positive way of talking about milk was a yawn.

So they looked at it a new way. They asked a group of consumers to do without milk for a week and then come back and talk about it. Bingo!

Suddenly they found an interesting story.

There were some things where *you just had to have milk!* A peanut butter sandwich. Cookies.

Suddenly there was exciting new drama where before there had been only the same old story.

So, as you construct all those great thoughts and sensational sentences, see what happens when you de-construct all of your good thinking.

Is there new perspective that can make the same old story slightly new again?

Or how about a new attitude? Like an upscale jewelry brand getting just a bit sassier.

New is good.

6. RE-ORGANIZE YOUR THINKING.

Hey, if it were easy, anyone could do it.

And they wouldn't need you.

Good writing is based on good thinking.

By this time, a lot has been said. Try to figure out what is really and truly the most important thing.

This isn't easy. Sometimes, every time you turn around, someone has something new to say.

Often, very bright people can tell you the exact opposite of what the previous bright person just said.

Keep reprioritizing. What's most important? In advertising, you cannot say everything, just the most important things.

When in doubt, think target. Hey, even when you're not in doubt, think target. Try to see, read, and think through the consumer's point of view.

And, with that in mind, look again at what you wrote. What was important to you, the person who wrote it, might not be that important to the really important person – the one who's going to read it.

FRESH BUT LOGICAL.
The strategy said that Chevy's competitive advantage was freshness.

Ever heard fresh before?

Well, the challenge was to find a fresh way to say "fresh."

And the good folks at Goodby did it. Simply. And memorably.

Fresh Mex.

Why will they buy your product in preference to the competition? For the brand, they'll need an emotional connection. For the product, they'll need a reason.

THIS SHOULD HAVE RUN LAST WEEK.

We're looking for a media buyer with at least 1½ years experience in television and print buying. If you're interested in placing ads rather than reading them, call David Cairns at 585-9992.

CHIAT/DAY

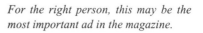

For the right person, this may be the most important ad in the magazine.

205

Dodge ⊕ Different.

A simple one-word theme can establish a long-term position.

HUNGRY? WHY WAIT?

A simple question can establish what your product is all about.

Raid

KILLS BUGS DEAD

A simple sentence can do it all.

Built for the Human Race.

A good theme will usually make a good outdoor board.

ALTOIDS WINTERGREEN

THE CURIOUSLY STRONG MINTS

THE CURIOUSLY STRONG MINTS.
A good theme will usually work with, and inspire, a variety of visuals.

Theme &

MOST GREAT ADVERTISING CAMPAIGNS have a great theme – a strong set of words that can give your campaign a "War Cry."

An advertising theme, whether it's a campaign line or a headline, will focus on the one thought you want your target to remember.

And, for that reason, it should be *memorable.*

It should have that certain something that makes it stick in the mind. Velcro!

By this time, you've probably written a few early theme lines and headlines and copy lines.

Sometimes it's hard to know which is which. Write it all down. . . everything.

Because the more you write, the better the chance you'll be right. Imagine the destination.

Let the Strategy give your thoughts direction and the Objective give you focus.

Try to think like the reader, not the writer.

Send your thoughts to the words that describe the benefit. Or the Problem.

Think. How do you get their attention, and what do you want them to remember?

Of all the things you've written, which of them is the right thing?

You may write two dozen theme or headline ideas (or more), yet you must end up with one.

How do you reach that goal?

How will you know you're right?

First, **it'll make sense.**

Second, **it'll feel right.**

Third, **someone else will like it.**

Fourth, **it will inspire more great ads.**

Let's try some variations on your theme.

206

Variations.

TAKE YOUR THEME as your new starting point. If you have a good Selling Idea, there should be a natural flow of *variations*.

Look for the *structural relationships* that make the communication work.

Write 'em down. You may need 'em later when you present your idea.

Let your thinking flow. Go with it.

Write various variations on your ideas.

Try different possibilities.

See where they lead.

Turn them inside out and upside down.

Play with the ideas. Have fun. Be prolific.

Get it all on paper.

It won't be all good, but at this stage, it's more important to just write it all down.

This is one of the most enjoyable parts of our business. . . enjoy it.

Respect your first idea, but don't fall in love with it right away.

Write Down Everything You Can Think Of!

See what generates additional thoughts.

Write 'em down.

If you have time, sleep on it.

Utilize the right-brain incubation process.

When you're done, sort it out and take a look at what you've written.

When you're through, certain phrases and constructions will emerge.

Some things will work better than others.

And, without seeing a single sentence, I'll tell you the one single trait that will distinguish your best writing... *rhythm.*

A Provocative Statement.
There are a lot of ways to ask it.

Secretary at Consulate General

A Simple Statement.
It can be powerful and effective.

HOW DO YOU KNOW YOU'RE RIGHT?
First, it'll make sense.
Second, it'll feel right.
Third, someone else will like it.
Fourth, it will inspire more great advertising ideas.

Rhythm.

ALL GOOD COPY'S GOT RHYTHM.

As a copywriter, your writing must *move* people – and much of it depends on the rhythm of your writing. You should look for:

1. SHORT, SIMPLE SENTENCES.

Good copy gets to the point.

One idea follows another.

It keeps the reader's interest.

Not only does this force your copy to be easy to understand, it creates a tempo. Movement. Cadence.

As Leo said, *"Great advertising writing, either in print or TV, is always deceptively and disarmingly simple. It has the common touch without being or sounding patronizing."*

Winston Churchill said, *"Little words move men."*

Or, as Ed McCabe said, *"Show me something great and I'll show you a bunch of monosyllables."*

'Nuff said.

ED McCABE'S MACHO STYLE.
Tough as a Volvo.
Hard-hitting and to the point.
Ed said, *"You Can't Eat Atmosphere."*
And *"It Takes a Tough Man to Make a Tender Chicken."*

2. ACTIVE VERBS AND A POSITIVE ATTITUDE.

Good copy should be written in the active voice. It should *move.*

In most cases, you should write in a positive, and assertive manner. Upbeat.

Every sentence with a passive verb should be examined critically.*

So should every sentence that contains a negative.

In "comparison advertising" and certain types of positioning, it may be necessary to be negative.

Certainly, you can still be positive when you're being negative. Particularly if you're a bit po-mo.

But remember, Avis said, "We Try Harder."

And "We're Only #2."

They didn't say, "We're not #1."

An upbeat attitude can help make products more desirable. We've shown this ad before, but it's worth looking at again. See what the attitude does. You just know you're going to have fun in these nifty new shoes from Reebok.

Active verbs and a positive attitude.

A Good Slogan Should Make a Good Button.

* DID YOU CATCH THAT?

That sentence should probably read, "Examine every sentence with a passive verb." Or, better yet, "Get rid of every passive verb."

**CONSTRUCTION
& JUXTAPOSITION.**

The ads above and below use both parallel construction and the *juxtaposition* of words to build strength and interest.

Bad/Good. Fish/Pig/Rose.

Drink like a fish.
Eat like a pig.
Smell like a rose.

3. PARALLEL CONSTRUCTION.

Good copy is well built.

Your sentence structure should be consistent.

Your phrasing should be consistent.

Verbs should generally be in the same tense.

Pronouns should be kept under control.

Is it first person plural (we), second person (you), or third (he, she, they)?

Be consistent. Consistency creates clarity.

The structure of your thinking will be reinforced by the strength of structured writing.

The classic ad below builds power with a series of sentences using parallel construction.

There are lots of examples:

"Better Things for Better Living."

"The Quality Goes in Before the Name Goes On."

"It's a Good Time for the Great Taste."

"What You Want is What You Get."

Many memorable sentences and many memorable ads use parallel construction.

So should you.

Parallel construction builds the case and makes this ad work harder.

MORE EXAMPLES:

"When You're Out of Schlitz, You're Out of Beer."

"The More You Look, The More You Like."

"Sometimes You Feel Like a Nut, Sometimes You Don't."

"Cleans Your Breath While it Cleans Your Teeth."

"Shaefer Is the One Beer To Have When You're Having More Than One."

"You're Not Getting Older, You're Getting Better."

"Does She or Doesn't She?"

EASY TO READ. EASY TO UNDERSTAND.

The ad above accomplishes a lot with clear simple writing that connects with some emotional truths.

The first truth is that reading about your bathroom is probably pretty dull. Wink. Wink. Nudge. Nudge.

So this headline is actually a bit of a put-on.

But wait. You just read the whole thing (parallel construction pulled you through it), you smiled and sort of agreed with the writer, who probably cried about the current state of his or her bathroom.

See how the rhythm of the thing carried you into the sale? So that you ended up a lot more involved thinking about it than you'd planned.

So, did you fill out the coupon? Well, if this ad was really about you – someone due to remodel a bathroom, it sure made you think about it.

And, of course, there's always the 800#. In bold.

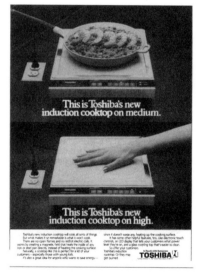

CLEAR CONSTRUCTION. CLEAR COMMUNICATION.

Not only is there a powerful visual demonstration (a hand on the cooktop), but the simplicity of the sentences makes it easy to understand this ad.

I don't know how an induction cooktop works (do you?), but easy-to-read writing makes me think I can.

And the parallel construction of the two headlines is the key.

The early epics of civilization were poems – so were many early ads.

4. ALLITERATION, ASSONANCE, AND RHYME.

Good copy sounds good.

You should make use of the phonetic characteristics of the words you use.

Alliteration – is the similarity of the first letter or sound of words, usually consonants.

For example, "Let It Be Lowenbrau" used a rhythmic double alliteration of the *L* and the *b* in "Lowenbrau."

This creates a distinctive theme that could be used by no other beer.

Assonance – is subtler. It relates to the internal similarity of words, usually vowels. "Invest in Karastan," has both assonance *and* alliteration.

Do you see which is which?

Rhyme.

Finally, rhyme has its reason.

A rhyme is memorable.

The early epics of civilization were poems for a very simple reason – they were easier to remember.

It was an oral tradition – poems could be passed along and remembered in a way prose could not.

For this same reason, a well-turned rhyme can nail your message in people's memories.

From   "Winston Tastes Good
        Like a Cigarette Should."
    (Sorry, I don't smoke, but it's in there.)

To   "Plop Plop Fizz Fizz
        Oh What a Relief It Is!"

The power of the poem is proven.

And it keeps your copy movin'.

212

Rhyming can make ordinary messages more fun and more interesting. Think about it.

None of the topics in these ads is that unique – a new nail polish, a bank loan, a fashion show, a cruise, an iced coffee, and a sauce that doesn't drip.

Yet, by using a strong and memorable rhyme, these messages get our attention – and they're easy to remember.

RHYME TIME!

"Rhyming forces recognition of words. You also establish a rhythm, and that tends to make kids want to go on.

If you break the rhythm, a child feels unfulfilled."

Dr. Seuss

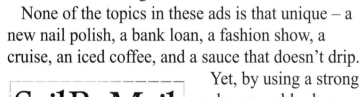

"Dare to Compare"

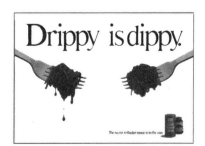

Naughty But Nice. *When this line was first proposed by copywriter Shirley Polykoff, the men in the room were troubled. Wouldn't women take it the wrong way? The provocative (for the time) line was one of the critical elements to Clairol's success.*

Times Change. *Once upon a time, people wouldn't think about talking about products this way. Then again, once upon a time, there was no such thing as a sports bra.*

Double and Triple Meanings *added extra power to this '60s ad for a Black "Anti-Machine" candidate in Chicago.*

5. PUNS, DOUBLE MEANINGS, AND WORD PLAY.

Good copy is clever. Sometimes.

When these devices work, they can make your copy richer and more interesting.

And they're fun to write.

But, BEWARE!

When they don't work, they're confusing.

Worse yet, you're giving the reader an excuse to not take you seriously.

Puns are fun, and double meanings feel twice as nice, but don't be clever at the expense of clarity.

The pun is *not* the lowest form of humor.

The lowest form of humor is a smart-ass ad that wastes the client's money.

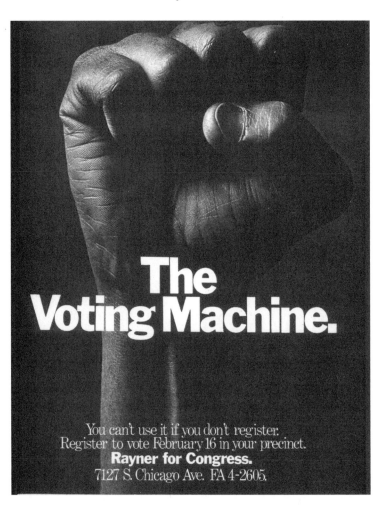

Outdoor is a great place for a play on words. People see it more than once.

HAIR TODAY.

Look at the fun you can have with some stock art, bright writing, and smart art direction. This campaign for a local hair salon won national awards.

Clever but Clear. The copywriter and art director made an ad for holiday ornaments at Pier 1 clever and appealing without sacrificing clarity. You see it. You get it.

Ads like these helped build the Soloflex image. But infomercials sold them.

PUNS, DOUBLE-MEANINGS, AND WORD PLAY.

When they work well, they speak for themselves.

Take another look at the campaign on the left. Visual puns, using stock art of famous faces, give this hair stylist a distinct and inviting personality.

There was a clear strong strategic approach. They dramatized the Problem– a bad haircut – in a charming way.

The writer and art director earned a few national awards as well. – free lance work that paid off big.

215

TWO OUT OF THREE AIN'T BAD.

SAM SCALI
Inducted into the Art Director's
Hall of Fame, 1984

ED McCABE
Inducted into the Copy Hall of Fame,
1974

MARVIN SLOVES

All of us at Scali, McCabe, Sloves would like to congratulate Sam Scali on his induction into the Art Director's Hall of Fame.

We're very proud.

We're also proud of the fact that Sam is not alone. He joins his partner, Ed McCabe, who entered the Copy Hall of Fame in 1974.

And that makes Scali, McCabe, Sloves something very rare indeed: an advertising agency with two founding partners in the Hall of Fame.

Both of these men are advertising legends for good reason. Together, they have created some of the most renowned advertising of all time.

If you're interested in talking to a great art director or a great copywriter about your advertising, Sam and Ed aren't hard to find. They still come to work every day.

Or, if you'd like to talk to the person who does most of the talking for Sam and Ed, call Marvin.

There is, unfortunately, no such thing as a Management Hall of Fame.

But Marvin Sloves is a great reason for creating one.

SCALI, McCABE, SLOVES, INC.

800 Third Avenue, New York, N.Y. 10022 (212) 421-2050 Offices in: Houston, Melbourne, Montreal, Toronto, London, Düsseldorf, Mexico City

6. GOOD COPY VS. GOOD GRAMMAR.

In general, good copy is good English.

Copywriters are allowed three exceptions to the general rules of good grammar:

1. Sentence Fragments.

For effect and brevity, sentence fragments can often make copy better.

And clearer.

Overuse will create a choppy effect.

Like this.

Sentence fragments can strengthen and shorten your copy with no loss of communication.

2. Beginning a Sentence with a Conjunction.

Because we often write one-sentence paragraphs.

And because we often have more than one thing to say.

Or for some other reason. . .

The use of conjunctions or connectors at the beginning of sentences is acceptable.

But don't overdo it.

3. Ungrammatical Usage.

As Will Rogers said. . .

"A lot of people who don't say ain't ain't eatin."

English is a wonderfully flexible language.

New words and usages emerge constantly.

When used for effect, slang and/or bad grammar is permissible. Sometimes, it's desirable.

Contemporary copy should reflect contemporary usage, realizing that an ad targeted at teenagers might not please high-school English teachers. But this should be done with care.

Writers have a responsibility to treat our language with respect. After all, we make our living with it.

NOW WHAT?

After you've done all that, what do you do?

You do it again. That's *Re-Writin'*.

& ReWritin'.

HOW DO YOU REWRITE RIGHT?

Chances are, you've little experience with the amount of editing and rewriting practiced by copywriters.

But a few new habits can help get you started.

THE MORE THE BETTER.

Tom McElligott's been known to write 200 headlines before getting the one he likes.

How many did you write?

Did you look at them with a critical eye?

Then did you write a few more?

The first simple rule seems to be that the more you write, the better the final results seem to be.

TIGHTEN YOUR WRITIN'.

Next habit. Solid structure.

Does your ad have a beginning, middle, and end?

Did you "tell 'em what you're gonna tell 'em?"

Is it clear to the casual reader?

With many good ads, a casual glance will tell you what the ad is about at the same time you want to know more. You shouldn't have to dig. Dig?

Most openings are overwritten. (After all, you were just getting warmed up when you wrote it.)

You must condense and distill.

You must be interesting, involving, and informative. *Immediately!* Not eventually.

Get the most meaning into the fewest words.

Create a rhythm and try to hold to it.

As you move through the middle, think strategy.

Is there a reason to buy this product?

Do you help people connect with the brand?

Which sentences and phrases deliver the Support most clearly and persuasively?

Build on those. Cut the rest.

Bad poets borrow.
Great poets steal.
Copy by Tom McElligott

Q. How many account execs does it take to change a light bulb?

A. I'll get back to you on that.

The end of your ad should wrap the package.

With a ribbon.

Reward the Reader. Ask for the Order.

Tell 'em what you told 'em.

DO IT AGAIN.

So far, so good. You've been tough, but fair. Congratulations.

But it's not enough to be tough.

You gotta be brutal.

VISUALIZE YOUR COPY.

You need another new habit.

Visualizing your printed copy.

Not words on a page, but type in an ad.

As you write body copy, you should begin to have an idea of how your finished copy should look.

CHARACTER COUNT.

As you develop the layout, work with the art director to generate a rough "character count." Here's how:

First, select the desired *type size.*

Type size is measured in "points."

This book is in 14 point type, "automatic" leading on this program, makes each line about 16.3 points.

This is 16 point. This is 12 point. This is 9 point. (Pretty small.)

Now look at the layout. Count the average number of letters on an average line and the number of lines.

A little math, and you've got your character count.

Set the margins on your word-processing program to the number of characters in each line and you'll start to see how your copy will fit.

Better yet, put the actual point-size on your screen – so you can really see what you're writing.

REQUIRED READING:
The Elements of Style by Strunk & White. Read this book.

Their Table of Contents provides a handy check list and guide.

You should pay particular attention to sections on style and composition.

Rules like the following should become either memorized or instinctive:

- Choose a suitable design. Hold to it.
- Make the paragraph the unit of composition.
- Use the active voice.
- Put statements in positive form.
- Use definite, specific, concrete language.
- Omit needless words.
- Express co-ordinate ideas in similar form.
- Keep related words together.
- In summaries, keep to one tense.
- Place the emphatic words of a sentence at the end.
- Place yourself in the background.
- Write in a way that comes naturally.
- Write with nouns and verbs.
- Revise and rewrite.
- Do not overwrite.
- Do not overstate.
- Avoid the use of qualifiers.
- Do not affect a breezy manner.
- Use orthodox spelling.
- Do not explain too much.
- Do not construct awkward adverbs.
- Avoid fancy words.
- Be clear.
- And – use a dash to set off an abrupt break or interruption and to announce a…summary.

The book is a lesson in itself. Every copywriter should own one.

& ReWritin'...

IT'S POSSIBLE TO WRITE good copy to almost any length. Long or short.

Most beginning writers overwrite.

Except for the ones who underwrite.

That's why this next habit is so important.

FORGET WHO WROTE IT.

If you're going to become a good rewriter… *forget who wrote it!!!*

You must become as objective as possible about your own work.

We fall in love with our own words (I do it all the time), and failure to be objective and tough-minded in the rewriting stage can be your downfall.

Even though you wrote every one of those wonderful words, that doesn't mean someone else wants to read them all.

Even though it was tough to write it the first time, you can still make it better the second time.

And the third.

Try to look at your words through someone else's eyes. It's the start of really teaching yourself to write for others.

COPYWRITERS WHO MAKE THE CUT KNOW HOW TO CUT COPY.

Here's a thought from Bill Bernbach: *"You must have inventiveness, but it must be* disciplined. *Everything you write, everything on a page, every word, every graphic symbol, every shadow, should further the message you're trying to convey."*

He's right. Rewrite.

And though you love to write, the rest of the world doesn't have time to fall in love with every word.

Someone has to cut the copy.

Let it be you.

220

As a final bit of cruelty, take a look at the part you like best, the part you really didn't want to cut.

It's often a piece of "business" or *"schtick"** used for extra entertainment, interest, or attention.

Your piece of "business" may be:

- A joke in the headline paid off in the body copy
- A joke in a TV commercial that's set up at the front and paid off at the back**
- A running gag in a vignette sequence
- Humorous background action in a TV spot
- A clever turn of phrase
- Etcetera

Remember, the objective of your ad's "business" is to help your client's business.

Bernbach observed, *"Creativity that doesn't reinforce the proposition in an ad or commercial isn't creative, it's disruptive."*

So take a look at your ad one more time.

Is it as strong and persuasive as you can make it?

How will it help your client's business?

Ask yourself these questions now. Someone else will surely ask them later.

If you can answer these questions satisfactorily, you're in business.

Though taste and writing habits may vary, these are the underlying principles of good copywriting style: *Readin', Writin', Rhythm, 'n ReWritin'.*

Review your work and your work habits.
And never stop.
Learn to cut your copy!
Be your own toughest critic.
Shorter *is* better.
Less verbal. More *visual.*

In conclusion…

write tight.

*

In the '60s, the Yiddish vaudeville term *schtick* was commonly used by copywriters. (Groucho Marx's cigar and eyebrow wiggle were his *schtick.*)

In advertising, *schtick* refers to a wide range of devices, both good and bad.

**

The final clever line at the end was also sometimes known as the *clitchik.*

14. Typing & Typography.

To improve your print writing,
widen the margins and narrow the
measure on your computer's word-
processing program.

Too many copywriters write with
narrow margins and wide lines.

That may be fine for letters,
novels,   and term papers.

But it's <u>not</u> the way to write copy.

A column of advertising copy is
usually 30 to 50 characters wide.

(40 is a good place to start.)

You'll notice that many of your
sentences break in the middle of
important phrases.

As you rewrite your copy, <u>adjust</u>
the words and phrases so that copy
"breaks" naturally.

If possible, "lines should be broken
the way they are spoken."

If the layout is in process, your
art director can give you an estimated character count.

To create readable copy, you must
make your copy relate to the page.

And to get it right, you need to work
with the art director.

It's a team sport, remember?

Historical Note: This is part of a <u>typewriter!</u> These machines were still being used when this book was first written.

It's bad enough having to deal with outrageous deadlines and whining account guys. Must you be asked to put up with insensitive typography as well? At Typesetting, we say there's simply no excuse for it. Type isn't just words. It's art. And it should be treated as such. Call Jay Higgins, 421-2264. Because it's time the breaks started going your way.

TYPESETTING
50 Clifford Street, Providence, Rhode Island 02903

TYPE & LAYOUT
by Colin Wheildon.

We really really like this book. In fact, I think I've purchased two dozen. I give them to writers and art directors.

Wheildon is an Australian art director who has spent a good bit of time studying readability.

Introduction by David Ogilvy.

Get this book. Read it. Use it.

Exercises:

1. RESET THE MEASURE ON YOUR WORD-PROCESSING PROGRAM TO BETWEEN 30 AND 50 CHARACTERS.

2. READ A TYPE BOOK.

3. PICK UP A MAGAZINE YOU CAN SPARE. TEAR IT APART.
PICK THE TYPOGRAPHY YOU LIKE BEST. PICK THE ADS THAT ARE EASIEST TO READ. PICK THE MOST INTERESTING. PICK THE THREE WORST, TYPOGRAPHICALLY.

4. PREPARE A PRESENTATION ON THE TYPOGRAPHY THAT YOU LIKE THE BEST.

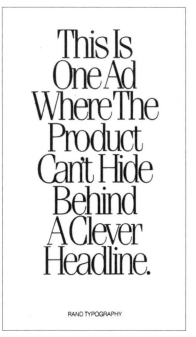

223

                    Sample Print Format.
Job Description Here:
Client Name
"Title Optional"

VISUAL: (Visual Idea Indicated Briefly)

HEAD: Headline Goes Here.

SUBHEAD: Subhead, if any, indicated.
(or, SUB) A subhead <u>before</u> the headline may
           be called a PRE-HEAD (or "EyeBrow").

COPY: Write your copy with a rough
           approximation of the column width.
               Use a second TAB to indent your
           paragraphs.

SUB: Additional Subheads Where Needed.

COPY: Then, add another line of space
           when you go back to the copy.
               Now, most programs have *italic*
           or **boldface**. Use it don't abuse it.
               And, of course, these days, the
           copy may go directly to layout.
               Know the correct format.
               And remember…

THEME: Good Copy Looks Good.

224

Sample Radio Format.

Client Name
"Commercial Title"
Commercial Length: 60"
Version/Date (optional)

ANNCR:	Writing radio's quite simple, really. Indicate who's talking on the left. And write it on the right. I'm the Announcer, but you can call me "ANNCR."
SFX:	DOOR OPENS
MAN I:	Hey, just dropped in to remind you…
ANNCR:	Of what?
MAN I:	…that in radio, people interrupt each other a lot.
ANNCR:	You mean like in…
MAN I:	…like in real life. Okay, cue the jingle.
MUSIC:	MUSIC UP
VOCAL:	Radio! Radio! Listen to the Radio! (MUSIC UNDER)
ANNCR:	That's right, <u>listen</u> to the radio…
MAN I:	And be sure to read your script at a nice pace.
ANNCR:	Naturally.
MAN I:	(TALKS FAST) Not so fast that you have to rush and sound like you're late for something…
ANNCR:	…and trying to get in every copy point.
MAN I:	(SLOWLY) And not so slowly that… uh… more music?
VOCAL:	(MUSIC UP) Your words are going to glisten Every time you listen to the R-A-D-I-0!
LOCAL TAG:	(10" - MUSIC UNDER)
ANNCR:	Write it right and the next radio commercial for an advertiser near you may be yours. Call 1-800-RADIO. Void where prohibited.

MUSIC BUTTON

Ready to write? Good. You've got a lot of opportunities coming up – to put principles to work – in print.

"If I had hair, I'd use Vidal Sassoon for men."

Geoffrey Holder,
Actor.
New York, N.Y.

Effective Surprise! That's what you want to create on behalf of your brand.

A QUICK CHECKLIST.
Here are some of the things we just talked about…

Build Your Vocabulary:
1. Find Your Verb.
2. Add Adjectives.
3. Pick Up the Pieces.
4. Organize Your Thinking.

Good Copy's Got Rhythm!
1. Short Simple Sentences.
2. Active Verbs and a Positive Attitude.
3. Parallel Construction.
4. Alliteration, Assonance, and Rhyme.
5. Puns, Double Meanings, and Word Play.

Print Principles.

THERE SEEMS TO BE A SHORTAGE of good print copywriters in this electronic media age.

Yet, print is the easiest medium to master.

It's relatively simple to produce.

There's a lot of it that needs doing.

And, it holds still.

Some books focus on types of headlines, or types of appeals. This book focuses on types of print *ads.*

Headlines and appeals will vary due to strategy and circumstance, but the underlying *structure* of print ads has remained fairly constant.

As far as this book is concerned, there are six basic types of print ad structures:

1. The One-Liner
2. News (Including Demos)
3. The Spiral
4. The Story
5. The Sermon
6. The Outline

And, of course, combinations of these.

Some may think there are more than six types and some may think there are fewer. (For example, ads that work and ads that don't.)

But you'll find this approach quite comprehensive.

You should try to become familiar with these types of ads and be able to write them as needed.

Remember, every good ad has a *structure.*

And there's more than one way to write one.

1. The One-Liner.

IT'S THE ESSENCE of the message.

One simple statement that says it all.

This is generally the best way to start writing on a project. And the most challenging.

Whether it's a theme line, headline, poster, outdoor board, or caption, this is the test of great copywriting.

Remember, let the visual do as much of the work.

The Double at Work. Turning around a familiar phrase freshens the message.

Classic.
This One-Liner by Hall of Fame copywriter Ed McCabe positioned the Horn & Hardart restaurants. The theme? "It's not fancy. But it's good."

The Two-Liner. Sometimes your One-Liner needs an answer.

We love this ad.
"Dot Your Toes and Cross Your Eyes." We can't read the copy. We don't care. Do you? The writer and the art director (and the model) teamed up to capture the spirit of these Sporto shoes.

Face It. Faces can say a lot about the benefits of your product and the personality of your brand.

CARAMEL KNOWLEDGE

PEOPLE OR PRODUCT?
OR BOTH?

There's no rule. Great advertising has been done with people, and great advertising has been done with "product as hero," like the ad below.

But there's one thing both kinds of ads have in common – the visuals do such a strong job, you don't have to say a lot.

You look. You like it.

Be careful! That's Chivas Regal!

Famous Faces. They can make you look good. It's one way brands get famous.

FACE VALUE.

People look at faces.

This is a powerful and natural human instinct.

We almost can't help ourselves.

For this simple, basic reason, we look back at ads that look at us.

Got a great face? You're on your way to a great ad.

Looking for an edge? There's an easy answer. Get people with an "edgy" look.

The European Tradition. *Posters have always been a more important medium. Here, a bilingual play on words for longtime advertiser Perrier.*

Double-Meaning Visuals. *Remember the Horn and Hardart ad two pages back? Here's an upscale version for a restaurant near a ski resort.*

The American Tradition. *Point of Purchase – like bank posters. Never miss an opportunity to build your brand.*

Get 'Em Quick! *With writing and visuals that communicate instantly.*

Strong visuals *make copy stronger.*

Simple ideas *work best.*

229

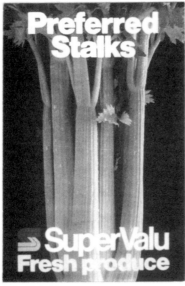

Produce Posters. How can you sell more fruits or vegetables at the point of sale?

Outdoor can put your message in front of a lot of people.

Assignment #11: Starting Your Agency.

CONGRATULATIONS! You just started an agency. Here are your four clients:

1. DENTAL FLOSS_____.

(Johnson & Johnson or a brand you invent.)

The Benefit. Flossing removes plaque from teeth and prevents gum disease.

The Problem. Unpleasant and inconvenient.

The Target. People with teeth (30+).

2. A FRUIT OR VEGETABLE_____.

Pick your own. You may advertise the vegetable generically ("carrots"), or you may give them a brand name ("UpDoc Carrots").

You should probably do a little background research on your chosen fruit or vegetable.

The Objective. Increase consumption.

First Assignment. In-store poster.

3. A SERVICE_____.

You may choose either:

Individual professionals – accountant, doctors, etc.

Service organizations – health or financial services (banks, brokers, etc.).

Other service jobs – baby-sitters, barbers, bartenders – maybe a unique service company (lawn care).

First Assignment. Bus bench back.

4. AN EXISTING BRAND_____.

Pick a product that you can buy in a store.

Buy it. Use it. Write ads for it.

List: Objective, benefit, target, and Problem.

First Assignment. Do in-store poster or "shelf talker." Can it be an outdoor board, too?

5. BE SURE TO WRITE A STRATEGY FOR EACH. Use a consistent Strategy format.

Assignment #11 (cont.): Themes & One-Liners.

NOW, let's do some writing…

6. WRITE A THEME AND A ONE-LINER FOR EACH OF YOUR CLIENTS.

Stick to the Strategy. Think Target.

7. WRITE A FEW MORE.

Remember, the more you have to choose from, the better your final selection will be.

8. WRITE VISUALLY!

You've probably been writing a lot of words.

Try thinking about the visual first.

All the ads you've seen so far in this chapter have had a strong visual.

Try to think of the visual first.

Find it or draw it.

Look at it. Think.

See what happens.

To find out more about flossing *and dental floss, ask your dentist, or write:* *American Dental Association Bureau of Health Education 211 East Chicago Avenue Chicago, IL 60611.*

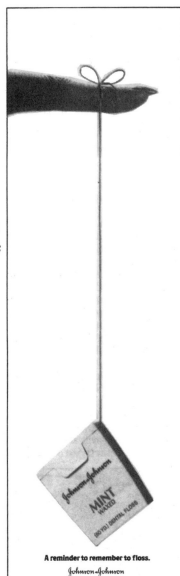

A reminder to remember to floss.
Johnson&Johnson

BACKGROUND: Dental Floss.

Flossing removes plaque (a constantly forming thin, sticky, colorless film containing harmful bacteria) and food particles from between teeth and under the gumline – where a toothbrush can't reach.

Tooth decay and periodontal disease often start in these areas.

How to Floss.

1. Break off about 18 inches of floss and wind most of it around one of your middle fingers.

2. Wind remaining floss around the same finger of the opposite hand. This finger will "take up" floss as it's used.

3. Hold floss tightly between thumbs and forefingers, about an inch of floss between them. There should be no slack. Using a gentle sawing motion, guide the floss between your teeth. Never "snap" floss into gums.

4. When floss reaches the gumline, curve it into a C-shape against one tooth. Gently slide it into the space between the gum and the tooth.

5. Hold floss tightly against the tooth. Gently scrape the side of the tooth, moving the floss away from the gum.

6. Repeat. Don't forget the back side of your last tooth.

Flossing Hints.

• Establish a regular pattern and time.

• Think of your mouth as having four sections. Floss half the upper teeth, then the other half. Do the same for your lower teeth.

• If you don't have good finger dexterity, you may find a commercial floss holder helpful.

• Ask your dentist for advice.

• Most children cannot floss their own teeth until about age 10. Even then, flossing should be supervised.

• Improper flossing may injure gums. Be gentle when inserting floss between your teeth and under the gumline.

• Your gums may bleed and be sore the first five or six days. As plaque breaks up and bacteria are removed, your gums will heal and bleeding will stop.

• Flossing can improve your breath – as it removes the bacteria in plaque.

Continuity, Frequency, Loyalty. *Promotions like this one, where Marlboro smokers save "points" and redeem them for branded products, can be successful for certain "badge" brands. Others can be used to "earn" free products, like a free sub or a latte. This type of program depends on a product that is used frequently. Do any of your brands have the potential for a loyalty program?*

Publicity, Public Relations, Direct Marketing, and Event Marketing. Here, Harley-Davidson turns their 95th Anniversary into a Big Event – with lots of PR, direct marketing involving their current customers, and an event that's newsworthy. When it's a strong brand and a strong idea, it can all work together.

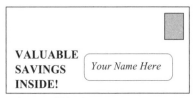

What would it take to get you to open the envelope? Think about it. And now start paying attention to the mail you get.

Assignment #12: Congratulations Again! Your Agency Just Grew.

SUDDENLY your ad agency has been asked to perform additional marketing services functions – everything, in fact, in The MarCom Matrix.

You really don't have the experience, but your agency needs the extra income and you don't want a competitor providing the service. So you say yes.

You might want to skip ahead to sections that talk about these specific areas, but, like so many things these days, your client isn't giving you much time.

So, here's what you have to do:

1. CREATE PROMOTIONAL EVENTS.

Do it for each of your brands.

The objective is to increase (promote) sales.

First, think about the behavior that will do that. Then develop a theme for your promotion that provides a call to action for that behavior.

For example, your theme could go on a display, a T-shirt, button, bumper sticker, or coupon ad.

If possible, try to build some brand equity with your promotion – all in one to five words.

2. PUBLICITY AND PUBLIC RELATIONS.

All of your clients want to be in the news.

How will you do it?

Think of a tactic (there's a list on the opposite page). Write a lead sentence for a press release that goes with that tactic.

If you want to think about this some more, read the tactics list again and skip ahead to Chapter Nineteen.

3. DIRECT MARKETING.

Each of your clients has two lists. One of current customers and another of people very much like their current customers.

All they need right now is a headline (a one-liner?) to put on the outside of their envelopes.

Can you do it?

5. EVENT MARKETING.

Well, can you turn any of your ideas into an event?

In a pinch, you can try a Grand Opening or an Anniversary. But work to develop something that really connects with your brand.

And, don't forget "cause marketing." Maybe there's a program, like Children's Miracle Network or a local sports team, where you can connect your brand with an existing event or series of events.

6. NEW MEDIA.

OK, each of your clients probably needs a Web site. But they probably have different needs.

Here's what you have to do.

A. Name the .com site – assume that their name has already been taken or is being used for something else, like corporate communications.

B. State the basic objective. In one simple, easy-to-understand sentence, state the basic purpose of each of your client's Web site.

HELPFUL HINT.

Remember the Domino's example from Chapter Two? It's back on page 82. You might want to take another look if you don't remember.

That example shows you how you can develop one basic idea through all these forms of Marketing Communications.

HERE ARE THE MOST POPULAR TYPES OF MARKETING PUBLIC RELATIONS TACTICS:

What can you do in Marketing PR? Here are thought-starters – A to Z – from *Value-Added Public Relations* (NTC/McGraw-Hill) by Thomas L. Harris, co-founder of Golin-Harris:

Awards – for example, "Best-Dressed" for a fashion marketer.

Books – like Campbell's recipes.

Contests – an opportunity for more product involvement – like a Bake-Off.

Demonstrations – can you present product "demos" in an interesting way?

Events – yours or someone else's.

Festivals – ditto.

Grand Openings – Great for retailers. Remodeling? It's a Grand Re-Opening!

Holidays – can you tie-in with a day (or month or week) or create your own?

Interviews – do you have a spokesperson who can make media appearances?

"Junkets" – is there a reason to bring the press to you? A fancy press tour?

Key Issues – can your brand connect with or support an issue or worthy cause?

Luncheons – feed 'em and pitch 'em.

Museums & Memorabilia – does your brand have a history? Publicize it.

Newsletters – these can double as direct mail to a variety of "publics."

Official Endorsements – does someone famous like your brand? Could they?

Product Placement – can put your brand in a movie or TV show.

Questionnaires – do a survey. Then, publicize the results. Think about it.

Radio – "Trade for Mention" contests.

Sampling – look for opportunities

"Thons" – marathons, telethons, bike-athons, walk-athons, and etc. link brands to worthy causes.

Underwriting – sponsorship of events

Vehicles – cars, trucks, hot-air balloons.

"VNR" – this stands for Video News Release. We'll talk about these later.

Weeks – like a holiday, only longer.

eXpert Columns – these are written by real (or invented) spokespersons who write about and answer questions about the product category.

Youth Programs – kids, teens, babies.

"Zone" Programs – target local areas.

Or buy a Volkswagen.

Volkswagen used the news. Bill Bernbach believed advertising should be "sociological," in tune with current events, reinforcing the feeling that the product was also in touch with the times. Above, an ad that tied into a gas shortage. Below, an ad that commented on a dismal economic picture. VW was even able to turn bad news into good news.

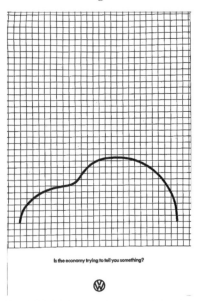

Is the economy trying to tell you something?

2. News.

PEOPLE READ PRINT for new information.

It's ugly, but it gets you there.

When an ad seems to contain worthwhile new information, it's a lot more likely to be read.

New information is usually a good reason to run an ad, whether it's a new product or new price. Yet, most retailers have sales, and new products (or product improvements) are not exactly front page material.

So, the copywriter's challenge is to make product news seem like more than the same old story.

The day after man landed on the moon, an ad appeared in newspapers across the country with a photo of the moon lander.

The ad was from good old Volkswagen. The one-liner headline? "It's ugly, but it gets you there."

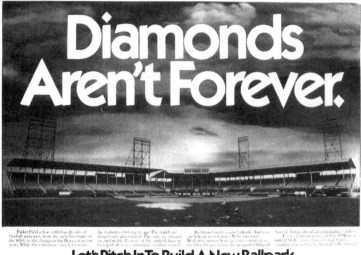

Let's Pitch In To Build A New Ballpark.

The Home Field Advantage. When you can connect with something of local importance, your message also gains in importance. Here, something as simple as a new baseball park contains the drama for a powerful message.

IS IT NEWS?

Many products compete for attention.

And, in many categories, the news is the same.

So it's easy to get lost in the blur.

Here's an example.

The two videotape ads below are quite well done.

Yet, it's hard to figure out which is which.

You must *differentiate.*

Or your good news will be no news.

Can you make your advertising make news? Above, a British glue creates a series of messages that stick in your memory. Below, a carpet store connects a news story (a Russian border dispute), with their products to freshen the message for their carpet sale.

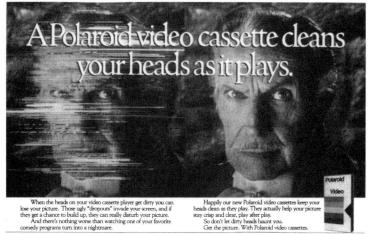

Two nice ads. But which is which, and who is who? It's crowded out there – lots of similar products, often in the same size packages wth similar benefits. Advertising is one of the major ways you can differentiate *your product from the competition.*

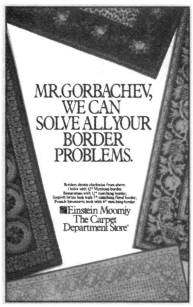

Vegetables in the News. A comment about broccoli by then-President Bush (W's dad), provided a unique advertising opportunity for canned Durkees French Fried Onions – just the thing for a broccoli casserole. Below, the slight alteration of an old phrase from the peace movement is a new advertising opportunity for the Dried Pea Council.

How much news is there in a drain opener or a car payment? Above, a copywriter did his homework and made a dull product interesting. Below, a writer and art director teamed up to turn a monthly payment into some breakthrough advertising.

DEMONSTRATE YOUR ADVANTAGE.

If you've got something to say, *show it!*

As far as this book is concerned, anything that demonstrates something is called a "Demo."

There are different kinds of Demos:

- There are *side-by-side* demos.
- There are *product usage* demos.
- There are *problem* demos.
- And many more kinds of demos.

As we will demonstrate.

The Claim. *Each of these ads seem to demonstrate by making a claim in a dramatic fashion. Above, a simple fact becomes more powerful with strong art direction and writing. Below, the media itself serves as the demonstration.*

Advertise Your Advantage. *Here's a side-by-side demo for house paint. Again,* visual reinforcement. *Saying it is fine. Showing it is better.*

This ad will self destruct in 5 minutes.

The life span of this ad is directly proportionate to your attention span for this page. But an ad in the Yellow Pages puts your name at people's fingertips day and night, 365 days a year, in 96% of all homes and businesses.

Which goes to show that the secret to long-living advertising may not be so much a function of what you say, or how you say it, but where you say it.
The Yellow Pages. They never stop selling.

Pacific Northwest Bell

Get rid of these handles,   with these handles.

Dramatize the Problem. Dramatize the Benefit. *Here's sort of a "before and after" demo for a small piece of exercise equipment. Note how the choice of media space – a nice wide horizontal format – helped to dramatize the message. How do you do a good Demo? It's all in knowing how to handle it.*

"Rams move to St. Louis; pick up new receiver."

Hello.
Southwestern Bell Telephone

New Information. *Here, a new pro football team coming to town provides an advertising opportunity for St. Louis advertisers.*

Irony and Sarcasm. They're not always appropriate, but under the right circumstances, with the right message, they can be very powerful.

Danger Brings Drama. With the right words, even a quiet photograph can be dramatic and dangerous.

THE "GOOD DEED" DEMO.

When you're demonstrating for someone else's good, you generally generate a positive attitude.

You demonstrate that you're the "Good Guy."

Here are some examples.

Certainly, when you demonstrate for a worthy cause, the result can be extremely powerful.

But you can generate some of the same feelings with something as simple as baby clothes.

A charming demonstration of a problem. The actual product – children's clothes – isn't that unique. Nor are the benefits dramatic – reinforced knees and clothes you can get on and off more easily. Yet, the copywriter and art director use charming visual demonstration to add drama in a humorous way.

In North Carolina, some of our greatest works of art never hang in a museum.

Anticipating the News. Here, Avis is ready for the winner of a tennis tournament, whoever that winner is.

TURNING OLD NEWS INTO NEW NEWS.

When you can make something old feel like something new, that's effective surprise.

These classic tourism ads for North Carolina take product features that have been around for literally hundreds of years and make them fresh with contemporary copywriting and art direction.

Each has an arresting visual with the counterpoint of contemporary copywriting.

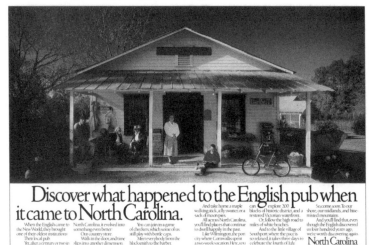

Discover what happened to the English pub when it came to North Carolina.

Some news doesn't last. But if it's part of a long-term campaign, it can still do a good job of building the brand.

This week, the teams driven to be number one are driving Number One.

Ads that Connect with the News. First, Hertz leverages Super Bowl sponsorship with a "salute" ad that congratulates Hertz for being Number One as much as it salutes the two top teams. And, of course, Hertz had two more ads ready, so that the day after the Super Bowl...

HOW LONG CAN NEWS BE NEW?

Legally, you can only say "new" for six months, but this ad for Maxwell House Coffee ran for over two years. How'd they do that?

Note how the writer generated a feeling of news and excitement with a rational copy story, yet never used the word "new."

This is very much a Hopkins-style ad.

Guess who did it? (Answer: Ogilvy's agency.)

By the way, do you know who first used the phrase, "Good to the Last Drop"?

Answer: Teddy Roosevelt!

Assignment #13:

1. MAKE "NEWS" FOR EACH OF YOUR FOUR PRODUCTS (FROM ASSIGNMENT 11).

Write at least one ad for each product:

A. At least one should feature *product news*.

B. At least one should use a *demo*.
  What kind of Demo is it?

C. One should relate to a *current event*.

2. FOR ONE OF YOUR PRODUCTS, CREATE THREE DIFFERENT DEMOS.

Describe them in a short paragraph or try to *visualize* them with a sketch and a caption.

EXTRA! EXTRA!
READ ALL ABOUT IT!

---

3. NEWS STORY.

Grab a news story from this week's news.

Then, figure out a way to turn it into an ad for some product involved in or related to the news story. (It doesn't have to be one of your current products, but if it is, that's even better.)

4. TESTIMONIAL.

Create a unique *testimonial* using a famous personality of your choice.

5. PRICE NEWS.

Write a *sale* or *coupon* ad for one of your products. Make it feel exciting.

6. GOOD DEED DEMO.

Do a *"Good Deed" Demo*.

Use a current client or, if necessary, select another product, service, or worthy cause that you can "tie-in" with your client.

...this ad ran. With News that reinforced their long-term brand position. Now, Hertz further leveraged their Super Bowl sponsorship with a "salute" to the #1 team. And, of course, this further reinforced their #1 position.

Late-breaking Product News. Here, a humorous attitude combined with a lot of product facts, creates news over a simple product introduction – California bottled water now available in Denver.

Some products lend themselves to "Good Deed Demos." Clearly, hard hats are one of them. Can you think of others?

These Rockport® dress shoes conquered the marathon.

Tony Post, marketing executive, has long believed that his Rockport dress shoes were the lightest, most comfortable, most shock-absorbing shoes you can wear. He recently ran 26 grueling miles to prove it.

He ran the world's biggest marathon in the Rockport wingtips you see here.

Some marathoners thought he looked a little silly. But when he finished, comfortably, in 5 hours, 2 minutes (beating over 24,000 runners) his shoes looked like winners.

We salute Mr. Post, who proved our point about Rockport Comfort Technology. Rockports are great looking dress shoes – but inside beats the heart of a long distance runner.

For the name of the store near you that sells the dress shoes that ran the marathon, call 1-800-343-WALK.

Rockports make you feel like walking™

Shoes in the News. Can you find a way to dramatize your product's benefits in the real world? And then, do an ad that tells the world about it.

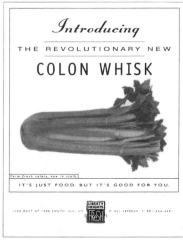

Introducing

THE REVOLUTIONARY NEW

COLON WHISK

Farm-fresh celery, now in stalk.

IT'S JUST FOOD. BUT IT'S GOOD FOR YOU.

Vegetables Are Good For You. This isn't exactly news – even if there's a new study that proves it. Think about it. How are you going to get people to eat their vegetables?

Assignment #14: Wanted: More News.

IT DOESN'T STOP. Your client is so pleased with your ad agency's work that he has… guess what?

Right. More work.

Now, we need to work a little harder to develop work that's even more newsworthy.

Here are a few more things you need to do:

1. CREATE A REALLY GREAT BILLBOARD.

One of your brands has secured the main billboard in town. It's big. And everyone sees it.

What are you going to do with that billboard?

And then, how can you leverage that billboard into something special? To help get you thinking, or should we say, "to help you use your noodle," here's a little integrated event Campbell's put together.

2. GOOD NEWS. A NEW STUDY SHOWS THAT YOUR VEGETABLE (OR FRUIT) _____.

Fill in the blank.

How will you dramatize this great news?

The budget will let you do a news release, a newspaper ad, and a local sports celebrity has agreed to pose with your vegetable.

Create a photo opportunity.

3. WANTED! A NEWSWORTHY PROMOTION.

Your clients just went to an all-day seminar. In the morning, they heard a speaker talk about how promotions can increase sales.

And, in the afternoon, they heard another speaker talk about how Marketing Public Relations (MPR) can generate lots of free publicity.

Now they want you to do it.

Create a promotional theme, write an ad that feels like "news," indicate at least three possible MPR ideas (don't forget to look at that MPR list on page 233), and write the "lead" for your press release.

4. YOW! YOUR SERVICE NEEDS A NEW DIRECT MARKETING CAMPAIGN. FAST AND CHEAP!

Suddenly, the budget can't afford those nice letters and envelopes, but they can afford postcards.

Create a cool postcard with an offer that will bring in new customers from the nearby area.

5. AN INVITATION TO EVENT MARKETING.

Two of your clients need to do booths for a trade show. Write a theme.

They're each having a very nice cocktail party on the first night of the convention (Monday). Write and design a cool invitation that will go to their best customers. (If you need more information on the convention, look up the trade group this client might belong to and find out about their convention. It's usually listed on their Web site.)

6. NEW MEDIA NEWS. AN E-MAIL PRESS RELEASE.

I know, I know, we all hate "Spam." But you can write an e-mail that people will click on.

What will you say in the message box?

How will you make your e-mail interesting.

And, where will readers go when they click to find out more – or do something cool.

How about a cool postcard for your service? *That's one of the most cost-effective ways to send your message through the mail. But, of course, there better be a good offer on the back of the postcard, too.*

The Trade and the Sales Force. *A brand like Lee knows that they're a big part of successful marketing. Which is the most important secondary target for your product? For example, with dental floss, it would be dentists and dental hygienists.*

And, at the same time, it makes you want to know more.

Basically, the copy repeats the premise in the headline.

If it's long copy, it keeps building, using good writing and strong Support to keep your interest.

Each time around, you try to add a little more – to reward the reader for his or her continued involvement.

A SPIRAL OFTEN STARTS WITH AN INTERESTING VISUAL.

Then, they follow it up with interesting copy. On the right, similar visuals dramatize the subject matter – the copy gets quickly to the point.

In one case, a health care provider wants to help you "stand up to osteoporosis."

In the other, a furniture retailer – features prices on orthopedic furniture "that won't break your back."

Bright writing. Front to back.

Even the media buy – a long skinny ad – helps reinforce the subject matter.

3. The Spiral.

THIS COPY FORMAT expands the information as it goes along. It says it. Then it says it at greater length.

The Spiral is very flexible – from headline to end-line, the story is stated and restated.

This approach is based on traditional newswriting principles. Reporters never knew where the editor would cut the story.

Copywriters never know when you'll stop reading.

The key is to repeat yourself without seeming to repeat yourself.

First, your headline makes the point, and then the copy makes the point again.

And then you sum it up.

But you need to keep adding something new – to keep it interesting.

This section was a Spiral.

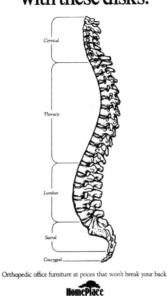

HOW NOT TO GET PLUCKED AT THE POULTRY COUNTER.

by Frank Perdue

Every day thousands of women go to stores thinking they know how to select a fresh chicken. Read on, and learn how little you know.

When you shop for chicken, you like to think you're getting the freshest chicken possible. Unfortunately, what you think you're getting isn't always what you get.

Not like the good old days.

Years back, it was easier to check out a chicken. Most women shopped in butcher shops where they could give their prospective dinner a pretty thorough going over.

But today most women shop in supermarkets. And approaching the modern supermarket poultry counter can be a bewildering experience. The consumer is faced with a sea of chickens. Chickens in a multitude of sizes, shapes, types and parts. All tightly wrapped in shiny plastic packages. And plastic can cover a multitude of sins.

Proceed with caution.

At a self-service supermarket poultry section, there is rarely a knowledgeable person standing by who you can turn to for advice. So when it comes to picking out a fresh chicken what do you do? Too many shoppers operate on blind faith. To them, Frank Perdue offers this advice: Don't. Use this information to guide you. And you'll always end up with a fresh chicken instead of a freshly defrosted one.

Ladies, please squeeze the chicken.

Many chickens are processed with a quick chilling system. Chickens that undergo this treatment are blasted with temperatures of 40° below zero. Between the wind and temperature, the chickens are exposed to a wind-chill factor of 80° below zero.

This often results in chickens with frozen or semi-frozen outer extremities. The wings for example. And the thin layer of meat on the chicken's back. So poke around and squeeze. If you hear or feel the chicken "crackling" it isn't from freshness.

Beware of borderline cases.

Sometimes frozen chickens aren't so obvious. They can arrive at your supermarket frozen like rocks. But after a few hours out in the open air, they'll defrost and feel completely fresh. So feeling isn't always believing.

If you have doubts about a chicken, go find someone and ask if the chicken was frozen or chilled when it arrived. Most supermarket personnel should be completely honest and open with you. Your continued business is more important than the sale of one chicken.

Watch out for stale chickens hiding in fresh wrappers.

Some chickens are wrapped at the processing plant and will appear on your poultry counter with a brand name printed right on the plastic wrapper. If you regularly shop in a supermarket that carries this type of chicken, keep a close watch on them. If chickens in plain clear wrappers start turning up among the others it could mean a couple of things.

Neither are in the best interest of you getting a fresh chicken.

It could mean that the chickens have been sitting around so long or handled so often that the packages began to look messy and dog-eared. And had to be re-wrapped. Or it could mean that the chickens went beyond the expiration date that was printed on the label. So the store dressed up the stale chickens in fresh clothes.

If you catch your supermarket pulling stunts like that you'd do well to find yourself a new place to shop.

Or just look for Perdue.

When you buy Perdue, you don't have to know all the ins and outs of the chicken business. Or be wise to any tricks of the trade.

Whether you buy Perdue chicken, Perdue Pedigreed Chicken Parts, the Perdue 'Oven Stuffer' Roaster, or the Perdue Fresh Cornish Game Hen, there's one thing you can always be sure of. No matter which one of them you get, you'll be getting the finest, freshest poultry obtainable. Frank Perdue makes sure of that. Just because his money-back quality guarantee is prominently displayed on every product he makes doesn't mean he wants you to take advantage of it.

IT TAKES A TOUGH MAN TO MAKE A TENDER CHICKEN.

SAYING THE SAME THING OVER AND OVER AND OVER DOESN'T HAVE TO BE BORING.

Here, Frank Perdue's agency helps Frank be interesting about something he loves – chickens.

Now, when you get right down to it, you get the point of the ad with the headline. Buy Perdue Chickens – Don't Get "Plucked."

But it keeps on going.

They tell you about this.

They tell you about that.

Guess what? They have good chickens – and they're a good value.

And maybe you learned something about chickens.

But, really, part of the point of the ad was that Frank Perdue had a lot to say about chickens.

And you got that point whether you read the ad or not.

We know, we know. You'll never ask for another thing as long as you live.

MIKIMOTO

SHREVE, CRUMP & LOW

***Bright, insightful writing** can make the point and still make you want to read more. Here, a lovely ad for a jeweler.*

SOMETIMES SAYING IT ONCE IS ENOUGH.

Here, a local hospital uses a bus card to announce a new service – or, rather, the return of something that doctors don't do much any more.

You see it. You get it.

There's not much to explain, and there's a "Take One" coupon with a simple offer – Free Registration.

The Counterfeit Mailbag.

The secret thoughts of an entire country were carried in leather bags exactly like this one. Except this one, a copy, isn't under lock and key in a museum. It's for sale.

I borrowed an original from a friend, a retired mailman who, like thousands before him, was kind enough to test it out, for years, on the tree-lined streets of small towns everywhere. Before you were born.

The test was successful; even though discontinued, it can't be improved upon. It's simply perfect as a device for carrying important ideas and feelings back and forth. And the same as with those old and scarce and beautiful mailbags, people will look forward to seeing what you've got inside.

The Counterfeit Mailbag. Containing one vast unzippered pocket, and another zippered. Shoulder strap and handle. Size: 15" long x 7" wide x 12-1/2" tall. Strong, soft leather that will only get better. A beauty.

Price: $275.

How to take care of the Mailbag.

The first scratch will kill you, but in fact. it's the first step in the right direction: patina.

So the sooner it gets scratched, nicked, bumped, dug, hit, squeezed, dropped, bent, folded and rained on, the better. Really.

When you receive your mailbag, it's so fiercely new looking I'm almost ashamed of it. But there's no choice. It would cost too much to pre-age each mailbag before sending it out to a customer. (Antiques cost more than new, for a reason.)

Here's my recipe for "accelerating" the aging process. First, spend one day (the day you get it) the way it is. Brand new. Then, the next day, scratch it all over with your fingernails. Lightly. This will horrify you, at first. Then, spray-mist it with plain water, lightly. Let it dry. The scratches will lose their rawness. They will look old. Repeat this treatment as often as you can stand to: once a week for 5 weeks. Then once a year. (Clean mailbag with plain water only. Not petrochemicals, not oils, not detergents, not mystery solvents, not leather "cremes." It will do just fine with plain water and will outlast both of us.)

CATALOG COPY.

Here's a place where you need spirals by the pound.

Every ad has to entice the reader, explain the product, and ask for the order.

This page is from The Peterman Catalog, which was quite successful for many years. Then it wasn't.

It's a tough business.

Next time you get a catalog in the mail, take a closer look.

You may learn something.

You may even buy something.

Assignment #15:

START SOMEWHERE INTERESTING and go where you should go. That's all there is to it.

First, figure out where to start. Then let 'er spin.

Believe it or not, the prunes have more fiber than the cereal.

If you've been eating bran cereal to get your daily fiber, we have a little suggestion. The tasty California prune. Because three prunes actually have even more dietary fiber than this entire bowl of bran flakes.

The fact is, prunes have more fiber per serving than almost any food you can name.

And if you add prunes to your cereal, you won't just be getting more fiber. You'll be getting different kinds of fiber.

Which is important. Because many nutritionists suggest that wheat fiber and fruit fiber is a healthy combination.

Besides, there's one more thing prunes can do for bran cereal. They can make it taste delicious.

Prunes. The high fiber fruit.

1. WHAT'S INTERESTING?

Pick one of your products and start with something a reader might find interesting – the benefit, the product, the Problem. Whatever. Like prunes being high in fiber.

Now, write a headline. Think target.

2. WRITE SOME COPY. THINK STRATEGY.

Next, write some body copy. It's easy. Really.

Your headline might focus on one part of the Strategy, and your copy flow will spiral through the important parts of your message.

3. MAKE A CHECKLIST.

After you write your ad, look at the way you spiraled through your Strategy.

Here's an example:

Part of Ad	Part of Strategy
Visual	√ Consumer Benefit
Headline	√ Product Benefit
SubHead	√ Support/Reason Why
Copy Flow	√ Consumer Benefit
	√ Product Benefit
Theme	√ Consumer Benefit.

Do it once, just for fun.

Spiraling through your Strategy will become instinct. Common sense will guide your Structure.

In a very natural way, you'll develop an underlying sense of sequence and structure. The key – just do it.

4. The Story.

ONCE UPON A TIME, this was a common format.

Many early print ads were stories, such as Caples' famous "They All Laughed."

Product stories, testimonials and case histories are types of ads that may take a Story approach.

Here, good writing is good storytelling.

FACT OR FICTION.

Whatever story you decide to tell, try to search for the "inherent drama" in your product and the people who use it. (Remember the Capo d'astro bar?)

With luck, you'll find a story worth telling.

And live happily ever after. Of course.

WAKING UP
(A True Hotel Story)

The client wanted to party.
So you didn't get back to your room until
after 1:00 in the morning.
You called the desk clerk to set up a 6:00 a.m. wake-up call,
then crashed.
Only five hours of sleep before the big presentation.
You would have liked more.
And you got it.
Because nobody called to wake you up.
Except your boss, at 7:55:
"Chuck, where are you? We're all in the lobby waiting.
The meeting starts in five minutes."
Somehow you got through it.
Nobody seemed to notice the little piece of toilet paper
you stuck on your neck where you cut yourself shaving.
Nobody said anything about the way you tied your tie,
with the back part an inch lower than the front.
And nobody could possibly have realized
what the inside of your mouth felt like
because you had no time to brush your teeth.
But you did.
Oh yes, you did.
There's only one thing to do.
Go to the hotel that knows
how to take care of business.

NEXT TIME RAMADA
1-800-2-RAMADA

TELL US A STORY.

Set the scene and establish characters.

Establish dramatic conflict, bring in your hero (usually the product or service), and then pay it off.

Try to make your story come alive, and make your ad an enjoyable journey.

Here's an "on the road" story, one that every business traveler can relate to.

In this ad, you can read yourself into the story. And maybe, just maybe, "next time," you'll try Ramada.

Over 120 years ago, Mr. E. McIlhenny had already discovered a way to improve T.V. dinners, microwave pizza, and frozen eggrolls.

Frozen food technology was not one of the foremost concerns for the denizens of Avery Island, Louisiana in 1868. In fact, the closest thing to refrigeration back then was winter. But, even then, Mr. E. McIlhenny was a man out to revolutionize the way people ate. A banker by trade and a gourmet by choice, Mr. McIlhenny devoted himself to improving the taste of foods. All kinds of foods. His culinary creativity resulted in the discovery of the liveliest condiment of all. The famed Tabasco® pepper sauce.

The founder, Mr. Edmund McIlhenny

Now, the last 120 years or so have introduced thousands of foods even Mr. McIlhenny could scarcely have envisioned. Things like T.V. dinners, microwave popcorn, boil-in-bag pasta, and frozen pizza. And today, we can only guess what Mr. McIlhenny would say about all this culinary progress. It would probably be something like, "Please pass the Tabasco® sauce." Which just goes to show that the more things change, the more they stay the same.

The lively taste of Tabasco sauce. Don't keep it bottled up.

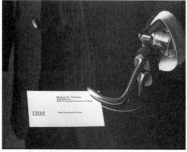

The man behind this hand is Michael Coleman.
The company behind this man is IBM.
There's a story behind both of them.
After the Marines and Vietnam, Coleman earned his MBA and began selling computers for IBM. Promotion followed promotion, and he now teaches our customers how to get the most out of their computers.
His success doesn't surprise us. People with disabilities keep proving that they are as capable as other workers. As reliable. As ambitious. And just as likely to succeed.
At IBM the proof is everywhere, in every part of our business.
The same is true at other companies.
Yet, some people just won't believe that the disabled can do the job. It has to make you wonder who's handicapped.
And who isn't. **IBM**

This powerful visual tells a story all by itself. And it says a lot about the company that runs the ad.

247

WHAT'S THE STORY?

Gossip can be an interesting way to tell your story. We all like "the dish."

Here, Old Navy gets their "fashion spokesperson" to give us the story on one of their latest items.

It's slightly Po-Mo. Even though you know that "it's just advertising," it's really kind of fun to read.

And, who knows, you might want a light-weight Russian anorak.

Below, there's nothing like life and death to give a story a bit of drama.

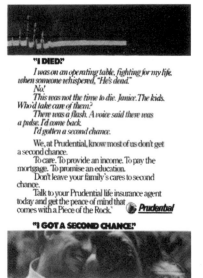

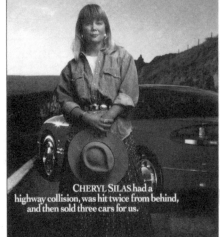
THE SATURN STORY.

When GM built the Saturn division, they had to develop a brand that would appeal to the people who were purchasing smaller foreign-made cars.

That meant that the brand couldn't feel like a GM brand. So, without being dishonest, they had to create "A Different Kind of Car Company."

They did it by focusing on people as well as cars. The people who made the car (in Spring Hill, TN), and the people who bought the car.

When you buy a car, you have a story.

And Saturn developed some very distinctive brand advertising based on these stories.

SUCCESS STORY.

Today, stories like this would never get through the legal department.

They were done before TV, but they still feel like TV commercials.

A comic book approach, like the Fleischmann's Yeast ad and the Charles Atlas ad on the next page, can be an effective way to tell your story.

Credibility might suffer, but you'll probably get great readership.

By the way, when George Gallup first surveyed newspaper readership, guess what part of the paper he found was read the most?

The comics!

One other thing…

"3 cakes of yeast a day?"
YUCHH!

Before there were health clubs, there were Charles Atlas ads in comic books. Can you imagine how many young boys could "read themselves into the story?" Will "comic book" ads ever make a come back? I wonder...

Assignment #16:

This assignment can be a lot of fun.

The "Store Story" helps you go from just writing ads to thinking about all the things it takes to make a business work.

1. WRITE A STORY FOR EACH OF YOUR PRODUCTS.

Try for a range of Story types: product stories, testimonials, case histories, fact and fiction.

Even a comic book.

Generally, you'll want it to be a story about how your product solved a problem – but try to look for fresh ways to tell your Story.

2. THE STORE STORY.

The engaging ad for Banana Republic is an excellent example of what we're talking about.

A. Create Your Store. You can create one from your imagination or pick your favorite shop (and maybe use this assignment to pitch some freelance). Here's a handy check list:

Store name.

What need does it fill in the market?

What products will you sell?

What services will you offer?

Who is your target customer?

(Don't forget the location.)

B. Write an Introductory Ad.

Tell the story of why you started your store.

C. Write a Product Story Ad.

It should be a good ad for your store as well as a good ad about the product.

D. Write a Customer Story Ad.

(Probably a case history or testimonial.)

E. Write a "Why We're Having a Sale" Ad.

Name the sale.

Any other promotional ideas?

Banana Republic: A Short History
    Chapter 1

Never buy clothing by the pound from someone you don't know...

It was the Summer of '77 when we came upon the Spanish Paratrooper shirts--shirts made to go through wars. Our kind of shirts. We were not retailers, but an artist and a writer who enjoyed dressing in our own way--in functional, well-made, natural-fabric safari-style clothing. We spotted those shirts in a damp warehouse in a dark Madrid alley and had them shipped home to the U.S. That's when we learned... never to buy clothing by the pound. When we unpacked the shirts, we also found a lot of old airplane parts...

Mel & Patricia Ziegler

THE PREMIER PURVEYOR
NOW AT NORTHBROOK COURT
OF TRAVEL & SAFARI CLOTHING

BANANA ★ REPUBLIC
TRAVEL & SAFARI CLOTHING C.

OPEN 7 DAYS A WEEK • NORTHBROOK COURT • CALL (800)527-5200 FOR A FREE CATALOGUE & INFORMATION.

CAN YOU BELIEVE THIS STORY?

It's how Banana Republic got started. Really!

Which just goes to show you. However your story starts, you can never be sure how it ends.

The moral of this story is this assignment is one of our favorites. Because it gets you thinking about how to put a business togethers.

That's our story. And we're sticking to it.

Save 20% On Our Watts Line.

Famous Labels You'll See At Pier 1 This Week.

Super Bowl Seats, Only $99.

PIER PRESSURE.

A store like Pier 1 has to keep generating traffic. That means they have to keep on generating reasons for customers to come visit. It's a tough job.

It means short-term retail action combined with long-term image building.

And ads that keep 'em coming back for more.

SERVICE SERMONS.

Are you in the business of delivering service or quality products? Then you might want to deliver Sermons on:

• Reliability
• Caring about customers
• Your corporate philosphy
• Commitment to doing a good job
Above, a Sermon from Avis.
Below, a Sermon from Porsche.

5. The Sermon.

WHEN ASKED HOW HE WROTE HIS SERMONS, the preacher replied,

"First I tell 'em what I'm going to tell 'em.
"Then I tell 'em. Then I tell 'em what I told 'em."

That's pretty good advice for a copywriter.

In the Sermon, the writer acts as an authority, not merely informing, but instructing.

Sermons are often written in the *"corporate we."* It personifies the corporation and builds a "one to one" dialogue with the reader.

Many successful advertising themes use this same "we" device. (We believe, we care, etc.)

You don't have to preach.

Sometimes, you're just a good friend.

To write a good Sermon, you must feel you have something worth saying.

Till death us do part.

It may be beautiful to die for love in a poem.

But it's ugly and stupid to die for love in a car.

Yet how many times have you seen (or been) a couple more interested in passion than in passing? Too involved with living to worry about dying?

As a nation, we are allowing our young to be buried in tons of steel. And not only the reckless lovers—the just plain nice kids as well.

Everyone is alarmed about it. No one really knows what to do. And automobile accidents, believe it or not, continue to be the leading cause of death among young people between 15 and 24 years of age.

Parents are alarmed and hand over the keys to the car anyway.

Insurance companies are alarmed and charge enormous rates which deter no one.

Even statisticians (who don't alarm easily) are alarmed enough to tell us that by 1970, 14,450 young adults will die in cars each year.

(Just to put those 14,450 young lives in perspective, that is about 4 times the number of young lives we have lost so far in Viet Nam.)

Is it for this that we spent our dimes and dollars to all but wipe out polio? Is it for this that medical science conquered diphtheria and smallpox?

What kind of society is it that keeps its youngsters alive only long enough to sacrifice them on the highway?

Yet that is exactly what's happening. And it's incredible.

Young people should be the best drivers, not the worst.

They have the sharper eyes, the steadier nerves, the quicker reflexes. They probably even have the better understanding of how a car works.

So why?

Are they too dense to learn? Too smart to obey the obvious rules? Too sure of themselves? Too *un*-sure? Or simply too young and immature?

How can we get them to be old enough to be wise enough before it's too late?

One way is by insisting on better driver training programs in school. Or . *after* school. Or after work. Or during summers.

By having stricter licensing requirements. By rewarding the good drivers instead of merely punishing the bad ones. By having uniform national driving laws (which don't exist today). By having radio and TV and the press deal more with the problem. By getting *you* to be less complacent.

Above all, by setting a decent example ourselves.

Nobody can stop young people from driving. And nobody should. Quite the contrary. The more exposed they become to sound driving techniques, the better they're going to be. (Doctors and lawyers "practice;" why not drivers?)

We at Mobil are not preachers or teachers. We sell gasoline and oil for a living and we want everyone to be a potential customer.

If not today, tomorrow. And we want everyone, young and old, to have his fair share of tomorrows. **Mobil.**

We want you to live.

A POWERFUL AD. A POWERFUL CAMPAIGN.

When this ad ran, one radio announcer was so moved that he read the whole thing to his listening audience.

Word for word. During drive time.

This campaign for Mobil from DDB set a new standard for taking the high ground.

We lose too many customers this way.

THE MOBIL STRATEGY.

It was a classic piece of business thinking. Mobil's reason for advertising was clearly stated: *"We sell gas and oil for a living, and we want everyone to be a potential customer."*

The emotion was supported by a touch of tough-minded logic.

Are you going to your folks for Christmas? Or are they coming to you?

Drive carefully. We want you to live.
Mobil.

SEASON'S GREETINGS.

A little grim, but the holiday season has some of the highest accident rates.

So, again, the advertising has a strong reason for being.

A SERMON CAN TALK ABOUT CORPORATE PHILOSOPHY.

This can be serious business

The ad on the right was done by Zenith, which was, at the time, a leading US TV manufacturer. Japanese TVs were taking over the market, and this ad threw down the gauntlet.

While the ad was viewed as a success, Zenith finally went under – and, last time we looked, the brand name had been purchased by a Korean Company.

Techniques and Tactics.

Often, a philosophical point is made with a *symbolic visual.*

Here, a bold American worker with arms folded and a challenging look made the point.

The reader is usually asked to think about something he or she may not have thought of – such as an aspect of *product quality* – or *corporate commitment.*

Print is often used to state the case.

Often, hard facts are used as Support for an abstract concept – tangibles as Support for intangibles.

If the company is serious about this sort of thing, the program is usually coordinated with the involvement of a high-level PR firm.

A SERMON CAN PRESENT A NEW WAY OF THINKING

A Sermon is supposed to make you think.

A Sermon is supposed to make you feel good about the advertiser – and good about yourself.

That's why we consider ads like this to have certain Sermon-like qualities.

"Training Wheels for the Feet." There's a nice little bit of philosophy that intrigues your mind.

And there's a "we care about your little one's little feet" attitude that elevates the advertiser and the product.

Product facts and philosophy.

In a Sermon, they work together to support the argument – and make us believers.

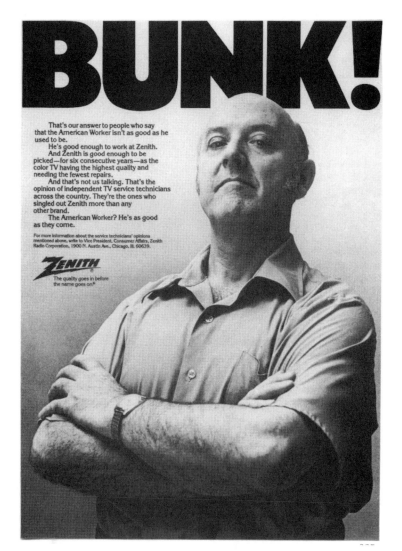

Introducing training wheels for the feet.

UNFARE.

Well, it's official.
40¢ to ride the CTA.

And hard as we try to explain or apologize, a lot of people won't listen.

To some it will be one more indication that "The System" is out to get the little man.

To some it will be the last straw. They'll stop riding.

And to some it will be one more strain on an already over-stretched budget. Well, we don't like it any better than you do.

But if we don't like it and you don't like it, why raise the fares? A good question.

In the first place, the CTA is required to meet expenses from income. We're not supposed to make a profit, but we're not supposed to lose money either.

Second, expenses are up. A new wage agreement with our drivers is the largest part of generally increased operating costs.

Third, ridership has declined. If use of CTA facilities had increased proportionally to our expenses, we wouldn't be operating at a deficit. But it didn't and we are.

In a nutshell, that's why the fare is 40¢. Well, at least transfers are still a nickel.

What can you do about the fare increase? Several things:

1) Grit your teeth and put up with it. Just like you put up with the increased cost of everything else these days (car insurance, parking rates, cab fares, and new car prices for example).

2) Ride the CTA as often as possible. In the long run, the more you use it, the less it will cost.

3) Here's the hard part. The CTA operates under the limitations of existing statutes. We must find other sources of income, such as subsidies. We will propose a program, but we will need your support. Frankly, we can't do it without you.

Certainly there should be better ways for a public service to increase income than by fare increases that put the heaviest burden on those least able to pay.

Once more, we're sorry. Please remember this as the new fares go into effect at 4 a.m. this Thursday.

And remember, we're in business to serve you.

We have to be. It's a cinch we're not in it for the money.

**CHICAGO
TRANSIT
AUTHORITY**

It's The Only Upward Mobility Some Women Ever Achieve.

If you're having trouble moving up or planning your career, attend one of our seminars. With the proper footing, there's no telling how far you'll climb.

Working Opportunities For Women. 647-9961.

DO ADVERTISING THAT DOES GOOD.

Bill Bernbach said a lot of things we should think about. Like this…

"All of us who professionally use the mass media are the shapers of society.

We can vulgarize that society.

We can brutalize it.

Or we can help lift it onto a higher level." It's something to think about.

One way we can add to the "uplift" is to seek out worthwhile advertising opportunities. Sure, they don't pay as much as the fat and sugar-laden products that are too much with us.

But there's another bigger payoff – feeling good about the work you do.

Assignment #17:

1. WRITE A SERMON FOR EACH PRODUCT.

A. At least one should feature a **symbolic visual.**

B. At least one should be a **poster.**

C. At least one should feature a **new way of thinking** about the product.

D. At least one should feature the **corporate philosophy** of your brand.

Free Lance!

FIND A WORTHY CAUSE TO WORK FOR.

Pick something you care about. Write an ad about it.

You might see if you can't get an assignment writing for them.

HERE'S A GOOD EXAMPLE.

Even though you can't read the copy in this small ad, you know what the whole ad's about by looking at the subheads.

You also know what the ad's about just by looking at it.

It's going to give you a number of good reasons to shop at Pier 1.

And you can read the bits of copy next to the items that interest you – without having to read the whole ad.

And, if you happen to be in the mood to go shopping for items like this, you just might read the whole thing.

"To encourage the feeling of accessibility, we often stick coupons or other reponse forms in ads.

It is not so important whether they really send in the coupons, as long as they feel they can.

A visible invitation to respond, whether it is used or not, adds another bit of believability to the characterization."

Howard Gossage

6. The Outline.

LONG COPY ADS with large amounts of information are often Outlines.

So are short ads that list key facts.

Brochures and catalogs are usually developed from Outlines, as well.

SUBHEADS TELL THE STORY.

A quick reading of subheads provides information to casual readers.

A variety of type "color" – **boldface,** *italics,* and •bullets can create additional interest. (Though not all in the same sentence, please.)

Small illustrations and captions add appropriate visual information.

By the way, more people will read the caption than the body copy.

THE OPENING SECTION.

This part lays out your story, with emphasis on *why it's in the reader's interest* to read the whole thing.

It's often handled with **A Boldface Subhead** that summarizes the whole ad.

THE CLOSING SECTION – AN INVITATION TO ACTION.

Reward the reader. He or she has invested time and effort. Offer an opportunity to do something.

Such as:

• Writing for a brochure or sales call
• Receiving a free gift or sample
• Or just coming in for a visit – store or Web site

He or she should be encouraged to **Act Now!**

Research indicates that an effective encouragement to action can have a dramatic effect on results.

And a good way to start is… *make an Outline!*

256

ONE TOPIC OR MANY.

An Outline ad can do a good job either way.

Above, the Andersen ad talks about how well their windows are made.

Below, First Interstate talks about all the things you can do with their product – money.

DON'T FORGET THE CAPTIONS!

They're read more often than body copy.

Every time you have a visual, think of a good thing to say. Or vice versa.

Every time you have a good thing to say, visualize it.

3 KINDS OF OUTLINES.

Here are three major types of Outlines:

Rational/Long Copy.

When there is a "considered purchase," one that involves a significant expenditure and where there is some "risk" in making a bad decision, an ad that presents all the reasons makes sense.

Think of The FCB Grid. The rational/high involvement quadrant (upper left) has many of these types of products.

The Andersen Window ad at the left is a good example. It provides a lot of reasons, clearly presented, and then even tells you how to find out more.

For a certain kind of product, this is a smart approach.

The Visual Outline.

There are a number of reasons for doing this type of outline.

Expanding on a simple topic. The bank ad on the left does this. Hey, it's a loan. But they use visual variety to involve you and maybe give you an idea for a loan that you hadn't had before.

Making a complex topic interesting. You'll see some of these examples on the following pages (right after the International Paper "How-To").

A good Visual Outline can help us work through technical reasons why.

Making an old topic new. Look at the ad for MedCenters, the one with the big cigarette butt, and you'll see a new way of telling the same old story. Be healthy.

Showing a lot of stuff. The Dodge minivan has a lot of features. A visual outline with captions lets you tell that story in an easy-to-understand way.

Want to know more? Focus in on the visual that interests you.

The "How-To" Ad.

This is a great all-purpose opening that "tells 'em what you're going to tell 'em" and draws in the reader who wants to know more.

Often, each section is reinforced with a small visual as well as a subhead.

Act Now! Turn the Page…

Read an outstanding "How-To" from International Paper produced by Ogilvy & Mather.

257

How to write clearly

By Edward T. Thompson

Editor-in-Chief, Reader's Digest

International Paper asked Edward T. Thompson to share some of what he has learned in nineteen years with Reader's Digest, a magazine famous for making complicated subjects understandable to millions of readers.

If you are afraid to write, don't be.

If you think you've got to string together big fancy words and high-flying phrases, forget it.

To write well, unless you aspire to be a professional poet or novelist, you only need to get your ideas across simply and clearly.

It's not easy. But it *is* easier than you might imagine.

There are only three basic requirements:

First, you must *want* to write clearly. And I believe you really do, if you've stayed this far with me.

Second, you must be willing to *work hard.* Thinking means work— and that's what it takes to do anything well.

Third, you must know and follow some *basic guidelines.*

If, while you're writing for clarity, some lovely, dramatic or inspired phrases or sentences come to you, fine. Put them in.

But then with cold, objective eyes and mind ask yourself: "Do they detract from clarity?" If they do, grit your teeth and cut the frills.

Follow some basic guidelines

I can't give you a complete list of "dos and don'ts" for every writing problem you'll ever face.

But I can give you some fundamental guidelines that cover the most common problems.

1. Outline what you want to say.

I know that sounds grade-schoolish. But you can't write clearly until, *before you start,* you know where you will stop.

Ironically, that's even a problem in writing an outline (i.e., knowing the ending before you begin).

So try this method:

• On 3"x 5" cards, write—one point to a card—all the points you need to make.

• Divide the cards into piles—one pile for each group of points *closely related* to each other. (If you were describing an automobile, you'd put all the points about mileage in one pile, all the points about safety in another, and so on.)

• Arrange your piles of points in a sequence. Which are most important and should be given first or saved for last? Which must you present before others in order to make the others understandable?

• Now, *within* each pile, do the same thing—arrange the *points* in logical, understandable order.

There you have your outline, needing only an introduction and conclusion.

This is a practical way to outline. It's also flexible. You can add, delete or change the location of points easily.

2. Start where your readers are.

How much do they know about the subject? Don't write to a level higher than your readers' knowledge of it.

CAUTION: Forget that old—and wrong—advice about writing to a 12-year-old mentality. That's insulting. But do remember that your prime purpose is to *explain* something, not prove that you're smarter than your readers.

3. Avoid jargon.

Don't use words, expressions, phrases known only to people with specific knowledge or interests.

Example: A scientist, using scientific jargon, wrote, "The biota exhibited a one hundred percent mortality response." He could have written: "All the fish died."

4. Use familiar combinations of words.

A speech writer for President Franklin D. Roosevelt wrote, "We are endeavoring to construct a more inclusive society." F.D.R. changed it to, "We're going to make a country in which no one is left out."

CAUTION: By familiar combinations of words, I do *not* mean incorrect grammar. *That* can be *un*clear. Example: John's father says he can't go out Friday. (Who can't go out? John or his father?)

5. Use "first-degree" words.

These words immediately bring an image to your mind. Other words must be "translated" through the first-degree word before you see

"Outline for clarity. Write your points on 3"x 5" cards—one point to a card. Then you can easily add to, or change the order of points—even delete some."

"Grit your teeth and cut the frills. That's one of the suggestions I offer here to help you write clearly. They cover the most common problems. And they're all easy to follow."

the image. Those are second/third-degree words.

First-degree words	Second/third-degree words
face ——————	visage, countenance
stay ——————	abide, remain, reside
book ——————	volume, tome, publication

First-degree words are usually the most precise words, too.

6. Stick to the point.

Your outline– which was more work in the beginning–now saves you work. Because now you can ask about any sentence you write: "Does it relate to a point in the outline? If it doesn't, should I add it to the outline? If not, I'm getting off the track." Then, full steam ahead–on the main line.

7. Be as brief as possible.

Whatever you write, shortening–*condensing*–almost always makes it tighter, straighter, easier to read and understand.

Condensing, as *Reader's Digest* does it, is in large part artistry. But it involves techniques that anyone can learn and use.

• *Present your points in logical ABC order:* Here again, your outline should save you work because, if you did it right, your points already stand in logical ABC order–A makes B understandable, B makes C understandable and so on. To write in a straight line is to say something clearly in the fewest possible words.

• *Don't waste words telling people what they already know:* Notice how we edited this: "Have you ever

wondered how banks rate you as a credit risk? ~~You know, of course, that it's some combination of facts about your income, your job, and so on. But actually, M~~any banks have a scoring system...."

• *Cut out excess evidence and unnecessary anecdotes:* Usually, one fact or example (at most, two) will support a point. More just belabor it. And while writing about some-

Writing clearly means avoiding jargon. Why didn't he just say: "All the fish died!"

thing may remind you of a good story, ask yourself: "Does it *really help* to tell the story, or does it slow me down?"

(Many people think *Reader's Digest* articles are filled with anecdotes. Actually, we use them sparingly and usually for one of two reasons: either the subject is so dry it needs some "humanity" to give it life; or the subject is so hard to grasp, it needs anecdotes to help readers understand. If the subject is both lively and easy to grasp, we move right along.)

• *Look for the most common word wasters:* windy phrases.

Windy phrases ————	Cut to...
at the present time ————	now
in the event of ————	if
in the majority of instances ————	usually

• *Look for passive verbs you can make active:* Invariably, this produces a shorter sentence. "The cherry tree *was* chopped down by George Washington." (Passive verb and nine words.) "George Washington *chopped* down the cherry tree." (Active verb and seven words.)

• *Look for positive/negative sections from which you can cut the negative:* See how we did it here: "The answer ~~does not rest with carelessness or incompetence. It lies largely in~~ having enough people to do the job."

• Finally, to write more clearly by saying it in fewer words: when you've finished, stop.

Edward T. Thompson

LET ME COUNT THE WAYS.

Here's a fun way to make multiple points.

Often, a product's superiority is an accumulation of minor advantages.

Try to combine this accumulation into one strong benefit statement.

Above, Purina convinces you that they have a better way to worm your dog.

Below, MedCenter Health Plan tells you how you can live longer with a very well designed visual outline.

How can you not read this ad? It looks interesting. It has fun visuals. And it has information with a benefit – live longer.

Outlines Can Make Products Interesting.
You see intriguing things. And you need to read.

Great For Washing Down Leftovers.

Clorox® Bleach Eliminates Bad Kitchen Odors
By Getting Rid Of The Old Food Bits And Drink Spills That Cause Them.

Under your sink or in your pantry there's probably already a bottle of Clorox Bleach. That's all you need to start getting rid of the odors. Just a little will freshen up even the biggest kitchens.

Eliminate lingering garlic and onion odors. It's as easy as wiping kitchen counter and sink areas with the Clorox Bleach Cleaning Solution (see below) once a week.*

Do you smell something fishy going on here? Deodorize your kitchen trash can with Clorox Bleach to stop the stench. A quick wash with the Clorox Bleach Cleaning Solution removes fish smells and other foul garbage odors, even from the filthiest cans.*

Let's see now. They have teeth, they eat constantly, and they never brush. No wonder disposals have such bad breath. Here's an easy way to keep yours smelling clean. First, fill your sink with the Clorox Bleach Cleaning Solution. Then drain and let water run for a minute to really rinse your pipes. That's all there is to it.*

*Spilled milk, old veggies, forgotten leftovers — it's hard to find a place in your refrigerator that doesn't trap odors. Get rid of them by washing shelves, drawers, and doors with the Clorox Bleach Cleaning Solution.**

You'll be happy to know that using Clorox Bleach is always an environmentally sound choice. In fact, after its work is done, Clorox Bleach breaks down to little more than salt and water.

***Clorox Bleach Cleaning Solution**
- Mix 3/4 cup Regular Clorox Bleach with one gallon of water.
- Rinse items first with water. Then apply Clorox Bleach Cleaning Solution and let stand for 5 minutes. Rinse well and let dry.

Limited space?
Try our handy quart and pint size bottles.

The Simple Solution For A Healthy Home.

Assignment #18:

1. PREPARE OUTLINES FOR EACH PRODUCT.

Each Outline should include:

A. Headline

B. Subheads

C. Visual(s) and appropriate captions

D. Introductory and **closing** copy

E. Offer or other response behavior.

2. TURN EACH OUTLINE INTO A BROCHURE.

How to write clearly

By Edward T. Thompson
Editor-in-Chief Reader's Digest

A FREE OFFER.

Some of the best Outline ads ever are this series for International Paper.

You can get FREE copies of the whole set by writing: **International Paper Co., College Survival Kit, Dept. FSE, P.O. Box 954, Madison Square Station, New York, NY 10010.**

Who Took My Copy of
Better Brochures, Catalogs & Mailing Pieces
by Jane Maas ©1984

AN EXCELLENT LITTLE BOOK.
It's packed with no-nonsense tips and techniques that will really help you put these critical marketing pieces together.

You can order one new for less than $10, and there are lots of used copies kicking around.

I'm re-ordering my replacement copy tomorrow. I have some brochures to write next month.

WHAT ABOUT HEADLINES?

As advertised, we didn't spend much time on "How to Write a Headline."

I believe the major obstacles to writing good print either come *before* the headline (Objective & Strategy), or *after* the headline (figuring out what's the best structure for your ad).

A good copywriter should be able to write a good headline.

What's a Good Headline?

Well, I guess a good headline is:

- Dramatic.
- Involving.
- Interesting.
- Informative.

Hey, it should be at least one of these. With luck, it will be all of them.

Many prefer the benefit to be in the headline. That's hard to argue.

Some say the headline should *"relate to the reader."*

Nothing wrong with that, either.

Whatever. Just so it works.

It can be a question, a statement, an announcement, a quote (like the famous Rolls-Royce headline), a title, or just the name of the product.

How do you write a headline?

Easy. Write a lot of them.

Then, pick the one you like best.

Sometimes it's short and sweet.

Sometimes it isn't.

Sometimes unselected headlines make good subheads or body copy.

Sometimes they become the headlines for follow-up ads in the campaign.

And sometimes you save 'em for later, because you never know…

Generally, a good headline should give a sense of what the ad is all about.

And, usually, other people say…

"Hey, that's a good headline!"

I guess that's how you know.

Assignment #19:

1. FIND EXAMPLES OF:

A. One-Liner.

B. News

C. Spiral

D. Story

E. Sermon

F. Outline

2. FIND THREE EXAMPLES THAT DON'T FIT.
What **combinations** were used?

3. PREPARE A PRESENTATION OF YOUR PRINT.
Select and organize the print work you've done.
Which ads worked best?
Which formats were you best at?
Which areas need work?

REMEMBER…

Good print ads are involving.

They tell you. And they sell you.

Just remember what Gossage said… *"People read what interests them. Sometimes it's an ad."*

Finally...

*"There's no rule that there are
six types of print ads."*

It's been a way to teach you the *structure* of print ads and help you develop some range.

We hope the lessons covered in this section will help you become a better copywriter.

But nobody can do it for you. That's up to you.

In addition, you really have to be aware of the increasing importance of visual communication and the entire range of media forms.

That's where it's headed. Logos, posters, comic books, and nonlinear design may be the print of the future. Deal with it.

Keep asking yourself whether you're saying what people should really be *seeing*. With a caption.

Now, we're going to shift gears a bit.

In the next section, we're going to talk about *writing* what people will be *hearing*.

Time to tune into radio.

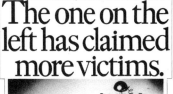

WHAT'S THE COMBINATION?

Of course, many ads are combinations.

Here's a Good Deed Demo and a Sermon – a fairly common combination.

The ad is for a life insurance company. It makes the point that a lack of exercise is a lot more likely to kill us than the electric chair.

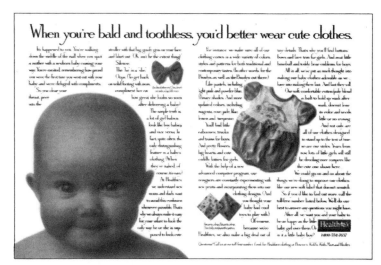

SERMON OR OUTLINE OR SPIRAL?

Who cares. It's a nice ad for baby clothes.

The point of this section is not to get you to categorize ads that have already been done, but to help you get a handle on the basic types of print advertising solutions available to you.

And I bet we've done that.

Next time you're faced with an advertising problem, you'll have a better understanding of the different ways you can solve that problem with a terrific piece of print. Right?

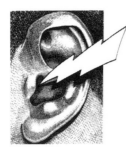

OTHER KINDS OF CREATIVITY.
Pep Boys wanted to reach buyers at their
time of greatest need – during nasty
weather. The agency asked station managers to report weather conditions – they
then ran ads at appropriate times. Sales
went up 55% to 92% in those markets.

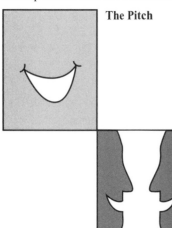

The Pitch

The Situation

Sound Advice for Radio.

RADIO IS THE **THEATER OF THE MIND**.

It doesn't play on a piece of paper.

Radio is an inside game.

It plays between the ears.

While print relates to the *reader,* radio relates to
the *listener.* For about 60 seconds.

TIGHTER TARGET AUDIENCES.

Target audiences are smaller and more defined:
Age, sex, and music preference are examples.

Radio offers distinct timing and geographic advantages. Like drive time. AM and PM.

Other types of targeting, such as ethnic group, are
more easily accomplished on radio.

Use this information to make your person-to-person
communication more personal.

THREE KINDS OF RADIO COMMERCIALS.

There are three kinds of radio commercials:

• **The Pitch** • **The Situation** • **The Song**
Combinations create variations.

1. THE PITCH.

It's simply an Announcer (ANNCR) talking to you.

Your two basic tools are: the announcer's voice
and your words.

Add anything else you want.

For example, sound effects (SFX).

2. THE SITUATION.

You create an event, a small drama that places your
product in a situation of your own creation.

It's often comedic, and limited only by your own
imagination.

3. THE SONG.

Radio was made for music.

Music can give your words new dimension.

One of the most satisfying experiences you may have as a copywriter is to help create a memorable piece of advertising music.

The Song

"Music and rhythm find their way into the secret places of the soul."

Plato

COMBINATIONS.

The three types of radio commercials can be combined. The major types of combinations are:

• Beds • Donuts • Tags • Vignettes

The Bed.

This is a Pitch with a Song in the background.

The Song might move to the foreground – usually to sing the theme.

The announcer talks, the music creates a mood and sometimes reinforces copy points.

"People don't hum the announcer."

Steve Karmen
Jingle Writer

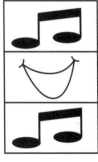

The Bed

The Donut.

This is a Song with a hole in it.

It's a Pitch in the middle of a Song.

It begins with a Song. Then the announcer pitches the product. This seems to make everybody feel like singing… so they usually do.

The Donut

The Tag.

The Tag is a Pitch at the end of a Song.

Usually the announcer (often the local announcer) tells you where to get the product or provides other information – such as a special promotion.

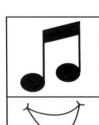

The Tag

The Vignette.

The Vignette is a flexible format that uses *all three* types – in any sequence.

You'll hear short Situations, and bits and pieces of the Pitch often held together in a Song.

These cost more and can be harder to produce, but, done right, can make quite an impact.

The Vignette

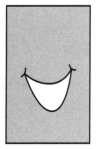

Radio Structure:

Context, Content & Conclusion.

IT'S SIMPLE. Beginning. Middle. End. In radio, it's helpful to think of *Context, Content,* and *Conclusion.*

Got it? Context. Content. Conclusion.

Let's see how they work with the three basic types of radio commercials:

THE PITCH.

In the Pitch, you establish Context at the beginning. You may work to establish the brand theme or the Selling Idea, or, often, you establish the Problem.

You also work to establish a relationship with the listener, with tempo, tone of voice, and attitude.

The middle moves to Content: information, reasons for buying. And so on.

The end is the **Conclusion**:

Stating the theme. Wrapping up the sale.

Providing purchase information.

Encouraging the listener to *act.*

In the Pitch on the left, a second, softer announcer track (usually with more echo) provides an answer to the main announcer. In this case, the phrase "Hear Here" (or is it "Here Here"?) is the device.

THE SITUATION.

The Situation has some structural similarities .

The Context at the beginning of a Situation is usually *place* and *personality.*

Who is speaking? *Where*? *What's* the Problem?

The Content in the middle of a Situation usually builds through *dramatic interaction.*

The Conclusion is often some sort of *payoff…* a punch line, a problem solved.

It's simple. Beginning. Middle. End.

Context. Content. Conclusion. Got it?

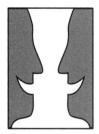

SITUATION COMEDY TEAMS.
Often, you'll find the same two characters in new situations.

Often, the commercials were written by the performers. Some famous radio comedy teams were: **Bob & Ray** (you may be more familiar with Bob Elliot's son, Chris), **Stiller & Meara** (you're more familiar with their son, Ben), and the legendary **Dick & Bert**.

Dick Orkin and Bert Berdis, both creative radio superstars, now work separately.

Orkin's "Radio Ranch and Home for Wayward Cowboys" demo tape should be heard by every writer. Their Web site is www.radio-ranch.com

Bert Berdis, a former agency creative director, is now at his own Bert Berdis & Co.

Collaboration. A good way to create situations.

If you're working on a radio project and find another writer who has a sense of humor you appreciate, you might want to give it a try.

The techniques are similar to the improvisational techniques used by comedy groups like Second City, where you take a premise and try to create a scene.

Watch some of those types of shows and try to apply those techniques to creating a Situation for your next radio project. Who knows?

You might be the next great Situation Comedy Team.

THE SITUATION
Molson Golden
"Fridge" :60 Radio

For Molson Golden, the same two characters would find themselves in new situations, usually involving his obsession with Molson Golden. She reacts.

Note the rhythm of the language – some of it may look funny written, but it's how people speak. Here goes…

SFX: Doorbell
HER: Hang on.
HIM: Hello?
HER: Hello.
HIM: Hi, I'm your neighbor, next door neighbor.
HER: Yeah.
HIM: I missed you when you moved in, I guess.
HER: Really?
HIM: I wanted to explain about that shelf in your refrigerator.
HER: The shelf? Oh, you mean the bottom shelf. The one with the whole case of Molson Golden. Boy, what a great surprise that was moving in.
HIM: It was my Molson Golden, my Molson Golden.
HER: Your Molson Golden.
HIM: Yeah, I had an arrangement with the person who lived here before you.
HER: Oh yeah?
HIM: I sort of rented one shelf in her 'fridge.
HER: You don't have a refrigerator?
HIM: Yeah, I'm a photographer. Mine's full of film, and I needed someplace to keep my Molson Golden.
HER: Oh yeah, I see.
HIM: Cool, clear, smooth. I'm sure you understand.
HER: Yeah, I love it. It was terrific.
HIM: It was terrific.
HER: Uh-huh.
HIM: What do you mean *was?*
VO: Molson Golden, from North America's oldest brewer of beer and ale. The #1 import from Canada. Molson makes it golden.
HER: It really was a shame you missed the party.
HIM: I feel like I was there in spirit.
VO: Martlet Importing Co., New York.

THE SONG
Popeyes Famous Fried Chicken:
"Dr. John" :60 Radio

This Song was written with New Orleans rock star Dr. John.

It captures the spicy personality of Popeyes – a spicy Cajun-style fried chicken.

There is an Intro, a first verse, a chorus, a second verse, another chorus, and a special ending, which in musical terms is called a coda.

In other versions, verses and choruses were "dipped" and an announcer added to present promotional offers.

A music-only version of the melody line was recorded to replace the singers, so the feeling and melody of the song was maintained.

A shorter version of the same song was used for TV.

MUSIC INTRO (Piano Lick)
Girls: Dr. John for Popeyes!
VERSE 1.
Dr. John: I was raised on Cajun Cookin', that New Orleans cuisine.
Girls: Oo.
Dr. John: And the folks at Popeyes Chicken… well they know just what I mean. Help me, Girls!
CHORUS:
ALL: Love that Chicken from Popeyes.
Dr. John: You'll dig the way it's fried.
ALL: Love that Chicken from Popeyes.
Dr. John: Feels so good inside
VERSE 2.
Dr. John: That New Orleans spice is *Oh so nice,* a scandalicious taste bud sin. So crunchy and spicy and juicy my Lucy, grab a piece and bite right in. Hey!
CHORUS:
ALL: Love that Chicken from Popeyes.
Dr. John: The best you ever tried.
ALL: Love that Chicken from Popeyes.
Dr. John: Your taste buds will be tantalized.
CODA:
Dr. John: And once you savor that eye-poppin' flavor, you'll say, this is some *serious* chicken!
(BUTTON)

THE SONG.

The Beginning of the Song is also called the Introduction or Intro.

In this section you establish musical Context – establishing tempo and musical attitude.

You may also use the Verse – the first one, to establish your context.

Then, you develop what you started. Content.

It may be a verse, it may be a chorus, or, today, it may move into a less-traditional musical structure.

Originally, advertising songs were sort of like show tunes – they may have been in many different styles, but they moved the plot along as well as made music. Today, unless you're purposefully corny, that may not work as well.

Give 'Em the Hook.

The End is usually the Chorus, which usually features your theme as the "Hook" in your Song.

While one hates to make rules, if you're going to work in this area, your Song better have a good "hook."

There should be a memorable musical phrase.

In pop music this is known as "the hook."

In advertising music, they try for the same thing. Only. . .

Music is very flexible. You may start with your Hook, establishing your theme at the beginning, or you might just repeat the Hook throughout.

So your Conclusion could also be your Context and Content. Confusing? Not if it sounds right.

Some musical forms, such as the blues, can be thought of as verse and chorus combined.

The list goes on. Whatever you do, it should have Structure. On the left is an example – a Song written with New Orleans' rock star Dr. John to capture the spicy personality of Popeyes Fried Chicken.

STRUCTURE: BEDS, DONUTS & TAGS.

The most common type of radio commercial is a Combination of the three basic types of radio commercials. Each has structure.

In the Bed, a Song is the background for a Pitch. A major concern is matching the structure of the Song with the pace of the Pitch.

For example, the words and musical mood should match. The tempo and attitude should match.

Another technique is to start with announcer only and bring in the music as you introduce the product.

In the Donut, the structure of the Song is usually already written for you. The usual concern is making your Pitch match the size of the "Donut hole" and the attitude of the Song.

You may want to write your Pitch copy to refer to the lead in lyrics. For example. . .

Dr. John (SINGS):

> 'Cause Popeyes does it right.

LOCAL ANNCR:

> That's right. Spiced right and priced right.

Donut Varieties.

There are a few. There's the Double Donut, with two holes, the Donut + Tag, with an additional Tag section. (The example at the right is a Double Donut with a Tag.)

There's something I like to use which involves *alternating* copy and singing...

ANNCR: Archway Cookies are made with good food.

SINGERS: Archway Cookies. . .

ANNCR: Like oatmeal, apples, dates. . .

SINGERS: The Good Food Cookie.

Finally, there's the Tag – the open place at the end of many radio commercials.

It's a smart way for retailers to use radio.

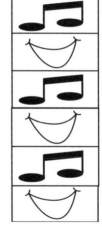

TWO DONUTS + A TAG.

Here's a commercial designed for local restaurants. It takes the "Against" position – positioning this local restaurant against fast food chains.

The Song is in a funky musical style – right for a place that serves ribs.

There are two Donuts and a Tag.

"Take a Break from the Chains" :60

MUSIC INTRO (One bar)

VOCAL: Take a Break from the Chains! (Take a break) Those uniform uniforms, it's all the same.

Those clever commercials and advertising claims. (Come On)

Take a Break from the Chains.

(Take a Break from the Chains).

ANNCR [DONUT ONE]:

At Jim & Johnny's in Oak Park, you get good food made in a real kitchen, instead of some assembly line.

Hey, a lot of places may cook up more food, but nobody cooks up better.

Real folks, real food, and real good.

Special dishes like Johnny's famous barbecued back ribs – best in town. Take a break from the chains at Jim & Johnny's, on Lake Street, in the heart of Oak Park.

VOCAL: Take a Break from the Chains (Take a Break) Those uniform uniforms, it's all the same…

ANNCR [DONUT 2]: This week, try Jim & Johnny's barbecue special.

VOCAL: Come on (Come On), Take a Break from the Chains!

ANNCR. TAG: At Jim & Johnny's on Lake Street, in Oak Park.

See how this works? The Song establishes the Selling Idea. The first Donut gives you the idea of the restaurant.

Then, the second Donut delivers a promotional message.

The Tag repeats and reminds you where the restaurant is located.

HOW TO PLAY TAG.

Some things you can do with tags:

• **Special Promotions** – you can change them quickly and add extra energy to your image.

• **Local address information.**

• **Local phone numbers.**

• **Announcements** – Happy Birthday to employees and customers, or anything that adds the personal touch.

• **Community Involvement** – use your local tag to increase local involvement.

VIGNETTE:

Golden Bear – "Where." :60

Here's a nice little example of vignette structure – a short song, the musical question "where?" punctuated by little situations.

SONG: Where . . .

GUY: Where can I find really good tasting food... I mean all across the menu?

SONG: Where...

GAL: Where can I get anything from a light salad to a great steak on my lunch hour... and still have time left for a little shopping?

SONG: Where...

GUY #2: Where can I get great breakfasts, you know really fantastic pancakes, perfect eggs and an endless cup of coffee or tea anytime of the day or night?

SONG: Where...

GUY #3: Where can I get a Senior Citizen's Discount on any regular menu item, from a sandwich to a meal?

SONG: Where...

GAL #2: Where can I afford to take the entire family and satisfy everyone's appetite?

SONG: Where... at Golden Bear.

ANNCR: At Golden Bear Family Restaurants you can choose what you like and be confident you'll like what you choose. Because we take extra care to bring you delicious wholesome food every day.

Whether it's breakfast, a sandwich, a whole meal, or one of our exciting specials, and you know why? Because what's really special at Golden Bear is *you.*

SONG: You can choose what you like; you'll like what you choose.

Where... at Golden Bear!

Address and offer information helps your spot work harder in the retail environment of radio.

So give those Tags a little extra effort.

LOCAL ANNCR: I'll repeat that. Give those Tags extra effort... starting *today!*

THE VIGNETTE.

In the Vignette, you can interweave all the different elements of radio. Here's a Vignette 60:

	Song Intro	Beginning
	Announcer Intro	
	Situation I	
	Musical Theme	
	Situation II	Middle
	Announcer	
	Musical Theme	
	Situation III	End
	Musical Theme	
	Announcer Tag	

HEY! YOU DON'T TALK LIKE YOU WRITE.

You're used to reading what you write.

With radio, you have to *listen* to what you write.

You may even need – um – new punctuation.

Tony Schwartz notes, *"If we use normal punctuation marks in written copy, it will be very difficult for someone to* sound *the words. Commas, semicolons, etc., are designed for the written word... There is a clear need for a system of oral punctuation marks that will indicate what people do when they speak...*

Spoken words that make complete sense when heard are incongruous when transcribed with written punctuation marks."

...AND MORE STRUCTURE.

Now let's examine two more bits of structure:

The *horizontal* dimension – Time & Tempo.

The *vertical* dimension – Sound.

Time & Tempo.

THINK OF RADIO as a *horizontal time line* sixty seconds in length. That's *Time.*

Now think of the pace at which you move along that line. That's *Tempo.*

TIME & TEMPO – THE PITCH.

For example, the Pitch. The tempo of your announcer's delivery can be a distinctive part of your commercial.

Readin', Writin', and *Rhythm.* Remember?

Hear how extra emphasis can be used for effect.

Pauses. . . can add. . . **importance**. . . to key ideas.

Use *repetition* of certain words or phrases to tie your script together. Because *repetition* works to build both rhythm and emphasis.

The parallel construction inherent in *repetition* can help you build a solid rhythmic script.

Repetition can help people keep track of what you're saying. Need we say it again?

How many words? That's up to you.

Depending on the tempo of the announcer, you can have almost as many words as you wish.

The real question is – *what's the right rhythm to deliver your message to the listener?*

Mood and attitude also affect tempo.

Your attitude can be tough and competitive. . . or. . . relaxed and friendly.

You can build excitement by pushing the tempo. Or you can add importance by moving more slowly.

Tempo is one of the major ways you can make your Pitch distinctive. And memorable.

TIME & TEMPO – THE SITUATION.

The Situation also has tempo.

The entire sixty seconds should have form.

Context. Content. Conclusion… bah-da-boom.

"I believe that the best commercials nearly always make people feel that the advertiser is talking directly to them."

Tony Schwartz

PERFECT PITCH.

Here's a pitch that Tony Schwartz designed to recruit new sales people for Bamberger's Department Stores.

Before writing the commercial, some of Bamberger's best employees were interviewed, asked why they chose Bamberger's as a place to work, and what they liked about their job.

They were also asked what radio stations they listened to.

Here's part of the spot.

ANNCR: Well, what are you doing with yourself now that the kids are all grown up and gone?

Wouldn't it be fun to go out and meet new people, maybe even start working again? You've got a lot to contribute.

And an extra paycheck could go a long way.

You know, there's a new department store opening in September at the Lehigh Valley Mall. Bamberger's.

And they really do need people like you. People who like to shop and who like to help other people shop.

And Bamberger's will have so many different work schedules – mornings, afternoons, evenings, full time, part time, weekdays, Saturdays – and they'll have employee discounts and nice benefits, too.

You know, Bamberger's really appreciates people like you, people who care and try.

So you probably won't stay at your starting salary very long...

Guess what? *Exactly the right kind of people showed up at Bamberger's – looking for jobs!*

"THE STRAW MAN."
Steve Steinberg, who taught radio at The Portfolio Center, suggests developing an imaginary competitor for your product – a "Straw Man."

You dramatize your advantage as you create a humorous situation. Here, Dick Orkin sells Breakfast at McDonald's as a waiter at "Chateau Le Foof."

McDonald's "Chateau LeFoof." :60

SFX: Bell

Waiter: Good morning, Mr. and Mrs. Whifflebottom.

Whifflebottoms: Good morning.

Waiter: Enjoying your stay at Chateau Le Foof?

Whifflebottoms: Quite.

Waiter: I assume you'll be joining us for breakfast.

Whifflebottoms: Breakfast?

Waiter: Yes, one boiled egg covered with poached salmon bits and set on a slice of dry toast all for the very reasonable price of seventeen dollars and forty-nine cents.

Mrs. Whifflebottom: No, no, we'll be going to McDonald's.

Waiter: McDonald's?

Mrs. Whifflebottom: They have a breakfast special for ninety-nine cents.

Waiter: Ninety-nine cents?

Mrs. Whifflebottom: Two farm fresh eggs scrambled in creamery butter, a toasted English Muffin, and crispy crunchy hash brown potatoes…

SFX: Feet exit

Waiter: I see, well have a good day then… Ah! Mr. HodNoggin!

HodNoggin: Morning.

Waiter: You'll be enjoying our delicious breakfast special?

HodNoggin: Breakfast special?

Waiter: Yes, an enormous boiled egg, smothered in a sea of poached salmon bits and set on a massive slice of dry toast all for only twelve dollars and forty-nine cents.

HodNoggin: No!

Waiter: Nine dollars and seventeen…

HodNoggin: No!

Waiter: Four dollars…

(continued on next page)

Beginning. Middle. End.

You need to feel the overall structure of your spot.

In the beginning, you must establish the Situation, introduce your characters, and perhaps the Problem.

You may wish to introduce the product. Context.

Then, you move to the middle where the product is a key part of the drama. Content.

And the end, with product as hero. Conclusion.

The tempo of all this action will also affect the mood and attitude. The spot on this page, done by Dick Orkin's Radio Ranch has the speed and tempo of an old-time farce.

Dramatic structure and comedic timing are key – here, a fast-moving situation with people stepping on each other's lines.

Or. . . perhaps a bit more laid back. . . warm and intimate conversation with background music reinforcing the mood.

The right tempo will give your Situation a sense of itself. At the right tempo, it will feel right.

TIME & TEMPO – THE SONG.

For the Song, tempo is also critical.

An average pop song lasts about three minutes.

Naturally, you can't stuff a whole song's worth of words and music into sixty seconds. Don't try.

Don't overwrite.

Don't rush the tempo of your commercial.

Don't try to squeeze in a few extra lyrics or a little more copy.

Find the tempo that's right for the mood and attitude you wish to convey. And stick to it.

Make your copy fit the tempo.

And to help you do a better job, let's talk about *natural rhythm.*

Natural Rhythm.

ONE OF THE BASIC PRINCIPLES of writing for the ear is… "natural rhythm."

What is it?

First, it's self-explanatory.

It means your writing and phrasing is built with the natural rhythm of the words you use.

Let's start by examining the natural rhythmic patterns of words and phrases.

For example, the word "emphasis."

Think of three notes in an even tempo.

Now, say the word "emphasis." The first note, the first syllable has extra *emphasis.*

Three notes with an accent on *one.*

"Emphasis" is a waltz. *Em*-pha-sis.

One - two - three.

Naturally, this varies with each word or combination of words.

Consider "serendipity" and "different."

Seren*dip*ity – two even notes, then three faster ones, with the "dip" accented.*

One-two-*three* and four. Ser-en-*dip*-i-ty.

For the word "different" you have a choice of two different natural rhythms.

*Differ*ent – two fast notes and a slower note.

One and *two. Diff*-er-*ent.*

Or… two notes with the accent on the first.

Diff-rent. *One,* two.

There's more than one natural rhythm.

Phrases have rhythm, too.

For example, "one of the best." This useful phrase has numerous natural rhythms.

You can emphasize *"one"* to create the phrase *"One* of the best…" *One,* two, and three.

HodNoggin: No! I'll be having scrambled eggs, an English Muffin and hash browns at McDonald's.
Waiter: Ah! Very good! (softly) You supercilious twit.
Mrs. McFarfel: Good Morning!
Waiter: Ah! Mrs. McFarfel, you'll be having breakfast here?
Mrs. McFarfel: No, I… But I…
Waiter: I've locked all the doors… You won't be going to McDonald's!
Mrs. McFarfel: Help! Help!
SFX: Clatter, yelling & commotion (continues underneath).
ANNCR: The incredible ninety-nine cent Breakfast Special – at participating McDonald's.

FIND YOUR RHYTHM…
The Motel 6 Campaign

Once upon a time, copywriter David Fowler, enjoyed listening to radio personality Tom Bodett on National Public Radio.

Then he was assigned a radio project for Motel 6. It was the perfect match – a folksy, no-frills radio personality that was a perfect fit for the no-frills product – Motel 6.

He wrote copy that fit Bodett's rhythm – from the opening, *"Hi, Tom Bodett here for Motel 6,"* to the final *"We'll leave the light on for you."*

It could happen to you.

Keep listening.

✳

UP BEATS & DOWN BEATS.

When counting musical beats, the *down beat* is the number of the beat (one - two-three-four, etc.) beginning with one.

The *up beat,* the in-between beat, is indicated as "<u>and</u>."

Thus, "One - two - three - four" indicates four down beats.

"One <u>and</u> two <u>and</u> three <u>and</u> four <u>and</u>…" indicates up beats as well.

You will find copy works well when some of your emphasis words hit on down beats.

And you will find that if you think of your copy rhythmically and match it to the music, it will fit more naturally.

SOUND: THE "VERTICAL" DIMENSION.

Radio is an acoustic environment.

You don't see it. You hear it.

You don't just write it, you shape it.

For example echo and sound effects can create differently sized space.

The tone of your announcer, the vocal characteristics of actors, and music... they all play a part in shaping the *vertical dimension* of sound.

Sound – The Pitch.

Even a single voice in the Pitch has vertical range. Even your copy goes up and down.

Inflections and intensity add additional dimension. Each sentence has an arc. You'll feel a rhythm as thoughts and words go up and down.

Each component of voice recording – presence, echo, equalization, and the voice tone itself – can help you build distinctiveness with a single voice.

Finally, an announcer should do more than read your words – he should "sound" them. (See opposite page.)

Sound – The Situation.

The vertical component of sound can be quite important.

For example, the voices in a Situation should have *tonal contrast*.

Unique voices will help establish your characters quickly and clearly. Dick Orkin's distinctive voice has been one of the key factors in his success.

Background noise and sound effects can also help you "set the stage" and shape your acoustic environment.

(continued on next page)

Or, you can string the words together into a four syllable adjective. "Oneofthebest."

(In musical terms, "Oneofthe" becomes a *triplet*. Three beats in one.)

Naturally, the words that come before and after also affect the rhythm of your writing.

And. . . you may wish to alter that rhythm on purpose – to create added emphasis.

When writing for music, you'll discover even more rhythmic potential, because the dimension that music brings offers even more rhythmic options.

As you become more aware of the natural rhythm of words, you'll find your writing improving.

You'll find natural rhythmic emphasis will merge into your message and strengthen your writing.

Naturally.

AN EXAMPLE FOR YOU.

Look at the natural rhythm of this Steve Karmen-written song for Budweiser:

> ***This Bud's for you!***
> *For working hard all day*
> *just like you always do.*
> ***So here's to you!***
> *You know it isn't only what you say,*
> *it's what you do.*
> ***This Bud's for you!***
> *For all you do, the King of Beers*
> *is comin' through.*
> ***This Bud's for you!***
> *You know there's no one else*
> *that does it quite the way you do.*
> ***For all you do – This Bud's for you!***

Horizontal and Vertical.

In addition, to these horizontal dimensions, take the time to examine the *vertical dimension* – it's in the vertical column on your left.

SOUND CONCLUSIONS.

And that's what radio is all about:

Pitches, Situations, Songs,
and **Combinations.**
Time and Tempo...
Natural Rhythm...
Sound.

And, of course, it all has **Structure.**
Beginning. Middle. End.
Context. Content. Conclusion.
Sound advice for radio.

Assignment #20:

FOR YOUR RADIO ASSIGNMENT, you have your choice of four products. Or more:

• **A Fruit or Vegetable.** Use the one you used in your print assignment.

• **A New Product.** Invent a new product, one that *solves a problem.* Describe it and name it.

• **A Beverage.** Pick a popular beverage – a beer or soft drink, or a less popular one. No hard liquor.

• **A Restaurant.** Try picking one of your favorite local restaurants. Pick up a menu. Look around at the customers. Ask what station they listen to.

• **Write a Strategy and Theme for Each.** Try for a really nice set of words.

Okay, here are the exercises.

1. THE PITCH.

A. Write a "Hot" Script.
Announcer and SFX (sound effects) only.
Thirty seconds. Lots of words. Good rhythm.
How many words?

B. Write a "Cool" Script.
Announcer and SFX only. 60".
Pauses... deliberate drama.
How many words?

SOUND *(Cont.)*
Sound – The Song.
Your final result will be better if you understand various vertical elements:

The Low End, bass drum and bass guitar, reinforces the basic tempo, rhythmic pattern, and the "root" of the chord progression.

The Middle Range is the center of your sound – melody and harmony.

This is the area where clutter can occur. Try to maintain acoustic "space" in the overall sound for your message.

Helpful Hints for the Middle Range:

• As Grammy-winner Quincy Jones notes, *"you don't put the instruments in the same sonic strata as the voice. You have to put instruments above and under, but let the lead voice make its statement uncluttered and clear."*

• When writing announcer copy to an existing music track, try to find a tone and tempo that "fits" the music.

The High End of your music track may offer additional opportunities:

• Distinctive percussion effects, some of which might reinforce copy points.

• Symphonic strings to give the track more size and an expensive sound.

Remember... **the voice that carries your message, whether singer or announcer, should have its own space; the music should surround and reinforce... not interfere.** Sound advice.

"Sounding."

"When you're working on the ear, you're working on sound. And once sound penetrates the ear, then you're working on the emotions of people.

Now, do I have to say *something to stir the emotions – or shall I* sound *something to stir the emotions?*

Certain words require to be sounded*, not said. 'What's new... whatsnew?'*

The second "Whatsnew" is slurred, but it is acceptable to you because it sounds right.

Therefore, in commercial copy, there are certain words, certain phrases, that are not to be said, they are to be sounded."

Bob Marcato, Announcer

Good Habits:

Here are a few habits that can help you develop your radio writing skills:

1. Read your scripts aloud.
Leave time for pauses and SFX.

2. Underline words you wish emphasized and indicate pauses… in your written script.
This can help your talent better understand how to read your scripts.

3. Familiarize yourself with some local audio studios. What equipment do they have available? Do they have sound effects and a music library?

4. Listen to the tapes of voice talent. Local and national.

5. Learn to announce. Don't be shy, you can do it.

6. Listen to jingle house sample reels.

7. Familiarize yourself with some of the local musical talent.

8. Who does the jingles you like best? Track down their sample reels.

9. Listen to the demo tapes of radio specialists: Chuck Blore, Ken Nordine, Dick Orkin, and Bert Berdis.

10. Listen to some old Stan Freburg recordings.

11. Finally, start producing some of your scripts in demo form.
Use friends at work as actors.
This can help you develop your production skills as well as writing skills.

www.wadio.com

WorldWideWadio
H O L L Y W O O D

LA: 323 957 3399 · NY: 212 768 9717

2. THE SITUATION.

A. Indicate three or four situations based on your **new product.**
What are the Situations?
What characters might be involved?
Pick the characters you wish to use.

B. Write Two Situations.
Use the same characters in both Situations.
Use the same "on strategy" copy as you talk about the product and the same theme.

C. If you want to make your commercial "funnier," read the next chapter. *Quick!*

3. THE SONG.

Take your **beverage.**

A. Write three possible "Hooks."

B. Indicate alternate rhythmic treatments of each with underlines.

C. Write a Song using an introductory verse, a chorus, a second verse, a closing chorus, and a coda. Tap your foot. How long is your song?

D. Write a Song with an alternate structure – most beginning writers write songs that are too long.
Hint: Try for two-line verses.

4. WRITE SOME COMMERCIALS FOR YOUR LOCAL RESTAURANT.

A. What ways can you localize your spot?

B. What times or special occasions can you use?

C. What special items or promotions will you feature?

D. Write two localized commercials. Announcer only. Assume someone at the station will read it.

E. Do an *Announcer Testimonial.* Assume the radio announcer has been to the restaurant and liked it.

F. Do a *Customer Testimonial* commercial – use customer comments and the local Announcer.

Yo! Mo Po-Mo!

PO-MO MAKES SENSE on a lot of radio stations.

Radio audiences are "tighter targets." And many of these groups are determined by musical preference.

See where this is going? In every market, there's a whole sector of the listening audience that's a bit mo' po-mo in their response to advertising messages.

So, while a certain attitude might be right for the radio spot you write for me and my need for comfortable shoes, it probably won't have the same attitude as the one that's right for you.

Clubs, clothing stores, restaurants, and all those other businesses that want your business… they may need to go a bit po-mo. So…

Let's think about how po-mo works in radio.

IRONY AND AN IRREVERENT ATTITUDE.

How do you do irony in audio? Some of this will very much depend on your voice casting.

Said one way, a comment is clever, said another, it's just kind of lame. Y'know?

So, one of the things you'll have to do is find some voices that can deliver that attitude for you.

One of those voices might even be your own.

Copywriter Mark Fenske has a sarcastic voice that you might recognize. You might want to check out some local comedians at the improv.

One thing though, onstage comedy involves an audience that's across the room.

You'll need talent that can make it work in the more intimate setting of radio.

If we sell, we might also need to make fun of the fact that we're selling. It has to hit the right note.

For example, Nike chose corny jingle singers to croon, "Hey There, Holiday Shoppers." That was smart po-mo.

NIKE I.E. CASUAL SHOES
"Feelings" :60

WOMAN: (To the tune of the song "Feelings" – Off-key) Feelings, nothing more than feelings, trying to forget my feelings of love. Feelings… Whoa, Whoa Whoa… Feelings… Whoa, Whoa Whoa … Feelings… Whoa, Whoa Whoa… Second Verse. Feelings, nothing more than feelings, you should try the feelings of I.E. Shoes with Nike Air. Tear drops rolling down on your face vanish with the feelings of I.E. Shoes with Nike Air… Whoa Whoa… Feelings, try them on for thirty days, if you don't love the feeling just bring them back to the store. **ANNCR:** I.E. Shoes with Nike Air, the second best feeling in the world… Whoa, Whoa.

Okay, now this was a Song.

Only this would probably not be the way to sell me comfortable shoes – or maybe it would. People of all ages pretty much hate "Feelings."

The irony and irreverent attitude still manages to convey the core message – the shoes feel good on your feet.

Without making a big deal of it, they also throw in a promotional incentive – try them free for 30 days, if you don't like them, bring them back. Whoa, Whoa.

THE PO-MO PITCH.
Comedy Central "Horror Movies"
Here's a Pitch from Comedy Central – with sound effects.

ANNCR: This is the sound of someone getting an ax buried in their skull (Hacking sound). This is a rat chewing on a pinky (Chewing sound). And this is a nailgun to the forehead (Thumping sound). What you've just heard is a horror movie – without all the boring parts. We cut out the foggy castle scene to bring you a human head exploding (Sound of explosion). We lost the unsuspecting teenager dialogue in favor of a power drill creating a new orifice (Drilling). People who enjoy this sort of thing – as we do – should check out Comedy Central's new show *Drive-In Reviews*. Where two guys who claim to be horror movie experts watch the very best of chop shop gore-laden slice-n-dice movies and make upbeat comments throughout. *Drive-In Reviews* premiers tonight (Give date and time) on the only all-comedy cable channel – Comedy Central. Comedy Central, where nothing is sacred – especially not ice picks rammed through spinal chords...

Okay, this is a bit po-mo, and also a good match with a certain narrow target. This spot is aimed at fans of this type of horror movie, mostly young guys.

But, again, the violation of normal standards of taste – the irreverence – is part of what makes this po-mo.

It was what it was – a radio commercial about buying some Nike products for the holidays – but, in making fun of old commercials – they got it right. And they got on your right side.

YOU UNDERSTAND WHAT WE MEAN –
EVEN IF IT'S DIFFERENT FROM WHAT WE SAY.
Po-mo works as subtext.

So, on the surface, you might be saying one thing when you're really saying another. Yes? No?

All of the traditional structural things we talked about in the front part of this chapter still apply… only there's another whole underlying structure – and some of messaging – it's sort of the opposite.

Many young marketers, club-owners, for example, get this, but there will be many other clients who really don't get it. So you may have a bit of a pre-selling, pre-education job to do – in addition to writing a spot that works.

THE RIGHT EMOTION FOR THE PROBLEM.

Thinking of getting your eyes lasered? Well, you might not want to hear a goofy commercial.

Unwanted facial hair, credit or insurance problems, an IT (Information Technology) School that can help someone get a better job, a public service spot for a group that needs volunteers.

The tone might be a bit po-mo. Or not.

You'll probably need a slightly different tone for a beach volleyball tournament … or travel to Europe for the summer.

How about apartment rentals, bank loans, and car loans… these are all messages that could be aimed at you and others in your target group.

You have to figure out how to tune the emotional dimension – so that people break into your message.

'Cause you "get it."

"NEW SCHOOL JINGLES."

Notice a lot of old rock 'n' roll in commercials?

One reason is that one of the best ways to connect with a target is by playing the music he or she was listening to at about the age of 14.

So stay tuned. All those songs you listened to a few years ago will probably be showing up again when it's time to sell you Buicks.

But there are other reasons, too – songs send much different signals than jingles.

Songs work nostalgically and subliminally – they create an emotional environment.

Jingles are overt, emphatic, and predictable.

As a result, we now have what Rick Lyon of Rick Lyon Music refers to as "new school jingles." Bob Seger singing *Like a Rock* for Chevy. Steve Miller singing *Fly Like an Eagle* for the Post Office, and someone digging up Randy Newman's *I Love to See You Smile* for McDonald's.

"New School Jingles" take the right songs and add their emotional content to a brand's message. One of the first to do this was Nike. Years ago, they introduced a new shoe with the Beatles' *Revolution*.

One of their most enjoyable TV spots was done during the LA Olympics, a music video to the tune of Randy Newman's *I Love LA*.

LISTEN AND LEARN.

Whether it's po-mo or no, you need to find lots of good radio to listen to, and, sad to say, there probably isn't a ton playing on your local station.

Mostly, that means award reels and production sample reels from the radio specialty houses.

We've reprinted a few of their names here.

You should get their reels and consider working with one of them. They know what they're doing, and they can teach you a lot. If you listen.

SOME CAMPAIGNS WORK EASIER IN RADIO.

Louie the Lizard is a bad stand-up comic – the translation from TV spots to radio for Budweiser is relatively easy – that's why there have been quite a few radio spots created using Louie.

PO-MO PITCH/SONG
Mr. Pickled Pig's Feet Eater :60
Compare this spot to the classic "This Bud's for You" on page 274. This send-up of all the "real hero" beer commercials, with overly dramatic music and sarcastic copy, is an award-winning Bud Light radio campaign called "Real American Heroes."

DRUM OPENING/MUSIC UNDER:
ANNCR: Bud Light presents Real American Heroes.
SINGER: Real American Heroes…
ANNCR: Today, we salute you, Mr. Pickled Pig's Feet Eater.
SINGER: Mr. Pickled Pig's Feet Eater!
ANNCR: Ignoring all you know about pigs and where they live and what they step in, you look at their pickled paws and say, "Yummy!"
SINGER: Lookin' tasty…
ANNCR: Craving only the most daring meal, you pass up the cow tongue, skate by the head cheese, dismiss the Rocky Mountain Oysters.
CHORUS: Rocky Mountain Oysters
ANNCR: But a pig's foot soaked in pickle juice, now that's good eatin'.
SINGER: Save me a pickle…
ANNCR: So crack open an ice-cold Bud Light, Mr. Pickled Pig's Feet Eater (SFX: CAN OPEN), because it takes guts to eat those feet.
SINGER: Thank you, Mr. Pickled Pig's Feet Eater!
ANNCR: Bud Light Beer, Anheuser Busch, St. Louis Missouri.

Radio Production.

SOME USEFUL THOUGHTS on producing radio:

1. Own a Stopwatch. Whether it's a feature on your digital watch or a big old clicker like your track coach used to use, you need one as part of your life.

2. Have your first copy cuts ready before you go to your recording session. Then, get ready to cut it some more. Really good voices sometimes need a bit more time to work with the words. Sound effects may last longer than you think. And you may find you need an extra pause to make a point.

3. Find a terrific audio production engineer. As soon as you can, find the best one you can and become friends for life. Look for someone with:

• **Good technical skills.** Not everyone has them.

• **A good sense of humor.** Is it funny? How do we make it funny? Where do we find that sound effect? Look for a good comedic collaborator.

• **Good judgement.** Again, you'll often be alone in the studio with this person. You often need at least one other set of ears you can trust.

4. Build your own talent pool. Get to know the voices in your market. There will be some good ones. If you hear a local spot with a voice you like, track him or her down. Then, as you write, you may be already hearing things in your mind. Many of the best radio production teams use a lot of the same people.

5. Listen to your mix on a small speaker. Hey, it sounds great on that big system. But in the real world, people are going to be hearing it in their cars, with the volume turned way lower than you have it in the studio. Most studios have a "worst case" audio set-up. Listen to that mix on that small speaker.

If it's still right – congratulations. Nice spot.

If not, aren't you glad you knew before you took it back to play it for your boss and the client?

HA!

A Quick Course in Comedy.

WHAT'S FUNNY? I'm not sure either.

But even comedy has a structural basis.

You can *build* comedy into your copy.

A mathematician who analyzed jokes called it "The Disaster Effect."

If it were true, it would be a disaster.

But it ain't. So you laugh.

If it really did rain cats and dogs.

If you really had a banana in your ear. (What's that? I can't hear you.)

The quick gasp. The slight pause between the punch line and the laugh.

These are all reactions to "The Disaster."

It isn't true, but it *is* funny. Sometimes.

Sometimes the truth is funny, too.

This is humor based on *humanity.*

The conditions we've all experienced:

- Growing up
- The first date
- School, friends, work

The characters we all know:

- The Braggart
- The Cheapskate
- The Good Ol' Boy
- The Jewish Mother (or Italian, or whatever)

"People like to smile, they like to laugh. No great psychology here... Increasingly today, we have to create a message wtih some entertainment value, some surprise, so we reward people for paying attention rather than just clicking the remote or turning the page."

Bob Scarpelli, Chmn. DDB Chicago (Agency for Bud's "Whassup")

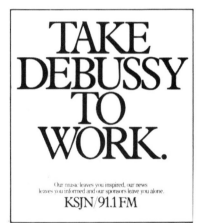

Our music leaves you inspired, our news leaves you informed and our sponsors leave you alone.

KSJN/91.1 FM

Fun with Puns. *Humor gives this small space ad a bright, friendly personality – making classical music sound inviting.*

Brand Character. *Actor Jim Varney leveraged some local gas company spots into a commercial empire. His comedic spokesperson talking to an off-camera "Vern," saying, "KnoWhutImean?" was virtually franchised to advertisers around the country. And this turned into a career that featured some feature films. Sadly, Varney died of lung cancer. Not funny. Know what I mean?*

I BRAKE FOR VERN. *KnoWhutImean?*

Do You Remember How It Feels To Wear The Wrong Clothes On The First Day Of School?

SOLANO MALL

Exaggeration and Humanity. They work together to make a point about back-to-school clothes. The exaggeration gets your attention, and then the humanity (remembering how you felt) makes the necessary emotional connection.

Speed bump.
The new Turbo

Drivers wanted. ⓥ

Funny Car. The Volkswagen personality is built into its ads as well as its design. The brand is clever and happy with itself, even though it has limitations in power and size. Quick, clever headlines – usually with a double meaning – drive home the brand's uniqueness and make you feel that the car itself is just a bit smarter than other cars.

0-60? Yes.

Drivers wanted ⓥ

Roundest car in its class.

Drivers wanted ⓥ

These are devices generally used to create humor:

1. The Double Meaning
2. Exaggeration
3. Incongruity
4. Humanity

Let's take them one at a time.

AH = ART

AHA = IDEA

HAHA = HUMOR

Something to think about.

Take some fat off your buns.
25% less fat, salt and calories than regular margarine. And zero cholesterol.

DOUBLE MEANING. DOUBLE MEANING.
One thing means more than one thing.
Buns/fat… evil/weevil. Get it? Of course you do.
When double meanings work, you build in extra interest and entertainment. On the double.

When we make Prince Spaghetti Sauce, we give you a choice. Because no two people have quite the same taste. PRINCE

Exaggerate the Difference. *Here, something as simple as a new variety of spagetti sauce is made new and clever by creating a visual exaggeration.*

EXAGGERATION FOR EFFECT.

Jimmy Durante was born with exaggerated looks. He said, *"If you're gonna have a nose, have a nose!"*

We have to create it.

Exaggerated characters, visuals, and situations can create comedy.

Overstatement and understatement are two other ways to use exaggeration.

Most of the things we advertise are part of everyday life and, often, if we don't add something, our messages will be dull.

Exaggeration can add drama, interest, and entertainment to those messages.

Totally.

On December 11th, giant lobsters will invade Downers Grove.

Find the Wow! *It's just lobsters at a Grand Opening. But look what happens when you add humorous drama and a bit of exaggeration. It makes the Grand Opening a little grander.*

PLEASURE IN PAIN
THE CURIOUSLY STRONG MINTS

Sex Can Be Fun. *Here, advertisers add interest to their products by dialing up the sexual references. Another issue, taste. How do these ads strike you?*

PANTY HOSE FOR MEN.

Who's the Humor For? *The ad above was done some time ago. On some levels, it feels a little dated. Yet, the target, a woman who wants a certain type of product, gets the humor – and the point. Below, we see a somewhat different angle at work – for anglers.*

What Pure, Unadulterated Sex Looks Like To A Walleye.

Wanna see a walleye pant? Then fish the most alluring shad bait yet hatched. With its gleaming, sexy exterior. And its unique come-hither wiggle when floating, swimming or diving. It's Phred's Shadeaux from Fred Arbogast. The lure that walleyes really lust for.

"You'd have a headache, too, if someone folded your forehead."

...because relieving a headache should be as easy as getting one.

Incongruity Can Get Attention. Here, an experimental newspaper ad uses the fold in the middle of the paper to make you think about a headache remedy.

Can Death Be Funny? Yes. This chapter features ads for food, insecticide, fishing, and seat belts, which involve the actual or potential demise of someone or something. In each ad, that "disaster" is part of the structure of the humor. It's also worth mentioning that humor often contains another "d" word. Danger. Funny isn't funny to everybody.

For example, eating meat offends many vegetarians. But cows telling you to eat chickens at Chick-fil-A is sort of funny. At least I think so. Do you?

WINE COLLECTING TAKES UP LESS SPACE THAN ANTIQUE CARS, IS QUIETER THAN HI-FI, AND TASTES BETTER THAN STAMPS

People always say that every man ought to have a hobby but they never mention the real reason, which is: it's the only way he can be alone at home.

Most men, therefore, will choose a hobby that is so bulky, messy, noisy, or boring that no one can bear to be near him; a high price to pay for solitude.

The wise man will forsake these self-tortures and take up wine collecting. It works just as well, no one will bother him: A) children do not drink and so are not interested; B) women love to have wine at the table, but they feel, quite rightly, that the collecting of wine is, like hunting, man's work. And so it is.

Wine collecting has one magnificent advantage over other hobbies: you can drink it. Also, it is neither expensive nor complicated to start. One may begin with two or three different reds and two or three whites; but which ones? To help you we will be happy to send you the labels of all thirteen Paul Masson table wines (plus a description of the delicious differences of each) to give you a collector's feel right away. Write: Paul Masson Vineyards, Dept. Y-1, Saratoga, California.

INCONGRUITY.

A favorite commercial began, *"Honey, let's take the penguin for a walk."* Humor creates a higher logic as it makes surprising new connections.

Above, with a curious juxtaposition, Howard Gossage encourages us to take up wine collecting.

Cows encourage us to eat chicken. And we are asked to "leave a light on" for criminals.

THIS WOMAN HAS
A SERIOUS SLEEP
DISORDER.

HER HUSBAND.

She may lose sleep from his snoring, but *he* could lose his life from lack of a good night's sleep. Sleep Apnea is a sleep disorder that affects primarily men. It causes them to stop breathing hundreds of times a night, resulting in fatigue, poor work performance, accidents and death. We can treat sleep apnea, and other sleep disorders. So, don't lose another night of sleep. Give us a call at (310) 967-SLEEP.

(F) CEDARS-SINAI SLEEP DISORDERS CENTER

The Human Condition. We forget to buckle up, we like to fish, and kids do the darndest things. We recognize this in ourselves, and in that recognition is the strength of this kind of humor.

"Mikey." This famous commercial for Life cereal has lasted for years. Why? First, the instant recognizability of the situation with characters we all know. Second, the warmth and likeability of the characters gives it staying power.

HUMANITY.

The first three devices are *external*.

Humanity is *internal*.

Often, the reaction is not a big laugh, but a small smile and the warm feeling of recognition.

The more you like people, the better you will be able to create this type of humor.

The easy way to use humor is to make fun *of* people. (Careful that you don't find yourself making fun of the same people you're trying to sell.)

Try to have fun *with* people. The ad above will resonate with a woman who is kept awake by her husband's health-threatening snoring.

But the key is to let them be in on the joke. Get it?

Well, that's how to be funny. I think.

When developing advertising humor, try to let it emerge from the product or product use situation.

Just as Leo Burnett sought the inherent drama of a product, you should seek the "inherent humor."

"Touching that truthful chord is at the root of all great humor."

Sharon Kirk

Made you look. Made you laugh.

285

HISTORICAL HYSTERIA.

A bit of history can be fun. You can use the past to make a comment on the present.

Each of these ads connects something from the past with a contemporary tone, and the result is interesting and humorous communication.

This instrument simplified romance, inspired pranksters and reduced insanity among farm wives.

A twirl of the handle got you Central, the "hello girl," and suddenly, with the world at the end of a wire, even the farm was no longer isolated. You can see this early telephone and a million other fascinating indications of a changing America at Henry Ford Museum and Greenfield Village in Dearborn, Michigan. For information, give us a call. Then pay us a visit and see how a nation grew up at the great American museum that's also great fun.

Henry Ford Museum & Greenfield Village.

Juxtaposition and contrast of major and trivial facts is Incongruity that gives this humorous headline impact and drama.

Guess what candy bar he would eat if he were around today.

SKOR

Rich, delicious Skor. Truly a total indulgence.

Historical Figures representing certain values or characteristics are Exaggerations that can communicate quickly.

You can't cover up a bad haircut.

7 South 8th for Hair

If you think being a Christian is inconvenient today, just look back 1500 years.

If you're ready to make the time and commitment that being a Christian sometimes requires, the Episcopal Church invites you to come and join us in the worship and fellowship of Jesus Christ. The Episcopal Church

IRONY & IRREVERENCE.

Above, a barbershop leverages a political scandal (that photo is Richard Nixon, who, as president, was involved in a "cover-up") to sell haircuts, while the Episcopal Church makes a serious point with humor.

Sarcastic humor is a part of our lives and a part of advertising. It's even a bit po-mo.

Often, a more serious point is being made.

This effect can be accomplished using all of the devices we've already discussed – double meanings, exaggeration, and incongruity.

What about humanity? Well, sort of… but since the point being made – such as in the Virgin ad – is often a bit on the nasty side, don't expect a warm toasty feeling.

But if you do it right, your ad *will* have more impact.

You don't get to be #1 by treating your passengers like #2.

1990 "Airline of the Year"
—Executive Travel Magazine

Sure mom, McDonald's sounds great.

The "Sure mom," ad and the one for someone "mediocre" are good examples.

You get the humor in the restaurant ad, and they don't have to make some competitive claim.

The "mediocre" ad makes its own connection.

In fact, they probably wouldn't want to talk to anyone who was dim enough to take them literally.

Likewise, someone who gets the "miserable wench" joke has the right attitude to perform in a Gilbert & Sullivan revival in a "wench" outfit.

Likewise, if you get the "Lemon" joke, you might feel OK with a VW.

Lemon.

SAYING THE OPPOSITE.

What happens when you "get it?"

You understand the double meaning. The irony.

You're amused by exaggeration. So even though it isn't true, you don't argue the point, but agree with the tangential truth. Ha Ha.

Are you a

MiSERABLE WENCH?

Would you like to be?

Now you can turn a bad hair day into an asset. Make pitted skin, poor demeanor and foul mouth work for you. We need miserable wenches and pretty maidens for The Pirates of Penzance. Open auditions will be Saturday and Sunday, March 23 & 24 at the UT Music Building East, Chorus Room 2.106 (Sat. 12-4, Sun.

1:30-4:30 p.m.) Bring sheet music from a Broadway show or opera, and resume and headshot if available. Be prepared to dance a bit. This popular musical comedy will run June 21 until July 7, 1996. For more information, please call the Gilbert & Sullivan Society of Austin at 472-4772 or 345-5950.

Humor makes an interesting connection.

When we "get it," we connect with others who also "get it."

The connection's deeper with the people you want to talk to, and the message is much more powerful.

The same picture hangs in tiny lake-bottom post offices.

Our members row. Warned since 1956. From left to right, it's Fat Rap, Husky Jerk, Count-Down, Original, and Jointed.

Humanization. We can also humanize things that aren't human. Like animals. Above, the humanization of game fish adds humor and story value to a fishing tackle ad. Below, "...Sparky opted instead for a quiet dinner at home."

Her invitation intrigued him, but Sparky opted instead for a quiet dinner at home.

All You Add Is ♥

Fun with Money. Here, American Express has the strategic objective of encouraging card use for everyday purchases. They have Jerry Seinfeld use his AmEx card for groceries, gas, and yadda yadda yadda

THE STRATEGIC USE OF HUMOR.

You already use humor strategically.

Your current use is for social strategy. To break the ice, to seem like a nicer person, or even to use humor as a hostile act. Think about it – "making fun" of someone may not be a friendly act.

By the same token, that's how advertising uses humor. We might want to "make fun" of the competition – like they do in those Daffy's ads.

We might want to use self-deprecating humor to make an AmEx credit card seem less ritzy and the *Village Voice* more fun-loving. See? It's strategy.

FOR EXAMPLE. . .

Let's say you're working on a lemon scented cleaning product. Here's what you could do:

• Work **double meanings** off the lemon characteristic – like "Lemon-aid."

• Create an **exaggerated** cleaning situation or an exaggerated "clean freak" type of character.

• Create a **human** and **humorous** situation where cleaning is important. Like your Mom is coming to visit your apartment…

• Juxtapose a straightforward message within some sort of **incongrous** situation.

Irony, of course, would be optional.

Assignment #21:

Pick a product. Any product. Have fun.

1. CREATING HUMOROUS DEVICES.

Make your fruit or vegetable funny.

2. CREATING MORE HUMOROUS DEVICES.

Take a look at your "client list." See if you can jot down humorous ideas based on:

A. The Product

B. Product features

C. Product-Use or Problem/Solution

D. A "Straw Man"

Remember the "ladder" from the strategy section? Look at the ladder (Attribute/Feature/Product Benefit/Consumer Benefit/Value) and see if you can find a place where you can make things funny.

3. WORD PLAY.

Write a silly limerick or a "Burma-Shave" poem for your product. (Note: Burma-Shave had little sequential signs which you read as you drove by. *"In this world/of toil and sin/the head grows bald/ but not the chin/Burma-Shave."*)

A short poem, please – 2 to 4 lines.

4. INCONGRUITY.

A. Think of a visual that features an incongrous juxtaposition featuring your product and write a straight headline. See what happens.

B. Do an ad with a gorilla in it. Or a banana.

5. CHARACTER STUDY.

A. Develop a comedic character related to some aspect of the brand, product, or usage.

B. Develop a character based on "The Problem."

6. WRITE A HEADLINE FOR THIS VISUAL.

"Egg on your face." Get it? Any product.

Fruits and Vegetables Can Be Fun. Humor has a lot of use when you're trying to add interest to something that people have seen a million times before. Here are two examples.

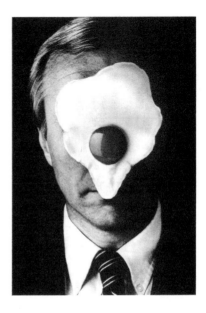

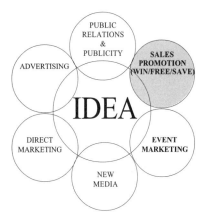

IDEA

- PUBLIC RELATIONS & PUBLICITY
- ADVERTISING
- SALES PROMOTION (WIN/FREE/SAVE)
- DIRECT MARKETING
- EVENT MARKETING
- NEW MEDIA

HOW TO THINK.
HOW TO GET A JOB.

First, we'll try to introduce you to the kind of thinking needed to solve sales promotion problems.

Then, we'll do some exercises that will give you a little bit of practice thinking promotionally. It's fun.

We think you're going to enjoy it.

Added Value.

As a bonus, we have "added value."

It's a piece by one of the top creatives at one of the world's leading sales promotion agencies – Frankel.

Colleen Fahey's article is *"Double Your Chances of Finding a Job: Start Your Promotion Portfolio Today."*

It has a lot of good advice. Read it.

Collect 'Em All! *This state license plate promotion for Wheaties was an early sales promotion success.*

PromoThink.

WIN! FREE! SAVE! Those are the three little words that launch an incredibly wide range of marketing tactics we call "Sales Promotion."

Basically, sales promotion uses some sort of incentive to stimulate (promote) a sale – and those three basic appeals are the building blocks.

It's free-thinking and inventive at the same time that it's demanding and disciplined.

The challenge is to make enough of an impact to achieve short-term sales results, while being affordable enough that you can actually make money on those increased sales.

Let's take a brief look at the sales promotion business and the role of creative thinking and writing.

A QUICK HISTORY.

Historically, much of sales promotion began with printing companies and design studios. They made money on the printing job (like a display), and they pretty much gave away whatever was designed and printed – after all, you can make a lot of money when you print a lot of cardboard.

Often, the creative thinking came from sales promotion account execs, a more free-spirited bunch than the usual ad agency account execs. The role of early sales promotion creative departments (remember, they were originally printers and design shops), was often to decorate rather than create.

As the business grew, it attracted ex-P&G brand people and agency groups. Now, every large ad agency has a sales promotion division or agency.

And as the marketplace matured and toughened, the use of sales promotion grew.

End of quick history.

TRADE & CONSUMER PROMOTION.

You see consumer promotions, but you generally don't see the ones to the trade – even though the dollars spent may be greater.

With trade promotions, wholesalers, distributors, and retailers are given an incentive (often discounts or other cash incentives, sometimes contests) to push the product on to the next member of the distribution channel – or the consumer.

Trade + Consumer. *Here, Am-Ex promotes restaurants that feature their card.*

In general, consumer promotions are thought of as "pull" – i.e., they "pull" product off the shelf.

Trade promotions are "push" – they "push" merchandise into the distribution channel.

(Note: This may not have a lot to do with writing, but it has a lot to do with thinking about the job. Remember, this chapter is titled "PromoThink.")

A big promotion may have elements of both pull and push. It may have a consumer component and a trade component.

SALES PROMOTION OBJECTIVES.

The objective is to increase (promote) sales.

The first thing you need to think of is where those sales come from. What kind of sales do you want?

More new customers trying the product?

Current customers buying and using more?

Getting store owners to stack it in the aisle, so that you get more impulse purchase?

Trial of your new or improved product?

BlockBuster Rewards. *This* continuity program *encourages additional rentals and rewards heavy users.*

WIN/FREE/SAVE.
A Quick Introduction to
Sales Promotion Tactics:

As you start learning to think promotionally, these are some of the basic tools you can use.

Realize that each simple tactic – such as a Sweepstakes – can have tremendous variety in the specifics.

Many of these decisions will be driven by things like the brand personality, "hot" trends with the target audience, availability of tie-in partners, budget, etc.

Here are the kinds of tactics you need to think about:

"SAVE" Tactics: Coupons, Rebates, Cents-Off, Free Standing Inserts (FSIs).

FSIs. Today, this is the most popular way to distribute coupons. FSIs are those sections full of 4-color ads with coupons – you'll find them in your Sunday paper.

Coupons are also distributed other ways: newspapers or magazine ads, direct mail, placed in or on the package, and even distributed electronically at point-of-sale (e.g., cash register receipts). They can go online or be linked to a "smart card" or membership card.

Rebates are cash refunds for purchase. They can be big (cars) or small (buy a certain amount and get money back). Though many buy because of the possibility of a rebate, most rebates go uncollected due to the hassle of filling out a form and mailing it in with proofs of purchase and receipts.

Cents-off Promotions can be done quickly, and they work.

Stack 'em and stick on the sign.

Not much creativity.

(Continued on next page)

WIN/FREE/SAVE *(Cont.)*
WIN Tactics:
Sweepstakes, Games, Contests.
These are similar but different:

Sweepstakes are strictly based on luck. They cannot require a purchase to enter, or it becomes a lottery, and that's illegal, unless you're a state lottery.

Games are also based on luck, but are more involving since they often require repeat visits for game pieces. This makes them a good continuity device.

McDonald's, which wants you to come back to their restaurants frequently, has used games for years.

Contests require some skill (usually, not much) to win the prize – often something involved with the product. Some contests, like the Pillsbury Bake-Off, may require quite a bit of skill. *(Cont.)*

How much can you afford to offer as an incentive to accomplish this objective and still make money?

That's a huge question. And remember that your competition is also meeting with their sales promotion people – with pretty much the same objective.

Now it gets interesting.

Adding Value with Branded Premiums. *Friskies aims at pet owners with a "$29.99 Value" Travel Kit for $12.99 and proof of purchase. Plus coupons.*

SALES PROMOTION STRATEGIES.

The sales objective and target are defined and *the strategy is the behavior you want to stimulate.*

Then the creative task is *get attention/add value.*

The attention part is, quite simply, letting your target know there's something going on.

The add value part is, well, it's the incentive.

And now it gets even more interesting.

Got Game? *Building on two brand equity properties, "Got Milk?" and "The Milk Mustache," milk marketers teamed up to offer an "under-the-cap" promotion, the "Milk Mustache Fame Game." Other promotional efforts included celebrity calendars and custom-published magazines.*

Add-ons & Tie-Ins. Marketers can get extra leverage by using one of their products as an add-on to add value in a promotion. Or they can team up with another compatible product in a tie-in. Sometimes both marketers share the costs, other times, the partner that adds the value gets a free ride – or a fee.

SALES PROMOTION TACTICS.

Sales promotion tactics are, essentially, all the different kinds of incentives that you can think of.

If it adds value and has the potential to increase sales, it's a candidate for a sales promotion tactic.

And, as you can see, even though they're based on three simple fundamentals, there's a wide variety of options that you can generate.

And that's what it takes to think promotionally.

FREE Tactics: Samples, Premiums, and Continuity Programs.

A **Premium** can be any additional item given free, or greatly discounted, to induce purchase of the primary brand.

A premium where the full cost is recovered by the money the consumer sends in is known as a **self-liquidator.**

If the premium chosen is "hot," this can be very effective in increased sales, and, if it's a branded premium, the premium itself can enhance brand image.

But, if your premium is "not so hot," you could find yourself with a warehouse full of them.

Bonus Packs. This is Save plus Free, providing "free" merchandise or more for less. Buy Two Get One Free. Buy One Get One Free. 20% more, etc.

Done right, it can attract new users and reward current users.

Done wrong, it can seriously cheapen the value perception of your brand.

Sampling is a powerful, though expensive, way to promote.

But if the product has a clear, easily demonstrable superiority, sampling may be worth it.

Promotions with Brand Equity and Kid Appeal. Pleasing a certain member of the family can add to a promotion ("Oh no, the Wiener Bank isn't for me, it's for…"). And if that promotion can reinforce brand values, that's even better. Here, Peter Pan Peanut Butter develops an obvious tie-in with a Disney re-release of Peter Pan, *and Oscar Mayer banks on their classic brand icon.*

(Continued on next page)

Continuity Programs can offer "free" product or unique branded merchandise. The most common is the punch card, offering a free product (coffee, bagel) or service (car wash, haircut, video rental) after a certain number have been purchased and a card punched or stamped.

This encourages repeat business and builds customer relationships.

Major brands, such as Marlboro and Pepsi, have tried continuity programs – some with great success.

"Drink Pepsi – Get Stuff" is an example.

And, of course, frequent flier programs are now a part of all airline marketing, with many other marketers tagging along by offering "free miles" on a whole range of purchases.

In-pack, On-pack, Near-pack.

Some premiums can be offered at the point of purchase. The Happy Meal is one we're sure you're familiar with.

For packaged goods, there are three ways of delivering premiums, referred to as **in-pack, on-pack** (attached to), or **near-pack** (nearby).

For some products, you can use the package itself as a premium.

Assignment #22:

WHILE THE BASIC TACTICS are pretty straight-forward, most writers don't get much practice thinking in a sales promotion mode.

So, you might want to go through these exercises.

Remember, your strategy is the behavior you want to occur. Your tactic motivates the behavior.

Whether you do these exercises or not, try to spend some time developing the mindset that you need to be a good promotional thinker. OK, here goes.

Exercise #1: Try/Keep/Retry.

This exercise is about how the function of the coupon or offer and the message can depend on the job you have to do.

SAMPLE CLIENT: Mama's Pizza Parlor. But it could be virtually any pizza place, restaurant, or retailer – even a professional services business like a dentist. Your prices are competitive, your product is fine, and you have lots of new competition. If you're on campus, you might want to use your favorite pizza place as the sample client.

ASSIGNMENT: Design messages and offers for each of those three purposes.

A. Get people to try Mama's Pizza Parlor.

B. Get current customers to keep coming back to Mama's Pizza Parlor (and maybe bring their friends).

C. Get former customers to come back to Mama's Pizza Parlor.

Assume you have a list of former customers and you can pull out those who have not been back in six months. If you're on a campus, some of this may be as simple as the fact former customers graduated.

Nonetheless, assume your database people can pull this group out of your customer list.

Now, let's think about how each of these may be very different in terms of target, purpose, and the way our offer is constructed.

A. Non-Users. Chances are, since we're talking about pizza, they like pizza. So they're probably getting their pizza somewhere else. And there's probably a geographic component.

Whether your business is sit-down, delivery, or both, you should probably concentrate your tactic on a certain geographic area.

You also need to have an offer strong enough to draw people in. And you might want to think about a "bounceback" – something to give them when they come in to get them to come back.

B. Current Customers. You know a few things. They know where you are. They like your pizza. And, if you've been doing a good job of keeping up a customer list, you've got their name and address.

• Develop two tactics – one that you deliver in-store and one that you deliver by mail.

Remember, they like you already, so you don't have to discount deeply for trial, but there may be some things you want to do to build your frequency (the number of times they buy your pizza) or the ticket size (the amount they spend).

C. "Rejector Base." You know something about these people, too. They know your restaurant. And they're not going there now.

First, you should probably find out why they're not coming back. So we can move along on this exercise, let's say you found out (or knew) that the main reason is Papa's Pizza Parlor opened up three blocks away six months ago. They dropped a lot of coupons. Now, a bunch of your former customers are eating their pizza. It's time for Pizza Wars!!

Remember, when dealing with a rejector base, you need to provide "A Reason for Retrial."

TRADE TACTICS.

These may be invisible to you but, in some cases, may cost more than ad expenditures. It's still Win/Free/Save – though it might be more accurately described as "Pay." Tactics include:

• **Dealer Contests**

• **Deals** – usually a straight price discount offered to a wholesaler/distributor or retailer to help push product through the channel.

• **Point-of-sale displays** (and display allowances – essentially paying the trade to put up the display).

• **Push money** (also called spiffs) – this is common in categories where consumers ask for recommendations (cameras, audio and video equipment, cosmetics, etc.) If there's a sales force involved, there's usually a "spiff."

• **Co-op** – (short for cooperative advertising) – marketers pay a percentage, (often 50% or more) of the retailer's ad cost, provided the marketer's brand is featured prominently. An example of a co-op campaign you've seen for years is Intel Inside!

By featuring those two words, the logo, and the little audio ID, the computer manufacturer receives partial funding for their advertising from Intel.

***Merchandising the Advertising** to the trade is a common tactic. In some cases, just telling them you'll be dropping an FSI coupon in their market will promote distribution and display of your brand. But a display allowance wouldn't hurt.*

SALES PROMOTION PROBLEMS.

As you work to develop successful sales promotion programs, here are some of the obstacles you have to overcome:

1. The Trade.

While your trade channel is in the business of making money selling your products, they're also in business selling *anyone's* products, so their loyalty to you is often short-term in the extreme.

To make matters worse, all of your competitor's are doing what you'd expect – they're competing.

So the trade has been trained to work you over for the best deal.

There are some other things driving your relationship.

You need them. They need you.

But it's going to cost.

The trick with trade promotions seems to be – just like consumer promotions – to deliver as much value to the trade as you can with as little cost to you.

This team performs.

For example, that was one reason NASCAR promotions went so well in the early days. It wasn't that your average housewife was more prone to buy Tide (though there are many couples who have a great time going to NASCAR events), it was that a NASCAR trip was a heck of an incentive to executives at southern supermarket chains.

2. Costs.

Even giving it away costs money.

For example, a simple effective technique like sampling generates costs in terms of: product costs, special packaging (often needed for "sample size"), distribution costs (shipping, etc.), and the actual delivery of the sample.

A sampling event in a single grocery store can cost over $100 a day – just to give it away.

(Continued on next page)

Got it? OK, start thinking.

Think about all the things you need to think about. For example, ways to deliver the message – in the mail, in the store, on the doorknob, under the windshield wiper, on a poster, etc.

Think about your options for this specific store. Then think how you might have to configure things if Mama's were a chain and you had to do something that could be replicated in all their stores.

Whether this is a real class assignment or not, you should spend some time thinking about it, because I guarantee that some version of this problem will be a real world assignment – very soon.

Exercise #2: Channels

Your client is your vegetable or fruit. Objective – increase usage of your fruit or vegetable. Design a promotion delivered in the following media channels.

A. In-store. Think up something that can be delivered at the point of sale.

B. Direct Mail or Co-op. Now we need something that can be sent to your store's customers. Remember, this could cost you $1 per mailing, given postage, printing, and other things involved.

What will be your offer? How many will you send out per store? Do you think it will pay out?

Or can you build a program where you become a part of your store's advertising? What would it be?

C. FSI. Create a full-page 4-color coupon ad.

D. Create a 1000-line newspaper ad (2 color) that might run on "Best Food Day" (usually Thursday). Your coupon redemption will be lower, so this ad better do something besides deliver that coupon.

E. Other Channels. OK? What else makes sense to stimulate sales for your fruit or vegetable?

Local cable? Bus bench backs? A blimp in the shape of an eggplant? Let's do some thinking.

Exercise #3: Adding Value

This is the key to building successful promotions.

Select any product you wish. Think of ways to add value to that purchase. For example, a fried chicken store could offer an extra piece of chicken or a Free Soft Drink. A cookie company might offer a special cookie jar. You get the idea.

If you go into the promotional field, this is the kind of thing you'll need to think of every day.

Exercise #4: Tie-Ins

A. Kraft Macaroni and Cheese & Spam. Every year, when I worked on Kraft Macaroni and Cheese, our group would have to do this ad – a tie-in with Spam. It would have a recipe (one year we did Spam-Ka-Bobs, bet you're sorry you missed it) and a coupon. (You had to buy both to get savings.)

Now it's your turn. Your assignment is to invent a recipe using Kraft Macaroni and Cheese and Spam (you can add other things if you want).

Name it. Design an ad promoting both products.

Add an offer (probably a coupon).

Wait, this assignment isn't tough enough – make it *Reader's Digest* size. (That's what we had to do.)

B. More Tie-ins. By now, you have a number of products in your client list. Time to think of some tie-in partners.

List current "clients" and then list some possible tie-in partners. Rough out an FSI (full-page, 4-color coupon ad – half page if it's a small client) with the tie-in, an appropriate coupon, and the offer.

Or do a "concept board."

Don't know what that is?

Read the next article.

3. Long-Term Brand Image.

A consistent policy of discounts and deals teaches customers your new price.

Many fast food chains, particularly pizza places, experience this problem.

Everyday prices become perceived as a "rip-off," and many consumers will only purchase with a coupon.

Many also feel it tends to devalue the brand – though many brands have established dominant market shares through aggressive pricing and dealing.

Though times can change things, too.

Recently, Suave, a price brand in the hair care category, has experienced a certain bouyancy in sales due to a general economic downturn.

For certain brands like Suave, bad times can be good news.

One more concern. Consumers continually exposed to "Fire Sale" promotional tactics may begin to sense that the brand is in trouble – and this contributes to a loss of standing with consumers.

Remember, a brand selection is, to varying degrees, a personal statement, and people like "winning brands."

4. Scattered Communication. The cumulative force of focused communications builds brands and consumer franchises.

Leo Burnett called it *"the glacier-like power of friendly familiarity."*

A chaotic sequence of deals and events can create noise in the marketplace, but it's not a message.

Over the long term, we believe that sales promotion management demands attention to long-term brand values and a consistent approach that will build good relationships with both the trade and consumers.

Budweiser's "Bud Bowl" and the Pillsbury Bake-Off are two good examples of promotional events that became a positive part of the brand heritage and reinforced relationships with both the trade and the consumer.

Professional Promotional Advice.

by Colleen Fahey, Sr. V.P., Group CD, Frankel & Company, generally acknowledged as one of the world's foremost sales promotion agencies. Clients include Coca-Cola and McDonald's. If you ever had a Happy Meal, Colleen has had an impact on your life.

DOUBLE YOUR CHANCES OF FINDING A JOB: START YOUR PROMOTION PORTFOLIO TODAY.
(Offers limited. While supplies last.)

By now, you've probably heard a lot of not-so-good news about the advertising agency job market. I started out in an advertising agency; I liked it a lot. Then I moved to sales promotion. I love it. And now for a little good news.

Promotion is still a growing business – gaining in size and gaining in stature.

Promotion agencies are expanding. International networks are flourishing.

Ad agencies are starting their own promotion divisions and buying promotion agencies. One is even integrating promotion specialists with their account and creative groups. This is lucky for you.

Because (personal opinion) promotion is about the most fun you can have and still be working.

UNEXPECTED CREATIVITY.

Promotion lets you be creative in unexpected ways.

You aren't constrained to the boundaries of a page or a thirty-second commercial.

You aren't even constrained by two dimensions. The medium for your idea can be anything from a hot air balloon to the great American T-shirt.

Your work is often molded, diecut, backlit, or in motion. You get to create premiums and prizes that have never existed before.

By now, a niece or nephew, or little brother or sister may be pouring their Heinz Ketchup from a dinosaur's mouth. We created that little creature.

In promotion, you get to use both your practical side and your wildly imaginative side, and because it's so varied, you never get stale.

Best of all, there's still room for new creatives. So take a look, start your book.

You may find, as I did, that you'll never give a thought to going back to advertising.

THE CHALLENGE: PROMOTING A SALE.

Promotion is the part of marketing that focuses on making a sale within a predictable period of time. You tell the customer what you're offering, you say what you want in return, and you make it clear how long the offer will last.

Not long afterwards, you'll find out whether your offer succeeded or failed.

In promotion, the most challenging task is to come up with a motivating offer.

The most fun job is to find the twist that makes the offer fresh and motivating. And the most gratifying part is to watch the results come in.

HOW TO THINK PROMOTIONALLY.

Your first step is to translate the objective (e.g., build sales 3%) into something the customer can act on. Here are some of the actions you would typically be trying to encourage a customer to take:

- Buy two packages at a time instead of one
- Come into a store or restaurant more times
- Buy several different products from the same manufacturer
- Buy a larger size

The next step is to get a good fix on exactly who your customer is.

This can be tricky. A product aimed at a child (who might think a whoopee cushion is the perfect promotion premium) might actually be purchased by his mother (who's more likely to be motivated by free school supplies).

A careful look at the audience will tell you where the offer will do the most good. Here are some broad groups our clients often need to influence.

- Mothers of young families
- Business people who fly constantly
- Affluent, single working women

The next stop for your promotional train of thought is the traffic itself.

Here's a partial list of tactics you can use:

- **A premium** is a gift offered free or at lower-than- retail cost in return for purchase, test drive, or visit.

A perfect example is McDonald's Happy Meal. The offer is simple: The customer buys a child's meal combination and, in return, the child gets a toy. There's even a premium that meets the needs of parents: a container that keeps the child busy with puzzles, jokes, and games so parents can enjoy a relatively peaceful meal.

- **A sweepstakes, game, or contest** offers a big, eye-catching reward to a few people, instead of a small one to everyone.

- **A bonus offer** gives the customer more of the product or service for the same price.

- **A coupon, rebate, or special price** reduces the cost of the product.

- **A continuity program or frequency program** is a long-term promotion that tries to keep people from switching brands. Airlines frequent-flier plans are good examples of these promotions. So are saving stamps.

WHERE DOES CREATIVE COME IN?

What makes the whole business creatively exciting is the next step: *figuring out how to combine tactics, embellish them, maybe add a bit of borrowed interest or make them work especially hard to enhance the brand's image.*

A Happy Meal becomes a Nintendo Happy Meal with spring-action Mario Brothers toys. It might even carry a tiny in-pack coupon book full of values for Mom.

A sweepstakes becomes the Benson & Hedges 100's Sweepstakes and gets the customer involved in choosing prizes that help highlight the product's most salient feature – its exceptional length.

Heinz Ketchup and Ore-Ida Fries get together to offer a free dinosaur head to grace a ketchup bottle top and encourage children to consume both products.

Borrowed interest is not a dirty word in promotional marketing. To be good at this part of promotion you need to be aware of what's going on in sports, entertainment, toys, and fads. Promotions that catch popular waves really create sales peaks.

The year I wrote this, we created promotions affiliated with properties like Batman, "Where's Waldo?" Nickelodeon, the Olympics, and several charities.

A HIT WITH YOUTH BASEBALL.

Oscar Mayer created an alliance with Youth Baseball that lasted three years and gave birth to many promotions that underscored its positioning as a wholesome, All-American product.

• One was a continuity program that rewarded baseball teams with baseball equipment in return for Oscar Mayer proofs-of-purchase.

• Another was a self-liquidating premium offer for a personalized Louisville Slugger.

• To assure trade support, the program allowed local retailers to make equipment donations to neighborhood ball teams in their own names, compliments of Oscar Mayer. (In return, retailers agreed to feature specials on Oscar Mayer products.)

The possibilities go on and on.

Remember, if you choose a movie, sport, character, or event to add appeal to your promotion, do it with any eye to extending the image of your brand.

HOW TO START A PROMOTION BOOK.

You can use your best ad ideas as jumping-off points for your promotion ideas.

What would motivate a customer to purchase your brand?

What will you give in return?

For your book, it's important that you show an un-derstanding of how to create an immediate impact on sales without confusing the long-term brand image.

Don't follow the ads slavishly, but you have to be true to the brand's identity.

Here's what I'd like to see in your book.

1. Take one promotional assignment and try three concepts that address it.

This will show me how much creative flexibility you have within the constraints of a single set of rules. That's important in sales promotion.

2. Pick your favorite one of these ideas and create the support pieces for it.

• An ad or FSI

• A display

• A TV commercial or radio spot

• The premium itself, a PR idea, a trade sell-in piece, or an especially original way of merchandising it. (This will help me understand your creative style and your ability to achieve continuity through different elements and to different audiences.)

3. Pick three products in at least two different business categories.

4. Do a "concept board" for each. If you see some natural extensions, you're welcome to include them. (This will let you show them off.)

WHAT'S A CONCEPT BOARD?

A concept board simply conveys the core idea.

It needs a theme, key visual, and quick bullets describing any important mechanics. Each concept should have a theme or "handle."

Theme lines are usually shorter than headlines – they announce the event and generally appear on all elements that carry the promotional message (e.g., floor displays, hang tags, and window banners).

Note to writers: a concept board usually doesn't give you a chance to showcase your writing. So put longer pieces into your book, too. Even though we spend a lot of our time writing bullets and themes, there are always clients who need longer copy for brochures, mailings, newsletters, and speeches.

WANTED: FRESHER THEMES.

You've seen lots of blah themes – retailers recycle them continuously: "Fall Festival of Values," "Sell-abration" and "Strike It Rich Sweepstakes."

Here are a couple of fresher approaches from my current pile (if you're reading this a few years later, we've moved on):

• *School's Baaack!* A fall promotion for Target.In two words, it conveys timing, merchandise, and a contemporary attitude.

• *Happy Hallowclean:* An October theme for Colgate toothbrushes and toothpaste.

• *With Our Compliments:* An everybody-wins sweepstakes offered through hotels or guests who paid with Visa cards.

WANTED: PROMOTIONAL LOGO DESIGNS.

Note to art directors: a theme will often appear as a design element that repeats throughout the promotional materials.

Here's a chance to show how you'd approach a design for a promotional theme. (It helps to tuck your roughs into the backs of the books, too. We like to see how you made your choices.)

HOW TO PRESCREEN YOUR IDEAS.

The CD will be trying to understand how you think, even more than how you execute a program. We're all looking for someone to think up ideas that haven't been thought of yet. Here are some of the ways we evaluate promotions:

• Is it clear how it will help sell product?

• Does it extend the image of the brand?

• Is the idea or the execution fresh and inventive?

• Does it communicate quickly?

• Do I wish I'd thought of that?

If your ideas pass muster, put them in the book.

Show your range. Big, flamboyant ideas are great.

So are small practical ideas – as long as they're a perfect fit. A fair number of ideas should show you were having fun while you were working on them.

Believe me, if you do this, you'll have far more promotion in your book than almost any fresh-out-of-school applicant we've seen.

And we'll be impressed with your commitment right off the bat.

If we're also impressed with your work, you could end up with one of the most demanding creative jobs in marketing.

And, no matter how often you explain your new job to your mother, she'll still tell all her friends you're in advertising.

About the Author. Colleen Fahey started her career in advertising in New York City. When she moved to Chicago, she decided to go into promotion for one year so she'd be a more well-rounded ad person She never went back.

Now in her 20th year in promotion, she is a key manager at what many regard as the world's leading promotional agency.

"Creatives" at Frankel come from widely diverse backgrounds.

"What they all have in common is an unwillingness to choose between being right-brained and left-brained. They want to be in on everything. So do I."

Good PR.

WANTED: WRITING SKILLS AND CREATIVITY.
Those are two of the major qualifications for a job in MPR – Marketing Public Relations.

Interested? You should be. Because MPR offers opportunity for creative people who like to write.

"THE HIDDEN WEAPON."

Here are examples of how successful MPR programs can be key to successful marketing.

National Soup Month? Campbell's pulled it off and stirred up a 36% sales increase.

A feature article in *Gourmet Magazine* titled "The Phenomenal Food Processor" was critical in launching the sales success of Cuisinart.

Ever see a movie called *E.T.*? Product placement of Reese's Pieces increased sales 65% the first month after the movie came out.

Herb Baum, former marketing head of Campbell's Soup, had this to say: *"The hidden weapon is PR… PR is probably more effective in changing consumer attitudes about products today than advertising.*

It is easier for consumers to believe a message if it's coming from an independent third party *than if you're shouting it in an ad."*

THE POWER OF THIRD PARTY ENDORSEMENT.

Notice how persuasive testimonials can be?

Or how when a friend recommends something it's going to mean more to you than an ad.

We look at the non-advertising part of our lives with a different mindset.

Of course, every ad will say good things about the brand being advertised, but we look at things like movie reviews, product reviews, articles, and the news quite a bit differently.

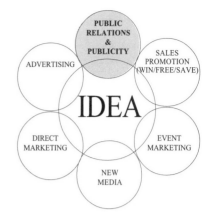

THIS CHAPTER WILL COVER…
MPR – Marketing Public Relations – a growing part of The MarCom Matrix.

MPR Tactics – A to Z…
Don't forget that list of popular MPR tactics on page 233 (From Tom Harris' *Value-Added Public Relations*).

AEROSPACE JORDAN MPR PLAN:
Nike knows how to get leverage with MPR. Here's their MPR program for the premiere of the second Michael & Bugs spot on the Super Bowl:

1/7 – Mailing of Letter and Stills
These confirm that Michael is back with Bugs and that his opponents are Marvin the Martian and K-9. Special targetting of major marketing writers, *USA Today* and *Ad Age*.

1/8 – Telephone Interviews
These are set up with Scott Bedbury, Nike Director of Advertising.

1/13 – PR Newswire Release
This goes to sportswriters with a new a new element – Marvin and K-9 are coaches for the Scream Team. Art from the TV spot is included. Entertainment writers are added to the target group.

(Continued on next page)

A Video News Release (VNR) is the TV equivalent of the press release.

It usually contains video clips that can be used by the station if it decides to pick up the story. Here's what Nike did.

1/18–FedEx Video News Release #1

• The Nike/Jordan VNR goes out with selected scenes from the commercial. (It isn't finished yet!) Plus…

• Copies of the first Hare Jordan spot.

• **"B-roll interviews."** Comments from Jordan and other Nike-contracted athletes: like Barkley and Sergey Bubka.

1/27–Satellite release of second VNR

This VNR includes the completed commercial (finally!), allowing news media to "scoop" the Super Bowl!

With this approach, it is possible that TV sports and entertainment media will pick up the story and play the spot free before it runs on the Super Bowl. That's right, free exposure!

The commercial is treated like news. This is exactly what happens on both sports and entertainment news features.

1/31 – Super Bowl Sunday!

As you can see, Nike kicked-off their campaign long before the kick-off!

THE HARRIS GRID.

Certain business categories are more "newsworthy" than others.

With that in mind, Tom Harris created this interesting model for developing your MPR strategy.

The Harris Grid categorizes by Media News Value and Consumer Interest.

MEDIA INTEREST		
	High News	Low News
C I O N N S T U E M R E E S R T **H i g h**	Computers **(A)** Cars Entertainment	Beer **(C)** Soft Drinks Athletic Shoes
L o w	Soup **(B)** Cereal Aspirin	Cigarettes **(D)** Car Mufflers Cookies

High News Categories.

"A" products should conduct high-visibilty campaigns, such as the announcement of new product intros and product improvements.

(Continued on next page)

We tend to believe a movie review more than an ad. And if an ad uses quotes from movie reviews (i.e., "third party endorsements") they have more credibility with us. Don't they?

Third party endorsements can be powerful.

Remember that wonderful headline in Ogilvy's Rolls Royce ad?

It was from a review in a British car magazine.

As Marketing PR exec Daniel J. Edelman notes, *"Public relations has the unique advantage of presenting the message in the context of the day's news. The impact can be enormous."*

TARGETS & PUBLICS.

Advertisers and agencies think in terms of target audiences or target customers.

Traditionally, PR thinks in terms of "publics."

These publics may be quite broad – everybody – or they can be a lot more targeted – "opinion-shapers" or software reviewers at a computer publication.

You know, "third parties."

Like good advertising, good Marketing PR is also "receiver-driven" communication – with one critical difference. Since the communication will be coming from a "third party," that communication has to be *newsworthy.*

Think about it. If you pay for the ad, you can put pretty much anything you want into that ad.

But when someone else is deciding what to put in their medium – whether it's a computer magazine, a food magazine, or a radio talk show – they usually have a lot to choose from.

These media "gatekeepers" are judging what content will be the most interesting to their readers, listeners, and viewers.

And it has to seem newsworthy to them.

Sure, *Advertising Age* and *AdWeek* may carry news about your just-breaking ad campaign, but for regular news channels, it's not news – unless, like Nike, you can figure out how to make it news.

HOOKS AND LEADS.

How do you "earn" newsworthiness? For a start, you'd better do it with your first sentence.

The "hook," or the lead, is the opening thought of a press release. It's the "headline."

PR firms spend a lot of time doing creative thinking on what is the most interesting angle for their press release. It is a key strategic decision. The right lead generates interest, the wrong one doesn't.

PR Style.

A press release (or news release) should feel like it's been written by an impartial news reporter.

In general, I write *terrible* news releases – they're too much like ad copy. That's an inappropriate tone in the world of PR.

On the right, some advice on how to do it right.

GETTING INVOLVED IN PR.

Big marketers have big PR firms with people who specialize in MPR. Usually, PR account execs are also "creative," in that they will write the releases.

Creativity is key in figuring out the right hook, but, as mentioned, what may be the right approach for advertising is the wrong writing style for PR.

Meanwhile, smaller marketers and advertisers may need you to do double duty – either writing the release or working with their PR person, who will usually be pleased to have your help. (But don't be upset when they "ruin" your writing.)

HARRIS GRID *(Cont.)*

"A" products, such as automobiles and movies, actually have "beat" reporters ready to help generate the publicity with media channels like auto sections in newspapers and car magazines, and movie reviewers in the newspaper and on TV.

"B" products (not as interesting to consumers) should realize that "new news" is necessary – such as announcing the health benefits of oat bran cereal.

"C" and "D" products need to consider linking to higher interest topics, such as celebrities, causes, and special events.

An example is Budweiser sponsorship of sporting events and involvement with concerts and festivals.

And, of course, Nike's involvement with Michael Jordan and Bugs Bunny turned their TV advertising into TV news.

That's MPR at work.

PR WRITING STYLE.

Remember, writing a press release is different from writing ad copy.

Here are some of the basics:

• **Write it like a news story.** You want it to be newsworthy. It should feel like news. Who. What. When. Where. Why.

• **Start with a strong lead.** Then, use an inverted pyramid form, emphasizing the most important stuff first.

• **Easy on the stylish stuff.** You want the reporters and editors to be the stylish writers – help supply them with good material – but don't compete.

• **Be accurate.** You need to be a good and trustworthy news source. Spell all names correctly. Get the facts straight and the quotes exact.

• **Be specific.** News is about facts. Use examples. Name names, give dates, times, addresses. Provide meaningful, hard information.

• **Do not editorialize.** Try to let the facts speak for themselves. Try to quote others for conclusions.

• **Vary paragraph and sentence lengths.** Be readable, not mechanical.

• **Be clear.** Remember, the language of the news reporter (your initial target audience) is simple, direct, and clear. Yours should be, too.

NEWS RELEASE FORMAT.

Here is standard format information:

• **Use standard format** – 8 1/2 x 11-inch plain white paper typed double-spaced on only one side.

• **Identify the organization** with name, address, phone number.

• **Name and phone number** of the contact at the top of the page.

• **Give a release time.** Most should be noted, *"For Immediate Release."*

If there is a compelling reason to specify a time and date, write, "For release at Time/Date." Be sure to include the date on which the release is prepared, either at top or in dateline.

• **Summary title or headline.** Put this above the story. Remember, this is just to give the editor an idea of what it's about. It should be intriguing and feel "newsworthy," but don't try to be a cute copywriter – skip the clever writing tricks. Leave the fun stuff to the editors.

• **Start your story about one-third down** on the first page. Your audience is used to looking at releases that look like that. Make it what they're used to.

• **Begin with the dateline.** Use the name of the city, town, or county and state where the story originated.

• **Complete a sentence before going to the next page.** Put "more" at the bottom of each continued page.

• **Page numbers.** Place page numbers on succeeding pages, along with a two or three-word "slug" identifying the story on the upper left corner of the page.

• **At the end of the story.**

Type "-30-" or "###" or "END."

• **Photos.** Attach a caption for each to the bottom border. The back of photo should be marked with a felt tip pen giving name, address, and phone number of contact person. Scans of photos may be supplied on disk or via e-mail in TIFF or JPEG formats. And remember, even though we've listed photos last, they can be the difference in getting your story into the news.

Howard Gossage and George Lois are two examples of creative advertising people with a flair (and instinct) for generating good PR.

To promote Rainier Ale (brewed in Seattle, sold up and down the West Coast), Gossage supported a "Hike to Seattle" that featured a character, Coach Stahl, who showed up in his office one day.

The first ad recruited a "team" to take the hike.

The next ad set them off, and after that, PR took over. Everywhere they hiked, it was news.

Gossage notes, *"The newspaper, television, and radio coverage was enormous. Front page stories with pictures – sometimes five-column pictures – and absolutely no reluctance to mention the client's name.*

I have a notion that this last may have stemmed from the fact that we didn't mention the product's name in the news releases except as an address to show the origin of the handout."

Recruitment ad.

Gossage even turned the responses to his Eagle Shirt ads into a book, *Dear Miss Afflerbach.*

On the East Coast, Goerge Lois not only knew how to generate noise with advertising, he was actively and effectively involved in many political campaigns – needing to work hand-in-hand with PR. He was a key player in such PR-driven causes as the effort on behalf of "Hurricane" Carter.

Gossage and Lois instinctively looked for ways to use PR to increase the impact of their ads – and they were often very successful.

Button for Fund-Raiser

MORE LEAD TIME & LESS CONTROL

First, you should also know that PR doesn't work as fast as advertising. You can create an ad, contract with the media, and have that ad on the air or in print in a matter of days or weeks.

With PR, think weeks or months – though newspapers may be able to respond fairly quickly.

Placement of an article or even just a mention in a magazine can take a lot of time.

The former marketing director of Yardley remembers spending summers going around to the major fashion publications with her Christmas products.

Sure enough, there was a nice product feature in each of the holiday issues, but this isn't something you do in October or November. Magazines are often working many months in advance.

PR can't be controlled as well as advertising messages. While you might be able to control every element in an ad, when you're working with "third party endorsement" much of this is in the hands of the writer, or reviewer, or host.

You have to be interesting, and, in some way, you have to be newsworthy.

TURF & TACTICS.

The MarCom Matrix has a lot of overlap. For example, tie-ins can be arranged by ad agencies, PR, sales promotion agencies, or the client.

But one responsibility is clear – *publicity designed for media placement is the job of PR.*

Here are some of the other things PR can do:

Sponsorships.

MPR may organize and supervise or be involved to maximize media publicity.

This covers everything from supporting concert tours, to leveraging local sponsorship of sport teams, to anything having to do with celebrity connections.

FINDING "THE HOOK."

When we introduced *The Book of Gossage,* we received nice coverage in *AdWeek* and *Ad Age.* But… that was it.

We sent copies out, but nothing happened. Then, Rich Binnel, former copy chief at Apple, gave me a wake-up call.

"Hey," he said. *"Gossage introduced the world to Marshall McLuhan, who is the 'patron saint' of* Wired. *Get a clue."*

So, we sent a release to *Wired* with that as the "hook." And, sure enough *Wired* did a piece on the book.

Just Your Luck

Throughout the 1950s and 1960s and until his death in 1969, Howard Luck Gossage shone as one of advertising's brightest talents - and harshest critics. *The Book of Gossage,* published this year, restores to print ample evidence of this legendary ad man's brilliance and vitriol.

The oversized paperback with its unorthodox page layout illustrates in detail how Gossage helped make household names of Land Rover, Qantas Airlines, *Scientific American,* and the Sierra Club - not to mention his pal Marshall McLuhan. With Gossage's handling, McLuhan was transformed, in two years, from an English professor with a cult following to the most famous Canadian in the world.

By finding the right "hook," we made the book newsworthy for *Wired.*

ARCHWAY COOKIES– GETTING THEIR 5¢ WORTH.

Archway Cookies wanted to increase off-shelf display. With the grocery trade as the original target, they developed a "cause marketing" campaign called "Cookies for Kids." For every package sold, Archway donated the 5¢-a-package advertising allowance to the local children's hospital.

(Continued on next page)

ARCHWAY COOKIES. *(Cont.)*
Initial Tactics.

It started with one hospital in one market – a few public-spirited chains were "early adopters."

Archway supported this program with additional advertising that publicized the local grocery chain's support with a sub-theme, "Be a Good Cookie," and a custom music bed for local radio spots.

Promotional materials were produced: In-store P.O.P. with the "Cookies for Kids" theme, and "Be a Good Cookie" balloons, buttons, and T-shirts.

The Program Grows.

Archway sales and PR people started to get involved with the local hospitals.

And then, because caring about sick kids is something you get caught up with, more Archway bakeries got involved in more markets.

A PR professional was hired to help coordinate the growing program.

Mentions of these events popped up on local TV stations, since there were public service aspects to the program.

Archway learned more about getting extra mentions from the local media.

A National Program.

Then, Archway ran into a national "cause marketing" program – the Children's Miracle Network (CMN).

Archway became a sponsor – and when the CMN Telethon rolled around, local Archway bakers presented checks.

(Continued on next page)

Integrated Electronic Support. Archway produced TV using national CMN spokesperson Merlin Olsen – with localized tags for participating chains.

One of MPR's important jobs is to maximize the "PR value" of sponsorships.

Trade Shows.

Trade shows may be done by PR or client sales or marketing groups. MPR is involved in the show, regardless, supplying press releases, and connecting with trade media who are also usually in attendance.

Cause Marketing.

Programs like Children's Miracle Network and Campbell's Labels for Education are proven performers in the marketplace.

They demonstrate that doing good can be good business. And MPR has the right focus to work with and coordinate these types of programs.

Event Marketing.

Though technically a separate area, this usually ends up having lots of PR involvement.

Much of the benefit of these programs depends on leveraging client participation effectively – not only at the event, but, hopefully, working to make the even newsworthy.

Startups.

When a new company is small, with little, if any, money for advertising, good PR is critical in helping the company and their "story" become known to the public – and the investment community.

High tech, for example, is very concerned with product reviews and coverage in the business press, which is as much related to investors as it is to customers or the public.

Some MPR professionals specialize in the high-tech or financial arenas.

PR professionals with these backgrounds and skills are much in demand.

It's all part of the growing field of MPR.

Assignment #23:

YOU CAN DO THESE, or just think about them.

1. Create a Customer Newsletter. Do this for any client – or do it for yourself. Make it feel like news.

2. Do a Press Release.
- First, list possible topics and hooks
- Choose the strongest idea
- Write it *exactly* in the format indicated

3. Travel. Pick a State. Travel accounts use a lot of PR – pick a state and do the following:
- Develop a theme – button & bumper sticker
- Get a calendar of events – think how to turn one into a big tourist draw, or start a new one.
- "Third-Party Endorsements." Make a list of the people who can "endorse" your state: locals, celebrities, those with a unique connection…

4. Sponsorship Exercise. Assume your local restaurant account is now a sponsor of a small local team (minor league baseball, a college team, etc.). Do:
- A billboard and a program ad
- Some tickets and a radio spot per game
- A Free Give-Away Day for one game

Now develop a Marketing PR package promoting both your restaurant and the team.

5. Event Exercise. Local Jazz Fest. A local Jazz Fest has just hired you. They have two well-known groups coming in, and the rest are local. They have no time and no money. Here's what you have to do:
- Name the Fest – assume it's where you are
- Design a Poster – leave room for sponsors
- Write a Press Release announcing the fest
- List photo opportunities – remember, you'll get better PR with a great photo.
- An Invitation to a kick-off Press Event

6. Design a Survey. What results might make news?

ARCHWAY COOKIES. *(Cont.)*

The next year, there was more advertising, sales promotion, and PR – all based around the Cookies for Kids theme.

The program evolved into an annual event featuring: public relations, advertising, promotion, cause marketing, and trade marketing.

Coordinators were assigned at each bakery. Workshops helped teach sales personnel how to implement on the local level. And – since cookies respond well to off-shelf display – sales went up.

From Tactics to Integration.

In retrospect, it was smooth, superbly integrated, and very successful.

It addressed Archway's important "publics" – customers, the trade, and Archway's own sales personnel.

It also did more good in the community than most.

It ended up as a well-integrated and executed Marketing PR program.

But the initial planning and implementation wasn't "integrated" in the classic sense. It began with a few folks on the local level trying to figure out something new to do with a nickel.

DO YOUR OWN PR

Here are some things that you might want to do to help give yourself a bit of "Good PR:"
- Get a good business card designed
- Get a great-looking fax cover sheet
- Produce a good résumé, with an interesting bio attached
- Draft #1 of a capabilities brochure
- Start thinking about the "publics" you'll be needing to influence
- Get involved with a cause
- Learn more about PR and MPR

DIRECT MARKETING COVERS:
- Direct Mail
- Catalogues
- Direct Response Advertising
- DRTV
- Telemarketing
  (Inbound & Outbound)
- Internet and e-mail based direct.

Direct mail is by far the largest part of direct and the one we'll focus on. But, as you might imagine, the Internet is viewed as an area of major opportunity.

CAPLES ON DIRECT WRITING.

"Get to the point. Direct writing out-pulls cute writing by a big margin. Don't save your best benefit until last. Start with it, so you'll have a better chance of keeping your reader with you. Don't stop by just telling people the benefits your product offers. Tell them what they'll miss if they don't buy it.

If you have an important point to make, make it three times: in the beginning, the middle, the end.

At the end, ask for action.

If people are interested enough to read your ad, they want to know what to do. Tell them."

On long copy…

"Fact-packed messages carry a wallop. *Don't be afraid of long copy.*

If your ad is interesting, people will be hungry for all the copy you can give them. If the ad is dull, short copy won't save it."

The Direct Approach.

IF YOU LIKE TO WRITE LETTERS, or think you might be good at writing letters, you might want to think about direct marketing.

This chapter will help you do exactly that.

In direct, the more you know, the better you do.

In order to make the most of that knowledge and the relationships that come from the initial sale, direct uses concepts like:

- **Database Marketing** – understanding how to use data and databases to get at the best prospects for your marketing.

- **LTV (Lifetime Value)** – understanding the true long-term value of a customer. Not just that first sale, but the lifetime of the relationship.

- **CRM (Customer Relationship Management)**– understanding how to make the most of that relationship from beginning to end.

100 YEARS OLD AND BRAND NEW.

Direct marketing has been around for more than 100 years, but some aspects of it are brand new.

For example, if you really think about all the things you can do on the Internet, a lot of it comes down to a single thing – *you can go one-on-one.*

If you start to think about the computer power you now have on your desktop, everyone can be a database marketer – whether it's just sending holiday cards or building a business from a good customer list.

ONE-TO-ONE MARKETING COMMUNICATION.

Direct marketing is built on the kind of effective one-to-one communication you find in a letter addressed to you, a catalog full of stuff that interests you, and a Web site that you enjoy visiting.

But that's the end point. Let's start at the start.

There are three critical factors in effective direct marketing.

WHO/WHAT/HOW.

These are the three critical issues:

• **WHO** is the most important thing.

• **WHAT** is the next most important thing to think about.

• **HOW** is the third most important thing you need to think about.

Let's take them one by one:

"The List" – the most important thing is WHO you are talking to.

The first truth of direct marketing is "you're as good as your list." You will have the best results with the best prospects.

That's why the first thing you need to be concerned with in direct marketing is how you're going to connect with the right people.

Direct marketing is expensive on a per-person basis. With postage, a good mailing could cost $1 a person – or more.

So… one of the first big jobs is making sure we're talking to the right people. Now you know why lists are so important. But wait, there's more…

Often, some of the best lists are those of people who are already customers. When someone is already a customer, or has already responded once to a certain appeal, you know even more.

The better you know who you are marketing to, the better you will be able to design your marketing appeals and the more effective your end result.

Now you know why the right list is critical in getting your effort off to a solid start.

ANATOMY OF A DIRECT MAILING.

Here's a mailing we got from Bose, one of the smart direct marketers.

Let's look at a recent mailing:

1. The Envelope.

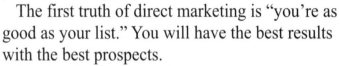

The objective of your envelope is to get your mailing opened for the right reason. This one asks the question "Why Go Another Day Without Great Sound? Presenting the Bose 12-Month Payment Plan." With a tasty photo of the Bose CD/Radio. Nice paper, too.

2. The "Wow!" Letter.

Open the envelope, and there's a nice letter – typed on both sides. The letter is mostly about the offer. (They assume we know about the radio by now.)

The "exciting information" is about an easy way to own the Bose radio.

The appeals are things like "Act Now and Enjoy Free Shipping."

They add up other "savings" like "No Interest" and "No Prepayment Penalty." But wait, there's more…

(Continued on next page)

3. Inserts.

The "Easy" insert lets you know that getting the Bose into your home (their objective) is easy as 1, 2, and 3.

When you open it, you'll find an easy-to-fill-out form – and an 800#.

But there's more in the envelope – something else to give it a lift…

4. The "Lift" Note.

Just in case you haven't heard everything you need to know about the radio, here's a simple but classy brochure.

On the outside, a testimonial, *"Without a doubt, the finest sound I've heard."*

If you don't do that, everything else is pretty much wasted. Right?

"The Offer" – the next most important thing is "WHAT is the incentive?"

Sometimes the inherent appeal of the product itself is enough.

For example, the Bose Radio.

It looks nice, it sounds nice, and they just sent you a message with your name on it.

But Bose knows they have to do more.

For example, they're going to let you try it FREE.

And, they're going to make it easy for you to purchase by offering easy payments.

See what they're doing? In addition to positive incentives, like telling us what a fine radio this is, they're reducing or eliminating barriers.

In fact, that's their biggest job.

And their offer – easy payments and no interest PLUS the Free Home Trial – is designed to overcome those barriers.

"The Message" – Finally, be concerned with HOW you communicate all this

This is also critical. *But remember,* if you're not talking to the right prospects, and if you don't have the right incentive, your good writing will not be as effective.

That said, let's look at what makes good direct. What makes it work?

LESSONS OF THE PIONEERS

Here's what John Caples (remember him?) and Bob Stone, one of the founders of the modern direct marketing industry, have to say.

Caples learned many of his lessons when postage was 3¢. People had more time, got less mail, and probably paid more attention to ads.

So you may not get the kind of responses Caples got 50 or more years ago, but the basics are pretty much the same. Here are some of his thoughts…

"Times change. People don't.

Words like 'free' and 'new' are as potent as ever. Ads that appeal to a reader's self-interest still work.

People may disagree about what self-improvement is important, but we all want to improve ourselves.

Ads that offer news still work.

The subjects that are news change, but the human curiosity to know what's new doesn't. These appeals worked 50 years ago. They work today."

Bob Stone adds these thoughts,

"Strong words like 'how,' 'what,' new,' have staying power.

They're flags, catching readers' eyes.

What counts, beyond words, is the hypothesis on which the headline is based – it must be based on a solid reason to buy."

Stone throws out a few more thoughts…

"Aim for orders, not just inquiries.

There's a big difference between curiosity seekers and customers, and you can't afford to forget it."

"You have to find your product's dramatic differences and link them to your prospects' needs and wants. And you must communicate in a one-on-one style that's readable and believable."

"There are only two reasons why people buy anything: to gain something or protect what they already have. Keep that in mind, and you're on the way to overcoming human inertia."

BOSE ANATOMY *(Cont.)*

On the inside, we can read some clear, classy "reason why" that tells us "we will enjoy music more."

That's the consumer benefit, our enjoying music more.

Patented technology is the reason why. There are more testimonials, reviews from audio magazines and more…

5. The Closer.

On the back of the brochure is "The Closer." An "Absolutely No Risk Involved Guarantee."

There's an envelope, too.

6. The BRE.

"BRE" stands for Business Reply Envelope. Bose makes it as easy as they can for you to pay the way you want to pay. So even though they know a high percentage will use the 800#, in direct, you have to play as many percentages as possible, to *maximize your return.*

A Quick Review.

Let's think about this mailing again.

Obviously, Bose has been doing this for a while (in direct, respect survival) – so what is their current objective?

They know that if they can get the Bose into your home, a combination of your satisfaction with the product and the hassle of returning it will make their direct marketing a success.

Here's a partial list of offers from Robert W. Bly's excellent book – *Power-Packed Direct Mail.*
- Free Brochure
- Free Booklet
- Free Catalog
- Free Newsletter
- Invitation to attend a Free Seminar
- Free Trial
- Free Use of a Product
- Free Product Sample
- Free Gift Certificate
- Free Consultation
- Free Estimate
- Free Cassette Tape
- Free Videotape (or CD or DVD)
- Free Gift (for providing names of friends who might be interested in offer)
- Free Special Report
- Free Sample Issue
- Send No Money Now – we will bill you
- Money-back Guarantee
- Enter our Contest and Win
- Enter our Sweepstakes and Win
- Enter our Drawing and Win
- Discount for New Customers
- Free Gift Item
- Surprise Gift
- Order Now – we won't bill you until…
- Order X amount. Get Y amount Free
- Free Membership
- Send No Money – pay in easy installments (Note: this was Bose offer)

"You start with several hypotheses. Each is tested with an ad that runs in a medium that reaches the right audience.

And the testing must be done within a narrow time frame."

Bob Stone

THE IMPORTANCE OF MAKING THE BEST OFFER.

When a baby joins a family, a new mother is usually made an offer by the company that makes Gerber Baby Food – Send us your name and address, and we'll send you coupons good for *Seven Free Jars* of Gerber Baby Food.

Gerber figured out this was the optimum offer.

Fewer jars would get less response (Would you go to all that trouble for one little jar?). And with more than seven jars, the incremental cost of that extra jar would not be worth the incremental response.

That's a simple example of developing the best offer. Yet working out the optimum results through test mailings and measuring results can be difficult and time consuming.

Direct marketers work very hard to find out exactly what works best. Then they stick to it.

TEST. TEST. TEST.

One of the things you're always trying to do in direct is try to get smarter. Often, you have to get smarter just to survive.

And once you do find something that works, you stick with it until you can prove something else is better. Direct marketers don't get tired of old ads – not if they keep working.

It's worth repeating. In direct, respect results.

Good offers pull better. Strong, clear benefit statements work better. Making it easier helps, too.

Try to find something that touches a nerve and makes a connection with the reader.

It worked then and it will work now.

TESTIMONIAL. TESTIMONIAL. TESTIMONIAL.

One of the best types of messages you can deliver is one from satisfied customers.

Good testimonials usually make good copy.

It's a form of "third-party endorsement."

After all, what advertiser doesn't have good things to say about their product?

Often the reader can relate better to a testimonial – because that person has a lot more in common with the reader than any advertiser ever will.

Think about lines like… *"I needed to lose weight." "I was skeptical." "We were paying too much in interest on our credit card bills."*

Statements like that often make a better connection than eloquent advertising copy.

And if you have a testimonial from an expert, like a reviewer or an industry leader, better yet.

BUT WAIT… THERE'S MORE!

Many of these ads use something called "The Turn" or "The Closer."

It sounds like a fairly good deal – that's when it's time to make it a better deal.

Set the hook. Often just the offer isn't enough.

Even Gerber, with seven free jars of baby food, offers mothers more. Advice lines. More coupons. Feeding tips. And so on. It's all part of Gerber's CRM – Customer Relationship Management.

RESPONSE AND CONVERSION.

Not everyone who takes you up on a Free Trial Offer – or even seven free jars of baby food – will become a permanent customer.

In "two-stage offers" (try and buy), the percentage of people who respond and buy is called "conversion rate." A high conversion rate is good. A low one, bad.

My friends at JuriSearch discovered that when lawyers who responded to their Free Trial Offer also took the tutorial (renamed "Fast-Track Productivity Training"), their conversion rate was two-and-a-half times greater. Wow. Big difference.

So, we turned that Free Trial Offer into a "Free Trial with Free Fast-Track Training Session (a $50 value)."

THE CRAFT OF CATALOGUE WRITING.

Direct marketers like Lands' End know how to make money from sending you a catalog of their goods.

Each square inch of that catalog has to earn its way – either by generating income for the item or by keeping your interest (some of the super-deluxe items featured in catalogs are really there for entertainment value – though even those $2,000 + items do sell).

A Rule of Thumb.

How much do you need to make on an item to make catalog sales worthwhile?

There's a "rule of thumb" in direct that says cost-of-goods should be about one-third to build a good business.

That means if you offer it in a catalog for $33, your basic cost should be no more than $11.

You should also remember that direct marketers generate significant savings by not having the expense of a store or salespeople – so, if they're efficient, you still get a pretty good deal.

Your Assignment.

Pick up some catalogs and study them.

Hey, you might even find something you like. And if you buy it, you'll get to experience a little "CRM" as they work to maximize your "LTV."

See, now you can speak direct.

Soloflex. The Original. They built their business with infomercials. Call Now!

Philips Electronics used the long form of an infomercial to explain their new television technology.

Callaway Golf sold expensive golf balls on outlets like The Golf Channel.

GOT HEADPHONES?

You'll be doing a lot of business on the phone – might as well get good at it.

I've recently discovered telephone headsets can help – you'll spend less time with your neck all scrunched up trying to keep the phone tucked in as you type.

You had to take the session to get the Free Trial.

The point is, some appeals, incentives, and behaviors result in better conversion levels.

And that's the point of direct – figure out what it's going to take to get people from A to B.

Anyone can give it away. You need to begin a sequence where the right people do the right thing for the right reason with the result of conversion (the sale) and the beginning of a relationship.

OTHER FORMS OF DIRECT.

A lot has been written on these topics – so it's silly to try to do it in just part of one chapter.

So we're just going to summarize very briefly.

Here are some of the other categories of direct:

DRTV (Direct Response Television) covers all those infomercials you see and shorter TV spots as well. If the purpose of the spot is to get you to respond – usually by calling an 800# – you're seeing direct marketing at work.

Telemarketing.

Inbound telemarketing is where the customer (you) responds to an 800# and calls.

Outbound telemarketing is where someone calls you – usually at dinner.

Radio. Though almost 50% of all radio commercials feature some sort of response mechanism (an 800# or store address), for a variety of reasons, radio is not currently regarded as a very good response medium. Though, for certain "hot" products with good margins, it does work.

The Internet. This is the new direct medium. From e-mail-based direct mail to doing business on Web sites, the Net is viewed, in many ways, as a whole new platform for direct marketing.

Hmmm.

Assignment #24:

THE INITIAL OBJECTIVE is to get you thinking about how to work effectively in direct. You may want to do some of these exercises, or you may just want to think about doing them.

1. The "Sweet Spot" Letter.

Here's an exercise from *Hitting the Sweet Spot.*

Write one (or both) of your parents a letter telling them why you need to stay in school one more year.

Think benefits. Think reason why. Think about reducing (or eliminating) barriers to agreement.

2. Create a Catalog.

Think of stuff you like. This should be easy, you've probably got a room full of it.

Put some of that collection into a catalog.

Name your catalog and write the cover copy that will make people want to read what's inside.

Now, pick an item or two and write brief but appealing copy for that item.

3. Offer Development – Season Tickets.

Your assignment is to sell season tickets.

It can be a campus sport team, a theater group, or a concert series at a club or venue.

List things you can add to make your offer more appealing and a better value.

Try to have at least five ideas.

Is there a "turn" or "closer?"

What can you do to encourage the reader to act immediately?

4. Create Your Own Database. Do a Mailing.

You've probably already got one.

It's in your address book or PDA – or maybe it's already in a computer file. Better yet.

Your assignment is on the next page. And you really ought to do this one.

START SAVING YOUR MAIL.
Not all of it. But if you get a mailing that you think is above average, save it.

If you see a catalog that almost makes you want to spend your money, keep it.

Start to evaluate how the best direct is working on you.

If you see some mailings more than once, give them new respect – something about those mailings is working.

Try to figure out what it is.

Find your Target. *I often buy hard-to-find jazz records. Guess who finds me?*

Today, technology can turn you into a
direct marketer. *With the right list, the
right software, and the right business
model, you can make almost any business
better – using the direct approach.*

**BOOKS ON
DIRECT:**
These days, all you
need is the title or
the author's name.
Some of these books
may be out of print,
but they are usually
available through an
online book service
– or the Direct Mar-
keting Association,
www.thedma.com

**Direct Mail Copy
That Sells**
*by Herschell Gor-
don Lewis*

**Power-Packed
Direct Mail**
by Robert W. Bly

Direct Marketing
by Edward Nash

Being Direct
by Lester Wunderman

**Tested Advertising
Methods**
by John Caples

A. Clean Up Your Database. Check the entries,
add updates. Double-check a few that are in doubt.

B. Design a Mailing. It could be:

• **A holiday card.** Design a card for an upcoming holiday. It could be a big one. Or not.

• **A family announcement.** A new puppy, an
award, photo of the family. Whatever.

• **Your own newsletter.** Design a masthead.
Write about how you're doing, scan in a photo or
two, add a few fun facts, a family update, and
perhaps some commentary. Proof it. Print it.

• **A fund-raising letter for a worthy event.**
Maybe you're already involved in something that
deserves support. A walk-a-thon, an upcoming
charity event. A fund-raising effort. Well, don't
just sit there, write a letter asking for funds.

And don't be shy about it.

C. Add a Response Mechanism.

It may be as simple as just listing your phone
number and address, or there might be something
more you can do – particularly if you're doing the
fund-raising version of this assignment.

D. Get the Envelope Right.

Get the right size envelope. Print labels, or figure
out how to print *on* the envelopes. (If you do that,
try to add some additional copy to the envelope.)

Get cool stamps. (The Post Office should have
nice-looking commemoratives). Or, if you've got
a lot of them (100 or more), find out how to get a
quantity mailing rate. (You'll be smarter knowing
what's involved.)

E. Do Your Mailing. Stuff. Seal. Stamp. Send.

F. See What Happens. You'll hear from people
you haven't heard from in a while, you'll probably
even get a phone call or two. Congratulations, you've
just done a direct marketing campaign.

Tune in to TV.

YOU ALREADY KNOW A LOT ABOUT TV. You've been watching it all your life. Now you have to start thinking on the other side of the screen.

Instead of consuming the images you see, you'll need to be creating them and producing them.

LEARNING PRINT VS. LEARNING TV.

Traditionally, advertising has been taught with an emphasis on print – for a good reason. It's much easier to evaluate early work on the printed page.

The layout for your print ad is a pretty good indication of how your ad is going to end up.

But TV can be very hard to evaluate until it's been produced. Want proof?

The ad industry has a rich history of expensive TV production screw-ups. Evaluating TV before it's produced has always been a risky proposition at best.

Variables like production budget, acting, video quality, music track, and all the other things that go into "putting it in the can" make a pretty good list of all the things that can go wrong.

There have been low-budget triumphs, big-budget busts – and everything in between.

Books about producing TV spots, like Huntley Baldwin's *How to Create Effective TV Commercials,* concentrate on how to do the big stuff right.

If you're doing big budget stuff, read those books – and find as many experienced people to work with as you can. Listen and learn.

Their experience is a result of doing a lot of things right, and – sad to say – seeing things go wrong along the way.

We're going to take a slightly different approach. Ready? Turn the page.

Until now, someone else has been filling in the frames for you. Now it's your turn.

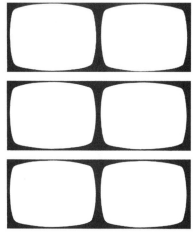

Huntley wrote a good book, though you may have to hunt to find a copy.

BIG TIME TV VS. FIRST TIME TV.

We'll begin the same way we did print and radio – with types of TV spots that can be done – regardless of budget. Then…. *instead of trying to teach you how to do big budget TV right, we'll try to teach you how not to do small budget TV wrong.*

Here's why:

1. First, you now have the tools to do TV.

They're on your computer – and the computer/video editor at your school, and the local cable TV station. The new video cameras are better than ever. So is the video editing software.

Back when I was using a typewriter to write the first version of this book, TV technology involved very expensive film and video.

You needed other skilled (and also expensive) crafts to help you produce your spot: film editors, music and sound experts, graphics and animation – even that new, very expensive state-of-the-art stuff called computer animation. Things change.

Now all of that technology is more accessible and more affordable. Things that used to cost $100,000 are on your desktop – or will be soon.

It's a new world.

2. Second, there are more opportunities than ever for you to do TV.

Maybe not for big budget TV spots, but with all the cable channels (local and national), Quick-Time videos showing up on Web sites, long-form video needed for corporations and education, and that music video for your friend's band… well, if you can get good at it, my guess is you can find a lot of it that needs doing.

Those are new reasons for starting to do TV as early in your career as possible.

Now here's why you should be careful…

Apple Computer & Final Cut Pro – just one example of the technology that's now available to create your own TV.

1. It will suck up incredible amounts of your time, energy, and resources (including money).

Yeah, you can do it. But wait until you see all the time and effort it takes.

If you're looking for a job, the amount of time you'll spend prepping, producing, and finishing a single spot compared to how you could spend that time preparing a book with lots of ads and scripts.

Given limited resources, it might be a bad idea, particularly if you're trying to do it on your own.

Then again, more and more programs are having students produce spots as part of a course. Good. Work hard. Do your best.

And realize that one purpose of these courses is to provide a safe place for you to make your mistakes – and learn further lessons from the mistakes made by your fellow beginners.

2. First time work looks like first time work.

Even fairly cool student stuff usually isn't very polished – not quite up to the quality of a local used car spot. Was that really your ambition? And, is someone really going to hire you based on something a notch above home movies? You get the point. "Whassup?" notwithstanding.
But, hey, you've gotta start somewhere.
We're going to work to give you the context and the tools to make good decisions at the beginning of your video career.

By the way, if you're already at an agency, you might be surprised at how much of this advice will also work for you.

Chances are, you've got a small budget, limited resources, and Ridley Scott and Joe Pytka are busy.*

How many times are we going to use "Whassup?" as an example? An independent low-budget film was the inspiration for Budweiser's "Whassup?" commercials. So, it can happen.

*Feature director Ridley Scott started out doing TV spots (he did Apple's "1984" among others). Joe Pytka is a top TV commercial director.

How do you invite the eye? TV is a visual medium. Your opening frames are like the headline to a print ad.

Visuals. Demos. Talking Persons. Slice of Life. "Punchy," is part of an audio-visual mnemonic* for Hawaiian Punch. They use a number of stylistic devices to serve up a single memorable message.

DUE TO THE NATURE OF THIS BURGER KING COMMERCIAL, VIEWERS ARE ADVISED TO WATCH AT THEIR OWN RISK.

Words and Pictures. You plan them in pre-production. *You produce those pictures during* production. *And you put them all together in* post-production.

We can't afford professional actors...

First Time TV Production. Lesson #1 – *if you're not rich, you'd better be smart.*

THE STRUCTURE OF THIS SECTION.

There will be three chapters and a bonus section:

21. Tuning in to TV/How to Think about TV.

This is the chapter you're reading now.

Thinking about TV is more complicated than print, because you're dealing with a very fluid audio/visual medium, and because the actual production is so critical – and so variable.

Yet, at its heart TV is simple.

Because, when you get right down to it, you need to make a simple point with people who aren't paying much attention.

22. Types of TV Commercials. There are a few basic types of TV concepts. We say there are six (and Combinations, of course). They can be done well or badly; expensively or cheaply.

We'll try to help you get comfortable with the range of possibility. The quality is your job.

23. Pre-production, Production, Post-production. These are the three key stages to getting a TV spot right. Each one is critical.

Or, to look at it another way, there are three times as many ways to screw it up.

23A. First-Time Production Tips. Here, we're going to try to *limit* your imagination. We'll help you focus on what is possible with relatively small budgets and limited production resources.

SOME GOOD NEWS ABOUT YOU.

As we said, you already know a lot about TV. Visually, you're very literate and sophisticated.

As a TV consumer, you're already very familiar with a wide range of techniques.

Now let's talk about how to create those messages instead of consume them. Here we go…

*****Mnemonic–** (ne mǎn ik) Short for "mnemonic device." A visual memory device. A common advertising technique for low-interest products.

How to Think About TV.

The Final Impression. *Have it clearly in mind – otherwise you'll be half-baked.*

TO BEGIN… START AT THE FINISH.

That's right, start at the finish.

First, concentrate on *the final impression* of your commercial. Imagine the destination.

Many writers spend too much time thinking about the beginning of a commercial.

They worry about gags, situations, openings, attention-getting devices, and the like.

Start at the finish.

You should first concentrate on the final impression of your commercial.

Try to have this clearly in mind before you start to write your commercial.

What do you want people to *see?*

What do you want them to *feel?*

What do you want them to *think?*

What do you want them to *learn?*

What do you want them to *do?*

To create the path…

first imagine the destination.

THE FINAL FRAME.

Think about how it's all going to end.

Often, the final frame is as simple as your brand's logo and your theme – maybe there's a nice payoff visual, too.

As you begin, try to keep that final frame in mind.

Next… a few more things to remember.

THE POWER OF ONE IDEA.

Maalox takes the generic problem of an upset stomach and generates ownership with a single, memorable idea, "The Maalox Moment."

The problem is dramatized and paid-off with the simple memorable slogan.

One goal is to break into the consumer vocabulary with a catch-phrase that dramatizes the need for the brand.

The advertising stays focused on this one simple, powerful idea.

It's even integrated into a consumer response program. If you have a Maalox moment, write: Maalox Moments, P.O. Box 8388, Philadelphia, PA 19101.

"Fresh Mex." *That's the Selling Idea for Chevy's Mexican Restaurants. A wide variety of "fresh" TV drives to that single-minded selling message.*

THE POWER OF STORY.

One of the many things they do well at Goodby, Silverstein is create TV spots that tell stories.

Here, they take their first assignment for Cracker Jack and tell us a tale on TV. It takes the old "prize inside" story to a new level using an "experimental extra extra large size" as the narrative device.

Stock boys try to stock it.

Families take the extra large size home and can't get it in the garage. Oops.

And, finally a little girl finds a prize inside her Cracker Jack – a pony! (Smile.)

They take a product (Cracker Jack) and a feature (prize inside) that everyone is familiar with and make it fresh and entertaining by creating a thirty second story with the product as the hero.

TV IS VISUAL.

This may seem like stating the obvious, but it's a huge shift for a writer.

You must learn to communicate with pictures. Words are not enough.

A good television commercial should communicate *with the sound turned off!* What will we *see?*

TV MOVES.

Next, remember that television *moves.* Again, seems obvious, but it's a new way of writing.

What *movement* will occur as you move from the beginning to the middle to the end? What will you write as you move along that visual path?

Finally, remember: *people aren't paying much attention.* You are. The client is. They aren't.

You must be perfectly clear, and, at the same time you must be intriguing or interesting.

This is a slightly Zen concept – you have to pay a lot of attention to create something that works with people who aren't paying much attention at all.

So…

Think of the *end* of the commercial *first.*

Think *visually.*

Think of how your commercial *moves.*

Think of a strong simple *selling idea.*

And remember…

your audience isn't paying attention.

These are things you should have in mind as you write for television.

Now, let's talk about *Structure.*

TV Structure.

FIRST, BEGIN AT THE END. What is it exactly you wish to accomplish? What are the final thoughts you want the viewer to remember?

Well, it's a pretty good guess that one of those things is… the brand.

Another good guess is that you'll want to communicate your Selling Idea.

You may have another job or two to do, too – a shift in attitude, a persuasive bit of support, or an overall emotional connection.

Whatever it is, it should be clear and simple.

With your final impression in mind, you're ready to begin at the beginning.

#1. THE BEGINNING.

For openers, you need an Opening Section.

It should, literally, "open the window."

It should provide the viewer with information about what's going on. Context.

You must begin your commercial so it's *easy* for people to understand. You don't want a "Huh?"

You want to be interesting, but not confusing.

That's what you *should* do.

Here are three three things you *shouldn't* do:

1. Don't overwrite.

Many commercials are overwritten in the opening section. This creates time problems that last for the rest of the commercial.

Too much time – or too many words – or too much establishing business – in the Opening Section creates a burden that will make the remainder of your commercial less effective.

Tell 'em what you're going to tell 'em. Quickly.

Better yet, show 'em.

The Final Frame. *The Brand. The Theme. The Call to Action.*

Direct Marketers know *what they want you to do. Call this number.*

Open The Door.

Say Hello.

325

Welcome to Miller Time. *It's a bar. It's a beer. It's perfectly clear.*

Intriguing. Involving. Intimate. *With the music of "Me and Mrs. Jones" playing in the background, Nike uses this extreme close-up to get us interested in one of their athletes, Marion Jones.*

Do you feel vibration?

A provocative question *helps generate relevant interest for Goodyear Auto Centers.*

2. Don't be confusing.

Many commercials are unclear at the beginning. While there is continuing pressure to be clever and original, an idea that took a long time to think up may take a long time for the viewer to understand.

As we mentioned, "Huh?" doesn't cut it.

Tricky visual or verbal footwork may be interesting – or it may merely be confusing. Remember, nobody's paying as much attention as you are.

Tell 'em what you're going to tell 'em. Clearly.

Better yet, show 'em.

3. Don't be irrelevant.

Many commercials are *uninteresting*.

This is not necessarily a function of dull words and graphics – or exciting words and graphics.

It's a function of your message not being *relevant* or *meaningful* to the viewer.

Consumers don't care how many meetings and rewrites it took you to sell the spot.

They're considering whether to change the channel, get a beer, or go to the bathroom.

And, like you, they've seen a few commercials.

You need to figure out what's interesting to *them* – not to you. That's the trick.

Tell 'em something that's interesting to *them*.

So...

You must be clear.

Quickly.

With *interest*.

That's for openers.

#²2. THE MIDDLE.

The middle section is often where you provide Support – the reasons, rational or emotional, for buying the product.

In my view, the basic question you must answer is "What sort of Support?"

How do you make your case to the consumer?

Even though that support might be an emotional connection, you have to do more than entertain.

You have to provide something that will help persuade the customer to select your product in preference to the competition.

Sometimes it's easy.

Sometimes you have just what you need:

• A convincing demonstration.
• Strong visuals.
• Great music.
• A meaningful emotional connection.

Sometimes it's tough.

And sometimes you have too much or not enough:

• No dramatic difference.
• A complicated message.
• A hard-to-visualize benefit.
• A low-interest product category.

Whether it's easy or tough, the middle of your commercial should relate to your Strategy – how are you connecting your target with your brand?

That connection will probably be a key part of the strategy. If it's a meaningful connection (interesting and relevant to the target), it should work.

Whether it's something in your Support section, something important to your target customer, or something that's just plain memorable, it should help you get where you're going.

Strategies are synergistic – so is good TV.

Driven to Keep Your Interest. *With no "hot" new models, Nissan brought back their "Z" car heritage in this engaging commercial starring a real doll – Barbie. They built the brand image while they were building new cars.*

Featured Personality. *Look who said "Hello." In this commercial, the GE Dishwasher really speaks for itself...*

dramatizing how "smart" it is in a clever spot with no spoken copy! Computer sounds and subtitles do the job.

As feature after feature is clearly and interestingly demonstrated, they really do "Bring Good Things to Life."

The style of this classic piece by Fairfax Cone is a bit dated. But the message is still fresh and appropriate. We put it here, because he reminds us to be clear.

Advertising is the business, or the art, if you please, of telling someone something that should be important to him. It is a substitute for talking to someone.

It is the primary requirement of advertising to be clear – clear as to exactly what the proposition is.

If it isn't clear – and clear at a glance or a whisper – few people will take the time or the effort to try to figure it out.

The second essential of advertising is that what must be clear must also be important.

The proposition must have value.

Third, the proposition (the promise) that is both clear and important must also have a personal appeal.

It should be beamed at its logical prospects; no one else matters.

Fourth, the distinction in good advertising expresses the personality of the advertisers; for a promise is only as good as its maker.

Finally, a good advertisement demands action. It asks for an order.

It exacts a mental pledge.

All together these things define a desirable advertisement as one that will command attention but never be offensive. Remember –

Reasonable, but never dull.
Original, but never self-conscious.
Imaginative, but never misleading.

And, because of what it is and what it is not, a properly prepared advertisement will always be convincing and it will make people act.

This, incidentally, is all that I know about advertising.

**Fairfax Cone
Foote Cone & Belding**

The Need to Be Clear.

ONCE UPON A TIME, we had a US President who lied and was forced to resign – Richard Nixon.

One of his favorite phrases was, *"Let me make one thing perfectly clear."* Often, he didn't.

Many of us were left with a funny feeling when we talk about making something clear. Like now.

Your TV spot needs to be perfectly clear.

Sure, you can be funky, hip, informative, sophisticated, or silly. But… *you must be clear.*

Are we clear about this?

The viewer will not give your commercial anywhere near the same attention that you, your boss, the account executive, or the client gave it.

Beware. This lack of clarity may not be clear to you, your boss or the people you work with. (After all, they have the same high interest level that you do.)

Another problem is that things that are important to people who make commercials are often not meaningful to people who watch them.

This is often not clear when you're in the third meeting and the seventeenth rewrite.

That's why the most common middle section problem is, in a sense, "inadequate Support."

Put simply, the commercial does not *persuade.*

What do you mean? How can this be? You've just finished persuading clients and account executives, how can this not be persuading?

This basic problem is given many names, but what it boils down to is what is shown isn't important enough to persuade the people watching.

Here's where your commercial should offer some sort of reason (rational or emotional) to buy.

And don't be afraid to say it again.

That's right, don't be afraid to say it again.

#3. THE END.

Now we finish where we began.

At the destination you first imagined.

In addition to providing necessary information, The end of your commercial should reward the viewer.

Whether it's a well-turned phrase, a great visual, a memorable musical theme, a warm, friendly feeling, or a punch line… tie the ribbon on the package.

Visually and verbally.

You must say it *and* show it.

Clearly, meaningfully, and *memorably.*

So your message stays with the viewer after the commercial has faded to black.

Remember, the objective of your commercial is to get people to prefer your product to the *competition* – the mission your commercial must accomplish.

And that's The End, my friend.

With all this in mind, let's talk about various types of television commercials.

To be continued… *Nike kept us involved by inviting us to view different endings to the commercial on a special Web site.*

Final Frames *should leave us with the right strategic thought about the brand.*

Focus – Front to Back. *Here, Chiat/Day stays focused on a single proposition restated in the final frame. "We treat you like a person. Not a prescription."*

329

Slice of Life.

The Talking Person.

The Demo.

The Visual.

Graphic Collage.

Types of TV.

ONE PROBLEM FOR BEGINNING COPYWRITERS (and some experienced ones) is a narrow repertoire, a lack of familiarity with the range of executional solutions available.

The objective of the next section is to help you become familiar with the range of TV commercial formats available to you. Naturally, creating categories creates room for debate.

But as far as this book is concerned, these are the six major types of television commercials:

1. **Slice** (short for slice-of-life)
2. **The Talking Person**
3. **The Demo**
4. **The Visual**
5. **Graphic Collage**

And of course. . .

6. **Combinations.**

We think you'll find these broad categories pretty well cover the range of options available in a useful and memorable way. Let's take a look...

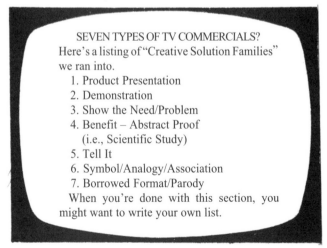

SEVEN TYPES OF TV COMMERCIALS?
Here's a listing of "Creative Solution Families" we ran into.
1. Product Presentation
2. Demonstration
3. Show the Need/Problem
4. Benefit – Abstract Proof
   (i.e., Scientific Study)
5. Tell It
6. Symbol/Analogy/Association
7. Borrowed Format/Parody
When you're done with this section, you might want to write your own list.

#1. Slice.

SOME OF THE BEST COMMERCIALS, as well as some of the worst, are "slice of life."

Comedy commercials, such as those for Alka-Seltzer and Volkswagen are Slice.

One of Volkswagen's best slice of life spots was at a funeral. You can see it on the next page.

The touching dramas of Hallmark and FedEx's surreal dramatizations are also Slice.

So are many "McDonald's Moments."

Short pieces of Slice strung together, usually with music, create the Vignette.

The first Vignette commercial was probably Dick Greene's "Tummies!" for Alka-Seltzer, with great music and a great theme – "No matter what shape your stomach's in."

How do you start slicing?

Imagine a situation where the product plays an integral and important part. Then write it down.

That's easy. The hard part is making it special.

Situations, characterizations, and dialogue.

Any way you slice it, you have to make Slice come alive to make it "slice of life."

SLICE OF REAL LIFE.
Copywriter Bill Heater was working on a pitch for the John Hancock account. Research showed that people only thought about insurance when undergoing some major life change.

The first spot was videotaped in his home and co-starred his infant daughter, Jenny Katherine. Copy went like this…

"I love you little Jenny Katherine.

I want to tell you something very, very important. Daddy got a raise.

That means I can buy you a sandbox, sliding board. What do you think? Think we should put some of it away? What do you know about the stock market?

I love you little Jenny Katherine. Guess what, Daddy got a raise."

Guess what? Daddy won the account.

"Real Life, Real Answers" grabbed little slices of life – of people in the middle of some important life change – and connected them with John Hancock.

Another spot featured a retiring football player – solid drama that felt real.

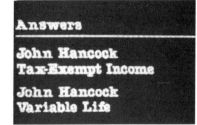

Answers

John Hancock
Tax-Exempt Income

John Hancock
Variable Life

The Saturn Story. Jobs come to Spring Hill, Tennessee, and they build a new American brand – the campaign continued with real customer stories.

Male Voice Over: I, Maxwell E. Snavely, being of sound mind and body, do bequeath the following:

To my wife Rose, who spent money like there was no tomorrow, I leave $100 and a calendar.

To my my son Rodney, who spent every dime I ever gave him on fancy cars and fast women, I leave $50... in dimes.

How to Slice.

Imagine a situation where your product plays an important part. That's the key.

The opening section should usually establish your situation. Scene and characters.

The middle section builds your sale.

It may be problem/solution, it may be a sequence of happy vignettes... whatever.

The key is that you slice your situation so that it's easy and interesting for the viewer to understand.

And it should be a situation that works toward selling the product, whether it's facts or feelings.

The closing section is the payoff.

At the end, we know why we should buy.

In the best slice of life, we can relate to the product and the situation in our own life – even if we need a sense of humor to do it.

Look at this classic Volkswagen commercial.

In the opening, we see that it's a funeral.

It's clear. It's interesting. And the "Last Will" voice over makes it both humorous and profound.

In the middle, we see a sequence of spendthrifts in big cars (get it) getting their just reward.

Then in the closing sequence, we see the virtue of owning a VW – with quite a pay-off!

To my business partner, Jules, whose motto was "spend spend spend" I leave nothing, nothing, nothing.

Finally, to my nephew, Harold, who oft time said: "A penny saved is a penny earned."

And who also oft time said: "Gee, Uncle Max, it sure pays to own a Volkswagen..."
I leave my entire fortune of one hundred billion dollars.

SFX: (Door opens, light goes on)
Mom: Okay now Harold, when you go away to college, you'll have to wash all your crazy clothes.

Harold: I thought you just put 'em in the machine and...
Mom: There's more to laundry than that. Today's clothes have changed.

Mom: Look at these things... new fabrics, new colors, you've got to use the right temperatures.
Harold: Sure, Ma...

Mom: See this tag...
Harold: Sure, you sewed them on all my clothes...

Mom: No, this one. Permanent press. Wash it in warm water.

Mom: This crazy thing is a bright color, and I don't want to see it all faded. Use cold water.

Harold: When do I use hot water?
Mom: With these Harold, white things.

Harold: I need three detergents?
Mom: No, Harold...

Mom: ...three temperatures, one detergent – All-Temperature Cheer.

Mom: It's specially made to really clean in all those temperatures.

Mom: Hot, warm, or cold. Use All-Temperature Cheer.

Mom: Fill it evenly... don't stuff!

Harold: Hey, Mom, it did work in all temperatures, this shirt looks groovy.
Mom: You're a good son, Harold.

ANNCR (VO): All-Temperature Cheer. For the way you wash now.

Mom: All-Temp-a-Cheer, Harold!

It's Alive!

IT'S A BIG WORLD – full of variety and possibility.

How and where do you find the most powerful connections? Tony Schwartz has a suggestion:

"An advertiser's research should deeply explore the actual experiences people have with products in real-life situations, and structure stimuli in the commercials in such a way that the real-life experience will be evoked by the product when the consumer encounters it in a store."

When I had to write that Slice commercial for All-Temperature Cheer, I was able to think of a grand total of one experience. But it was real.

As the brand started growing, we did some research. Women remembered going through a similar experience, or, if their children were young, they thought they would one day. The spot wasn't just about All-Temperature Cheer – it was about them!

IT'S A SMALL WORLD, TOO.

IBM shows us that computer technology is making the world smaller with humorous juxtaposition. French nuns discuss their online issues.

Here, we see that even people who are not like us, have problems and issues that are very similar.

This connects us to the product in a real and powerful way.

KODAK.

These warm, human vignettes slice life into images that Visualize the Benefit. Pictures to remember.

SLICING THE COMPETITION.

Here Ikea uses slice of life vignettes to dramatize their cost advantage – no salesmen, no warehouse guys – so you save.

#2. The Talking Person.

THE TALKING PERSON is, simply put, the *personification* of your message.

It's your selling message. In person.

Ask yourself. Who is this person?

A celebrity? A distinctive character?

An enthusiastic consumer? Maybe even the client himself... like Wendy's Dave Thomas.

How do you add dramatic dimension?

The right visual environment.

The right props.

The right words.

It's important to add *visual* information to the *verbal* information your Talking Person provides.

Don't feel limited to only one person, either.

Dialogue can add additional dramatic interest.

The Talking Person can be part of a Slice commercial, such as the continuing character dramas of P&G and others.

How do you get started? Easy.

Think of what you want to say.

Then, think of the perfect person to say it.

It may be some*one* or some*thing* that represents the inherent drama of your brand, like Leo's "critters."

Finally, add appropriate *visuals*.

It walks. It talks.

It's advertising with *personality!*

Product Presenter. For years, Josie the Plumber sold Comet Cleanser in a Slice/Demo.

A Real Person. The founder of Wendy's projected the spirit of the brand.

Squeezing Out a Selling Idea. Hate him or love him, Mr. Whipple is the vehicle for delivering the memorable selling line, "Please Don't Squeeze the Charmin."

Who Needs to Talk? The character of Charlie Chaplin's "Little Tramp" was the perfect vehicle to introduce IBM's line of PCs. At the time, a big success.

PROBLEM/SOLUTION.

"Problem/Solution advertising is as old as advertising itself, simply because the basic function of many products is to solve people's problems.

But avoid the temptation to make the commercial all problem; the solution is what you are selling."

Luis Bassat
European Creative Director

335

A Po-Mo Logo. *Jack, of the well-known Jack-in-the-Box sign, was brought back from the junk heap and turned into a hip, though not particularly well-spoken spokesperson for the brand – about what you'd expect from someone whose head is an overgrown Ping-Pong ball.*

An Entertaining Way of Delivering the Strategy. *American Express wanted to communicate an ordinary idea – use your American Express card for everyday purchases. Clever spots featuring comedian Jerry Seinfeld kept you watching while they made their point.*

The Maytag Repairman.
He's lonely because Maytag's are dependable. Inherent drama at work.

Remember, the Talking Person doesn't have to be a real person. Charlie the Tuna, Morris the Cat, and Tony the Tiger are all excellent Talking "Persons."

Celebrities can work, particularly if they bring some unique characteristic that connects with your brand.

Mr. Butkus & Mr. Smith
Famous Lite Beer Drinkers

BUTKUS: *I tell ya, trying to get cultured isn't easy. We just went to the opera, and didn't understand a word.*

BUBBA: *Yeah. That big guy in those tights sure could sing.*
BUTKUS: *Well, at least we still drink a very civilized beer. Lite Beer from Miller. Lite tastes great.*
BUBBA: *But us impresarios drink it because it's less filling.*
BUTKUS: *We can't afford to get filled up. Tomorrow night we're going to the ballet.*
SMITH: *Yeah, sure hope they do it in English.*

Everything you always wanted in a beer. And less.

ANNCR (VO): *Lite Beer from Miller. Everything you always wanted in a beer. And less.*

Your Talking Person can even be part of a Slice commercial – or present a unique Demo.

Simply put, it's the Selling Idea. In person.

Or how about two?

TWO TALKING PERSONS ADD DRAMA.

Two Talking Persons add dialogue.

They talk to the customer and each other.

On the left, some Lite comedy from Miller – a pioneer in getting good advertising performances from athletes.

Today, we see it all the time, back then it was groundbreaking.

ANACIN "COAL MINER."
(A tough, good-looking actor who talks like a tough, hard-working coal miner gives Anacin's story extra impact.)

He's Lying. *It's Joe Isuzu, the lying car salesman for Isuzu. Outrageous lies. Hilarious commercials. Not sure they worked. But everybody remembered them. And... he's back!!!*

MINER: *Tell ya what, you go down a half-mile shaft... It's dark... Damp...*

TALKING PEOPLE, PRODUCTS, AND PROBLEMS.

Can you make your strategy talk?

Who/what would be the best vehicle to deliver your Selling Idea? Answer that and you're on the way to finding your Talking Person.

For example, after an extensive talent search, the people who wanted to sell McCulloch Chainsaws found the perfect spokesperson.

'bout 12 million ton o' rock on top ya. An' ya getcha a headache. Wheeh!

He was unique, humorous, and clearly qualified as an expert in the category – Barney the Beaver!

MCCULLOCH 10" TV

BARNEY: *You've got power. Sharp teeth. Even a chain brake. Next to a guy like me, you've got everything.*
ANNCR: *See the feature-loaded McCulloch 310 at your McCulloch dealer.*

Buddy, ya better have ya some Anacin. Yessir!

ANNCR: *Anacin. More medicine than any regular strength pain reliever.*
MINER: *More medicine, 'at's good. But what's better is not havin' no more headache down in the hole.*

Wal-Mart knows the power real people can bring to advertising. Here, a satisfied customer endorses their batteries.

Famous People are Real People, too. Here, Jane Seymour in her real-life role as a mother speaks for Gerber Baby Food, and Steve Ballmar, in his real-life role as President of Microsoft and "FOB" (Friend of Bill), delivers his message.

One of the strengths of testimonials is simple but obvious – the people in these ads are the most like your customers – so it's easy for your customers to identify with the people in the ads. And, if those people like your brand, well maybe I might like your brand, too.

And that makes it easy to make your point. Looking for an idea? Talk to people who use the product – and really like the product. Testimonials can be a strong place to start.

The Maysle Brothers have been experts at this type of commercial. Here are some of their thoughts:

THE TESTIMONIAL.

Real people out there like your product and they'll tell you why. See what they say.

(By the way, actors can act like real people, too.) Television can be a window on reality. Open it.

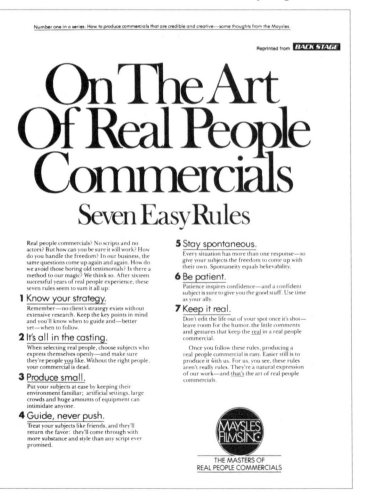

Number one in a series: How to produce commercials that are credible and creative—some thoughts from the Maysles.

Reprinted from **BACK STAGE**

On The Art Of Real People Commercials
Seven Easy Rules

Real people commercials? No scripts and no actors? But how can you be sure it will work? How do you handle the freedom? In our business, the same questions come up again and again. How do we avoid those boring old testimonials? Is there a method to our magic? We think so. After sixteen successful years of real people experience, these seven rules seem to sum it all up:

1 Know your strategy.
Remember—no client's strategy exists without extensive research. Keep the key points in mind and you'll know when to guide and—better yet—when to follow.

2 It's all in the casting.
When selecting real people, choose subjects who express themselves openly—and make sure they're people you like. Without the right people, your commercial is dead.

3 Produce small.
Put your subjects at ease by keeping their environment familiar; artificial settings, large crowds and huge amounts of equipment can intimidate anyone.

4 Guide, never push.
Treat your subjects like friends, and they'll return the favor: they'll come through with more substance and style than any script ever promised.

5 Stay spontaneous.
Every situation has more than one response—so give your subjects the freedom to come up with their own. Spontaneity equals believability.

6 Be patient.
Patience inspires confidence—and a confident subject is sure to give you the good stuff. Use time as your ally.

7 Keep it real.
Don't edit the life out of your spot once it's shot—leave room for the humor, the little comments and gestures that keep the <u>real</u> in a real people commercial.

Once you follow these rules, producing a real people commercial is easy. Easier still is to produce it with us. For us, you see, these rules aren't really rules. They're a natural expression of our work—and that's the art of real people commercials.

MAYSLES FILMS INC

THE MASTERS OF
REAL PEOPLE COMMERCIALS

#3. The Demo.

TELEVISION IS UNIQUELY SUITED for visual demonstration. Consider.

How can your product be demonstrated visually? Demonstrate. Dramatically.

There are many types of Demo:

SIDE-BY-SIDE.

The traditional Side-by-Side, compares your product with another.

BEFORE/AFTER.

The Before/After dramatizes both The Problem and the benefit.

PRODUCT PERFORMANCE.

The Performance Demo is another related type of Demo. It dramatizes how well your product works.

For example, Timex Torture Tests.

Before *Vlasic's New Big Pickle Slices.*

After *Vlasic's New Big Pickle Slices.*

Guy on porch eating pizza...

with lots of Tabasco Sauce.

Mosquito bites guy, flies away...

"Timex takes a licking and keeps on ticking."

IN-USE & NEW-USE.

The In-use Demo shows how the product is used, and how the product works. Like an infomercial.

The New-Use Demo shows people new ways to use the product. Like a recipe or serving idea.

And remember…

Demos can be real or symbolic.

...and explodes.

TIMEX TORTURE TESTS.

For years, Timex had demonstrated the durability of their inexpensive watches with visually dramatic demos – like this one with a water skier.

Then, as market opportunities appeared they were able to grow into areas like watches for kids with an already established reputation as a durable brand.

THE CHEER DEMO.

On the right is a demo first done at a P&G sales meeting. The technical staff wanted to show the ability of Cheer's formula to remove stains in cold water.

As Leo Burnett, Cheer's agency, was looking to develop a new campaign, they came up with a graphic re-creation of that sales meeting demo – with a comic actor doing the demo accompanied by music.

The result was interesting, powerful, and very effective. Variations of this demo format ran for years.

Incidentally, the actor, Jobe Cerny, is also the voice of the Pillsbury Doughboy.

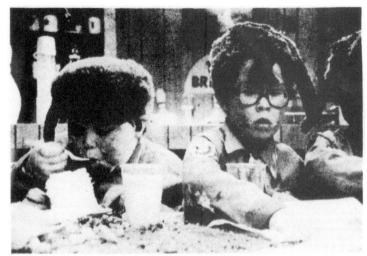

"Torture Tests."

YOU CAN DRAMATIZE product performance by dramatizing the Problem – or you can dramatize the product usage Situation.

Above, a humorous "torture test" for Mr. Big Paper Towels.

Other examples would be a graphic representation of a new product technology or a humorous overstatement.

Demos can be based on:
• Test Results
• Sales Figures
• Popularity
• Uniqueness
• Whatever…
Visual Demonstration is the key.

Don't just say it.
Show it.
Demonstrate.
Dramatically.

DEMOS THAT BECOME BRAND ICONS.

The Energizer Bunny keeps on going (durability).
Sprint is so clear you can hear a pin drop (clarity).
Good demos are clear – and they keep on going.

THE DEMO THAT ISN'T THERE.

We begin with a Chicago snowstorm. Then we
see the cars of Chicago Bulls buried under snow.

We see more fancy cars buried under the snow.

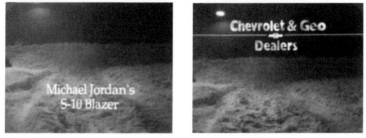

Then we pan to an empty space – Michael
Jordan's Chevy Blazer is gone. We just dramatized
the problem – and the solution.

MCDONALD'S HATED THIS BURGER KING COMMERCIAL.

In fact, they even sued to stop it.

Here, a little girl compares the size of
the McDonald's and Burger King beef
patties – and encourages us to go to
Burger King.

Over the years, Burger King has consistently worked to demonstrate the difference between broiling (them) and fry-
ing (McDonald's).

ANNCR (VO): A very very big message for grown ups.
LITTLE GIRL: Do I look 20% smaller
to you? I must to McDonald's. When I
order a regular burger at McDonald's,

GIRL: they make it with 20% less meat
than Burger King. Unbelievable!

GIRL: Luckily, I know a perfect way to
show McDonald's how I feel.
I go to Burger King.
SINGERS: Aren't You Hungry for
Burger King Now?

341

DEMONSTRATE. *DRAMATICALLY!*

(Music Up)
ANNCR: (VO) Watch closely… you're about to see something you've never…   *… seen before. Here comes Fuji Film*   *with color pictures so true to life…*

it's a real breakthrough.

Fuji Film.

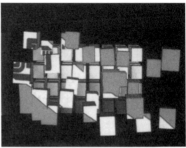

Fuji's advanced technology has developed a precise color balance.

The better the color balance,

the truer the picture.

Consistently brighter… clearer.

*With Fuji, seeing is believing.
So see for yourself.*   *Get Fuji Film. And get the true picture.*   **(MUSIC OUT)**

#4. The Visual.

TELEVISION IS A VISUAL MEDIUM.

Imagination begins with images.

How can you create interesting imagery for your brand? How can you *visualize* the benefit?

Or the problem?

How can you show what you say?

Remember, your audience can move, too.

You can fly them through space, so they see the Big Picture. You can shrink them, so small things seem larger.

Just imagine. See?

Here, an egg on wheels gets put back together again by State Farm – a metaphor for car insurance. See?

STATE FARM "EGG."

NEW WAVE WOMAN: New Wave shouldn't be recorded on punk tape.
ANNCR: Maxell, it's worth it.

ANNCR (VO):
Handle with care.
That's what...

this familiar emblem really says. And you'll get one like it when you insure your car with State Farm – the biggest car insurance company there is.

Then wherever you drive, whether your need for claim service is large or small...

You'll have a friend nearby to handle everything with care. See your State Farm Mutual insurance agent

soon and have your car marked for careful handling. You'll be surprised at how little it costs...

probably less than you're shelling out now.
THEME: *"And like a good neighbor, State Farm is there."*

STATE FARM.

Here's Keith Reinhard's story on how he came up with this classic commercial:

"State Farm complained, 'You can't see insurance, so the logo is critical. But it's not big enough and it doesn't stay on the screen long enough.'

My solution?

Sixty solid seconds of logo!

I used the familiar State Farm bumper sticker to create a simple visual metaphor for the auto accident, then the full restoration of the logo to represent the car's like-new condition.

Simple? You bet.

But that simple spot won me my first Clio for State Farm.

Simplicity is the essence of unforgettable advertising."

Today, Keith Reinhard is Chairman of DDB. And a good egg.

343

COLOR.

As mentioned earlier, color can be used as a core Selling Idea. Very visual.

Dockers dramatized the subtle colors of Dockers pants – brown, grey, khaki.

Levi's used obvious music – blues – in concert with filmed tone poems that celebrated casual and contemporary fun in Levi's. When these spots hit, they were some of the coolest things on TV.

Volkswagen promoted special limited edition VWs with custom paint colors. Here, a color called "Vapor."

The product itself can be visualized very dramatically. Logos and other product graphics can reinforce your selling message.

Many brands use visual mnemonics to make themselves memorable.

Many image campaigns rely on visual impact and unique, memorable imagery.

Consider…

What is your product's visual "world?"

Study the images associated with your product.

Try to create new combinations – new relationships – that's where you may discover The Visual.

Visuals are an international language. Beauty. Smiles. Art. Fashion. Children.

Remember, the world *is* shrinking.

The visual speaks to everyone.

Show what you say. See?

VISUALIZE CONCEPTS.

Here, a complicated concept is made simple.

If everyone knew your house was for sale, you wouldn't need a broker.

With a humorous visualization, Century 21 makes this concept both easy-to-understand and important – if you're thinking of selling your home.

VISUALIZE PROBLEMS.

What did you have for breakfast?

Kellogg's Nutri-Grain Breakfast Bars visualize the problem of "too many donuts" in a humorous and relevant way, as people "wear" their breakfasts.

Here, a donut around the waist causes a problem on the subway.

Visual Gags. Traditionally, the Yellow Pages has inspired great visualizations and great advertising. After all, it's the book that has everything in it.

This recent award-winning campaign presents visual puns. In the one above, a squad of Marines performs various dances – Rock Drills.

The theme line – "If it's out there, it's in here."

"I NEVER MET A METAPHOR I DIDN'T LIKE."

A few more examples: On the upper right, a tragic toast visualizes an important message.

Michelin's babies dramatically symbolize the importance of safe tires.

"Mr. K," a smiling (but silent) Japanese car executive (based on a real person who helped Nissan develop cars for the US market) appears as an upbeat icon – with a dog – to symbolize a warm and friendly brand spirit – and love of cars.

DRINKING AND DRIVING CAN KILL A FRIENDSHIP

Powerful Message – Simple Graphic.
This TV commercial from the Ad Council is an example of public service advertising at its very best.

And animated Scrubbing Bubbles visualize the cleaning process of Dow Bathroom Cleaner. They don't say much, but they sure have fun doing a job that people don't enjoy much at all.

In a tough product category, they've helped Dow Bathroom Cleaner clean up.

Scrubbing Bubbles. A memorable visual representing a unique product Feature. Then again, lots of bathroom cleaners foam. Here, they take a generic feature and make it a unique Selling Idea.

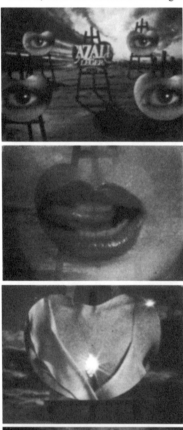

The Eye of The Artist.

VISUAL IMAGINATION can bring new dimension to your story. When the artist's eye looks at ordinary objects, they are no longer ordinary.

Here surrealism approaches perfume, beverages, and even Wendy's hamburgers – with the weird comic vision of director Joe Sedelmeier, who did "Where's the Beef?" and FedEx.

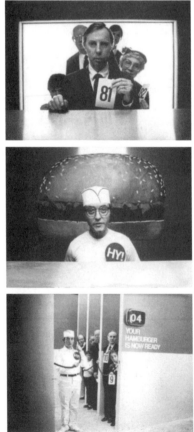

The strange sequence on your right dramatizes waiting for a burger at a "non-Wendy's."

It's advertising, and, in a curious way, it's also art. Surreal art.

Just as Renaissance nobles and merchants commissioned portraits, modern corporations can be patrons of the arts in their advertising.

And the quality of the art itself communicates much about the quality of the advertiser.

One way or another.

Assignment #25:

PICK THREE PRODUCTS. They can be from previous exercises or new ones. You may already have a Strategy and theme. Whatever.

The objective of this assignment is to help you develop range and flexibility in using TV formats.

Naturally, your ideas will not be of equal quality, since some TV approaches will "fit" better with some products. Don't worry – just try to do the full range of approaches for each product.

1. PRODUCT #1_____.

  A. Develop a **Visual.**

    Write a 10" TV spot.

  B. Develop three **Talking Person** ideas.

    Write a 30" spot using the best idea.

  C. Write a **Slice** 30".

    Single situation or Vignette.

  D. Do a **Demo** 15".

    What kind is it?

2. PRODUCT #2_____.

  Same as above.

3. PRODUCT #3_____.

  Same as above.

KEEP IT STRONG AND SIMPLE.
Even an expensive and complicated product like Lexus (made by Toyota) can be dramatized with a simple Demo.

A rolling steel ball dramatized their engineering and workmanship.

Advertising can create new context. Nissan quickly recreated Lexus' Demo using one of their less expensive models.

From steel ball to hard ball.

TV SCRIPT FORMAT

PRODUCT NAME:
"TITLE"
LENGTH:

VIDEO INSTRUCTIONS IN ALL CAPITAL LETTERS, SINGLE SPACED.	**AUDIO:** Copy indicated in upper and lower case. Double spaced.

#5. Graphic Collage.

THERE'S ANOTHER TYPE of commercial out there – "Graphic Collage." This type of commercial has two key differences.

1. "TRACK-DRIVEN" VIDEO.

This type of commercial tends to be "track-driven." The audio portion (copy and music) is often done first – the video (and the edit) develops from that.

Most MTV music videos are done this way, and this has influenced the way commercials are now done.

In addition, today's audience is able to process video information at a much faster rate and is used to the non-linear nature of track-driven edits.

2. EXISTING VIDEO IMAGERY.

Instead of creating a commercial from scratch, the production process often involves using a number of existing images.

Footage is often re-used – such as "hero" product shots. In many cases, such as local auto dealer spots, preproduced material is provided.

Often, part of the job is "picking up the pieces." Some elements you may have to work with:
- Logos and graphics.
- Existing footage.
- Existing music.
- Other elements from previous commercials.
- Other miscellaneous materials including:

slides, photos, ads, news footage, and anything else that's lying around and seems to be paid for.

Many local commercials are put together this way, and a surprising number of national ones.

The re-editing of other people's footage with new audio tracks is also used in presentations and pitches – in what has come to be affectionately known as the "Rip-o-Matic" or "Steal-O-Matic."

Pick-Up Art Can Be Convenient.
AM-PM advertises hot dogs, drinks, and low prices with a collection of images in the "pick-up" animation style used by Monty Python's Flying Circus.

348

Simple or Complex.

A GRAPHIC COLLAGE can be as simple as inter-cutting between film and titles – like the Goodyear commercial on the right.

Titles add an intellectual counterpoint to the message and give it new meaning.

Or a Graphic Collage can be rich and complex.

Here is advertising developed by Wieden + Kennedy for Black Star Beer, which features a montage of "historical" advertising footage for a beer that never existed before.

It was "Po-Mo with a budget." The brand-new ads featured ironic (and very funny) send-ups of old-time beer advertising cliches.

Words and Pictures. *Intercutting builds messages needed for tires and car repair.*

It's in the Edit.

YOU MAY START WITH WRITING, but you finish with editing – and all the other techniques of "post-production."

A strong music track, great graphics, a good editor, and your own imagination can combine to create a rich video tapestry.

In general, the better the material your start with, the better the edit you end up with.

"HEROES" AND "STOCK."

Many major advertisers have large libraries of produced footage which are cut into new commercials or used to produce additional spots.

For example, many food and beverage marketers already have "hero" shots of beverage pours.

There are also services that provide "stock footage." Need a wheat field? Or a rocket? Or a sunset? Chances are, someone has shot it already.

The Layered Look. Now you can stack video images in layers, similar to the way they constructed old-time animation with cels – only now it's with computers.

Grids and Graphics can make it happen.

"Supers" & Titles.

"SUPER" IS SHORT FOR "super-imposition." It's what you say on screen. Titles are either supers used at the beginning of a spot or full-screen supers that may be used anywhere.

Though TV is driven more by the visuals than the words, there can still be important opportunities to let the strength of the words move the video along.

In addition, supers and titles cost much much less than most other forms of video.

Usually, they can be done on a computer or the character generator at the editing house – which is part of their computerized editing set-up.

But remember, the screen isn't like the printed page, you have to limit your words.

Powerful minimalism positions Tuborg against all other beer advertising.

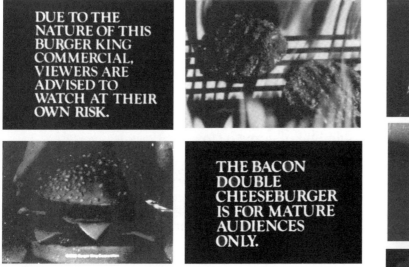

Titles and Appetite Appeal. These were the ingredients for this simple but effective execution in Burger King's "Aren't You Hungry?" campaign.

351

GIRL: Daddy, smell my flowers!
DAD: Ohh, my sinuses.

SPOKESMAN: When sinus trouble strikes, reach for Nasitene. Only Nasitene has fast-acting muchinol.

Watch as nasal passages open…
(Energizer Bunny walks past chart…

…and walks past spokesman.)
ANNCR: (VO) …still going. Nothing outlasts the Energizer. They keep going and going and going…

#6. Combinations.

MANY TELEVISION COMMERCIALS are combinations and variations of these commercial types. Here are some examples:

SLICE / DEMO / DONUTS.

It's very common to use Slice to establish the problem your product solves.

Then, you stick a Demo in the middle.

Finally, a little Slice of happy ending.

TALKING PERSON/ DEMO/DONUTS.

Look at the structure of the Band-Aid spot on the right – it uses a Talking Person (a young one) with a Demo in the middle.

That's the commercial that "solved the problem" we discussed way back in Chapter Eight.

ETCETERA.

Talking Persons emerge in Slice commercials. Visuals, such as mnemonics, are also often integrated into Slice commercials.

Or they may be cut into a Graphic Collage.

Think of the elements that created the "Punchy" mnemonic. A cartoon Talking Person, with a memorable line of copy: *"How would you like a nice Hawaiian Punch?"* And then… well it's not exactly a Demo, but you sure do remember it.

And, of course, the Energizer Bunny has their pink Visual/Demo/Mnemonic appearing within other familiar formats – even another Demo, like this fake commercial for a sinus remedy.

LOOK FOR NEW COMBINATIONS.

Remember, these formats are not designed to put limits on your imagination, rather, they're there to give your imagination some useful reference points.

Combining formats can help you create interesting new ways to do terrific TV.

BOY: *Wanna see the cut under my BAND-AID bandage?* *Mommy said keep it covered and it'll be all better faster. Wanna see it?* *Hey*

Where'd *my cut go?* **ANNCR V/O:** *Only Johnson & Johnson has proven…*

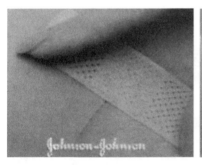 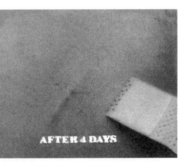 

that BAND-AID Brand heals cuts faster. *Up to twice as fast as uncovered cuts.* *BOY: It was here. Honest, I mean it.*

ANNCR V/O: *Cuts covered with BAND-AID Brand* *are proven to heal up to twice as fast. Only from Johnson & Johnson.*

Assignment #26:

Let's try some Combinations.

You may use ideas from previous exercises. Or new ones.

1. TAKE ANY TWO IDEAS FROM THE PREVIOUS ASSIGNMENT.
Combine them into a TV spot.
What kind of combination is it?

2. DEVELOP A MNEMONIC.
Write a :30 Slice commercial using it.

3. COMBINE A TESTIMONIAL WITH A DEMO.
Write sample "testimonial" comments.
How would you produce it?

4. CREATE A COMMERCIAL FROM ONE OF YOUR FAVORITE PRINT ADS.
What format(s) did you use?

Collage + Mnemonic. This spot for Agree uses basic visual tools – beauty shots and product visuals – cut to a strong rock music track. There's a simple mnemonic for the "Turn Up The Volume" Selling Idea – an Agree logo on the Volume knob of a stereo. It's a nice contemporary way of stating the benefit.

Slice, Visual, Demo, even Real Spots! The Energizer Bunny keeps going through a range of commercials – most of them imitation versions of formats we're familiar with – two women talking about coffee, soap in a shower, and even a real commercial for Purina Cat Chow, then owned by the same company that owned Energizer Batteries. The fake brand names were fun, too. Trés Cafe, Nasitene, Alarm, and my favorite – wine from Chateau Marmoset.

TV Production.

COPYWRITING IS A CRAFT. So is producing TV.

Like so many things in our business, it's something you learn by doing. It's not easy.

Even something as simple as opening a bottle and pouring can be expensive and complicated if you want to do it well.

Your best initial resource is people who've done it already: producers, directors, editors, and other more experienced writers and art directors.

Another good resource is sample reels – from com-mercial production houses and award shows.

Study them. How were the commercials you liked constructed? What worked? What didn't?

Hang out. Watch. Learn.

Finally, do "animatics."

Animatics are rough versions of TV commercials. Originally, they were storyboards put on videotape with a sound track, but new technology is providing other ways to do that.

Producing animatics for research or presentation can teach you important principles of producing and editing TV commercials. It's particularly good training for producing soundtracks.

Producing TV *is* easier said than done.

But the only way to learn is to do it.

In this section, we'll cover:

• **The Three Stages of Production** – pre-production, production, and post-production.

• **"The Winking Dog Syndrome"** – Early production problems, and how to recognize them.

• **Bonus: Your First TV Production** – some early words to the wise – and a few ideas. Hope they help.

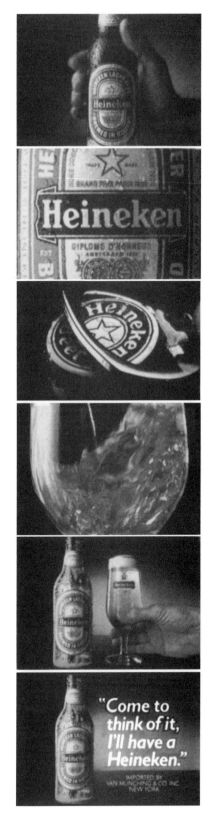

355

Production Values.

THAT'S WHAT WE TRY TO PUT ON THE SCREEN. All the things – small and large – that are involved in producing television, they all add up to production values.

You should be thinking about production values every step of the way. Because you can add to them every step of the way.

THE TIME/MONEY/QUALITY TRIANGLE.

This is an age-old "truth" that can help you today.

You can't have all three. (Unless you're very lucky.)

Need it fast? Well, it will cost more. The more you rush, the more you pay – and the more risk that the quality of your final result will suffer.

Got limited money? Well, in general, the more time you can spend, the more you can save. Though, of course, time is money, too.

Got no time and no money? Well, even if you're smart and lucky, the quality probably won't be all you'd wish.

And then there's quality. A strange factor. You know that you want the commercial for the expensive sports car to look terrific. But if the spot for the bargain store looks like they spent too much, you're might be suspicious that it isn't quite a bargain. Then again, if it's too cheesy, you might not want to go.

We'll start with these two thoughts:
• You want the quality of the final product to be appropriate for the job you're trying to do.
• In general, the more time and attention you can spend on the front end, in *pre-production,* the better the overall production will go.

Let's keep this in mind as we work our way through the three stages of production.

Production Trip. The "spontaneous" documentary feel of this Nissan SUV commercial took advance planning: travel for equipment, crew, and talent; local permits; and getting film back for processing.

Pre-Production, Production, Post-Production.

THERE ARE THREE CRITICAL STAGES in the production of every TV commercial. Each one can "make or break" your spot.

PRE-PRODUCTION. PART ONE.

Pre-production is pretty much what you think it is – it's all the things you do before you produce.

Here are some of the critical things you do:

Bids and Budgets.

How much will it cost? It's a critical question – with a lot of variables. Do you get a cute puppy from the animal shelter or the best animal trainer in Hollywood?

And just in case you think getting the best you can find will solve all your problems, don't. A friend had an absolute disastrous shoot with Lassie. Go figure.

Basically, you have to identify all of the cost items and get production bids from the suppliers that you think are right for the job.

Casting and Talent.

Sometimes the production house handles some of this, but it's a critical agency decision – often, the client is involved in final approval.

There are often additional cost issues involved.

A dozen union actors on-camera could cost your client a bundle. Sometimes it's enough to move the shoot overseas. If your script has a lot of people in it, that's another thing that will be discussed.

Legal Clearance.

You may be adjusting your script due to concerns raised by the client legal department.

And, most important, choosing your…

PRE-PRODUCTION NOTES.

When you send a board out for bid, you need Pre-Production Notes.

In some ways, this piece of paper is as important as your script. The bid will be built on a combination of your script (and board) and the "Pre-Pro Notes."

Your notes should contain things like:

Deliverables. What do you want? Film delivered to you or the completed spot?

If you'll be handling the editing and post-production somewhere else, you only want a bid for producing the film.

This is also a good place for describing the kind of spot you want. Bright and light-hearted. Modern and cutting-edge. Give 'em a clue.

Sets/Location. Where do you want to do this? In a studio or on the coast of France. Location and set issues will be a critical part of the bid.

Talent. This will help guide those in charge of arranging the casting session.

It will also be critical for how much this commercial may cost in residuals. One principle? Three? Extras? (If they react to the product, they're principles.)

Props & Misc. Who provides product? What other things will be needed?

Special Effects/Post-Production/ Misc. Music? Sound effects? Pre-score or post-score? Computer effects?

Let 'em know what else is going on.

You'll get better, smarter bids. And if someone has a problem remembering what was asked for and promised, you've got your Pre-Pro Notes.

Great Casting helps make the humor work in this "Got Milk" commercial. The actor has just eaten a peanut butter sandwich and cannot answer a big quiz question because he don't "Got Milk."

I'm sure there's a longer list than this, but these were the ones I could think of:

Bidding Too Many Companies.

Bidding takes time. If you let a job out for bid with more than four, you're abusing the relationship.

If you can't make up your mind, talk to some people with more experience and try to get a handle on who you should be bidding.

Bidding too many companies short-term can hurt your reputation long-term.

Bidding the Wrong Companies.

Pay attention. If it's comedy, pick a production house that knows how to do it – with the right casting, direction, and film techniques.

If it's specialized table top, with motion control and familiarity with the right kind of specialists, like prop-builders and food stylists, get those companies.

Don't look for them to learn a new specialty on your job.

Try to focus on the right companies for this particular job. Try to avoid a political situation, where some people have to be bid for the wrong reasons.

If you do get in that situation, I have no advice for you. It happened to me once, and all I can tell you is that honesty was not the best policy.

The only reason it wasn't a disaster is that the production company knew that they weren't right for the job and showed some class and turned it down.

Don't count on this happening for you.

Unrequested Bids.

What if they want to bid anyway?

Well, sometimes it's hard to stop that sort of thing, but what will you do when that company comes in with the low, low bid and you don't want to use them?

See the problem?

You need a gatekeeper, and you need to be able to say, "No, not this time."

Even if you really mean, "Never!"

Producing Too Fast.

Time pressures keep getting worse.

Sometimes there is an air date that can't be changed. So I'm not telling you to go slow. But I will say this…

(Continued on next page)

Production Suppliers.

The major types of suppliers you'll be selecting are:

• **Production House.** This company will be responsible for the film and video. There services may or may not include post-production.

This supplier could be a major film production company with well-known directors or a local cable station – or anything in-between.

• **Audio or Music House.** If music or special audio effects are a part of your production, you'll want to get these specialists involved. In some cases, music production may have been a part of the initial presentation to the client. If you're using an already existing piece of music, you may be negotiating for music rights as well.

• **Post-Production.** This is primarily editing and finishing, but it may include some sort of special effects. For example, if your commercial combines live action and specialized animation, you may be choosing one company to produce the film and then another to create special effects on that film.

PRE-PRODUCTION: PART TWO.

Once your major suppliers have been chosen, it's time to put them to work. Here are some of the things you'll be looking at:

Schedules and Logistics.

It's rolling now. You'll see when things have to be done. Even though you may have hired the company for the director, you'll begin to appreciate what a good producer can do.

Approvals.

Talent needs to be approved. Locations. "If we pick this location, there will be an extra hour of travel. And that will cost…"

"Now that the bid's approved, we'll need the first third…" And so on.

Props and Misc.

Stylists and "PAs" (production assistants) will be doing things and asking questions you may not have thought of, like "What color napkins do you want?"

You may need to arrange for boxes of product, or uniforms of a certain size, or logos, or trucks, or who-knows-what to be shipped to arrive in plenty of time.

You start to realize: There are a lot of things to do. And any one of them could cause a huge problem!

One more thing. Pre-production is over.

You are now in production.

PRODUCTION. STAGE ONE.

You're still prepping, but now the meter is starting to run at a good clip. (You'll see in the bid what everyone is getting per hour and per day.)

Some of what they're doing, they do all the time (book the caterers, book the lighting package, book the crew). So no big deal.

And some of this is brand new. (Get a dozen hardware store owners to show up at the shoot, get little souvenir clap boards with their names on them done up, and put an extra PA on to make sure everyone gets there from the airport. Oh yeah, and what about make-up and wardrobe?)

The thing that you realize about production is that *you're doing something that has never been done before.* Sure, plenty of TV commercials have been done before. *But not this one!*

You start to realize all the things that can go wrong.

Suddenly, here comes that well-intentioned last-minute comment from the client based on your revision because of the comment from legal.

Everyone is rushing around, as efficiently as they can to see that everything shows up at the right place at the right time. In the middle of all of this, here is my advice on *the one thing you must do...*

THINGS YOU SHOULDN'T *(Cont.)*

• **Try to build in as much lead time as you can.** Remember the TMQ triangle.

• **Hold on to your "turn-a-round time."** Try to build it into the schedule.

• **Build in a "weather day."** Or don't shoot outside.

• **15% "Contingency."** Things happen. Budget for it. Tell your client that it's responsible business practice. It is.

• **Compare Bids.** Did they miss anything? If there's something too low, up that item to where it ought to be – then make them live with their bid.

• **Have a procedure for overages.** They're going to happen – even if your procedure is "no overages," make sure it's spelled out ahead of time.

• **Tell 'em what you want.** Don't overdirect, but be clear as you know how to be about what you want out of the production. Don't get carried away by the bells and whistles and nice treatment (they're making money off you, of course they're going to treat you nice). Remember, when it's all done, they're gone, the checks are cashed, and you're the one whose reputation is riding on the job.

• **It's in the details.** Prep. Prep. Prep. Props. Talent. Location. Shot list.

• **Stay on top of it.** *During pre-pro, everything is important.*

Prep Your Props. *These custom street signs help make this commercial work.*

Wide Shot

Medium Shot

Two Shot

Close Up Shot

Here are some of the shots and angles that you need to edit a spot. This simple Slice spot for Apple – two men in an office trying to set up a computer – needs a number of different "set-ups" to create an interesting spot. We don't realize how many different angles get used to put together a simple spot – until we have to do one ourselves!

SHOT LIST AND SCHEDULE.

You need to get a shot list. You must do this.

Look at the board. Look at the script.

Try to see the final edit in your head.

What shots will you need to put this together?

First, what are all the shots that you'd like to have to put this together? Establishing shot. Close-up. Reaction shot. Product shot. Etcetera.

Second, what is the minimum you'll need to be able to deliver the spot you promised – instead of having to consider a new career so early in life.

This is serious. What are the shots?

When during the day will these shots be done.

You have a right to expect a shot list from your director. The director needs to put it down and tell you what he or she will do and when it will be done.

During the day to come, you will certainly focus on making sure each shot is as good as it can be, but you also must focus on getting it all "in the can."

(Yeah, it's often video now, so it's not really "in the can," but old phrases die hard.)

A Word of Warning.

Directors particularly like great establishing shots which they usually do at the beginning of the day.

In general, they'll do the widest stuff first and the tightest stuff (like the final product shots) last.

That's good, you get the whole thing lit and then you break it down as you move in closer.

But… if too much of the day is going into that shot, you may have a problem. That's why you need to *insist* on a shot list and schedule – this is the production company's guarantee of what they will do and when they will do it.

It is also, frankly, a bit of protection if things go awry. But we don't want protection, we want a great spot.

Here's how you can help make it happen.

PRODUCTION. THE SHOOT!

First, your day often starts very early.

Often, the set has to be lit. Though much of the prepping has already been done, the lighting crew and equipment are usually hired for the shoot day.

Here's where the shot list and schedule come in.

People should tell you when they will be shooting – this will vary according to the needs of the shoot – and the budget.

Get there early – before you have to – and find somewhere to be in view but out of the way – let them do their job.

The director will have much on his or her mind. If there is "synch-sound," one of your major concerns will be how the lines are read. Try to have as much of this as possible worked out beforehand. Let the talent know the reading you like, let the director know the reading and attitude you want.

There's probably no avoiding a bit of comment from you when they're finally shooting, but the more you can get those thoughts and opinions into their heads beforehand, the happier you'll be.

Production Protocol.

There will probably be a number of folks from the agency and client. That's normal.

But there's one rule during the shoot.

Only one person talks to the director. It may be you. It may be the producer. But it's one person.

You can't have a bunch of people and a bunch of opinons adding distraction.

Fortunately, these days, you can all sit in front of the monitor, see what's going "in the can," and get that one point of view pulled together.

You get to have a point of view. You get to have it the way you (or the client) wants it. *But only one person talks to the director.*

*Check out **The Shot List** for this commercial for Lee Jeans...*

Dad sits down...

...pops the button on his jeans...

...which shoots past the kids...

...ricochets off the goldfish bowl...

...and shoots past Dad, who's joined the kids, knocking the painting askew.

Bob Ebel is great with kids. Here's a frame from one of the spots he directed for Oscar Mayer. But when you work with a specialist, you need to let him do his job. So, you need to make sure the director knows what you're looking for, and then let the director do it. After all, that's why you hired the director in the first place.

How'd They Do That? Here, production and post-production works together. A dancer leaps into the air, and we see her suspended in mid-air as we circle around. Very Matrix. This effect was the result of setting up synchronized cameras around the dancers and grabbing the shot at just the right time. Then, taking all of the shots from the individual cameras, and intercutting them at just the right point in the master shot. Get it? The producers of this commercial for The Gap really had to have it together every step of the way – from pre-production, through production, to post-production.

"IT'S A WRAP." OR IS IT?

"Wrap" (not rap) means the shoot is "wrapped up." That means you got everything you wanted to get.

The means you were paying attention to the shoot, the director was paying attention to you, the talent was performing, and the crew was doing their job.

If everything went smoothly, or as smooth as it ever goes, you may actually be done on time.

But if it didn't go smoothly, or perhaps you were pretty ambitious and the production company agreed, even though they might have known they wouldn't get it done on time, you may be dealing with…

Overtime.

Overtime is expensive. There may be a bit of it in the budget already. It may also be time to use a bit of that contingency we mentioned (don't use it all up now, there's still a long road ahead).

You don't want overtime, but you may be dealing with it – like it or not.

If things look like they might go that way, get the account exec and the client ready with whatever they feel the proper response is. (You'll already have a clue during lunch, when you compare your proposed shooting schedule with the actual schedule. A client that will not pay overtime might motivate the production company to get a move on.)

What I'm saying is, stay alert and anticipate.

Fortune favors the prepared mind.

Ultimately, you get what you need.

It's a wrap – and the beginning of post-production.

THE POST-PRODUCTION PATH.

Basically, the post-production consists of stringing together and synchronizing all the audio and visual elements and assembling them into one final spot.

But there's more to it than that.

It's a marvelous combination of art and technology.

Once post-production was exclusive territory, using complicated film-editing equipment, processing, and difficult-to-implement optical effects.

Today, computerized editing equipment and programs, like Avid and Final Cut Pro, make the process much more accessible.

On some levels, almost anyone can do it. But the best in each specialty still command (and deserve) top rates and are much in demand.

In the beginning, you can become familiar with the basic post-production process on your computer or the video facility at your agency or school.

Is it complicated? Sure.

But it's simple, too.

The analogy would be food and cooking.

The better the recipe (concept), the better the ingredients (audio and video), and the better the cook (director, editor, audio engineer, and you), the better the final result. Bon appetit.

POST-PRODUCTION. ELEMENTS.

You have audio and video. Here are the basic elements you'll be working with:

Audio Elements:

There are four kinds of audio elements.

Direct Voice (Synch). This is dialogue (and sound) that is recorded with the video. It is synchronized – and it's called "synch" for short. If you lose synchronization, things are "out of synch."

A major consideration is clarity and quality – audio recorded at a low level or with a lot of background noise can cause you problems later on.

Voice Tracks. These audio elements are things like announcer copy, etc. They are usually recorded later at an audio studio.

There may also be other audio elements that have been pre-recorded.

PRODUCTION ON THE RUN.

Chevy's "Fresh Mex" campaign has commercials "done fresh today." The result is pretty nuts.

"This commercial was made today." That's how it begins. They use funky hand-drawn supers in hot colors to give the video tape a fresh funky feel.

Then, they try to add a little bit of visual proof, and make some point about the freshness of the food at Chevy's

And, in a fresh way, without doing all the fast food cliches you've seen a million times, their whole commercial drives home the point – Fresh Mex!

The Production Challenge.

It's simple, you have to do a spot in a day. Get up early. Shoot it. Edit it. Run it. And then… think of what you're going to do tomorrow.

Fortunately, they didn't have to do it every day.

For example, years ago, I worked on Popeyes Fried Chicken and we had a reel of audio "bites" done by the actor who did Popeye's voice.

Music Tracks. These audio elements are usually done separately by a music house. Often they are maintained as two separate audio elements – the music track itself and the vocals. This way, you can preserve your options in the final audio "mix."

Today, tracks are usually done in stereo, though it is a "compatible" stereo, without the amount of separation you'd find in a record.

Creating music for commercials is exciting, creative, and can be hugely enjoyable. I've had the privilege of working with some of the best people in the commercial industry as well as a few members of the Rock and Roll Hall of Fame.

I have one piece of advice. Listen to it on a small speaker. Don't be deluded into thinking that those who will hear your spot will have the benefit of hearing it cranked up through a state-of-the-art system using speakers as big as a garage.

Put it on something that cost less than $200. And you might even want to listen from the next room.

Do that. It will still sound great on big speakers.

Pre-scoring and Post-scoring. As you might imagine, *pre-scoring* is doing the track before you do the video (and then "cutting to the track") and *post-scoring* is doing the music after the video.

Even when you pre-score, you may want to go back to the track and add musical effects to reinforce certain bits of video.

Sound Effects. Most audio studios have libraries of standard effects – and, in some categories, like screeching car brakes, they're quite good.

Other times, you may have to create something – using computers, other sounds, sampling, and any other trick of the trade you think might work.

Video Elements. These may start with the film or video that you shot, but there are many other sources for video.

Animation and Computer Animation. This is a whole different way of generating video. In the case of film and tape, you shoot what exists. In the case of animation and computer animation, you are creating something that has never existed before.

Film and Video. In addition to what you shoot, you may find yourself dealing with "library footage."

For example, hero product shots or other pieces from previous commercials. You may also find yourself looking for "stock footage." Why go to the volcano when you can pick up some film already shot?

Other Graphic Elements. Logos and photos are just two examples. Today, these can be treated and restored, and even animated.

Those are the elements you'll be working with. You already understand the concept of "better ingredients." So now let's put them together.

POST-PRODUCTION. ASSEMBLY.

Editors are technological artisans. They use technology, but the best of them do it with art.

As you edit, you'll see that subtle timings of just a frame or two (video goes at 30 frames a second, film at 24 frames a second) can make a difference.

You may be tempted (or forced) to do some of this yourself, but, if possible, spend as much time as you can with those who are already accomplished. You'll learn a lot about what it takes to put a spot together.

Simple or complex. You may have something that is simplicity itself. In that case, try to make it as clear and clean as possible.

If it's complex – with lots of layers, graphics, and effects, both video and audio – you'll see how much can be done. Not only that, it's fun.

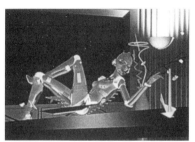

ROBOT: Even in the year 3000, the question will be "What's for dinner?"

In a super commercial for the Super Bowl, a shiny computer-generated robot with the voice of Kathleen Turner tells the world about the advantages of tin cans on behalf of their industry group.

Technology takes a straightforward product message and makes it new and exciting. In many ways, the video technology – shiny and state-of-the-art, is the message itself, repositioning tin cans as a modern packaging product.

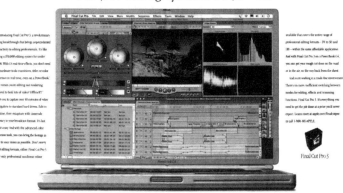
Truly Amazing. For those of us who worked with earlier forms of film and video technology, the capability (and incredible low price) of today's technology is a wonder. Then again, you probably take it for granted.

Nike Knows Music. This "Bo Knows" commercial, with multi-sport athlete Bo Jackson, was cut to a track by Bo Diddley.

Was it clever compositing that produced these video visuals for IBM, or did they just build a real big desk and file cabinet? If you do it right, no one will know.

It's truly amazing to see the flexibility and possibility that technology has opened up for all of us.

But, again, the more you can spend time with truly accomplished editors and audio engineers, the better your work will be and the better you will be.

Audio Mix and Sound Design. While the audio and video are ultimately put together, they're usually treated separately, with specialists in each area.

One of the new fields in audio is what is known as "sound design." Simply put, this utilizes all available audio tools: music, sound effects, and computer generated sounds, to assemble the ultimate audio track. Try to find the reels of some good sound designers and you will see that added level of impact and interest good audio can produce.

Video Assembly. The edit you see on the Avid has to be finished. Usually, this involves going back to the original visual source material and assembling a final spot using the highest quality video image (Avid edits are usually done with lower quality video that is derived from your originals).

Often, assembly and "rendering" can take many hours. In addition, this is the time that final tweaks like color correction (making the logo greener) can be made. All I can say is keep paying attention.

"The Winking Dog Syndrome."

LET ME TELL YOU A STORY. When I first started at JWT Chicago, I paid attention to everything that went into production. And I paid attention to what came back. The dog food spots were often disappointing.

They weren't as good as the storyboards.

Then I looked at the storyboards again. The dogs were smiling in anticipation, laughing. . . *winking!*

In the finished spots, the dogs were. . . dogs.

The Winking Dog Syndrome is still with us, perhaps not as obvious, but that makes it harder to catch.

Consider. . . will everything in the frame show up in the shot in the same proportion? Or, does your board have a slight case of "rubber pencil?"

Does the storyboard show the time it takes to get from one frame to another? Or, is there a lot of copy in one frame with not much happening – and then frames with a lot of action and not much copy?

Will real actors smile as broadly as those storyboard cartoons? Get the idea?

They say every dog has his day – just so it isn't the day they shoot your commercial.

MORE PRODUCTION PROBLEMS:
Winking Dogs aren't the only examples. Let's talk about a few other production problems. Some happen on the shoot, and others happen as you're getting ready to produce your spot.

Rubber Pencil.
The board shows angles and proportions that don't exist and can't be shot.

Too Many Words.
The ever-popular 33-second script. Twenty pounds in a ten pound bag. And nobody's able to make the cut. The result? Blahblahblah.

Making Fun of the Customer.
Gee, everyone laughed at the casting session. Is your target ugly idiots who act goofy and like to be laughed at? Then your spot should do very well.

"Let's Do It Both Ways."
This is a major symptom of the dreaded "Ad-Man's Disease." Too much film – too few decisions. Now you get to edit.

"The Spinach in the Trombone."
My term for creative last-minute ideas that seemed clever at the time, but look strange, stupid, or simply inappropriate after the film is shot.

There's a good example in the movie *Nothing in Common*. Granny's going away on a long trip. They decide to have her say "goodbye" to her cat. Watch the reaction of the Creative Director, played by Tom Hanks.

Bonus:

Goofy Angles. Goofy Testimonials. Here, Snapple goes a bit po-mo with Wendy the Snapple receptionist and testimonials based on customer letters.

Nothing like a stupid mascot outfit for a bit of entertaining video and good brand identification at this "training session."

And Wendy visits a Snapple family with lots of corny reality. Goofy and corny is OK if it's real, and we're all in on the gag.

Your First TV Spots.

THINGS WILL GO BETTER if you work within your capabilities – the capabilities of your equipment, your talent, your resources, and your budget.

Sure, we want you to hit the heights and win at The One Show. But we also want you to come through for that first client who trusts you.

And, even if it's a student project, trust me that you will get a better grade if you look like you knew what you were doing – instead of getting that sad but kindly smile and the encouraging "nice try" comment when what you did really didn't work very well.

With that in mind, here are some approaches that could serve you well. We call it…

STUPID CAMERA TRICKS.

Shoot some testimonials.

You'll probably want what they call a "three-quarter" shot – not straight into the camera, but off-axis. Try to get the lighting nice, and you might want to get a strong simple background – perhaps with the brand colors.

Or, if you've got interesting background action – like tires being changed, or a busy office, do that.

Be careful with the sound! You don't want background music going on. You'd be surprised at how loud that couple at the next table can be – at exactly the wrong time. Use a "lavolier" mike if you can.

I've found that it helps to give the testimonial people a few run-throughs – film them all and have someone taking notes, if possible.

Tell them it'll be "like playing catch." They'll respond to your question. Repeat the sequence and, usually, the second or third run-through you'll get the good takes. But don't forget to film the rehearsal – sometimes the first take is the only good one.

If there's a particularly good line (nice language, nice phrasing), you might consider asking them to turn to the camera and deliver that line. Cut the best of 'em together, add a front and your theme line, and, chances are, you've got a spot.

Lock down the camera.

Get a wide angle – maybe like a security camera – and see if you can make it happen that way.

Get a medium angle – then cut or dissolve in sequence and make your point that way.

Can you do it in one take?

Did you see the movie *Angel Eyes?*

Look at the opening scene – one long take.

Doing it in one take will be interesting enough that it will go past the rough spots. Maybe.

Move the camera.

OK, maybe you can't do it all in one take, but if you can get the lines delivered to the camera as you're moving, and you've got good movement on the front and end of each scene for "cut points," you might be able to have something nice

Can you do it on the move? Look at *West Wing*.

Many of the new video cameras have a "SteadiCam" feature that will let you move around without the camera shaking all over the place – though you still have to be smooth and good.

By the way, don't forget to settle down a bit when you need to make a serious selling point. I'll repeat that. Don't forget to settle down a bit when you need to make a serious selling point.

Cut to the music.

Get a strong music track and cut to the beat.

To do this, you need to generate as much good video source material as you can – you'll be amazed at how many scenes and shots you'll use up with aggressive cutting. You'll need a good editor.

A Convenient Camera Angle (in a convenience store, of course) sets up this little drama where a Coke deliveryman tries to grab a Pepsi and knocks over the whole display case.

ANNCR: (VO) If a year of civilization has taken its toll, we recommend one week at Club Med…

Time Moves Ahead. The Camera Stays Still. Here, we see the gradual tanning and relaxation of a guy enjoying and evolving on a Club Med vacation.

A Nice Payoff for Club Med without spending a ton of money – unless, of course, you wanted the production trip.

The Art of Being Artless. A TV spot for the price of a TV dinner.

Supers and Stock Footage do the job.

Supers over static shots.

Design a shot that's fairly empty, or has action in just a part of the frame, and deliver your message with supers and a voiceover.

Lock it down. Speed it up.

Lock down the camera in front of a place where there's good action – whether it's the weather (cool clouds rolling past), or people going in and out, or working, or building something – then, if you can rig a "speed up" editing sequence (hopefully not frame by frame), you could have something interesting. Or not. Then you find out you've wasted a day.

Look Ma, no camera!

Or, you could try a few things that hardly use any video at all. For example, the SouthWest Airlines commercial at the right uses…

Title Cards and Stock Footage.

Many retail concepts that depend on price information can work well with… the price information.

Stoopid Animation.

Use old-fashioned art cards, graffiti, ransom notes for supers, or some other funky graphic style.

Maybe with a bit of very limited animation.

Have fun with the sound track.

It could be very hip.

Switcher Fest.

The gizmos on the editing equipment that make all those effects are called switchers. Learn what they do and use them to build your spot.

Take basic graphics, art, supers, and logos and try to build something interesting.

Even a simple piece of video can be manipulated in a number of interesting ways. Have the editor or video technician show you the possibilities.

Pick up some "Pick-up Footage."

Remember, the better the ingredients, the better the final dish. See what you can cook up.

Anything from the polished shots provided by car dealers, to stock film (you can find stock houses that provide film as well as photographs), to old home movies and "funniest home video" clips.

All of the Above.

It's a new world. You have opportunities and possibilities that never existed before.

Become familiar with the production process, develop good habits from pre-pro all the way through post-production and who knows what you can create?

Assignment #27:

1. **PRODUCTION INVENTORY.**
   Write a quick summary of production resources that are available to you – video and audio.

2. **REAL WORLD EXERCISE.**
   Write the *cheapest* commercial that you can think of. 30 seconds. Any product.

3. **ONE-TAKE EXERCISE.**
   Write, design, and choreograph a spot you could shoot in one take for a local restaurant or bar.

4. **REAL WORLD EXERCISE** #2.
   Write the *second cheapest* commercial you can think of. 30 seconds. Plus two 10 second spots.

5. **BUILD YOUR BOOK EXERCISE.**
   OK, write a commercial based on one of your print ads using one of the techniques suggested in this section. 30 seconds. Plus two 10s.

STAY CALM.

Or, as they say in *Hitchhiker's Guide,* "Don't Panic." It's hard enough to write good television without feeling like you've got to invent the wheel.

The difference between a car salesman selling an old Oldsmobile in your home town and the latest 4-wheel drive spot from the slopes of Mt. Kilimanjaro is one of degree.

Your first assignments may not be very exotic. You'll be asked to sell condominiums with slides from the brochure before you'll be asked to sell Caribbean vacations on location.

Budgets will vary accordingly.

Your problem is your opportunity. The writer on the big national account is *expected* to do terrific work. Or it's over.

Think how amazed they'll be at the excellence of *your* commercial.

Think about what a great job you'll do *despite* the obvious limitations.

And, for you, it's only the beginning. Take 'em on a trip… just imagine.

HOW CHEAP CAN YOU DO IT?

A Minneapolis agency used the TV color bars for a local supermarket – red for apples and tomatoes, yellow for corn and bananas, etc.

Motel 6 used a black screen to make the point that all rooms are the same when you're sleeping.

For reservations call
505-891-6161

Small budget commercials can have big impact – and they'll know it's because of you, not the budget.

Remember, *you're the added value.*

TV Terminology:

Note: Video technology is changing rapidly, with new formats and new capabilities at every stage of the production process. These terms are accurate, but underlying technology may change.

ANNCR: Abbreviation for Announcer.

ANNCR: (VO) or **ANNCR (VO):** Announcer, Voiceover

A-ROLL: The first roll of a multi-element edit or mix. Video or audio.

ASPECT RATIO: This is a major new concern. It is the ratio between horizontal and vertical for the image. With all the new formats (and HDTV coming on), there are a number of different Aspect Ratios out there. Stay alert!

ASSEMBLY (VIDEO ASSEMBLY): Combining elements and adding effects.

BG: Abbreviation for background, as in **(MUSIC BG).**

B-ROLL: The second roll of a multi-element edit or mix.

CU: Abbreviation for close up.

DAILIES: The film from the day's shoot.

DISS, DS, or **DISSOLVE**: Fade from one scene to another.

ECU: Extreme Close Up.

FADE: In audio, to reduce volume. In video, it usually means **FADE TO BLACK.**

FX: Abbreviation for effects – sound effects / special effects / video effects.

INTERLOCK: Old way of editing film. The edited film and sound track were "locked together" on an editing machine. Today, video is already "in synch."

MATTE: Originally a film process which combined filmed images by cutting mattes to match the shape. Today it can be done electronically. Often used as a verb.

MCU: Medium Close Up.

MIX: The combining of audio elements in a soundtrack.

MORTISE: Area, usually geometric, containing a second image. Also used as verb.

MOS: Film shot without sound.

NEGATIVE: The original film stock is usually negative.

NEGATIVE TRANSFER: Turning the film negative into a positive video image.

OFF-LINE: Inexpensive editing – editing to prepare the edit. Avids are off-line.

ON-LINE: Expensive editing – final assembly and optical effects.

ROUGH CUT: Usually an early cut or the Editor's first cut.

SFX: Sound Effects.

SUPER: To superimpose. As in "Super the Title on the end shot."

SYNCH: The synchronization of audio and video. "In-synch" and "out-of-synch."

TWO-SHOT: A shot with both characters in it.

WIDE SHOT or **LONG SHOT**: A scene shot from a distance.

WIPE: An optical effect. There are many types of wipes.

Onwards...

AS ORIGINALLY PLANNED, this book should be over by now. But it kept on growing…

Why did this happen?

Why can't a book that was simply supposed to be about writing ads stay simple?

Objective, Strategy, Tactics.

Strategy, Structure, and Style.

Readin', Writin', Rhythm, and Re-Writin'.

Beginning, Middle, End.

Well… the answer is simple.

Once begun, the practice of your craft becomes a journey… not a destination.

And, like it or not, the world keeps on changing.

So here's some extra baggage this book picked up while it was first written... and rewritten… and...

Anyway.

Hope some of this comes in handy along the way.

This is a backbone.

You can't run a good advertising agency without it.

It often makes you say an honest "no" to a client instead of an easy "yes."

It means giving service instead of servility.

Very often, the result is outstanding advertising.

YOUNG & RUBICAM

*"A BILLION DOLLAR HAMMER
POUNDING A 10¢ THUMB TACK."*

Some thoughts on our business from the San Francisco ad man **Howard Luck Gossage,** a brilliant copywriter who was also a relentless critic of advertising.

"Since ours is a competitive business in an open economic system, our services and facilities are for sale to the highest bidder; and the highest bidders are just those who have the highest profit margins – usually because they have little intrinsic worth – most of their value is contributed by the advertising they buy so freely."

"Advertising is not a right, it's a privilege. Our first responsibility is not to the product but to the public."

"Is Advertising Worth Saving?"
Yes, if we can learn to look at advertising not as a means for filling so much space and time but as a technique for solving problems. And this will not be possible until we destroy the commission system and start predicating our work on what is to be earned rather than what is to be spent."

Tell the Truth.

THIS IS A CHAPTER my friends told me to write.

As they read early drafts of this book, each said it in their own way. . .

"Talk about telling the truth."
"Be sure to mention the need for honesty."
"You've got to put in a chapter about telling the truth."

Why is this?

Why should a book about writing talk about something we all should have learned a long time ago?

Because all too often in our business, the truth will be unclear.

Is the product *really* better?

Is the price *really* lower?

The people who tell you are honest men.

They believe they're telling you the truth.

Yet, they may not know – for they were told by someone else. And who is to argue?

The search for advantage in business encourages misrepresentation, overt and subtle.

And your writing is at the cutting edge.

The pressures to tell people what they want to hear are equally strong.

"The client says," says the account exec.

"My boss says," says the client.

"Research says… Legal says… My wife says…"

"Will this ad work?" they ask.

"Yes, of course," you say. As you silently pray.

Bernbach said, *"You and I can no longer isolate our lives. We must practice our skills on behalf of society.*
We must not just believe in what we sell.
We must sell what we believe in."

This is a business shot through with fear and anxiety. The unknown is always with us.

You deal with sales projections made by optimists and budgets approved by pessimists.

Your copy is examined by lawyers who don't want any trouble and often offered for approval to client bureaucracies who won't make a decision that isn't backed by a stack of research and legal precedents.

Their guiding thought is, *"Don't get any on ya."*

Meanwhile, consumers believe as they please and really aren't paying attention.

Because frankly, it isn't all that important.

Is this truth? No. Merely reality.

So, what can you do?

First, be honest.

If you think it's true, say so.

If you think it's wrong, say so.

If *you* were wrong, admit it.

And learn from your mistakes.

Second, search for the truth.

Dig for the facts of the matter.

This business thrives on hearsay.

You're not obliged to believe everything you hear.

If it sounds too good to be true, it probably is.

Finally, don't be afraid. It won't change a thing.

"The very bulk of advertising is its own worst enemy because somewhere along the line our immunity starts building up against imitation...

Thus we see that as the immunity builds up, it costs more and more to advertise every year."

Howard Gossage

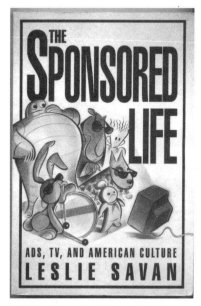

THE SPONSORED LIFE

ADS, TV, AND AMERICAN CULTURE
LESLIE SAVAN

Did You Know the Village Voice *has an advertising columnist? They do. This is a book of her columns. Provocative.*

IMMUNITY & BELIEVABILITY.

In a recent survey, advertising ranked behind toxic waste and political corruption on a list of "least liked" things.

So much for the good news.

Often, one of your biggest challenges will be to get people to believe what you have to say. Even if it's true.

Consumers have heard it all before, and they've been burned before. We're stimulated to buy more than we can afford, so we all learn early in life to resist as a matter of economic survival.

So we've all built up our immunity.

Howard Gossage had the right idea.

"People read what interests them. Sometimes it's an ad."

So did Julian Koenig...

"Tell the truth.

Make it interesting."

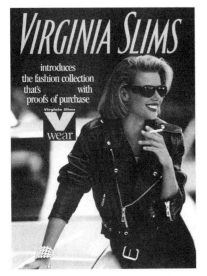

LEADERSHIP IN INTEGRATED MARKETING COMMUNICATION.

Traditionally, cigarette marketers have been innovators in advertising and marketing techniques.

Banned from some advertising media, they have led the way in such areas as event marketing and direct marketing.

This continuity-building promotion from Virginia Slims offers fashion items – like this leather jacket – with proofs of purchase.

A Word from Our Sponsor.
The ad on the right is part of a well-written campaign that has been controversial from its inception.
What's your opinion?
And, if you were assigned this as a project, what would you do?

By the way, here's my opinion.
A major influence on young people smoking is a desire to be adult.
So... seemingly public-spirited messages that tell kids "you can't smoke till you're a grown-up" is actually sending a very different sort of message. See what I'm saying?

Everyone looks on the surface and sees a very OK and "adult" message. Underneath the surface, it seems to me there is still an ongoing seduction of the target – young men and women looking to become more "adult." Savvy. Cynical. Probably more effective than many realize.

TOBACCO has been part of the American economy since Colonial days.

Cigarette ad budgets have always paid for some of the best talent and the best work in our industry.

Today we know more about the the health problems caused and aggravated by the use of cigarettes.

"Light my Lucky" These artful ads project both youth and a defiant (perhaps death-defying) attitude. How do you feel about that?

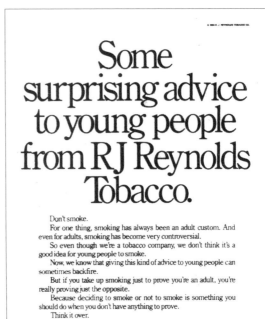

Some surprising advice to young people from RJ Reynolds Tobacco.

Don't smoke.

For one thing, smoking has always been an adult custom. And even for adults, smoking has become very controversial.

So even though we're a tobacco company, we don't think it's a good idea for young people to smoke.

Now, we know that giving this kind of advice to young people can sometimes backfire.

But if you take up smoking just to prove you're an adult, you're really proving just the opposite.

Because deciding to smoke or not to smoke is something you should do when you don't have anything to prove.

Think it over.

After all, you may not be old enough to smoke. But you're old enough to think.

R.J. Reynolds Tobacco Company

We're not allowed to tell you anything about Winston cigarettes so here's a stuffed aardvark.

LOW TO MEDIUM TAR
DANGER: Government Health WARNING: CIGARETTES CAN SERIOUSLY DAMAGE YOUR HEALTH

We're not allowed to tell you anything about Winston cigarettes, so here's a man blowing a raspberry.

LOW TO MIDDLE TAR As defined by B.M.Government
DANGER: Government Health WARNING: CIGARETTES CAN SERIOUSLY DAMAGE YOUR HEALTH

The Joke's on Who? Here are some bright, funny ads from England that make fun of cigarette advertising restrictions. What do you think?

Ethical Exercise.

You're a Creative Director at an agency.

They're good people. They try to do good work. You like it there, and you're doing well.

They have some cigarette business. You don't work on cigarettes, and you told them when you joined.

Suddenly, a Group Creative Director leaves. They ask you to take over the group – it's a big promotion.

Well, guess what, one of the accounts in this group is a cigarette – which is very important to the agency.

The parent company also has other brands, some of which are also with the agency.

There are international relationships as well.

It's a good creative group, with good people, and they're not going to break it up. What do you do?

NO ORDINARY JOE.
This memorable campaign used engaging art of the Camel character, Joe Camel.

While cigarette advertising is only supposed to target adults, some have claimed this image appeals to children.

As a result of pressure, the campaign was pulled.

What do you think?

ANTI-SMOKING ADVERTISING.
What is the role of advertising in either starting or stopping?

Clearly, you can write powerful anti-smoking advertising using negative appeals ranging from death to bad breath.

Which is the most effective for a younger audience?

You're in the target. What strategy would you recommend?

"Our corporate goal is to do good work... it's a lousy business if you can't do good work."

Jay Chiat

Few products are like the safety pin... so good to start with that they never have to be basically changed. At Young & Rubicam, people are always on the lookout for ways to make good products better, just as they are always trying to make good advertising better. Both are important if you are interested in keeping ahead of your competition.

Problems.

HERE ARE my three favorite problems:

"Running Laps,"
"Moving the Problem," and...
"The Tar Baby."

There's also one very good question...
"What Business Are You In?"

RUNNING LAPS...

When you're "Running Laps," you're working hard, but not really going anywhere.

Do you get the feeling that the problem was identified a while ago? It was.

Only no one will recognize it.

Meanwhile, you keep on moving on with no real idea of where you're going.

Many reasons and motives create this advertising version of the Gerbil Exercise Wheel.

Sometimes, it's as simple as bad judgement and bad decisions by the people in charge.

Sometimes, it's people who find it hard to acknowledge obvious answers.

And sometimes, people aren't as interested in solving the problem as you might think.

It gives them something to do.

It reinforces their importance as decision makers for one more pay period.

Another nasty example – clients who've become disenchanted with their agency and are getting ready to move the business.

Meanwhile, you work away. Running laps.

How do you know when it's "Laps" and when it's just a tough problem and you just have to keep on working at it? You don't.

That's one of the problems.

BUT… if you get the nagging feeling you're going over the same ground as you keep passing the solution to the problem, you may be "Running Laps."

Meanwhile, be hopeful. Sometimes people get tired enough to acknowledge the obvious.

Try to be one of the last ones standing.

Many copywriting careers have been built on endurance and enthusiasm.

Sometimes, someone else not burdened with the baggage can get it solved quickly and simply.

Don't be envious – try to become wiser.

And sometimes… you just have to tell yourself you're getting good exercise.

Running laps.

Moving the Problem.

IN ADVERTISING, we're constantly being asked to "solve problems." Usually the answer to the problem is, you guessed it, an ad.

So we write a great ad.

And we solve the problem.

Or do we? All too often, events reveal that we really haven't solved the problem at all.

We have merely *moved* it into another area where the problem sits unsolved.

> *"It's an operations problem."*
> *"It's a distribution problem."*
> *"It's a pricing problem."*
> *"It's a product problem."*
> *"We don't know what the problem is."*

Before you run the ads and spend all that money, take a look around.

Did you solve the problem?

Or did you just move it?

The Tar Baby.

It's organizational Fly Paper – with all the entrapping potential of that cute little fellow Ol' B'rer Rabbit punched in the nose. Know the story?

You never know when you'll meet one. But unlike B'rer Rabbit, you'll usually have plenty of company.

With a Tar Baby, everyone gets stuck.

Account execs – probably a couple, just to add to the confusion.

Definitely more than one level of client decision-making, to complicate matters further.

And research. Lots of it… badly used.

Enough data so everybody can collect a bundle of binders to make it look like they're helping.

Add uncertainty, complexity, and season well with underlying panic.

It's a mess, and you're stuck in it.

If you're not *in* one, sometimes it's fun to see one grow down the hall.

The layouts fill wastebaskets.

Storyboards by the pound.

And meetings abound.

As meetings get longer, people seem to get dumber. Or number.

Send out for more research – and maybe some pizzas – 'cause we'll be working through the weekend. Again.

Suddenly there are too many people, lots of opinions, no real answers, and a problem that might not be solvable.

That Briar Patch starts to look good.

An outdated or overpriced product is a prime candidate. There are others.

If you think you see a Tar Baby sitting in the path… ***watch out!***

He's gonna getcha.

THAT'S NOT ALL FOLKS!

These are just some of the more common problems in the advertising business.

There are more.

They're common as fleas – and they will always be with you, no matter what collar you wear.

Some you will solve. Some you won't.

Just remember, if there weren't problems, they wouldn't need you.

"What Business Are You In?"

IT'S ONE OF the classic questions of marketing.

As the business school parable goes, the railroads were once all powerful in America – but they didn't realize what business they were in.

They weren't in the railroad business, they were in the *transportation* business.

By not realizing this, they became an outdated industry. So it goes.

Ask yourself the same question,

"What business are you in?"

The advertising business? Marketing? Communications? Promotions? Customer Relations?

You're in all of those businesses, but the bottom line is . . .

YOU'RE IN THE BUSINESS OF BUILDING BUSINESSES.

You're in the business of helping companies talk to customers. You're helping merchants and manufacturers – and all the people who work there.

And... you're helping the people you talk to.

You're in the business of helping people find products and services of genuine benefit.

All in all, it's a job worth doing.

The Career-Building Business.

Ads can be an opportunity to win awards and professional recognition.

Often, small advertisers and pro bono accounts offer big opportunities.

Here is an award-winning ad for Elmer's Minnows – an account that hooked 15 awards in two years.

Contrary To Popular Belief, A Music Teacher's Main Competition Isn't Other Music Teachers.

Your Competition Can Help Define Your Business.

Don't take too narrow a view of who you're competing with.

These music teachers understand what business they're in.

New Business Is Where You Find It.
Here, 3M, a company in the business of innovation, tells the story of the accidental discovery of Scotchgard.

Their success is no accident.

How a dirty old sneaker made living rooms livable.

Common Cents.

LET'S DEAL BRIEFLY with one very important aspect of your job. MONEY.

In general, the purpose of your job is to sell goods or services. The amount of money spent selling is an *investment* by your client.

He's entitled to expect results from that investment. And he's entitled to expect that you will treat every one of his dollars as though it were your own.

Your job is to help people make money.

Not only is this ethically correct, you will reap an additional benefit if you do it well – the trust and friendship of the people you work with.

Because here's one more truth.

Everybody loves a profit center.

Not a lot of dough for a full day in Israel.

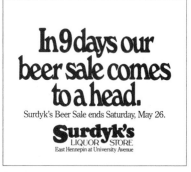

In 9 days our beer sale comes to a head.

Surdyk's Beer Sale ends Saturday, May 26.

Surdyk's LIQUOR STORE
East Hennepin at University Avenue

Retailers need good advertising. Become an effective and dependable source of good retail advertising and you'll have a friend for life – or until business is bad.

Let's talk money. It's something that concerns everyone. If you can train yourself to become an interesting and persuading writer on financial topics, there's a lot of work for you. Some may be a bit of a grind – insurance and investment brochures, etc., but a lot of it is fascinating and exciting. Remember, this is a field that does a lot of direct and collateral in addition to advertising.

Come To Surdyk's Beer Sale. The Place Will Be Crawling.

Fishing Opener Beer Sale. May 10-26

A dozen free nightcrawlers to the first 1,000 customers. Great beers at greatly reduced prices. It doesn't get any better than this.

A jolly good price. *Clear but cheerful. Right for the season. Quality presentation of a low-priced item.*

PRICE CAN BE NICE.

One of the things you will be called upon to advertise is price. Here are some excellent examples of advertising that uses price, discounts, coupons, and Free Trial Offers.

A Hard-Working Newspaper Ad. *Clear but cheerful. Right for the season. Quality presentation of a low-priced item.*

Free Offer with Class. *Sort of. Here's a humorous ad offering a Free Trial Membership at a local YMCA.*

Coupons Can Be Fun. *In addition to delivering a value to the consumer, you're also delivering a message for the brand. You can be humorous and generous at the same time. Each of these coupon ads connects in a meaningful way with a brand benefit, feature, or attribute.*

Discounts come in many shapes and sizes. *A unique shaped ad, like this one, can give your message a little extra impact.*

TO _____ FLOOR _____

FROM Bruce Bendinger   EXT 1840 DATE 9/29/80

SUBJECT WHAT I LEARNED FROM AN ACCOUNT EXECUTIVE

A number of years ago, a good friend and business partner taught me a lesson.

"Principles," he said. Repeatedly.

"Decisions have to be made from principles."

We have to make a lot of decisions in this business.

And there are always a lot of factors complicating those decisions.

How do we decide?

How do we choose between conflicting demands?

How do we build a point of view from an abundance of opinion?

Then, how do we sell it?

Principles.

Opinions vary. Principles remain constant.

During the time we worked together, our work and our decisions were shaped by one basic principle.

The agency must work in the best interests of the client's business.

That is the principle on which decisions must be based.

Not short term gain. Or "points."

Not profit or "profitability."

Not expedient personal politics based on client opinion or bias.

Not more comfortable or less controversial relationships.

Not easier meetings.

Not "safer" work.

This principle will unify a creative group. Enabling a variety of skills, view points, and personalities to focus on a common objective.

It fosters improved team work and more productive discussions between account and creative groups.

It ultimately generates the respect and trust of every client worth having.

Finally, it allows you to be utterly fearless.

When you know in your gut why you're doing what you're doing, your arguments will be strong, your logic will be tight, and your presentation will have the presence that only comes with conviction.

Naturally, you will never win every battle, or sell every recommendation the first time.

But as time goes by, the client's business will move forward.

Because every one will be united by a shared belief and a common goal.

Because the lessons you learn as you try to achieve that goal will make you wiser and more capable.

Because the feelings of mutual respect and partnership will grow, even though meetings may feature intense disagreement and controversy.

That is the lesson I learned, and it has served me well.

It is yours if you wish it.

BB/5C/929

P.S. The account executive was Bob Barocci, who became President of Leo Burnett International and then went on to head his own agency. Thanks, Bob.

Building Your Book.

DURING YOUR FIRST YEARS in the business, you must do your job *and* build your book.

Sometimes these aren't the same thing.

In that case, you will reap the additional benefit of building your capacity for overwork.

Your book represents your ability. It 's worth all the time and effort you can spare.

A GOOD BOOK LOOKS GOOD.

Neatness and organization count.

Remember, you do meetings.

Presenting your book is a meeting.

KEEP EVERYTHING AND FILE IT.

You should have comps or stats of your best unproduced work, as well as proofs or stats of *all* your produced work.

Some of these may be large – invest in some inexpensive storage from an art supply store.

Develop a filing system for old ad ideas that never went anywhere (you never know).

MAKE COPIES OF YOUR BEST PRINT.

As years go by, samples age. In the old days, we did slides, now scans will be better, and they can be made quickly into customized presentations.

CHOOSE YOUR CHOICEST COPY.

If it isn't produced, make sure you have a clean, crisp print-out. Neatness of presentation counts.

Need a piece of choice copy?

Write about something you love.

There should be a fairly long piece of copy that shows you're a *great* writer.

MAKIN' BOOK.

by Rhonda Huie (former Associate Recruitment Manager, Leo Burnett.)

What do I look for in a beginner's portfolio? Ads, of course.

I don't look for the short story you got an "A" on, or your GPA, or what fraternity you were in. I don't look for cute pictures of you and your dog.

I don't even look for articles from the school newspaper that demonstrate your ability to produce work on a deadline.

I look for ads. Smart ads. Interesting ads. Ads that make me want to go out and try the product.

Ads that make me happy, or mad, or misty. In other words, ads that are better than most of the produced work you'll find out there on any given day.

I don't care if you have a degree in advertising. Or any degree at all.

All I care about is if you understand what is interesting about a product, and if you can translate that into something that will make a consumer stop and think, "Gee, that looks like something I really ought to check out."

Good ads don't have to be cute or clever. I have a rubber stamp in my office that reads, "Use a pun, go to jail."

I don't want to see how many cliches you can come up with that relate to your product. I want to see that you're smart – that you've considered all the possible ways to relate your message, and that you've had the sense to pick the most innovative, intelligent, interesting one.

Let's get down to brass tacks.

Your Portfolio.

Your portfolio should consist of four or five campaigns of three or four ads each. Throw in a few one-shots if you'd like.

Make sure that you choose a wide variety of goods – everything from a big ticket item to something like toothpaste.

Pick things you know about – go to your medicine cabinet or under the sink, and look at what you buy.

Then, try to use the reasons you buy those things in your advertising.

If you want to be a copywriter, words are all-important.

(Continued on next page)

Talk to your customers as if you know them. How would you try to convince your best friend to try your brand of shampoo? How would you describe your bank to a person new to town?

How would you persuade your boyfriend or girlfriend that spending $1,000 for a new stereo makes more sense than a trip for two to Aspen?

I'll bet you wouldn't say things like "phenococabromolide" or "known for many good reasons."

And, while you may not be able to draw a straight line, you should have some kind of layout.

The best ads are the ones where the copy and the art direction augment each other for an even stronger message.

Advice for Art Directors.

If art direction is your goal, you'll want to show you have interesting new ideas on how to present products.

Type is important, too.

What really counts here are the ideas.

And don't think you can get away with bad headlines just because you're into art. I don't think you can have a great visual idea without first knowing what you want to say.

The best young art directors – the ones that get hired – write great headlines.

Keep Improving Your Book.

Once you have a book together, get opinions, professional opinions.

Don't ask your mother if she likes it – unless she just happens to be a Creative Director. What's important is what people in the industry think.

Listen to them. Take their advice.

Change things. Keep at it.

It may take a while for things to click, but when they do, you'll wonder why it seemed so hard back in the beginning.

Your book is what has to sell you, not the other way around. It's the only gauge we have of your talent.

It's the only thing that will get you a job in a creative department.

If you have a great portfolio, it won't matter where you went to school or who you know.

(Continued on next page)

INVENT PROJECTS.

A good idea will usually make a good ad. Do it.

DEVELOP A "SCRAP FILE."

This is not cheating!

Studying and saving other good work will help you learn to make yours better. Finally...

FREELANCE.

Some call it "Moonlighting," some call it "Freelance." Some of this work is, literally, free.

Neither resent this fact nor despair. You are performing a useful economic service – revitalizing the economy, helping provide jobs and sales for new, struggling enterprises, and helping ambitious politicians build careers so they can hire expensive consultants to tell them what to do.

Most important, you will be developing your skills, making new contacts, and, of course. . . *building your book.*

David Ogilvy agrees, *"If you need more income than your agency is willing to pay you, make up the difference by moonlighting... I've been moonlighting for 30 years."*

Nonetheless, discretion is advised.

Book-Building Exercises:

1. Review and Update Your Book.

(If you don't have a book yet, an outline for your first sample book is on the following page.)

2. Have Your Book Evaluated.

This is a good way of meeting people.

3. Write Additional Samples.

Write ads designed to build your book.

4. Freelance.

New businesses, relatives, worthy charities, etc. Start to build a clientele.

Sample Sample Book:

IN MOST CASES, the work in your sample case will be the most important factor in your getting a job. It's worth all the effort you can put into it.

The following is an outline of what a good sample book might contain…

1. An Ad for Yourself.

It can be a letter, a résumé, or something more unusual. Make it bright and brief.

2. Two Parity Products.

Take two existing products with little or no competitive difference. (Like a beer or a bank.)

Each product should have: A short strategy statement and a three-ad campaign.

3. Two "Unique" Products.

Pick affordable consumer items that you think are really special.

Write a strategy and a three-ad campaign for each.

4. Do a Long-Copy Ad.

Show people you can write.

5. Some "One-Shots."

A few individual ads that are really terrific.

6. Something That's "More than Advertising."

How about a button, T-shirt, POP, etc. Show some IMC ideas that reinforce your ad ideas.

7. New Products.

No science-fiction. It should be possible with today's technology and appeal to today's market.

Your new product should have: a name, a strategy, and a three-ad campaign (two in one medium, one in another – e.g., two print, one TV.)

NOTE: If you've had anything published or produced, like something in the college paper, or a brochure for your uncle's business, put it in the *back* of the book. It won't hurt. But probably won't help, either.

MAKIN' BOOK *(Cont.)*

If your book is awful, it won't matter where you went to school or who you know.

The hardest thing in the world for me is to tell someone they're just not good.

When you walk through my door, I want you to have the right kind of book.

I want you to have smart, gutsy, innovative work.

I want you to be great. That's what I look for in a great portfolio.

(P.S. A year after writing this, Rhonda took her own advice and got a job as a writer at Ross Roy.)

SAMPLE STORYBOARD SCRIPT.

If you're an art director who wants to demonstrate storyboard technique, here's a 30" TV script to help you do just that.

1. ESTABLISHING SHOT
   SUPER: YOUR NAME:
   Hi, my name is (Your name).

2. ACTION SHOT
   And I do storyboards.

3. FAMILY IN KITCHEN
   I can do families in kitchens.

4. FASHION SHOT
   And models in limbo.

5. WIDE SHOT
   Wide shots…

6. TIGHT SHOT
   Tight shots…

7. ANIMATION
   And even animation.

8. CUTE KID W. HAMBURGER
   Cute kids with hamburgers.

9. SPACE LOGO
   Logos in space.

10. ACTION SHOT
    And, I'm fast!

11. ACTION SHOT CONTINUES
    SUPER: Name & Phone Number
    Call (Your Name)
    at (Your Phone Number).

CREATIVE SCHOOLS.

You might need a bit of "post-grad" work to get your book good enough. These are some places that can help:

✴ Creative Circus

(www.creativecircus.com), Atlanta, GA

For aspiring copywriters, Creative Circus Web site claims, "At the Circus, writer's don't just write – they take 26 letters and turn them into magic. By the time they graduate, a blank sheet of paper isn't a wall. It's a doorway."

They offer advanced work in design, photography, art direction, and copy.

✪ Miami Ad School

(www.adschool.edu), Miami, FL

They also offer course work in account planning – plus a unique network of satellite locations that allows students to work in New York, Chicago, and Minneapolis after the first year.

✆ Portfolio Center

(www.portfoliocenter.com), Atlanta, GA

Offers course work in design, photography, art direction, copywriting, and illustration.

☆ University of Texas

(www.utexas.edu/world), Austin, TX

In addition to offering an excellent undergrad program, this university has added a grad program with a creative emphasis. Their Advertising World Web site is one of the most comprehensive advertising sites anywhere.

❢ VCU AdCenter

(www.adcenter.vcu.edu), Richmond, VA

An innovative program developed by Virginia Commonwealth University, it has students work in agency-like groups.

Students at the AdCenter are equally divided among art directors, copywriters, account managers, and planners.

❧ And Others...✍

The Academy of Art College in San Francisco, **Advertising Arts College** in San Diego, **Art Center College of Design** in Pasadena, **BrainCo** in Minneapolis, **AdEd** in Chicago, and **SVA (School of Visual Arts)** in New York are other places where you can keep growing your creative skills.

And building your book.

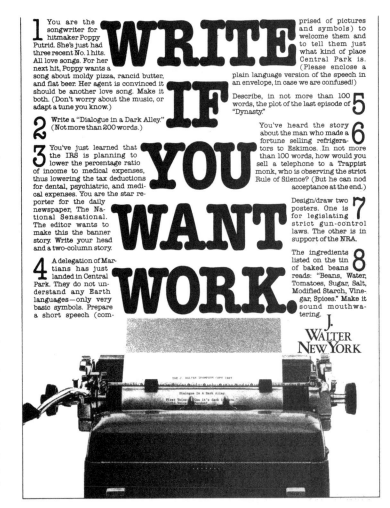

Above, a copy assignment for beginning writers from J. Walter Thompson.

On the next page, you can see some excellent self-promotion ads.

The writers and art directors who created these ads won awards and got jobs. *That's* effective advertising.

Check it out. *This is Jelly Helm's famous application for a job at the Martin Agency. Effective direct marketing in action.*

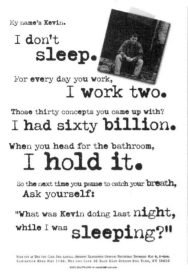

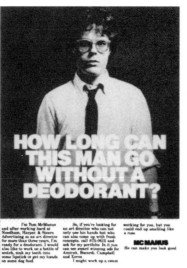

GOOD READING:

CMYK is a magazine dedicated to student work in advertising and design. You'll see great work that may inspire you to do great work.

There are useful articles from some of the top people in the business and the latest winners from student award shows. It's a good read and a good resource – probably the best place to look at current student work from all the best programs.

You can order a copy from their Web site, www.cmykmag.com – and also read some of the articles from back issues.

A Book on Your Book.

It's a book called *How to Put Your Book Together and Get a Job in Advertising* by Maxine Paetro.

It's the book on how to do exactly that.

You'll find it packed with good advice from someone who has helped many young advertising people get their start.

Even if you're not lucky enough to meet Maxine in person, you can benefit from her experience.

Available from The Copy Workshop. You can get it by calling (773) 871-1179 or by going to www.adbuzz.com

HOW BAD DO YOU WANT IT?

When you're just starting out you may not be sure what you want. It's understandable.

But you also need to understand that the young writers and art directors who created these ads want to do this more than anything.

If you do decide to go for it, you need to know that you'll be competing with other dedicated talents.

It's a tough business. You may need to do a bit more work after you graduate to get the job you want.

Alex Osborn. The "O" in BBD&O.
Inventor of "BrainStorming." Author of
Applied Imagination. *Cool guy.*

BRAINSTORM GUIDELINES:

1. Suspend Judgement. No negative comments. No critics. Evaluation and criticism is postponed during session.

2. "Free Wheel." The participants have to let go of traditional inhibitions.

Wild ideas are encouraged. It's easier to tone down an idea than think one up.

3. Quantity not Quality. The objective is to generate the most ideas you can think of.

4. Cross-Fertilize. Participants are permitted and encouraged to work off of other people's ideas.

Authorship is not a concern.

Ideas are tossed around in the group and new versions are developed.

TO: _____
**YOU ARE INVITED TO
ATTEND A BRAINSTORM
MEETING ON (DATE)
AT (PLACE) AT (TIME).
THE PROBLEM/TOPIC IS**
_____

Looking forward to seeing you.
JOHN DOE (Phone #)

Notify participants of the meeting and topic in advance – it enables them to start thinking about the topic. If you have useful background materials, they should be included as well.

Team Creativity.

BrainStorming & "The Brain Wall."

THIS SECTION IS ABOUT having creative ideas with others. "BrainStorming" is a technique that was developed in the 1930s by Alex Osborn of Batten, Barton, Durstine & Osborn.

It's a method of unlocking creativity in people in such a way as to generate a lot of ideas in a short amount of time.

"The Brain Wall" is a variation I use (as do many others – under a variety of names), and it's covered in the upcoming sidebar.

For a brainstorming session, you'll need a group, a group leader, large sheets of paper, and a room with lots of space. In general, it's good to let people know the topic ahead of time – to prepare.

Here's how BrainStorming works:

THE SIX STAGES OF BRAINSTORMING.

1. The Problem.

The group leader states the problem. For example, *"Today, we're going to talk about new ways to sell hamburgers. The hamburger business is suffering from no news and increasing concerns about eating red meat. Plus, there are too many burger places."*

The problem to be addressed is discussed, initial questions are answered, and the problem is discussed by the group in more detail.

2. "How To..."

Now, we step away from the problem and restate it in a "How to" format. The problem is…

"How to end the Ho-Hum Hamburger."

"How to establish the Tradition of the Hamburger."

"How to put more fun on a bun." And so on.

They are written on large sheets of paper, in large letters, and displayed around the room.

This stimulates more thoughts.

This opens participants' minds to the possibilities, and is usually upbeat and stimulating.

All statements from this point on are written down and displayed prominently.

3. "How Many Ways..."

The group selects the first statement to be Brain-Stormed. The selected statement is written down in a "How many ways…" format. *"How Many Ways Can We End the Ho-Hum Hamburger?"* Etc.

Solutions are called out and written down.

As ideas dry up on the first restatement, you may move to another.

The ideas are numbered, reinforced, and built on as you move into the session.

Now, take a step back. Pause and leave the Basic Restatement up on the wall.

It's time to get the group ready to "storm."

4. The Warmup – "Other Uses For..."

There should now be a short session to "step away from the problem." About five minutes.

Participants throw out ideas like "Other uses for…" a paper clip, an ash tray, whatever.

The idea's to get the mental muscles warmed up and create a positive, freewheeling atmosphere.

For naturally "creative" people, this stage can sometimes be eliminated, as they'll be "chomping at the bit."

📌 The Brain Wall.

For major advertising projects, here's a technique I like to use. I call it "The Brain Wall."

It's not a formal technique, like Brain-Storming or Synectics, just a general approach to creative problem-solving within an agency creative group.

(If you're in a student agency or Campaigns contest, your team will be the "creative group.")

Others use this technique – under many different names. Here's all you need:

1. People. Art, copy, even account executives and people from the Research Department.

2. Flexible Leadership. Don't force your will on the group (at least at first). "Go with the flow" as you look for the strongest lines of development.

3. Paper (not too big) and Markers (lots). Get everything possible on paper. And get as many possible pieces of paper on the wall. Index cards can work. 3x5" or 5x7". Post-Its are OK, too.

4. A Room with a Cork Wall or a big piece of Fome-Core. It could be your office or a conference room. You should be able to leave the stuff up on the wall.

A good-sized piece of Fome-Core can work – it's light yet big and it can be set aside if it's in the way.

5. Pins and Thumbtacks (Tape, too.)

6. Multiple Meetings. People need time between meetings to think and work.

Here's how it works…

Meeting #1.

The assignment is presented.

"Just got the account."

"We need to show the client some new product ideas."

"If we don't come up with something new, we're going to lose the account!"

Note the use of the word "we."

This begins to build a group approach to the problem.

The problem is discussed.

Perhaps the AE or research person gives some background. Relevant material is shown or handed out.

A business summary and competitve ads can also be helpful.

(Continued on next page)

A good set of handouts for the first meeting gives it substance – but... not just piles of data.

If the time is right, you might kick it around in a pleasant, casual, and optimistic way. Set the tone.

And set a time for the next meeting.

Meeting #2.

Everybody gets together and you go around the room. Thoughts and impressions are stated, shared, and put up on the wall as Headline Ideas.

Some may be rough layouts or key frames. Or scrap. Or samples.

Put 'em up.

At first, they will be placed randomly on the wall.

As the meeting develops, ideas and approaches will begin to "cluster."

Move them around and start to organize them: Benefit Ideas. Target Consumer Ideas. Graphic Ideas. Theme Ideas. And so on.

You might want to add some "Title" heads for each cluster.

You will see the thinking begin to pattern. Strengths and lines of development will emerge.

Often, certain people will show up with a similar approach – they may actually have the same idea.

Terrific. This helps defuse the authorship issue, and you can begin to form creative teams.

After all the ideas are up, ask for new thoughts or variations.

People should work off of each other to stimulate new lines of thinking.

Put 'em up.

Now, take a deep breath and head into the second part of the meeting (a short break here is fine).

In this part of the meeting, ask for reaction to others' ideas.

At first, compliments only.

Strengths are reinforced.

Initially, people are asked to refrain from "selling" their ideas. (That's for the next meeting.)

For now, they can only be positive about *someone else's* idea.

(Continued on next page)

But even with people eager to begin, an additional shift in perspective can be helpful.

Then, the group leader turns to the basic restatement and the "Storm" begins.

5. BrainStorm!

The Leader reads the restatement and calls for ideas. Write them down as quickly as possible and put them up on the wall.

Displaying ideas stimulates additional ideas.

Laughter and noise should be part of it as ideas are continually written down.

As it slows, take a short time out – a silent minute. Stretch. Let people look at the ideas that are displayed around the room.

The flow of ideas should start up again.

Then, select another restatement.

And do it again.

Ideas are continually generated, written down, and built on. The leader is also allowed to contribute ideas as well (but don't get in the way of other participants). The idea is to keep the storm going.

In a good session, one feels like one is riding a surging mental wave.

Traditionally, the leader then ends the session with a technique called "The Wildest Idea."

6. The Wildest Idea.

The group takes the wildest idea and tries to turn it into something useful.

This tends to brighten up the session again, and a few more ideas are usually generated.

Usually, it will become obvious when the session has run its course. One-and-a-half to two hours is good for a first session – a morning or afternoon is usually plenty.

Don't make them marathons!

Everyone is thanked and given positive feedback. Now it's time for that next step – evaluation.

"AFTER THE BRAINSTORM."

Evaluation is a critical, logical left-brain process. The search is for *quality* in the *quantity*.

And naturally, the next steps are up to you.

The BrainStorming technique has been quite helpful over the years in generating fresh, new perspectives and new ideas. It has also generated new variations on the technique.

SYNECTICS™ & "STORYBOARDING."

"Synectics" is a copyrighted technique developed by W. J. J. Gordon and George Prince.

It's a more focused version of BrainStorming, concerned with practical problem solving.

Specific exercises, such as analogy metaphor and discontinuous stories, are used to stimulate fresh, rich beginning connections.

It is practiced by Synectics, Inc., and licensed users around the world – casual, nonlicensed versions of Synectics' techniques are commonly used in "idea sessions," or BrainStorms.

A related technique is "StoryBoarding," which relies on visual display. It's not like a TV storyboard – it's more of a visual outline. It looks like this...

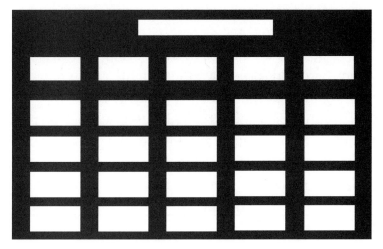

BRAIN WALL *(Cont.)*

Leadership at this point can be tricky, particularly if the group has never worked this way before.

There can be initial discomfort.

But if you promote a positive attitude toward everyone's contribution, you can solve the problem *and* strengthen your group.

Don't expect the problem to be solved at this meeting – but the beginnings of an answer may appear.

You're accelerating the ideation process – creating an "Input Soup."

Keep an upbeat attitude. It's the beginning of the journey– don't expect the problem to be solved right away.

Next Steps.

Compliment the group. "A lot of good ideas here." Etc. Indicate ideas you think are particularly interesting.

Give out some assignments ("pull this together... expand that idea," etc.), but keep it flexible.

If possible, leave the ideas up on the wall. Save them for the next meeting.

Meeting #3.

This is the watershed meeting.

Unless the problem is complex, or wideranging, it's the meeting where you "pull it together."

Generally, you'll start to see some developed approaches, theme lines, a few new ideas, and some ad roughs.

Major lines of thinking will start to become clear.

Here's how to handle it. Take down the old cards and put them in a pile(s).

Let people present.

First, the new work is put up on the wall. Then the best of the old – with your comments.

Now, people can sell their ideas and promote their point of view.

Enthusiasm is encouraged.

When everything has been presented, take a deep breath and say, *"Wow"* (or words to that effect).

Look around at all the good work. Talk about what you like, and why.

Gently ignore ideas that, in your judgement, aren't working.

(Continued on next page)

Give people permission to work on those ideas further, if convictions are deeply held – but it's time to start thinning the garden.

Focus on the strongest approaches.

Hopefully, it will become obvious.

Now, start to organize it into a Presentation. You can kick it around in a pleasant, casual, and optimistic way, or turn it into a real "Let's Win One for the Gipper" type of team effort.

Make an outline of the order of presentation for your next "work session" with account executives or clients (or both), and proceed to develop a final presentation in whatever way is typical for your agency or group.

The Brain Wall can be a fun way to build a strong campaign –

And a better, stronger group.

A HELPFUL THOUGHT.

Remember, in most cases, there will be only one winning idea. (Though often two or three ideas might go into the next round of research.)

Here's a positive way of discussing a negative subject. Share your disappointment ahead of time that there's going to be a lot of good work and probably more than one good answer – but only one "winner."

Many contributions will not be "bad" ideas, just good ideas that didn't make it.

Happens all the time.

Try to make everyone feel better about the inevitable and positive about their contributions.

There are other business uses for these techniques – as part of annual marketing meetings and to help people in structured jobs stretch their mental muscles.

Companies are finding it's very productive for groups of people to be creative and have good ideas.

Under proper circumstances, it can be an effective way of dealing with business problems.

If you're interested in learning more, there are books with techniques and guidelines as well as the training programs available (see Reading List).

A TRUE STORY.

One day, I ran into someone who'd been involved in the successful campaign "Weekends Are Made for Michelob." I asked him about it.

"Well," he said, *"We had a lot of things up on the wall… one said 'Weekends are Special' and another said 'Michelob is Special.'*

So we put them together."

And that's where that campaign came from.

Do these techniques work?

Certainly they don't work every time, and they probably don't work for everybody.

But they've worked for me.

In a wide variety of circumstances, I've seen this technique identify the key issues of a difficult advertising problem and solve that problem with a variety of approaches.

I've seen relationships revitalized, new talent identified, and sad to say, those in the group not pulling their weight exposed for all to see.

This approach should only be used when the problem is big enough to allow for the presentation of a number of alternative solutions.

Inviting too many people to work on a small problem can be demeaning.

But on the right project, it can help develop an upbeat team spirit within a creative group.

Not only will people enjoy working together more – they'll get better with each new problem.

And in this business, the more problems you solve, the better you get.

Learn to solve problems – it's problems that keep us all in the business. Hey, if we didn't have 'em, there'd be nothing to do.

I remember my freshman year at JWT.

Sears had just assigned us a new battery.

"I was thinking," said Tom Hall, "a battery doesn't wear out… it *dies.*"

Marion Dawson looked up from strumming his baritone ukelele. "Let's call it The DieHard."

And they did.*

Advertising is a team sport. The better we learn to work together, the better we'll do.

Together.

A TEAM SPORT.
Art and copy work together.

Creative teams, account management, media, research, and clients all play their key role in creating work that works.

An engineering team developed a better battery for Sears. Sears went to their agency at the time – JWT/Chicago – and the agency named the product and designed the graphics for the product.

And it was a hit.

READING LIST:
Some books about BrainStorming and group creativity.

Applied Information
Alex F. Osborn
Charles Scribner & Sons, 1957

Your Creative Powers
Alex F. Osborn
Charles Scribner & Sons, 1948

Synectics
J. J. Gordon Williams
Harper & Rowe, 1961

Creative Thinking and Brainstorming
S. Geoffrey Rawlinson
John Wiley & Sons, 1981

*

Years later, I found out that Marion had been kicking ideas around a bit earlier with his baritone uke and Howard Rieger, the talented art director who developed the original DieHard graphics. Howard insists he had the idea first – and the uke's not talkin'!

BrainStorming Exercise:

ORGANIZE a BrainStorming session.
- Pick an assignment:
  - New Product
  - Fund-Raising Project
  - Original Party
  - Etc.
- Get everyone together in a room with all the tools that you need.
- Follow the steps and **BrainStorm!**
- Implement the best idea, if practical.

Brain Wall Exercise:

GOT A BIG PROJECT? Start a Brain Wall.

Find a room. Find a wall. Or get a big piece of Fome-Core. Then, fill 'er up!

IF THIS IS WHAT YOU THINK ABOUT VOLVOS, YOU'VE GOT ANOTHER THINK COMING.

THE NEW VOLVO 850 GLT

Coming October 24

Slow and Steady Wins the Race. Brand equity builds in the mind of the consumer. Ultimately, this allows advertising that builds on itself and resonates with consumers' existing feelings.

QSCV = Food, Folks, and Fun. McDonald's does almost every kind of advertising – with quality and consistency.

When working on Apple, you are following in the footsteps of many wise, talented, and creative people. They also got massive headaches. (From The Communicator's Guide to Success and Survival *by Chris Wall.)*

Campaigns.

THIS IS ABOUT making it all work together. That's what turns advertising into an advertising campaign.

Advertising rewards those who do it right over the long haul – the effect of advertising is cumulative.

Each ad builds.

Which leads us to a few final truths –

"You're not in the business of making ads, you're in the business of building businesses."

And…*"Good ads don't sell bad products."*

The campaigns we'll cover were good ads for good products. They had strong, Selling Ideas.

Each built a unique "brand personality," one that people came to regard almost as a trusted friend.

Each ad connected with the core selling idea, making their messages cumulatively stronger with each additional ad.

Even when they changed, they evolved, building on the past, not rejecting it.

Each campaign had a look – a "graphic rhythm" that builds recognition and awareness - even if the ad isn't read!

Together, all these things build "brand equity" – the result of all the things people know and feel about your brand.

None of this is done overnight.

Not even at FedEx.

It's *"Keeping Everlastingly At It,"* as N. W. Ayer has done since 1869.

Here are a few examples of successful long-term advertising campaigns and one relatively new one.

Each has some lessons to teach us.

396

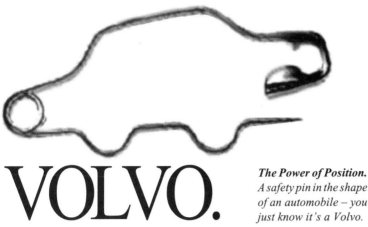

VOLVO.

The Power of Position.
A safety pin in the shape
of an automobile – you
just know it's a Volvo.

THE INITIAL SELLING IDEA of Volvo's campaign was *durability*. It was the first step in a logical and well-executed series of ads that helped build Volvo into one of the major imported auto brands.

In the beginning, Volvos were relatively well-built – particularly compared to American cars of that time. As a result, they lasted longer than most other cars. That was the Support for their benefit – Volvos lasted. Not very stylish, but they lasted.

Look at the first two ads – "Fat Cars" and "Payment Book." Each played a slightly different angle on the same key product feature – durability.

Support for the message was product-based. Their were reasons Volvos lasted longer. Ads were smart, but very logical with reason why copy.

Then, as other cars became more durable, and Volvo became a more upscale brand, their durability message began to evolve…

**A NICHE CAN BUILD
A BIG BUSINESS.**

Find the right niche in the marketplace and you can build a dominant brand – your competition lets you keep it.

But remember, that niche has to translate into a genuine consumer benefit, and the product must deliver.

In the case of Volvo, a longer-lasting car was the original benefit.

Early work was done by Hall of Fame copywriter Ed McCabe. Most ads were single page black and white.

Above, durability translates into a logical economic benefit.

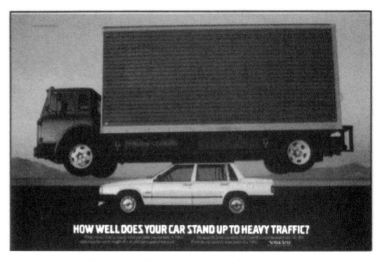

…to one of *safety.* It was an evolution.

Since durability of construction contributes to this additional benefit, they could add this new message on top of the old one. They leveraged existing brand equity into this new position. Theme: "Drive safely."

Their advertising evolved to dramatic demos of the strength of their cars' construction. Crash-Test TV and dramatic print demos all drove to add the safey benefit to the existing durability benefit.

As they became a manufacturer with more cars and more features, they broadened their approach, to extend individual product-specific benefits, like style and speed, while maintaining the overall position.

**THE VOLVO TURBO
AS MOST COMMONLY
VIEWED FROM A
BMW 318i.**

The positive of a Volvo Turbo may not be its most attractive feature, but it's the one BMW 318i owners will be seeing a lot of. In an independent test of 0 to 60 acceleration, the intercooled Turbo from Volvo beat the 318i by almost two seconds.

Results like this have prompted *Car and Driver* to call the Volvo Turbo "a missile."

And *Road & Track* describes its handling and performance as "Exemplary."

So before you run out and buy the ultimate driving machine, test drive the intercooled Turbo from Volvo.

It could prevent you from becoming one of those BMW owners with 20/20 hindsight.

THE TURBO+
By Volvo

VOLVO "Margit" :30
ANNCR: (VO) She was a physical therapist working with car accident victims in a hospital in Sweden 40 years ago. Yet Margit Engellau continues to save lives the world over. The reason? She instilled her horror of accidents in her husband... who happened to run a car company called Volvo.
You may never have heard of Margit Engellau, but maybe you've seen the monument they've built her.
Historical facts reinforce the safety component of Volvo's brand character. Strong appeal to a key target – women.

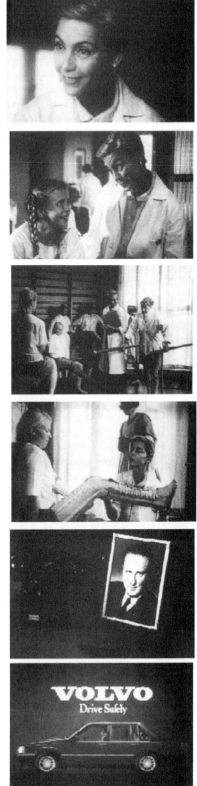

With the broadening of their line, Volvo also had to promote other benefits of other models – such as a sport sedan and a station wagon.

In some areas, success was modest, as they had built a Brand Character, that appealed more to "soccer moms" than the sports sedan buyer.

But their consistent, intelligent execution maintained their brand character through model changes.

Now, with improved styling and a broadened base, they're working to expand their brand with a campaign called ReVOLVOlution.

Whether they do or not, Volvo is an excellent example of building a brand position through both consistent execution and intelligent evolution.

SO AERODYNAMIC, THE AIR JUST SLIPS RIGHT PAST IT.
HOW UNFORTUNATE FOR THE AIR.

RE**VOLVO**LUTION THE NEW VOLVO S60

Advertising the Advertising.

Introducing with Impact.

*Communication beyond advertising –
even creating new media vehicles.*

Macintosh.

APPLE COMPUTER established itself as a dominant force in the computer industry with Macintosh. They also established themselves as a dominant advertiser.

One reason is that Apple's top people were deeply involved in the ad program. This had two results.

First, their marketing communications stretched beyond advertising, even including new media.

Second, it was a deep and accurate reflection of the company. They were their ads. The ads were them.

A UNIQUE TONE OF VOICE.

Apple has a tone of voice that speaks clearly to their target – a target that includes you and me, as well as a lot of people who aren't like us at all.

Look at the graphic rhythm, a friendly serif type face that is contemporary, yet comfortable and a personal tone of voice that speaks to the individuals who make the purchase decision.

We've added a piece by Chris Wall, when he was at BBDO/LA (Apple's agency at the time).

It describes Apple's tones of voice.

As you will see, it works for a wide range of material: television, print, brochures, direct mail… all done with a consistent and consistently tasteful point of view.

If you find that tone of voice now stretching to other computer companies, like IBM, well, Chris and Steve Hayden, who wrote the classic "1984" commercial for Apple, are now directing the creative for IBM.

Let's take a brief look at the range of Apple's work and then their underlying tone of voice.

THREE THEMES.

Over the years, Macintosh had only three ad themes: *"The computer for the rest of us." "The power to be your best."* and *"Think different."*

They basically had only one typeface (Garamond @ 80%), and a design integration of product, packaging, corporate communications, and advertising.

ANNCR: (VO) *This is a highly sophisticated business computer. And to use it,*

THE INTRODUCTION.

Everybody remembers "1984," the introductory commercial for the Macintosh. It ran once (during the Super Bowl), but it set the stage for the product introduction in a dramatic and memorable way.

all you have to learn is this.
(THICK STACK OF MANUALS DROPS

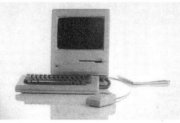

The follow-up TV and print was product-oriented and high-impact. Magazines carried 8-page inserts or multiple ads (like an entire issue of *Newsweek*).

PR had the Mac on the cover of magazines.

Sales promotion was a "free test drive."

INTO SCREEN WITH A THUD)

This is Macintosh from Apple. Also a highly sophisticated business computer. And to use it, all you have to do is learn this (ONE THIN MANUAL FLOATS IN) Now... you decide which one's more

sophisticated. Macintosh. (SFX)
The computer for the rest of us.

"Trade Secrets" :60
(OPEN ON HALLWAY, CAMERA PANS TO MEETING.)

Foster (VO): *...and we should be on the shelves by the first.*
Goodman (VO): *Six months ahead of everyone else.*
Secretary (VO): *I'm sorry, Mr. Gordon. It's John Karlson on the phone from Los Angeles...again.*

Gordon: *Ask him to hold please.*
Goodman: *Karlson?*
Gordon: *He's from Batten, Barton Durstine and Osborn.*

Foster: *Decorators?*
Gordon: *(chuckles) Ad agency for Apple.*
Woman: *Apple Computer?*

Gordon: *Yeah, they want to do a commercial about us.*
Woman: *Us? Why?*
Gordon: *We've got six offices networked to every desk... people who wouldn't touch our old PCs are hooked on the Mac system. They think it's a great story.*

TOUGH PROBLEMS & A WINNING POSITION.

Excellent as the work was, Macintosh needed more than good MarCom. There were problems.

The PC world had a much larger installed base – more programs, more users, and cheaper computers.

The advantages of Apple's GUI (Graphic User Interface) were slipping with the development of Windows. Macs were priced higher than PCs, which were just fine for normal office work.

Worse yet, the Mac product line was slipping.

For example, they were late with a good portable.

During this time, Apple switched agencies – to BBDO/LA. The campaign, "The power to be your best," worked to address their problems with business.

It was a good theme line – it defined the benefit, particularly for the business user, and the Slice commercials did a good job of communicating the Mac's benefit to a business. But it was too late – most companies already had PCs.

Apple was simply not the choice of business – with one big exception – desktop publishing.

The Mac's superior graphics capabilities helped it establish a leadership position in the "niche" market of print production and design.

402

Apple's system was an inherently better graphics platform, and the Mac became the system of choice for a whole range of graphics-oriented business.

Other areas of the arts – music and, much later, video – were also "Mac-friendly."

Their graphics programs became the standard. Even if most of the company used PCs, the division doing graphics and design used Macs.

Goodman: Would we get to be in the commercial?
Gordon: No, because we won't do it.
Goodman & Woman: Why not?

Gordon: Over the past 15 months, we've doubled our productivity and cut development time by a third.
Goodman: That's what I mean.
Gordon: Why would we go on national TV and tell our competition exacly how we did it?

In addition, Apple's business-oriented ads had them caught up in a "me-too" message. Apple needed to differentiate – with products as well as messages.

They went back to their roots – back to their original agency, Chiat/Day (which became TBWA/Chiat/Day) and the executive who had helped make those first "insanely great" products, Steve Jobs.

Goodman: Oh, it's a good point.
ANNCR: Macintosh has the power you can measure in results.

They started over. Design became important again.

And their ad messages became a reflection of who they were – instead of who they wanted to be.

Gordon: I'm sorry, Mr. Karlson, we'd love to help, but our attorneys just won't permit it.

I think, therefore iMac.

THINK DIFFERENT.

The result? The iMac and "Think Different."

They changed the product, adding dramatic and colorful styling – a startling change from a world of grey boxes.

They changed the price, making models that were competitive on price and performance.

They changed their distribution, taking a page from Dell and Gateway, opening "The Apple Store."

Finally, they changed their advertising. In addition to product-oriented ads introducing their dramatic new models, they added a high-impact campaign that featured photos (and film) of famous individuals. Very individualistic individuals.

Einstein, Gandhi, John Lennon, Amelia Earhart, and others, such as Miles Davis and Paul Rand, told us to "Think Different."

It was a perfect connection with the Mac's core consumer – an individual connected with the arts.

And the Macintosh was special again.

"Do you want to spend the rest of your life selling sugared water or do you want a chance to change the world?"

– Steve Jobs to John Sculley, 1983

"You're hired. Here. This is due tomorrow."

– Steve Hayden to you, date unknown

The Communicator's Guide to Success and Survival.

by Chris Wall, BBDO/LA

Preface.

It's the best of times.

It's the worst of times. It's Apple.

Seldom in your career as a communicator will you have the opportunity to work with products that are so good and so clearly different in vision from their competitors.

Never again will you have the chance to work so many hours on so many tasks that are so vaguely defined, that can change at the drop of an offhand remark by an industry pundit; where your clients applaud your great work on Monday and tell you on Tuesday that you were totally off the mark.

Working on Apple is like trying to nail Jell-O to a bulletin board – like driving on a freeway where the posted maximum is 75 and the posted minimum is 85.

1 Apple year = 5 human years = 35 dog years.

Working on Apple, you will have the chance to make your career, win major awards, and make a real contribution to the success of a Fortune 100 company. You will also have the opportunity to destroy your personal relationships, raise your blood pressure, and take advantage of those psychology benefits in the health insurance.

The good news is, Apple will do incredibly exciting advertising, take calculated risks, and give you the chance to do the unexpected.

When working on Apple, you are following in the footsteps of many wise, talented, and creative people. They also got massive headaches.

This piece was written by Chris Wall when he was at BBDO/LA.

It provides an excellent view of what it takes to develop a long-term stance and tone of voice for a brand.

It is reprinted with his permission and our apologies – we really had to cut it down. Sorry. But, as Chris says, "write copy to fit the layout."

The good news is, we kept the insights.

Unlike the rest of the book, this article was set in "Apple Garamond." That's Garamond condensed 80%.

Chris is now at Ogilvy, working with Steve Hayden on IBM, so if you see some IBM stuff that seems a little Apple-like, well, you'll know why.

This was written in 1991, as the early version of Windows was being introduced – the technical comparisons are now out-of-date. And how do we explain to you who Leona Helmsley was?

405

The bad news is, they will change the assignment on you, they will change the assignment on you again, and quickly dismiss great advertising if it doesn't say exactly what they believe it should say in exactly the way they think it should be said.

Apple exists in an industry where monumental change takes place overnight.

Where the life of even a successful product can be less than a year.

Don't expect a lot of time to develop your ideas. (They develop entire products in a matter of months, so it's not unreasonable for them to expect you to do an ad in a week or two.) The faster you can develop your communications, the quicker you can adapt to change, the greater success you will enjoy.

The purpose of this guide is to give you a little perspective on Apple communications and help you understand the basic ingredients that go into any successful Apple ad.

I. The Apple Voice.

The very best Apple communications have one of the most distinctive voices in all of business communications.

It sounds a whole lot like Steve Hayden in a good mood.*

It isn't easy to pick up the Apple Voice.

The Apple Voice has three basically different moods that you need to understand. All three can be found occasionally in a single piece.

*The Apple Voice can be funny, serious, hopeful, glib, wise, practical, but can never, ever sound like Leona Helmsley.***

1. The Hopeful, Optimistic Apple.

This voice is serious, intelligent, and human. It has the quality Steve calls *ponderosity.* It has a profound quality and relates the way Apple builds products to the ambitions and aspirations of our readers and viewers.

It espouses that one person with the right tools and a great idea can accomplish anything, and that people working together with the right tools can change the world and make dreams come true.

This is not b---s---. The people at Apple believe this. The people who have written really great Apple communications believe it.

If you have a point you want to make and you can make it with this voice, it is almost impossible to go wrong.

* Steve was head of BBDO/LA and a long-time Apple creative force, beginning at Chiat/Day, Apple's first agency.
** Leona Helmsley ran some New York hotels. Their ads featured Leona. She was a b----. But that wasn't why she went to jail.

It makes people feel good about Apple. It gets test scores that are off the charts. Best of all, it truly reflects the spirit of Apple people and the products they make.

This voice belongs to Apple, and you are its custodian. This is the voice you will use if you're working on an education ad. For an example of this voice, see *Industrial Revelation, MacWorld, I'm Different,* and most education print ads.

An Apple computer is a basic, practical tool for just about any human being. But most people don't realize all the things an Apple Computer can do.

2. The Practical Apple.

This voice wants you to know why the particularly bright engineers at Apple build computers the way they do. How those computers work. And why the way they work is better than the way other computers work.

This is the voice that easily relates complex technology to real-world benefits.

It works very well in business ads, new product ads, and in product television spots.

Examples of the Practical Apple can be found in *Manuals,* most of the product TV spots, *Testing 1-2-3, Testing 4-5-6,* and the original Macintosh introduction insert.

3. The Radical Apple.

This is the nitroglycerin of Apple communications.

Funny, flip, roguishly smart, and confident that we have a better way of working. The best thing about this voice is that it attracts lots of attention. It is fun to read and watch. And it has a certain charm in a world of bland, predictable corporate communications.

The worst thing about it is that it is taken as arrogant and condescending.

Without this voice, Apple would never have created perhaps the single most successful ad of the last decade – *1984.*

Don't be afraid to use this voice.

Just use it with care.

Examples where it has worked well include the print ads *Just what the world needs...* and *Welcome IBM. Seriously.* And the TV spots *Testing 1-2-3, Testing 4-5-6,* and *1984.*

Where it backfired was the *Lemmings* TV commercial and *The Berlin Wall* print ad.

It's a good idea to handle the Radical Apple Voice with care.

II. The Apple Advantage Points.
The Evidence for Any Argument.

In 1989, a lot of people spent a lot of time defining the Apple Advantage Points (also known as the "points of light"). These points serve as the outline for the body copy of any Apple ad thusly:

1. Powerful technology that is easy to use.

Although this point wasn't discovered until 1989, it's really the basic idea behind Apple since the days in the garage.

Macintosh – with its simple, graphic interface – made the personal computer useful to millions of people who couldn't or wouldn't invest the time to learn the peculiar syntax personal computers had borrowed from their mainframe cousins.

Everything about Macintosh was designed around a real-world metaphor – the desktop. Instead of you having to adapt to the way the computer works, the people who designed Macintosh adapted it to the way that you work.

This was a revolutionary concept.

Ultimately, it is this philosophy that continues to distinguish Macintosh from other computers and Apple from other computer companies.

Each subsequent version of Macintosh has increased the power and sophistication of its technology enormously with only a small increase in complexity to the user.

2. Thousands of programs that work together.

Prior to the arrival of Macintosh, every computer program worked differently, according to the whims of its author.

The command to save a document in one program could be the command to erase a document in another – even though you were using the same machine.

On a Macintosh, programs are consistent, and they work together. Although there are thousands of Macintosh programs, there is only one way to print, open, save, or close a document. You can copy information from one program and paste it into almost any other program, so you never have to do the same work twice.

3. Built-in networking.

At its most basic level, Apple makes it easy to connect a Macintosh to other computers so you can share information, send electronic mail, etc.

You can use a very sophisticated, complex network without a lot of training.

This gets back to Apple Advantage #2; networking software works exactly like all other Macintosh software.

4. Growth without disruption.

In the DOS world, each subsequent iteration of the operating system has required users to get new versions of their applications. Or, a new version of a program would be incompatible with previous versions and would have entirely new commands. This is disruption.

In the Macintosh world, it's much simpler. The Mac interface is basically the same today as it was in 1984. New features have been added, improvements have been made, but the basic way of working is still the same.

The basic benefit of this is that you can add new features and capabilities as Apple improves the system software – quickly, easily, inexpensively, without enormous interruptions in your business.

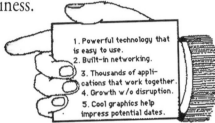

If you have trouble remembering the Apple Advantage Points, just write them down on a small piece of paper. If you think of any new points, be sure to include them.

III. The Basic Reader Perspectives.

Every Apple ad is written to one of two perspectives.

1. The User Perspective.

People who use computers want to know what's in a Macintosh computer for them. You can talk to them with any Apple Voice that is appropriate.

They care about the emotional appeal of Apple as well as the practical. The User Perspective is in the Chiat/Day spot *Basketball* and more practically focused spots like *Macintosh Office* and *Manuals*.

2. The Management Perspective.

These guys don't care about the hopeful, optimistic Apple. Spare them anything remotely philosophical unless, of course, you relate it to a practical benefit. The benefit to them is that people use Apple computers more and get more done with them with less training. *Testing 1-2-3* is a particularly successful example of this perspective.

IV. Three Ways to Explain the Advantages of a Macintosh.

When it's all said and done, you've got three choices:

1. Product.

Explain how a Macintosh works. Demonstrate point by point why it does what it does and how that differs from other computers. Show it. Explain it. Demonstrate it. This is your basic new product ad.

2. Task.

Explain why a Macintosh is a better way to accomplish any particular task. For example, Macintosh is a better way to work with numbers not only because it has great spreadsheet programs (any computer has them) but because it's easy to learn and set up (so you spend more time working and less time learning); because all the programs work together; because it makes it easy to work with other people. And so on.

3. People.

Explain innovative ways real people are actually using Macintosh.

V. The Basic Arguments Against Macintosh (Circa 1991).

(NOTE: This is a discussion of the counter-arguments to the following four "Arguments Against Macintosh:"

1. It's not affordable. 2. It's not compatible.
3. It doesn't connect. 4. No applications.

Many normal, well-groomed people
are confused by the technical aspects
of buying a personal computer.
It is our job to help them.

VI. Art Directors Who Write, Writers Who Art Direct.

You are inheriting a unique tradition of advertising.

Apple ads are frequently better written and more interesting than the articles in the magazine in which they appear.

It is your responsibility to maintain that tradition.

Any copywriter good enough to get a job working on Apple knows the basic cliches of copywriting. Lots of fragments for emphasis. Clever word plays and jokes.

Quite simply, the use of phrases like "quite simply."

Use them to help make your points. But don't kid yourself into thinking these little devices are a substitute for hard facts, insightful analysis, and passionate reasoning.

Detail is everything. Apple ads have achieved no small measure of notoriety among copywriters for the bright, amusing quips in the legal copy. At first blush, they seem to just be one of the more charming manifestations of the Radical Apple Voice. But they tell the reader something very important: that everything in an Apple ad is written to be read and enjoyed, that Apple, as a corporation, pays attention to the smallest detail.

I'm a copywriter, so this has mostly focused on writing.

Art directors are also responsible for good writing. They should read the copy and, if it isn't as good as they think it can be, they should say so.

Much of the print work of the late 1980s was influenced by the clean, dramatic Apple look. As an art director on Apple, you are following in the steps of the best: Lee Clow, Yvonne Smith, Houman Pirdavari, and Brent Thomas, to name a few.

It never hurts to study their work and measure yours against it.

Don't fall into the trap of changing the Apple look just for the sake of change.

Every time someone played around with the "Apple look" to "make it better" we have come away with something far less satisfying than we had before. I know, because I've fallen into this trap.

Apple ads should be beautiful and consistent. The best Apple ads of 1983 bear a striking resemblance to the best of 1986, which look a lot like the best of 1989.

It's wonderful to win an award for an ad. It's far better to win two awards: one for the great individual ad and one for the great campaign.

Art direction is just as important as great writing. Maybe more so.

The beauty of Apple ads isn't just "an art problem." Copywriters are responsible, too. That means you should do things like write copy to fit the layout.

Don't present a layout with half as much room as you need and wind up with an ugly ad filled with eensie-weensie type.

This sound obvious. But it's amazing how often a really good concept winds up weak and unsatisfying because the members of the team don't work together.

VII. Apple. Where the Future Is Tomorrow, Every Day.

The next decade is going to be at least as exciting as the last – technologies are going to come together very quickly – computer, telephone, television, fiber optics, cellular, photocopy, laser printing, maybe more.

Imagine a Macintosh with a television, cellular telephone, and VCR built into it, small enough to fit on your desk. Or in your briefcase.

I'm not letting you in on anything confidential, you can see most of the pieces today at any MacWorld Exposition. It's just a matter of time – and not much, at that – before some-one will pull it all together for you, eventually at a reasonable price.

In the next few years, it's important that we help Apple win not just market share, but mind share. We must expand and redefine what "" stands for that is consistent with our "computers for people" heritage.

We must protect those values and attitudes, and we must find new ways to express them as others clamor to jump on our bandwagon.

If we do, if we continue to make Apple communications relevant, dynamic, and innovative, we will help Apple become one of the first great global brands of the 21st Century.

Chris Wall/BBD /January 1991

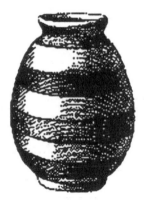

*Doing a really good job on Apple advertising for a few years has helped
many copywriters and art directors have long, rewarding, highly paid careers.
Making it possible for them to indulge in exotic, expensive, utterly pointless hobbies
like collecting ancient pottery or everything ever made by the Franklin Mint.*

MYER-EMCO.

THIS WAS A RETAIL CAMPAIGN for a small chain of stereo (now audio-video) stores in Washington, DC, that helped move them from #3 to #1.

The campaign was originally based on the strong central idea that Myer-Emco provided the highest quality equipment supported by the best stereo service department in town.

They even tested equipment before you took it home!

This unique combination of quality and service, and their well-earned local reputation, led to a simple straightforward position and Selling Idea.

"Washington's Leading Stereo Store."

At the time, they were #3 in the market, and the stereo business was exploding with mass merchandisers and heavy discounting.

They grew with a small but consistent ad campaign and *only one sale a year.* (No kidding.) Here's how they did it.

STAGE ONE.

It started small and simple. But classy.

• **Read All About It.** Ed Myer, the head of Myer-Emco, wrote a booklet – *The Insider's Guide to Stereo Component Buying.*

We promoted the free booklet in our advertising.

• **Small Space Print**, with nifty headlines based on unique selling points from the booklet. The first year, these ran mostly in the upscale city magazine.

• **Radio Commercials**, usually funded by co-op money, used each individual brand to feed to Myer-Emco's quality position.*

• **Promotions.** A Free Turntable Clinic, which let people get their turntables checked, was a consistent traffic builder. Then, when cassette tape decks became popular, we added a Tape Deck Clinic.

It Is Better to Give Our Receivers.

Choose from our large inventory of world famous receivers from $199.00. Checked in Myer-Emco's labs, backed by Myer-Emco Service. Sounds like a great gift idea from Myer-Emco.

MYER-EMCO
Washington's Leading Christmas Store

Washington/1212 Connecticut Ave., N.W./293-9100
Virginia/Willston Shopping Center, 3900 Patrick Henry Dr., Falls Church/536-3900
Maryland/11611 Old Georgetown Rd., Rockville/468-3000 In Baltimore call 366-3574

The Selling Idea. Myer-Emco had their own labs to check audio equipment (and the best service department in town). This knowledge was the reason why stereo equipment from Myer-Emco was a better value. They also offered free courtesy services – bring in your turntable for a check-up (and probably buy a new needle). This was back when people played records (flat round black things with a hole in the middle.)

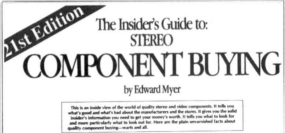

21st Edition

The Insider's Guide to:
STEREO
COMPONENT BUYING
by Edward Myer

This is an inside view of the world of quality stereo and video components. It tells you what's good and what's bad about the manufacturers and the stores. It gives you the solid insider's information you need to get your money's worth. It tells you what to look for and more particularly what to look out for. Here are the plain unvarnished facts about quality component buying—warts and all.

The Client Wrote This Brochure. It criticized inflated "list" prices and some other common practices in the stereo business. Ed Myer was an audio engineer by training, so he was able to write with knowledge and authority. It helped establish credibility for Myer-Emco's "expertise."

True Co-op Story. I was asked to write a bunch of radio commercials for a very expensive reel-to-reel tape recorder – not exactly what anyone would buy for their home system. Years later, I found out their government sales division had sold a bunch to the CIA, and, as a result, they had a lot of co-op money to spend.

413

We stuck with this program for almost two years, adding a few radio stations and gradually increasing the impact and frequency of our print – adding the newspaper and going to larger sizes.

Business increased slowly but steadily while the competition outspent us with advertising that featured screaming discounts.

There was also steady PR, with Ed Myer becoming a source of audio expertise for reporters.

The contrast between the intelligent brand personality of Myer-Emco and the "Everything Must Go" attitude of the competition served to further reinforce Myer-Emco's position – so when they did run a sale, *"Once a year and only once a year, Myer-Emco has a sale...,"* it blew the doors off.

During that time, a major competitor went out of business and Myer-Emco made their move…

A Few Good Words About Tape Decks From Myer-Emco. The Tape Deck Experts.

Here are a few things you should know about tape and tape decks.

They'll help make the deck you've got play better, and your next purchase the best one yet.

Head Alignment. The physical adjustment of the tape heads to the tape. This is an adjustment that is checked at our free tape deck clinics.

Cleaning. Proper cleaning can double the life of your tape heads. Dirty heads can cause a loss of music. We recommend the Discwasher Perfect Path, and its new C.P.R. cleaners. Clean at least once a week.

Bias. This critical internal calibration must be adjusted at time of purchase for the specific type of tape you will use for recording. Bias can affect performance by as much as 40%! All decks purchased at Myer-Emco are checked and calibrated for the type of tape you'll use. Many stores do not perform this important service.

De-Magnetize. This simple maintenance procedure eliminates residual magnetism that builds up in the recording/playback heads and tape guides. Once a week, or once for every 90 minutes of recording.

Denon! The Best Cassette Yet. We may be biased, but the new tape cassettes from Denon are the best we've found for quality, consistency and value.

Recording Meters. Measure recording or playback strength. Inaccurately calibrated meters are one of the major causes of distorted or fuzzy recordings.

WOW and Flutter. Not a new rock group. An old problem caused by variations in tape speed due to lower quality manufacturing, and in some single-motor decks, improper mechanical adjustments.

Dynamic Range. Also called "signal-to-noise ratio." This is a measurement of the ability of a recorder (and a particular recording tape) to reproduce both the softest and the loudest parts of the music without noise or distortion.

Nakamichi BX1. A new exciting deck which has tested well in our laboratories, and which should become the hit of the season. A Nakamichi for $299.

Lux KX 101. A cassette deck that not only incorporates Dolby B, but also Dolby C, for an additional 10dB improvement in signal noise. Nice at $499.

Yamaha K-200. An excellent cassette deck. And for good reason. One of our most popular. It has the same two-motor high-precision transport system as in more expensive Yamaha decks. $220 and quality built.

Free! Tape Deck Check. Bring your tape deck into our Maryland or Virginia store and let our stereo experts check it out. We'll check your head alignment, frequency response, distortion, dolby system, tape speed, WOW and flutter. (Sorry, no portables.)

We hope this advertisement has been helpful and informative. If you have any questions about tape and tape decks, come in and visit us at any of our three full-service stores. We'll be glad to help.

MYER-EMCO
Washington's Leading Stereo Store

Maryland/11611 Old Georgetown Road, Rockville, Maryland/468-2000 In Baltimore call 366-3574
Washington/1212 Connecticut Avenue, N.W., Washington, D.C./293-9100
Virginia/Willston Shopping Center, 2930 Patrick Henry Drive, Falls Church, Virginia/536-2900
We honor the American Express and other major credit cards.

The Deck the Halls Deck.

Choose from our large inventory of world famous cassette decks from $169.50. Price includes 2 Maxell blank cassettes. Sounds like a great gift idea from Myer-Emco.

MYER-EMCO
Washington's Leading Christmas Store
Washington/1212 Connecticut Ave., N.W./293-9100
Virginia/Willston Shopping Center, 2930 Patrick Henry Dr., Falls Church/536-2900
Maryland/11611 Old Georgetown Rd., Rockville/468-2000 In Baltimore call 366-3574

A MYER-EMCO CHRISTMAS.

Advertising works better when it runs at the right time. Ed Myer was an experienced retailer, and he knew when to make noise in the marketplace.

So, instead of a retailer running ads in desperation because business is bad, we were able to run ads with confidence when business was good.

Certainly, we don't always have that luxury, but it's definitely a better way to do advertising – if you can.

"Washington's Leading Stereo Store" was the right line, but a bit flat-footed. So we did variations like "Washington's Leading Christmas Store."

Along the way, Myer-Emco print and radio started to win awards – sort of a Christmas bonus.

STAGE TWO.

We maintained the focus of the campaign, but added *impact* as our budget grew.

• **Print Advertising.** Myer-Emco began running full pages that continued to reinforce their expertise. Some examples. . .

• **Tape Talk.** Myer-Emco responded to the move to audiocassette players with this informative and helpful long copy print ad.

It also promoted a new event that was added to the Turntable Clinic – a Free Tape Deck Check.

• **Bigger Holiday Promotions.** This was the big season, we heavied up during the busiest time.

Give Your Ears Some Christmas Presence.

Choose from an inventory of more than 200 different speakers from $72.50 to $1900.00. Sounds like a great gift idea from Myer-Emco.

MYER-EMCO
Washington's Leading Christmas Store
Washington/1212 Connecticut Ave., N.W./293-9100
Virginia/Willston Shopping Center, 2930 Patrick Henry Dr., Falls Church/536-2900
Maryland/11611 Old Georgetown Rd., Rockville/468-2000 In Baltimore call 366-3574

"HEAR HERE" :60 RADIO

ANNCR: Myer-Emco thinks you could use a new set of speakers.

(ANNCR)(Hear Here)

ANNCR: Perhaps something small like the Yamaha mini-speakers.

(ANNCR) (Hear Here)

ANNCR: or… something a bit larger. Now there's Boston Acoustics for less than $150… that might fit quite nicely.

(ANNCR) (Hear Here)

ANNCR: Extra extension speakers for the bedroom. Or a brand new pair for the living room stereo. The new JBL speakers or the Acoustat Three.

(ANNCR) (Hear Here)

ANNCR: Select your next speaker in the home-like comfort of Myer-Emco's listening rooms.

And when you speak to Myer-Emco's stereo experts… they listen.

(ANNCR) (Hear Here)

ANNCR: Find the speakers that will be pleasing to your eye… and *music* to your ears at Myer-Emco, Washington's Leading Stereo Store.

MINI-CAMPAIGNS.

This radio commercial combined with the print ad started to make some impact.

We did more radio and small space print and turned this effort into a mini-campaign.

The Tape Deck Check.

This was another mini-campaign, based on a new in-store promotion.

Cassette tape decks were becoming more and more popular.

In addition to continuing the Turntable Clinic for the still big record-based audio market, we used this event to reinforce Myer-Emco's expertise with this "hot" new stereo component.

The early cassette decks often needed service – this was another reason to get your cassette deck from Myer-Emco.

"Myer-Emco To Go!"

When car stereos got hot, Ed was ready with another service, which we branded as "Myer-Emco To Go!"

Again, leveraging their expertise and reinforcing their leadership position by specializing in higher-end audio products and installations.

- **Hear Here/Print.** We dramatized selection by featuring a visual variety of the speakers offered and reinforcing Myer-Emco's leadership position.

- **Radio Ads.** We kept the distinctive sound of our spots, continuing to add stations (reach) as well as increase frequency. Various components were advertised in the Myer-Emco style using co-op ad dollars.

- **Promotions.** We developed a seasonal promotion, "Have a Myer-Emco Christmas," supported with print, radio, and direct mail. An engaging mailer, sent to a growing list of Myer-Emco customers, featured a wide variety of items, many selected for appropriateness as gifts.

It made an already strong selling season even stronger.

HAVE YOURSELF A MYER-EMCO CHRISTMAS.

This was the effort that moved Myer-Emco into the #1 position.

There was strong seasonal advertising, direct mail with current customers (this mailing), and a promotion.

We turned a small demo clearance into a major event with radio advertising.

All of this stimulated the Christmas shopping traffic that helped make it the best year ever for Myer-Emco.

Ed Myer. *It helps to have a smart client.*

PRE-CHRISTMAS RADIO.

Though we tried to keep it to one sale a year, every once in a while there was a chance to grab an extra selling event.

Here, we turned a small demo clearance into a big deal – which also served to stimulate Christmas shopping traffic.

Radio was the primary medium.

Again, it was the right time to run the right advertising.

"SALE BEFORE CHRISTMAS" :30
ANNCR: [Christmas Music Under]

*'Twas the sale before Christmas
and all through the store.
The samples were moving
from off of the floor.*

*Components were nestled
all snug in their shelves.
While shoppers went shopping...
just for themselves.*

*Ma in her Gucci
was looking quite nifty.
"Look, Pa," she said,
"We can save 10 to 50."*

*So visit our stores,
if it's bargains you seek.
But hurry, my friends.
It's only this week.*

*Myer-Emco's Pre-Christmas
Clearance Sale. At Myer-Emco.
Washington's Leading Stereo Store.*

WHY IT WORKED.

We all want our campaigns to take the client to #1. Here are the reasons this one worked.

Start with a quality product.

Ed Myer was smart. He leveraged his audio expertise into an advertisable point of difference.

When a company's good, the ads work better.

And it's usually easier to write good advertising.

Establish leadership as quickly as possible.

We were not the #1 store by volume. But we were, by our definition, the *leading* store in quality. (Myer-Emco had, in fact, a national reputation.)

We weren't shy about doing a bit of pre-emption, turning a *niche* into a "#1" claim.

Differentiate dramatically.

We used both creative and media differentiation.

If we'd played the competitors' game, with large screaming price/item print and hard-sell TV, we probably would have been buried.

Our classy print and low, slow radio were unique – and they reinforced our quality position.

Consumers noticed we were different.

Stick with it.

The first year, it was hard to know how well the campaign was working.

Business was good, but not great. It would have been easy for a nervous client to change.

We kept it up for two years and were able to tap into the *cumulative* power of a good campaign.

Be lucky.

Two big audio retailers punched each other out, discounting themselves out of business, while degrading their brand images with their own money.

We had the quality position to ourselves.

And Washington, DC, is an unusually affluent market – without the economic pressures common to other areas. (Think of it as your tax dollars at work.)

McDonald's.

"NONE OF US IS AS SMART AS ALL OF US."
That was one of the guiding thoughts at McDonald's, where fifty years of teamwork and focused execution built one of the world's great brands.

CORE VALUES. QSCV.

You know what you're going to get at McDonald's – they have incredible consistency, based on a simple but powerful set of shared values – QSCV. That stands for: Quality, Service, Cleanliness, and Value.

In-store execution makes it work.

They combine work from top ad agencies with smart marketing at the store and regional level.

There are over 100 regional McDonald's co-ops.

The result is a wide range of work on a wide range of products and promotions that usually manages to be both consistent and effective.

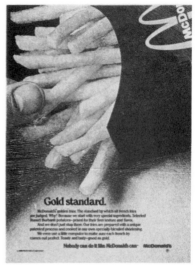

Gold standard.

CONSISTENCY & QUALITY.
When advertising presents a promise, the product needs to deliver.

One of the keys to McDonald's success has been a consistency of execution at the store level.

You know what you're going to get.

CREATIVITY IN THE STORES.
Know where the Big Mac came from?

Or the Happy Meal?

Or Breakfast at McDonald's?

They were all created by local McDonald's operators. They're always comparing and sharing new ideas.

McDonald's is the result of a whole network of smart people who keep looking for better ways to do things.

THE POWER OF A NEW IDEA.

A milkshake mixer salesman named Ray Kroc ran into a little California restaurant called McDonald's.

They'd combined assembly-line techniques with a limited menu and low prices. And the "QSR" (Quick Service Restaurant) business was born.

At first, Ray Kroc thought about how many mixers he could sell. Then he developed a vision for the brand we know as McDonald's.

419

You Deserve A Break Today. A simple theme served up in advertising that connected the fast food idea with American family values.

"Grab a Bucket and Mop." McDonald's employees do a song and dance about keeping the store clean. McDonald's franchisees lived it. This not only advertised McDonald's cleanliness, it reminded Americans that McDonald's was also serving up the American Dream to their franchisees.

Kids had their own campaign and their own long-term advertising property – Ronald McDonald and all his menu friends.

EARLY ADVERTISING.

Then another person entered – one who shared McDonald's vision – Keith Reinhard, a young CD at a Chicago agency called Needham, now DDB.

Keith is now Chairman. He was deeply involved in two classic early campaigns, "You Deserve a Break Today" and "We Do It All For You." The brand grew – in almost every direction – the result is awesome.

NATIONAL AND LOCAL ADVERTISING.

From the beginning, McDonald's worked on both a national and local level, with both a national ad fund and programs funded by the regional co-ops.

It also built a dynamic tension, where successful agencies could add more McDonald's co-ops.

As McDonald's grew, they added a second national agency, Leo Burnett, plus niche agencies, like Burrell, for ethnic advertising. They also used a number of sales promotion agencies.

CHILDREN'S ADVERTISING.

In addition to the part they play in the national advertising, children have their very own campaign, featuring Ronald McDonald.

And it pays off in the store. A child wants to go to McDonald's and get a "Happy Meal" with a toy or game-oriented packaging.

McDonald's also has other younger targets – Teens and another "niche" with its own budget – "Tweens."

PROMOTIONS.

Much of McDonald's advertising supports their promotions.

They run price promotions, but they try not to, since it lowers the price perception of the meal.

Often, they'll try to promote special "limited time" menu items – to stimulate an extra visit.

"Big Mac Attack" focused on Big Mac sales. "Mac Tonight" focused generating more traffic during a slow period – dinner.

"McBreakfast at McDonald's" created a whole new meal opportunity for every restaurant.

And one promotion that's running all the time is the Happy Meal – with periodic movie tie-ins.

Games like "Monopoly" help bring customers in more often. (And, if problems arise, public relations resources are in place to handle these things as well.)

OTHER MEDIA.

McDonald's has the resources to try almost anything – from outdoor boards to the sign behind the cash register – not to mention place mats and all the stuff you need for a kid's birthday party.

Their MarCom efforts give attention to every dimension of the McDonald's experience.

Local tie-ins, event and sport sponsorship, ethnic advertising, and community support – with a full staff of regional marketing support to help make it happen – they're virtually everywhere.

A WORLD BRAND.

Today, McDonald's imagery is universal – the outdoor boards below, from the US and Canada, barely need words.

QSCV translates. Their growth is based on superb operations that delivers to customers – worldwide.

And they keep on looking to serve up new ideas – wherever they are.

Breakfast at McDonald's created a whole new sales opportunity. The Egg McMuffin was invented by a franchisee.

Games Generate Extra Visits as customers come in to collect game pieces. By the way, the publicity is fresh, but if you're reading this a few years from now, you might not know that there was a large scandal when it was discovered that a person at the company supervising the games was giving the big prize pieces to friends and relatives. McDonald's (and their crisis management team) handled this problem quickly.

Local Promotions. Here, a national promotion – SCRABBLE – ties-in with a local radio station.

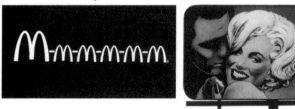

Good Sports. *Larry Bird and Michael Jordan appear in a spot together. McDonald's is a "heavy user" of sports celebrities – including local efforts using local pro athletes.*

Family Values. *Every family member goes to McDonald's at some time or other. They use this to weave stories that build on existing and real connections.*

Strong Connections Make Simple Communications. *The consumer already has your message stored in their memory.*

PROBLEMS.

It's not a perfect world – even for McDonald's.

Not every product is a winner – the Arch Deluxe was a major failure in developing an "adult" product.

And there are other issues ranging from fat content, to the minimum wage, to the environment.

In many areas, McDonald's has responded very positively to the pressures facing today's marketers – large and small. It hasn't been easy.

For example, moving from styrofoam to recycled and recyclable packaging involved a massive logistical effort – but they did it.

WHAT'S THE POINT?

There are quite a few, actually.

Graphics. Look what a good logo, consistent graphics, and strong visual skills can produce.

Design can be a powerful identifying element.

Creative Teamwork. Not just the ad agency, the whole company. See what happens when everyone gets involved in making things better.

Where would McDonald's be without the Happy Meal, Big Mac, and Breakfast at McDonald's?

New Opportunities. They have the resources to do a lot of things. And they do them.

Just about anyplace you look in The MarCom Matrix, McDonald's has been there. Big stuff. And small stuff.

If you're trying something new – an Hispanic ad program, or big screen animated point of sale, or a grassroots local promotion, chances are they've already done some of it. Learn from them.

Best Practices. Ever heard that phrase? It's one that is used a lot by business consultants.

If you're going into advertising or marketing, you can find a lot of those best practices at The Golden Arches. And, chances are, they're doing it near you.

Starbucks.

ADS? WHAT ADS? You'll find a Starbucks almost everywhere (well, not yet, but it's getting there), and you'll find most of the communication in their stores.

LOCATION. LOCATION. LOCATION.

They'll tell you those are the three most important things in retail – and it's true.

But there were a lot of businesses not doing much business in those same locations.

So let's say you got in a time machine before there was a Starbucks, and you got a thousand MBAs to look at all of the data about coffee and tell you how successful Starbucks was going to be.

Those MBAs would have looked at that data – with low growth or no growth, aging demographics, low margins – and they would have shaken their heads sadly and told you that, clearly, the data said there was no opportunity. Sorry, none. Forget it.

THE MILAN EPIPHANY.

Now, a young man from Seattle is on a trip to Italy – he notices the popularity of corner espresso bars.

Returning to Seattle, **Howard Schultz** asks the small coffee roasting company he works for if they'd be interested in expanding into retail locations.

They decline, probably they'd seen the data, too – but they tell him he can try it if he wants to. He does.

A designer/merchandiser named Harry Roberts gets involved and they open 'em up. Great graphics, smart merchandising, good coffee, and a nice place to drink it are just the beginning. They start communicating.

Starbucks markets and communicates intelligently to all of its targets – from their employees, to their customers, to the investment community.

Let's look at what they've brewed up.

Nice Logo. *That's how it starts – with a good choice of corporate colors, a deep and inviting green. Starbucks is the name of an old coffee family (like Folgers), and it was already the name of the coffee company Howard Schultz worked for.*

Nice Store. *Good looking. Good location.*

OVERVIEW.

The target for this early message was the investment community and anyone who happened to have a retail location that might be good for a Starbucks.

"Starbucks Coffee Company is a Seattle-based privately owned and operated chain of over 100 retail outlets, merchandised around two concepts: espresso bars, and stores offering whole bean coffees and brewing accessories. Starbucks is committed to dominating the specialty coffee market in each city where they establish operations.

Quality, service, speed, and cleanliness are the vehicles of Starbucks' success in implementing this strategy.

Each aspect of Starbucks' identity has been developed to reinforce the convergence of the often-contradictory ideas of high quality and high speed. The products which are the cornerstone of this identity are ..."

OVERVIEW (Cont.)
Coffee.

The freshest, highest quality arabica beans, ground on-site and prepared and offered according to the strictest standards of quality and freshness... The Company believes coffee brewed at Starbucks' espresso bars will become the criterion by which every other cup of coffee is measured.

Food.

The stores serve fresh pastries and assorted savory items throught the day. All food items are prepared off-site, very fresh and at good values.

Other items sold include...

Decor.

The upscale decor is European and contemporary. Each store is small, normally no larger than 600 to 1,200 square feet... Limited seating is provided. Lighting is bright, but friendly. Many customers return at least once every business day. The staff knows many of them by name.

Well-Communicated. *A key dimension of the Starbucks product is the people who serve it. Internal communications and training are critical. Because a commitment to quality demands a commitment to people and a company culture that is rich with shared values and team spirit. This company magazine communicates that commitment.*

Well-Sampled. *"Star Bucks" are handed out regularly to stimulate customer traffic. Since it's a location-driven business, the primary marketing communication tool is something that invites them in for a Free Cup of Coffee – and not just any cup – you want your customers to try the best you have.*

Well-Merchandised. *Here's an inside spread from an in-store brochure. It's also an in-store poster. This product story encourages the customer to become more of an expert on the product. This doesn't just make the sale, it starts to build the relationship. Now, you can be more knowledgeable as you order your coffee just the way you like it.*

Well-Packaged. *Starbucks doesn't miss a sales opportunity.*

Shopping bags, beans, cups, grinders...

Each one is an opportunity to make the point that Starbucks is a special place – and each one is also an opportunity to build the sale and extend the Starbucks experience into the consumer's home.

A Latte to Love

From tasty vanilla lattes to steaming cappuccinos, there's a latte to love at Starbucks.

Ads That Get Response. Hey, Free Latte!

Adapt and survive.

Try Starbucks on ice.

A Poster. An Ad. A Seasonal Promotion. This handsome advertising introduces the thought of iced coffee for the summer months. Smart marketing has to fight the seasonality of hot beverages. Answer? Have a great cold beverage.

OH YEAH, ADVERTISING.

Actually, it's *communication*. Major MarCom.

If it's an ad, it has a very advertising-like point to make. Come in and have a free cup. It's summer, try iced coffee.

But looking at ads misses the point of how Starbucks is communicating – they're particularly good at using a key media element – *their store environment*.

There's music – you can buy a CD – no big thing.

Just sip your coffee and here's a little flyer on their book clubs. It's *total immersion*.

Enjoy a sip of seasonal delight.

Christmas Card? Well, actually, it's a coupon for a Free Ginger Latte.

Coffeehouse Culture!
It's a Book Club – a tie-in with Starbucks and a local library. Concerts, poetry readings, and so on. Whether you go or not, you feel like it's what a coffeehouse should be.

Starbucks Monthly Book Clubs

co-sponsored by the Chicago Public Library

Read all about it. Check out the titles listed below at your local Chicago Public Library and then join in at your neighborhood Starbucks every second Tuesday of the month. Relax with friends as you enjoy warm beverages and engage in discussion with experienced book club leaders.

Discussion starts at 7:00pm, dates & titles below:

Tuesday October 9th
To Kill a Mockingbird

Tuesday November 13th
Harry Potter and the Sorcerer's Stone

Tuesday December 11th
The Corrections

At select Starbucks locations:

Not every path leads to another job as a copywriter. One of the writers down the hall at Leo Burnett was Don Novello. Today, he is, among other things, Father Guido Sarducci, an actor, and the voice of the guy in *Atlantis* who blows things up. So, you may end up being a copywriter – or an animated character. You never know. Here's a funny spot Don did for the San Francisco Art Institute.

Father Guido Sarducci: How would you like to sit around all day long, drinking espresso with friends and talking about stuff you know absolutely nothing about?

If the answer is yes, you'd like to do that, perhaps you should become an artist.

You get to wear old clothes all the time, and if you don't want to talk to somebody, you say to him, "Hey, I don't feel like talking to you now, I'm an artist."

You see, that's what artist means.

You could do whatever you want to.

Right here I have a chart – this is the rising times of various occupations.

Doctor, 6:30 in the morning you got to get up. How about that?

Lawyer gets to sleep 15 minutes more; a quarter to seven.

Engineers, 7:30. Big deal.

But artists, on the average, don't get up until a quarter to noon, even better than priests, 10:30, 11:00.

(Continued on next page)

Next Steps:

THE ESSENCE OF THE JOURNEY IS PROGRESS…

Next Steps…

Yet, in our business, we often seem plagued with slow, clumsy decisions multiplied by last minute deadlines.

Too often, we deal with institutional inertia alternating with intense periods of panic and uncertainty. Reactions instead of actions.

Does this sound familiar?

Are you reacting instead of acting? Try this…

While you cannot control previous events, you can get in touch with current events.

Think about things as they are…

Now, think about possible future events and actions you could take which *might* make things better… take a deep breath.

As Louis Pasteur said,

"Fortune favors the prepared mind."

Vaccinate yourself against the future.

Where do you want to go?

What are *your* Next Steps?

For example…

Before you write an ad, you should have a sense of what you want the ad to do.

In every meeting, look for the new things that need doing. Seek the chance to do them.

Do not expect too much. Find the small steps that will help put things on track.

And do not be too big to take small steps:

Improve the copy. One more time.

Find a way to do more. Show how that big idea works as a small piece of POP.

Do another ad. Do another campaign.

Do it again. And again.

By focusing on Next Steps, you will begin to manage change – whether what you need to change is someone else's mind or your own habits.

There is change with every next step.

Do not avoid tough problems and tough accounts.* Look for them.

Solve a few, and it can make your career.

People may even begin to seek you out to help them with their problems.

Naturally, they will be people with problems, generally a pre-occupied sort, but, then again, *if people didn't have problems, they wouldn't need you.*

I still remember the new business campaign a young writer had written for his former agency.

The theme... "We're Looking for Trouble."

It was targeted at clients with problems – just the type searching for a new agency. Smart.

Sadly, his agency decided to play it safe.

Happily, he quickly got a new job with that campaign as the centerpiece of his book.

I bet he's doing quite well.

He understands the business.

Savor each challenge and do not despair that you cannot solve every one – it's a tough business.

Many impossible problems, particularly in tough times, are just that… impossible.

And many smart, talented, imaginative people have found satisfaction somewhere other than the advertising business.

Remember, you're being paid cash money to give it your best shot. Give it gladly.

You'll do a better job.

And you'll feel better doing it.

Develop a healthy appetite for tough problems and your reward will be more of them.

San Francisco Art Institute

Looks like I missed the boat there, but you don't have to.

You could become an artist.

Write to San Francisco Artist Institute and ask for a folder and maybe they'll send it to you. Who knows?

---

*

These can often be confused with impossible problems and accounts, which should, of course, be avoided.

Experience alone will help you tell the difference between the tough and the impossible.

Unfortunately, this new wisdom is often acquired after the fact.

As your journey progresses, so will your career. Hopefully.

It can be a good living *if* you can develop an appetite for hard work and constant frustration.

This will be punctuated by the brief satisfaction of a job well done and the lasting satisfactions that come with helping to make a business grow.

Your reward will be a growing wealth of knowledge and experience, a job that may pay fairly well, and friendships that often last longer than the jobs and the agencies.

Now this book is over.

The Next Steps are yours . . .

What is your Objective?

What is your Strategy?

What is your Style?

What tactics will you use to help your client's business? Think about it.

Think about how you can help your friends and business partners.

Help them, and you will help yourself.

It's a team sport.

Give your gift.

Good luck.

Bruce Bendinger

Words:

Advertising and marketing has its own vocabulary – here are some common words and acronyms, and their generally accepted meanings in the industry.

A

AAAA: The "4 A's." American Association of Advertising Agencies.

AAF: American Advertising Federation.

"A" Counties: Larger urban counties.

A & B Roll: The use of two rolls of film or videotape to achieve some sort of **wipe** or **dissolve** between the two. Now done electronically.

Account Executive: The person who is in charge of running a piece of business (the account) at an advertising agency.

ADDY: Advertising award given by local ad clubs/regional advertising groups through the American Advertising Federation.

ADI: Area of Dominant Influence. Market definition based on TV viewing.

AFM: American Federation of Musicians. The musician's union.

AFTRA: American Federation of Theater and Radio Artists. Performance union for talent appearing on audio or videotape.

Animatic: Rough commercial, usually a storyboard laid off onto videotape and the frames matched to a rough soundtrack. An animatic which uses photos is also called a "photomatic." An animatic which uses pieces of other commercials is commonly known as a "steal-o-matic" or "rip-o-matic."

Aspect Ratio: Horizontal/vertical proportion of video image.

Attention: An initial objective of an advertisement.

Attitude: The feelings people have towards a product or service.

Audio Mix: Combining or "mixing" audio elements to produce final soundtrack.

A/V: Audio Visual Presentation. Once exclusively slides with an audio track, this now refers to a number of formats, with PowerPoint currently dominant.

Avid: Commonly used video editing system.

B

"B" Counties: Smaller urban and suburban counties.

Bait and Switch: Illegal practice of baiting customers with a low-price on goods which they are then unable to buy or discouraged from buying.

Bells and Whistles: Usually special video effects. Or extras in general.

Benefit: In advertising, this is usually short for "consumer benefit," the positive result the consumer receives from use of the product or service.

Bite: A short segment of audio.

Bleed: When the "live" area of an ad, such as the photograph, "bleeds" off the page. A non-bleed ad has a white border around it.

"Blooper Soap": Description of overdone reading of copy. It refers to an old comedy tape in which the announcer ends up shouting every single word of the phrase "Blooper Soap Is Real Good!"

Boilerplate: Standard legal copy, often used on coupons.

Bold Face: Type style that is darker and heavier than the regular "reader" face.

Broadside: One page promotional flyer, folded for mailing.

"Buckeye": Description of crude, obvious approach (except in Ohio).

• **Bullet Points:** Way of listing multiple points in presentations or print ads.

Burke: A type of "day-after recall" research supplied by Burke Research in Cincinnati and used by P&G and other package goods marketers.
It is often used as a verb. To "Burke" something. Or "it won't Burke."

Business to Business: Advertising of products and services from one business to another (as opposed to consumer advertising). "B to B."

C

Call-Outs: Small captions next to items or features in an ad.

"C & D" Counties: Predominantly small town and rural counties.

ChromaKey: Way of "Matting in" backgrounds by shooting foreground actors against a Chromakey blue or green. On film, the technique used is "UltiMatte."

Clearance: Procedure of submitting scripts or storyboards to TV networks for approval before they are shot. Also "Network Clearance."

CLIOS: Advertising industry award competition. There are many.

Color correction: Technical process of altering color values of film or videotape.

Comp: A "tight" or comprehensive layout, including type.

Contingency: Part of production budget (10-15%) set aside for unknowns.

Copy: The words in an ad. (Of course, this word has other meansings as well.)

Copy/Contact: Dual job. An account executive/copywriter who works directly with the client. Once common on small or specialized industrial accounts.

© **Copyright:** The exclusive right to a publication, literary, dramatic, musical, or artistic work. The copyright to an ad is generally owned by the advertiser, and a copyright symbol plus the year of publication must appear on the ad.

Cut: Going from one scene to another with no intervening effects. May be used as a noun ("nice cut") or a verb ("It doesn't cut").

D

Dailies: Film that was shot that day. One usually views dailies the day after they were shot. Also used to refer to all the film from the shoot.

Demo: 1. A demonstration in a TV commercial. 2. A rough version of a jingle submitted by a music house. 3. A sample tape submitted by a film house. 4. Short for "demographic profile."

Demo Rates: Lower rates which apply to the production of music demos. If the music is approved, their may be additional money due.

Demographics: Statistical data about target consumers, i.e., age, income, family size.

Dissolve: Fading from one scene to another.

Dog & Pony Show: A big presentation for a client or prospective client.

Dominance: Often an objective in many areas of advertising. In media – dominant space or schedule. In business – dominant share.

Donut: TV or radio spot with a "hole" in the middle for local or promotional use.

DTP: Desktop publishing.

Dub: 1. A copy of an audiotape or videotape. 2. To substitute a new voice track. (A voice replacement may also be called an "overdub.")

Dummy: Mock-up or layout of brochure or other multipage piece.

Dupe: Tape copy. Same as **dub.** Can be noun or verb.

E

Echo: Audio effect which gives the voice and acoustic space more size.

Effects: Term referring to a wide range of audio and visual (optical) techniques.

Empty Suit: Executive who adds little.

Emulsion: The part of the film that holds the image. It's on one side.

EQ: Sound equalization or re-adjustment.

Eye Camera: Research device used many years ago, which measured the dilation of the pupil when a person looked at an ad.

Eyebrow: A small pre-head at the top of a print ad.

F

FCC: Federal Communications Commission.

FDA: Food and Drug Administration.

Fill: Lighting used to "fill in" dark areas.

Focus Group: Research technique where 6 –12 consumers discuss product and/or advertising. Often observed from behind a one-way mirror.

Four Color: Full color printing derived from 4 separate plates. Usually called CMYK: cyan, magenta, yellow, and black (K).

Frame Count: Numerical record of the number of frames in a commercial or a part of a commercial. Often used for animation or music scoring.

Frequency: Media statistic measuring the number of times various percentages of an audience see a commercial.

FSI: Free Standing Insert. Media vehicle for delivering coupons in newspapers.

FTC: Federal Trade Commission.

FX: Common abbreviation for **effects** in scripts. Sound or video.

G

Generation: A measure of how far removed a dub is from the (analog) master. The master is first generation. The dub is second generation. A dub of that is third generation. There is a gradual diminution of quality – which varies. This has become less critical as we've moved to digital reproduction.

GRP: Gross Rating Points. A way of buying and measuring media based on the cumulative number of ratings points (usually Neilsen ratings).

H

Headline: The words that make the initial connection in an advertisement.

Hook: The part of a song (or jingle) that "hooks" your memory.

Hype: Generally negative statement describing empty claims and enthusiastic selling with no substance. Sometimes used as a verb meaning add excitement or energy, e.g., "hype-up the product shot."

I

ID: A short commercial message. Usually 10 seconds. . . or less.

Image: 1. Result of factors that add up to how people think and feel about a product. 2. Adjective used to describe advertising that is more attitudinal than factual.

Impact: Initial attention-getting.

Inherent Drama: Advertising philosophy of Leo Burnett. He believed it could be found in every product or service.

ips: Inches per second. Audiotape speed. Faster speed = better quality.

J

Jive: Slang for phony, empty, trying to be hip but not.

Jump Cut: Type of edit where continuity is sacrificed for effect.

K

Keyline: Final assembly of type and art for printed piece. Also called **paste-up.** Most of this is now done on computer.

L

Layout: Graphic representation of an ad. Can be rough or tight.

Lead Time: Amount of time needed to complete a job.

Leading: The amount of space between lines of copy. Pronounced *ledding.* (Typesetters used to put bits of lead between lines of type.)

Leakage: In recording, occurs when extraneous sound "leaks" into the microphone.

Left Hand Side: Scene and action description in a TV script.

Library Music: Pre-recorded music used for a fee. Also known as **stock music** or **needle drop.**

Local Tag: A part of the commercial, usually at the end, with no pre-recorded announcer. Local station announcers then read appropriate local **tag** copy.

Locator Copy: Address information in a tag.

Logo: Identifying graphic treatment or device for product or service. Short for "logotype."

M

"Marionette Effect": Actors become phony – saying words they would never say.

Master: Usually refers to first generation video assembly or audio mix.

Matte: Film or video effect where one image is overlaid onto another. A matte is used to block out the underlying image.

Maven: Yiddish word for "expert."

Mnemonic: Memory device usually used to register product name or benefit.

Mortise: A cut-out area in which a second image appears. Also used as a verb ("Mortise in a product shot").

Multing: Repeating vocal or instrumental parts on additional tracks to create the sound of a larger group. Short for multitracking.

N

NAB: 1. National Association of Broadcasters. 2. Newspaper Advertising Bureau.

NAD: National Advertising Division of the National Advertising Review Council. A self-regulatory body which reviews advertising.

NARB: National Advertising Review Board. Reviews decisions of NAD.

Needle Drop: Also known as **library music** or **stock music**. Originally, you paid each time you dropped the needle on the record.

Neilsen: Refers to data from A. C. Neilsen Company. Usually refers to TV viewership but may refer to retail sales, or even box office results.

Negative: The film in the camera is negative film.

Negative Transfer: Process of putting film negative onto a positive videotape image.

Nine Wheel Logic: Type of support which seems to prove a point, though it doesn't. (There is a more complete definition on page 151.)

O

Objective: The mission or goal of an advertising or marketing program.

Off-Line: A type of tape editing that is free-standing.

On-Line: Tape editing where all elements and effects can be used.

Opticals: Various visual effects (dissolves, supers, etc.) performed during the final part of the post-production process.

Out-of-home: Any ads which appear outside the home (e.g., bar posters, stadium signs).

Outdoor: Advertising which appears outside. Also **out-of-home.**

P

Paste Up: Same as **keyline.**

Penetration: The depth or degree of presence felt, usually expressed as percentage. Examples: Market penetration (% distribution) Media penetration (% of target).

PDQ: Pretty darn quick. A rush job.

"Permission to Believe": Concept credited to Leo Burnett. It allows the audience allows itself to go along with your message. This may be real, though minor ("peas picked in the moonlight") or totally made up (Keebler Cookies "made by elves").

P.I.: Per Inquiry. Type of advertising, usually television, in which the media is compensated depending on the number of orders or inquiries.

POP: Point-of-Purchase. Also called "POS," Point-of-Sale.

Portfolio: Folder containing samples of writer's, artist's, photographer's, or model's work. Also known as the "book."

Post-production: Activities which occur after production, i.e., editing, mixing, optical work, and final assembly. Also called "Post-pro."

Post-scoring: Writing the music *after* the film is edited to match or reinforce visual timings and cues in the edit.

Pre-production: Activities necessary to get ready for production. "Pre-pro."

Production: The actual filming or recording of a commercial.

Psychographics: Psychological description of target consumer, e.g., nurturing mother, adventurous, sensate, etc.

Q

Qualitative: The non-numerical aspects of a situation – i.e., attitudes, "image," and types of research – which give a "feel" but are not statistically accurate. For example, **focus groups.**

Quantitative: Numerical data. Market share, customer demographics, etc. These are "hard" research numbers from large sample research.

R

® Registration Mark: Indicates name or logo is legally registered and owned.

Reach: The percentage of an audience reached by a media buy.

Reason Why: Facts which support consumer benefit or product performance.

Right Hand Side: Voice script broken out for reading.

Rough: Anything in rough form: layout, mix, edit, etc. Sometimes spelled "ruff."

Rough Cut: The initial edit of a film or tape without optical effects. In the days of film editing, splices and other marks of assembly are visible.

Rough Mix: Early mix of audio elements.

S

SAG: Screen Actor's Guild. Performers' union for actors in filmed commercials.

Sales Promotion: Use of incentive to stimulate purchase behavior.

Schtick: Yiddish vaudeville term for a piece of "business." For example, Groucho Marx's cigar and eyebrows were his *schtick.*

Scratch Track: Rough version of music or audio track.

SFX: Sound Effects. Sometimes used as an abbreviation for Special Effects.

Share: Percentage of market held by a brand.

Share of Voice: Percent of ad weight held by brand in product category.

Side Light: Lighting that comes predominantly from the side.

Side by Side: Type of comparison commercial or Demo.

Slogan: Phrase used to advertise a product. Usually the theme of an ad campaign. Many products have numerous slogans, some quite old.

Slogo: Slang. A combination of slogan and logo.

Small Space: Print advertising utilizing small-sized media spaces.

SMPTE: A standard electronic time code used in video editing. SMPTE stands for Society of Motion Picture and Television Engineers, the professional group which established the code. Also known as **Time Code.**

Spec: 1. Short for "Specifications." 2. Short for "Speculative" – work done to get new business, usually with no payment from the prospect.

Spread: An ad covering two pages. A full page spread uses two full pages. A horizontal spread uses two horizontal half pages.

SRDS: Standard Rate and Data Service. Publishes media rates – primarily magazines.

Stock Music: Pre-recorded music which can be used for sound tracks for a small licensing fee. Also known as **library music** or **needle drop.**

Stop Motion: Animation created by images or objects moved and filmed frame-by-frame. A form of stop motion using clay is called "Clay-Mation."

SubMaster: Master wihtout certain elements, usually supers (video submaster) or announcer (audio submaster) which will be used in the final version or versions.

Super. Words "super-imposed" over the picture. Also used as verb (to super-impose words over the picture).

T

Table Tent: Point-of-purchase signage that sits on a restaurant table or bar-top.

Tag: Copy, often localized, used at the end of the commercial. Usually used to supply purchasing information – offer details, address, etc..

Target Audience: The audience to whom you are aiming your media message.

Target Market: Group of people in the marketplace who are best prospects for your product. Also "target consumer," "target customer," or just "target."

TBD: To Be Determined.

Telemarketing: Marketing done via phone. Can be "inbound" or "outbound."

Time-Code: Numerical code, such as SMPTE, used to indicate frame of videotape.

™ **Trademark:** Symbol used to distinguish a product, usually protected by law and indicated by a ™ symbol. Any word, symbol name, or device used to identify goods and distinguish them from those sold by others.

Transit: Advertising associated with mass transit.
Bus cards inside busses, the outsides of busses, and kiosks at bus stops.

Turnaround (Time): Time necessary to implement revisions.
Usually integrated into a production or approval schedule.

Turn-key: An event that includes all materials required so that the program is easy to implement, i.e., you just "turn the key."

TV Safe: Area of TV screen for clear title read.

Typo: Typographical error.

U

UltiMatte: A matte of the film image is generated along with the negative.

UltiMatte Blue: The background color on which UltiMatte is shot.

UPC: Universal Product Code. Those bar stripes on packages.

USP: Unique Selling Proposition. (For compelete definition, see page 34.)

V

VALS: Research which emphasizes Values and LifeStyles.

VCR: Video Cassette Recorder.

VFX: Video Effects.

VHS: Popular 1/2" video format.

Video Assist: Video Hook-up on a film camera that shows what's filmed.

Videotape: Tape used to record video. Used in many formats. Common formats *were* 1", 3/4", and 1/2" (BetaCam). DV (Digital Video) is now used widely. Current common home use format is VHS. This is an area of major change.

VO: Voice Over.

W

Wipe: Graphic video effect which provides a transition from one scene to another. Examples: Clock Wipe, Flip Wipe, and Page Wipe.

Work for Hire: Unless otherwise specified, creative work that is paid for is the property of the person or company that pays for it, not the creator. The work is regarded as "work for hire."

X-Y-Z

X-Acto™: Type of razor-blade knife used in mount rooms.

YUPPY: Name for Young Upscale Professional. Also YUPPIE.

This sort of nicknaming of target markets and consumers is fairly common.

Zap: Change channels.

Zoom: Film or tape production term, to move in or out on subject – usually with a "Zoom" lens. Used as noun or verb ("Zoom in on the product").

Some Numbers . . .

SOME AUDIO AND VIDEO NUMBERS.

Audio Tape Speed is measured in inches per second – "ips."

30 ips was used for highest quality audio mastering.

15 ips was used in most professional audio studios.

1⁷⁄₈ ips is the usual speed of audio cassettes.

Note: with the shift to digital audio and CDs, this is much less relevant.

Film Speed: Film is normally 24 frames per second.

Tape Speed: Videotape plays at 30 frames per second.

Time code matches up with this speed. For example, 01:04:03:22 indicates one hour, four minutes, three seconds, and 22 frames.

30" (or **:30**) **TV Commercial:** About 29 seconds, with fade up and fade to black.

30" (or **:30**) **Radio Commercial:** 30 seconds in length.

60" (or **:60**) **Radio Commercial:** One full minute.

10" (or **:10**) **ID:** About 9 seconds – if you push it, 9.5.

Billboard: From 3 to 8 seconds of audio. Usually used with a still photo or graphic.

PRINT NUMBERS.

Agate Line: Unit of print space – 1 column inch wide by 1/14".

There are 14 lines to 1 inch.

Column: Different newspapers may have different column widths.

Point: Type size. There are 72 points to 1 inch.

Index:

Here's where some of the stuff is located. Want to find a Bernbach or Gossage quote, or something on Marketing Public Relations? This might help.

Some words, like "advertising," "copywriter," and "creativity" appear throughout the book on too many pages to index. And we didn't see much point in listing minor brands that appeared once or twice – so you'll find Nike, but not the Dried Pea Council (which happens to be on page 236).

So not every brand name, agency or ad topic is indexed.

If there are topics you think should also be indexed, send us an e-mail.

Hey, there's always the next edition.

A

*www.adbuzz.com **Our Website.** You can save on books, find hot links, see QuickTimes of great spots, and hear MP3 files of cool commercials. We're still building it, so visit every once in a while. And, if you have a suggestion or contribution, send it along. Thanks.*

I

IBM: 38, 52, 247, 334, 335, 366, 405
ideas: 106-112
inherent drama: 40, 130, 247, 335
Integrated Marketing Communications, (IMC): 61, 73, 79

J

Jobs, Steve: 403, 405
Jordan, Ned: 26, 30
JWT (see Thompson, J. Walter): 24, 66, 105, 367, 388, 395

K

Karmen, Steve: 265, 274
Keebler: 41, 43, 144, 152
Kellogg's: 17, 40, 42, 52, 165, 195, 291, 344
Kennedy, John E.: 124
Klaff, Gary: 111
Koelker, Mike: 90,
Koenig, Julian: 45, 195, 375
Koestler, Arthur: 106, 109, 112
Kroc, Ray: 419
Krone, Helmut: 116, 119-121, 140

L

laddering: 130, 289
Lasker, Albert: 20
layouts: 18, 120-121
Learn-Feel-Do: 96-97, 98, 103-4
Leverhume, Lord: 98
Levi's: 70, 182, 344
Levy's: 46

Listerine: 29
Lite Beer: 51, 136, 154, 336,
Lois, George: 48, 59, 116, 134, 140, 181, 185, 306
"Look at All Three": 31
LTV: 103, 310

M

M&M's: 35
Macintosh: 61, 73, 164, 400-412
MacManus, Theodore: 28
Man Nobody Knows, The: 28
mandatories: 372
Marcato, Bob: 275
MarCom: 402, 421, 425
MarCom Matrix, The: 5, 74-78, 79, 82, 122, 179, 232, 303, 307, 422
market segmentation: 54,
"Marketing is Everything.": 62
marketing public relations (see MPR)
Marketing Warfare: 51, 63, 139
Marlboro: 41, 64, 152, 182, 294
Matthews, John: 108-109
Matthews, Leonard S.: 6-7
Maytag: 43, 336
McCabe, Ed: 208, 216, 227, 397
McCann-Erickson: 374
McDonald's: 52, 72, 75, 99, 183, 272, 279, 292, 294, 298, 299, 331, 341, 396, 419-422
McElligott, Tom: 188, 193, 218
McKenna, Regis: 62
McLuhan, Marshall: 79, 81
meetings: 118, 189
merge/purge: 340, 361
Michelob: 108, 394

Acknowledgments.

THE RED PENCIL BRIGADE. A number of courageous professors and students participated in the class-testing of this latest (3rd) edition. Their comments helped make this a better book.

The professors and their schools are: **Dan Cahalan** of the University of Montana, **Renee Gravois-Lee** of Quinnipiac College, **Joe Bob Hester** of the University of North Carolina in Chapel Hill, **Ray Seide** of UCLA, **Sarah Shaw** of the University of Minnesota, and **Birgit Wassmuth** of Drake University.

Thanks to all. And to all the students in those classes, the offer still stands, just write me at thecopyworkshop@aol.com

THIS BOOK IS THE RESULT of many lessons from agency professionals and clients. Thanks for your help and experience. (You know who you are.)

A few people are entitled to specific thanks:

H. J. and **Babette K. Bendinger** who taught me that life is a team sport.

Dave Berger and **Norm Brown** of FCB for help on early versions and **The FCB Library** for valuable assistance. **The Leo Burnett Company** for a terrific four year education. **Howard Cutler** and "Adopt a School." **Ken Jones** and **Jim Gilmore** of MSU, and the late **Prof. Larry Baricevic** of St. Louis University.

Cynthia Burns, formerly of the Kellogg School at Northwestern, and **Paul Geisler** of Kimberly-Clark, for help and assistance in the Strategy section.

Apple Computer (particularly Rich Binell), for their support of a strategy seminar that resulted in great improvements, and **Chris Wall,** formerly of BBDO/LA, for his wonderful piece on Apple.

Norm Grey (formerly of **The Portfolio Center,** now head of **The Creative Circus**), for hosting a week to class-test and work on the New (2nd) Edition.

Roy Sandstrom for type and cover design.

Harant Soghigian and **"Sam" Macuga,** agency professionals dedicated to quality. Thanks for the use of 8 Quince Street on Nantucket, where the initial version of this book was written…

To **Alan Quarry** for the Canadian translation.

Much thanks to **Kevin Heubusch** for industrial-strength proofing and to **Last Minute 'Lizabeth** for coming through once again.

To **The Copy Workshop Crew,** for going above and beyond every day…

…and most of all… **Lorelei.**